FINANCING LOW-INCOME COMMUNITIES

FINANCING LOW-INCOME COMMUNITIES

Models, Obstacles, and Future Directions

Julia Sass Rubin
EDITOR

Russell Sage Foundation ◆ New York

The Russell Sage Foundation

The Russell Sage Foundation, one of the oldest of America's general purpose foundations, was established in 1907 by Mrs. Margaret Olivia Sage for "the improvement of social and living conditions in the United States." The Foundation seeks to fulfill this mandate by fostering the development and dissemination of knowledge about the country's political, social, and economic problems. While the Foundation endeavors to assure the accuracy and objectivity of each book it publishes, the conclusions and interpretations in Russell Sage Foundation publications are those of the authors and not of the Foundation, its Trustees, or its staff. Publication by Russell Sage, therefore, does not imply Foundation endorsement.

Library of Congress Cataloging-in-Publication Data

Financing low-income communities : models, obstacles, and future directions / [edited by] Julia Sass Rubin.
    p. cm.
  ISBN 978-0-87154-711-8 (alk. paper)
 1. Financial services industry—United States. 2. Poor—United States—Finance, Personal. 3. Banks and banking—Customer services—United States. 4. Consumer education—United States. 5. Community development—United States. I. Rubin, Julia Sass.
  HG181.F6447 2007
  332.2'80973—dc22

                                                                2007014439

The paper used in this publication meets the minimum requirements of American National Standard for Information Sciences–Permanence of Paper for Printed Library Materials. ANSI Z39.48-1992.

Text design by Suzanne Nichols.

RUSSELL SAGE FOUNDATION
112 East 64th Street, New York, New York 10021
10 9 8 7 6 5 4 3 2 1

CONTENTS

To Evgenia, Gregory, and my beloved Raisas

ABOUT THE AUTHORS

Julia Sass Rubin is assistant professor at the Edward J. Bloustein School of Planning and Public Policy at Rutgers University.

Rachel G. Bratt is professor in the Department of Urban and Environmental Policy and Planning at Tufts University and a Visiting Scholar of Housing Studies at the Joint Center for Housing Studies at Harvard University.

Kathleen C. Engel is associate professor of law at the Cleveland-Marshall College of Law at Cleveland State University.

Marianne A. Hilgert is a masters student in the Division of Family Studies and Human Services at Kansas State University, and previously worked as a research assistant for the Division of Consumer and Community Affairs at the Federal Reserve Board.

Jeanne M. Hogarth is manager of the Consumer Education and Research Section in the Division of Consumer and Community Affairs at the Federal Reserve Board.

Robinson Hollister is Joseph Wharton Professor of Economics at Swarthmore College.

Jane Kolodinsky is chair and professor in the Department of Community Development and Applied Economics at the University of Vermont.

Patricia A. McCoy is George J. and Helen M. England Professor of Law at the University of Connecticut School of Law.

Daniel Schneider is a doctoral student in Sociology at Princeton University. He previously worked as a research associate at the Harvard Business School.

Lisa Servon is associate professor at Milano, the New School for Management and Urban Policy, and director of the Community Development Finance Project.

Peter Tufano is a senior associate dean and Sylvan C. Coleman Professor of Financial Management at Harvard Business School.

Marva E. Williams is Senior Program Director for LISC-Chicago.

ACKNOWLEDGMENTS

THIS BOOK originated in the spring of 2002 in a coffee shop in Cambridge, Massachusetts. After patiently listening to my ideas about the field of community development finance and my desire to expand the academic work in this area, Rachel Bratt suggested organizing a research conference on the topic. Ruth Clevenger, Dede Myers, and Elizabeth Ann Rodriguez, community affairs officers of the Cleveland, Philadelphia, and New York Federal Reserve Banks, championed the idea and brought it to fruition with their sponsorship. Nora Fitzpatrick and Marty Smith contributed their time and expertise to making it a success. The conference was graciously hosted by the New York Federal Reserve Bank on December 9–10, 2004.

The chapters in this volume began as research papers first presented at that conference. I want to thank the contributors, as well as Michael Barr, Michael Stegman, and Michael Swack, for their thoughtful and informative papers, and for their patience in accommodating my many editorial requests. I also want to thank the discussants—Timothy Bates, Ray Boshara, Ellen Brown, John Caskey, Carla Dickstein, Elaine Edgcomb, Mark Pinsky, Jane Schuchardt, Ellen Seidman, Susan Wachter, and Alan White—for their ideas, which greatly improved the papers. Finally, I would like to thank the two anonymous reviewers for their excellent suggestions and the Russell Sage Foundation for its support of the project. Eric Wanner, the Foundation president, and Suzanne Nichols, the director of publications, were a real pleasure to work with.

I also want to thank Leah Apgar for her amazing research assistance, and my colleagues at the Edward J. Bloustein School of Planning and Public Policy at Rutgers, for their immense enthusiasm and support. I cannot imagine a better or more enjoyable work environment.

My greatest gratitude, as always, goes to my family—Raya Sass Rubin and Abe Rubin; Senya Fishman; Ann and George Stankiewicz; my sisters, brothers, nieces, and nephews; my wonderful husband, best friend, co-author, and editor extraordinaire, Gregory Stankiewicz; and our beloved daughter Raisa Rubin-Stankiewicz. Thank you for your love and for making everything else in the world meaningful.

March 2007
New Brunswick, New Jersey

CHAPTER ONE

Introduction

Julia Sass Rubin

ACCESS TO affordable capital and basic financial services is a critical component of healthy communities. Without them, individuals cannot pay bills, save for retirement, or buy a house. Developers need capital to build and rehabilitate housing, commercial properties, and community facilities. Entrepreneurs need equity and debt capital to start and expand their businesses. Yet low-income communities and individuals have always had limited access to financial services, affordable credit, and investment capital. This has hampered efforts to improve conditions in these areas.

Numerous products, programs, organizations, and policies have been designed to address the financial exclusion of low-income individuals and communities. Similar to those readily available to more affluent communities, these include loans and equity investments to create and improve businesses and finance community facilities, nonprofit organizations, and housing developments. They also include basic financial services, such as check cashing, savings and lending accounts, and financial education.

The specialized financial organizations that serve low-income communities are known as community development financial institutions (CDFIs), and include community development banks, credit unions, loan funds, and venture capital funds. CDFIs provide low-income communities with financial products and services, act as a conduit between them and conventional financial organizations and markets, and advocate for policies that empower and protect them.

The important role of government and public policy has been a constant thread in community development finance. The first U.S. developmental financial institutions—savings associations formed by African Americans in the seventeenth century—came into existence in response to laws that codified slavery and discrimination (Immergluck 2004). In the late 1880s, in the aftermath of slavery's abolition and in the face of ongoing discrimination by mainstream banks, African Americans formed the earliest development banks (Immergluck 2004).

Over the last forty years, government and public policy have played a more positive role in helping create and grow the current field of community development finance. Many of the oldest community development financial institutions trace their roots to the first community development corporations (CDCs), which were the result of President Lyndon Johnson's War on Poverty and the 1964 passage of the Economic Opportunity Act.[1] In 1966, New York Senators Robert Kennedy and Jacob Javits introduced amendment I-D to that act, creating the Special Impact Program (SIP). Kennedy and Javits saw SIP as differing from the earlier war on poverty programs in its strong focus on specific distressed communities and its emphasis on economic development as a way to alleviate poverty. To demonstrate these principles, Kennedy and his staff created the Bedford-Stuyvesant Restoration Corporation, the first community development corporation in the country. They ensured that $6.9 million, more than 25 percent of the total 1966 SIP appropriation, would go to fund the Bedford Stuyvesant effort, and organized a coalition of community residents and influential business leaders to steer the corporation (Parachini 1980).

Bedford-Stuyvesant became the model for other SIP program recipients. By 1970, more than twenty-five organizations nationally were receiving federal assistance under the SIP program (Zdenek 1990). In 1972, Title VII legislation, labeled Community Economic Development, further formalized the SIP program's structural components. CDCs funded under Title VII received grants for administrative overhead and program investment funds. The recipient organizations engaged in a broad range of activities, including business and economic development, labor-training activities, and housing and community development (NCEA 1981).

Through trial and error, these early CDCs pioneered some of the community development financial tools and models that currently make up the field. Bedford-Stuyvesant, for example, ran a small business lending program that initially focused on creating jobs by attracting large businesses into the neighborhood. When this resulted in the recruitment of only one IBM plant, Bedford-Stuyvesant instead began using the loan fund to support neighborhood entrepreneurs, in the process creating one of the first business-focused community development loan funds. Bedford-Stuyvesant also helped pioneer housing-oriented lending, by administering a $100 million home mortgage pool targeted to its neighborhood and funded by a group of New York City banks (Moy and Okagaki 2001).

The Job Start Corporation of London, Kentucky, was one of the SIP CDCs that used federal funds to begin its own business ventures. Given the limited business experience of those running the CDCs, and the generally high rate of new business failures, this approach proved an expensive and ineffective way to create community jobs. In 1972, frustrated with the failure of this approach, Job Start began investing capital in outside entrepreneurs in exchange for an equity stake in their enterprises, creating the first community development venture capital fund (Miller 1994).

The Bank Holding Company Act of 1970 enabled bank holding companies to invest in community development if the primary goal was to benefit low- and moderate-income people. This prompted the creation of Shorebank, the first community development bank in the country. Had this legislation not been enacted, Shorebank would have been set up as a credit union (Grzywinski 1991).

Public policy also has provided community development financial institutions with the tools necessary to accomplish their work. The passage of the Home Mortgage Disclosure Act of 1975 (HMDA), which requires financial institutions to file annual reports on home mortgage applicants and borrowers, made publicly available data on whether financial institutions are serving the residential credit needs of their assessment areas. The Low-Income Housing Tax Credit of 1986 provided investors a federal tax credit for investing in low-income housing developments, substantially reducing the costs of financing such projects.

More recently, public policy played an important role in the dramatic growth of the field of community development finance during the administration of President Bill Clinton. Clinton strengthened enforcement of the Community Reinvestment Act (CRA), which Congress had enacted in 1977 to encourage regulated financial institutions to fulfill their "continuing and affirmative obligations to help meet the credit needs of the local communities in which they are chartered" (NCRC 2005, 1). New CRA regulations, enacted in 1995, recognized community development financial institutions for the first time as qualifying investments and borrowers, giving commercial banks a significant incentive to finance CDFIs.

President Clinton also championed the 1994 creation of the U.S. Treasury Department's CDFI Fund, which finances CDFIs and banks that increase their investments in CDFIs. The CDFI Fund has been a critical source of difficult-to-obtain equity capital, enabling CDFIs to grow in asset size. The fund also has helped increase private sector investments in CDFIs, due to its policy of requiring a private match for its capital. More broadly, the fund has raised the visibility and legitimacy of CDFIs, thus opening other federal and state government funding sources to them (Pinsky 2001). The Clinton administration also was responsible for the New Markets Tax Credit program, which was enacted as part of the Community Renewal Tax Relief Act of 2000. The program's initial allocation will leverage $15 billion in private and public sector capital for investments in low-income communities.

The community development finance field is very cognizant of the importance of government support. It actively lobbied to shape and enact these Clinton administration initiatives and has continued to advocate for their preservation during the G. W. Bush administration. Many CDFIs also see advocacy on behalf of low-income communities as a critical part of their missions. This includes state-level efforts to increase regulation and consumer protections, such as laws curtailing predatory lending and fringe banking. It also includes broader efforts to impact policies ranging from workforce development to environmental protection, and to increase the availability of funding for community development finance, such as state-level development of tax credits and CRA legislation.

The eight chapters that follow acknowledge the roles played by public policy both in helping to create the lack of capital in low-income communities and in trying to mitigate this lack of capital. Each chapter summarizes and analyzes what is known about a specific topic, provides a blueprint for what future research needs to address, and makes public policy recommendations. The book is divided into three sections: creating personal assets, building institutions, and evaluating progress.

CREATING PERSONAL ASSETS

The lack of financial services and access to capital in low-income communities hinders residents' ability to accumulate assets, a critical component of financial stability and sustainability for individuals and communities. Assets act as a buffer, enabling households to weather short-term income fluctuations related to loss of a job or unexpected health expenses. They also serve as a capital reserve for starting or expanding a business.

This section, consisting of chapters 2 through 4, addresses the role of finance in the empowerment and enrichment of low-income individuals. It does so by examining asset creation; the contribution of financial education toward poverty alleviation, and the role of microenterprise development in building personal wealth.

The most direct form of asset accumulation is via savings. In chapter 2, Daniel Schneider and Peter Tufano review data on U.S. household savings, especially by less-affluent households, and discuss theories of savings and the impediments to savings. Americans overall are poor savers, but low-income Americans have a particularly difficult time. The impediments to savings include a combination of factors that influence behavior by households and financial service firms.

For example, most Americans take access to saving and bill paying accounts for granted. This is not the case, however, for the estimated 56 million, primarily low-income and minority adult Americans who do not have a bank account (General Accounting Office 2002). Many of these individuals are forced to use high-cost check-cashing services to meet their most basic financial needs, greatly diminishing their ability to save and build assets.

The chapter discusses a number of innovations that might increase savings, largely adapted from experience with more affluent financial services consumers. Some of these innovations are surprisingly simple, such as making it easier for low-income individuals to sign up for employer 401(K) plans. These innovations either stimulate the demand for savings by providing incentives for families to save or making it easier for them to save; or they stimulate the supply of savings by making it easier or more cost effective for business organizations to serve this population.

Education of all forms is both an asset in its own right and a tool for obtaining and accumulating other types of assets. In chapter 3, Jeanne Hogarth, Jane Kolodinsky, and Marianne Hilgert focus on financial education in particular, providing a snapshot of the current state of financial education in the United States as it relates to low-income communities. Decreasing union membership, more temporary employment, disappearing employer pensions, and declining employer-provided health coverage have meant that individuals, particularly those who are low income and working poor, are increasingly bearing financial risk. This has raised awareness of the importance of financial education and of the need for such education, under the premise that well-informed, well-educated consumers should make better decisions for their families, increasing their economic security and well being and minimizing the chance that their assets will be depleted through predatory financial practices.

Hogarth, Kolodinsky, and Hilgert examine whether financial education leads to greater financial security. There is increasing evidence that it makes a difference in consumers' attitudes and behaviors, but most of these studies have focused on household-level behaviors. Personal debt levels have been reduced and savings and assets have been increased—but virtually none of these outcomes have been related to neighborhoods, communities, or economic development more generally.

The chapter concludes with a brief case study of consumer education initiatives at the Vermont Community Development Credit Union to examine whether financial education outcomes go beyond individuals. The findings hint at the potential relationships between financial education and community involvement and provide some hope that financial education programs really are making a difference in communities.

One much-touted avenue of asset creation is self-employment through microenterprise. In chapter 4, Lisa Servon reviews the challenges facing the microenterprise field in the United States, and suggests strategies for addressing them. U.S. microenterprise programs provide business training or small amounts of credit ($35,000 or less) to businesses with five or fewer employees, and sometimes both. As the U.S. field nears the end of its second decade, experts and practitioners agree that it faces difficulties. There also appears to be relatively widespread consensus on the nature of the problems. These include a lack of standardized data, decreased funding from some key sectors, increased competition, and difficulty in reaching the target market.

Servon argues that, if the microenterprise field does not make some significant changes—at both the program and field levels—it will neither sustain itself nor approach its potential. Strategies to address these challenges fall into three broad categories: restructuring, innovation, and accreditation and standardization.

BUILDING INSTITUTIONS

Chapters 5 through 8 examine ways that institutions can serve low-income communities by providing personal financial services; capital for the production of community facilities, housing, and businesses development; and protection against predatory financial practices. In chapter 5, Julia Sass Rubin profiles community development loan (CDLFs) and venture capital funds (CDVCs). Like all CDFIs, community development loan and venture capital funds experienced tremendous growth in numbers and scale during the late 1990s. Since 2001, however, the economic and political environment has become significantly more challenging, making it increasingly difficult for these organizations to obtain the subsidized capital necessary to continue operations. Rubin discusses the factors responsible for the reduction in bank, foundation, and federal government support for CDLFs and CDVCs. She then reviews potential new sources of capital, including state governments, public and Taft-Hartley pension funds, individual investors, and the capital markets. Rubin also discusses the increasing pressure on CDLFs to find ways to use market-rate capital and on CDVCs to demonstrate market-rate financial returns. Rubin concludes by discussing ways that both CDLFs and CDVCs are redesigning and repositioning themselves in response to environmental pressures.

In chapter 6, Marva Williams looks at alternative depository institutions (ADIs), consisting of community development banks and community development, low income and mainstream credit unions. ADIs can play an important role in providing affordable financial services and loans in underserved, lower-income communities. Williams explores the evolution and recent performance of ADIs and finds that, though community development and low-income credit unions and community development banks do serve low-income communities, mainstream credit unions generally do not. Williams proposes public policies designed to encourage them to do so. She also discusses the importance of developing impact methodologies for ADIs and the need to continue advocating for conventional banks and savings and loans to improve their performance in lower-income neighborhoods.

In chapter 7, Rachel Bratt reviews the history of affordable housing production, focusing on how public, private, and nonprofit-oriented programs have attempted to fulfill the three essential components of the housing finance process—raising equity; securing debt financing; and, in the case of lower-income households, creating mechanisms to maintain the long-term affordability of the units. A home is the most important asset that most American families own. As housing prices and rents continue to climb in much of the United States, production of affordable housing is falling further behind demand, making this basic need increasingly out of reach for millions of low- and moderate-income Americans.

Bratt presents an overall assessment of the mechanisms and programs for financing affordable housing from four political perspectives and vantage points. She concludes with proposals for what should be done about homeownership for low-income households and what is needed to stimulate the production of rental housing affordable to low-income households.

In chapter 8, Kathleen Engel and Patricia McCoy focus on predatory lending. Low- and moderate-income individuals who have been able to purchase a home face the risk of losing it at the hands of such lenders. Predatory lenders market abusive loans to financially unsophisticated homeowners who have home equity but do not have a relationship with conventional lenders. As a result of predatory loans, neighborhoods that once were stable become littered with abandoned and neglected homes, resulting in increased crime, falling home values, rising demands for social services, and lower tax revenues.

Engel and McCoy describe how the rise of securitization, deregulation of price terms, affordable lending incentives, bank closings, and historical credit discrimination together fueled the rise and institutionalization of predatory lending in the 1990s. They then evaluate different possible approaches to redressing predatory lending, including industry self-regulation, consumer education and counseling, Community Reinvestment Act oversight, criminal enforcement, existing private causes of action, and a suitability proposal.

EVALUATING PROGRESS

The last section of the book consists of chapter 9, in which Rob Hollister discusses appropriate means of evaluating community development financial institutions. He begins by reviewing methods of evaluation and examples of attempts to evaluate the impacts of CDFIs. A major theme of the chapter is that there are a variety of parties interested in such evaluations—including foundations, governments, and private investors—and that the method of evaluation should be shaped to the appropriate perspective of a given party, while attempting to ensure that the party has realistic expectations about what an evaluation study may be able to provide.

Hollister reviews the strengths and weaknesses of an array of methods that have been used or suggested to evaluate outcomes associated with CDFI activities and details several quality attempts at such evaluations. He reviews recent developments in evaluation of CDFI performance and concludes by stressing that, in many situations, monitoring activities regarding performance may be more useful than attempts to establish and estimate impacts.

CONCLUSIONS

Low-income individuals and communities face numerous obstacles as a result of their financial exclusion. The community-based financial institutions that are trying to help them overcome these obstacles have accomplished a great deal. However, these communities and institutions still are confronting serious challenges going forward. The climate for community development finance has become significantly more difficult over the last six years, even as the needs of low-income communities have grown and the resources available to meet those needs have diminished.

In the face of these challenges, industry leaders are telling community development financial institutions that they must "grow, change or die" (Pinsky 2006). It already is clear that some prominent and pioneering CDFIs will not survive the transition, but the industry as a whole cannot afford to fail. This book is intended to help facilitate the growth and change that must take place. It identifies information gaps that need to be addressed in moving the field forward and lays out potential directions that private and public institutions can take to minimize and address the financial exclusion of low-income communities.

NOTES

1.   Although community development credit unions came about as a result of the War on Poverty, the first credit unions were introduced to the United States from Europe and Canada in the early 1900s (Immergluck 2004; Isbister 1994).

REFERENCES

General Accounting Office. 2002. "Electronic Transfers: Use by Federal Payment Recipients Has Increased but Obstacles to Greater Participation Remain." Report to the Subcommittee on Oversight and Investigations, Committee on Financial Services, House of Representatives (GAO-02-913).

Grzywinski, Ronald. 1991. "The New Old-Fashioned Banking." *Harvard Business Review* 69(3): 87–98.

Immergluck, Daniel. 2004. *Credit to the Community: Community Reinvestment and Fair Lending Policy in the United States.* Armonk, N.Y.: M. E. Sharpe.

Isbister, John. 1994. *Thin Cats: The Community Development Credit Union Movement in the United States.* Davis, Calif.: University of California Center for Cooperatives.

Miller, Thomas. 1994. *Of These Hills: A Review of Kentucky Highlands Investment Corporation,* Unpublished manuscript.

Moy, Kirsten, and Alan Okagaki. 2001. "Changing Capital Markets and their Implications for Community Development Finance." *Capital Xchange,* July 2001. Washington: Brookings Institution.

National Center for Economic Alternatives (NCEA). 1981. *Federal Assistance to Community Development Corporations: An Evaluation of Title VII of the Community Services Act of 1974.* Washington: National Center for Economic Alternatives.

National Community Reinvestment Corporation (NCRC). 2005. "Policy." Accessed at http://www.ncrc.org/policy/cra.php.

Parachini, Laurence F., Jr. 1980. *A Political History of the Special Impact Program.* Cambridge, Mass.: Center for Community Economic Development.

Pinsky, Mark. 2001. "Taking Stock: CDFIs Look Ahead After 25 Years of Community Development Finance." *Capital Xchange,* December 2001. Washington: Brookings Institution.

————. 2006. "Grow, Change, or Die." Speech delivered to the Community Development Society, St. Louis, Mo., June 26, 2006.

Zdenek, Robert O. 1990. *Taking Hold: The Growth and Support of Community Development Corporations.* Washington: National Congress for Community Economic Development.

PART I

Creating Personal Assets

CHAPTER TWO

New Savings from Old Innovations: Asset Building for the Less Affluent

Daniel Schneider and Peter Tufano

"[We should] focus on the 100 million who are investors and not try to cover 'pre-investors' who should focus on saving."
—Financial services executive, private discussion with author, 2004

ALTHOUGH the rich and poor both have the need and the desire to build financial assets to enable them to meet important life goals, there is a false dichotomy that is captured in the epigraph. Taken from an exchange with a successful financial services executive, it signifies the perception that the rich invest, but the masses at best only save. What differentiates the wealth-building activities of the rich and the rest of society to justify this semantic distinction? Is it because the less affluent tend to save in banks and the rich invest in mutual funds and hedge funds or because the less affluent tend to buy low-risk products and the rich buy higher risk products? If so, then would a rich person's holdings in bank products or money market mutual funds not constitute part of his or her investing strategy? Is planning for short-horizon goals just saving and long-horizon goals investing? Trying to differentiate saving and investment based on institutional features seems to be an impossible task.

This is because, in the financial system, a dizzying number of terms describe the same function and seemingly different products and institutions often serve identical needs. To see past these institutional definitions, the functional approach to defining the financial system (Crane et al. 1995) suggests that activities can be decomposed into the set of core functions they perform. Saving (or investing) addresses two such functions: moving money across either time or space and risk management. In either activity, the saver-investor moves money across time because she reduces her consumption today to consume more tomorrow, perhaps when it is necessary to fund a child's education or to retire. By saving or investing, she engages in risk management to protect herself from various risks (such as unemployment or poor health) or to diversify her investments.

Along these dimensions, saving by the poor and investing by the rich are identical. These functions (moving money across time and space and managing risk) are timeless and common to all people. In part, this likely explains why some prefer to use the broader term asset building, though even this ignores important risk-management motives for saving.

Adopting a functional approach to understanding the problems of helping less affluent families to save leads us to consider a broad range of institutions and possible solutions. Supporting saving for the less affluent is not a banking problem or a mutual fund problem; it is not merely about time deposits or about stocks and bonds. Rather, it is a generic problem that can best be understood in terms of simple root causes: diseconomies of small scale and poor information flows. It is a problem whose solution is likely to be found in many different institutions and products.

Adopting a functional approach might mistakenly seem to suggest a naiveté about institutional details or an ignorance of the differences between saving by the more and less affluent. To the contrary, we recognize that though the need to save may be common to rich and poor, their specific preferences—and the institutions that vie to serve them—are not alike. As we will discuss, government policies encourage asset building among the more and less affluent, financial service firms have distinct preferences about which families they choose to serve, and these families may have different risk tolerances that lead to different goals and practices.

Regardless of risk profile, saving appears to have important benefits for families. Michael Sherraden (1991) hypothesized that the ownership of assets would result in certain economic, social, and political benefits. It is important to note that he attributes these effects not to the high income associated with asset holding but rather to the ownership of those assets. Table 2.1, adapted from Sherraden (1991), and Deborah Page-Adams and her colleagues (2001), summarizes these findings.

The positive effects Sherraden discussed have been documented in a number of studies. Assets in the form of homeownership have been shown to increase residential stability, lead to higher levels of property maintenance, increase social and political participation, and produce greater marital sta-

Table 2.1   Hypothesized and Observed Effects of Asset Holding

Asset Effects Hypothesized by Sherraden	Homeownership Effects	Financial Asset Effects
–Improve household stability –Create an orientation toward the future –Stimulate development of other assets –Enable focus and specialization –Provide a foundation for risk taking –Increase personal efficacy –Increase political participation –Enhance the welfare of offspring	–Decreases residential mobility –Raises property values –Increases home improvement, property maintenance –Increases involvement in neighborhood organizations –Decreases instances of domestic violence –Increases marital stability –Leads to better health outcomes –Leads to stronger economic position –Creates more favorable life outcomes for children	–Increases marital stability –Leads to better health outcomes –Leads to greater economic security –Raises educational attainment by children

Source: Adapted from Sherraden (1991) and Page-Adams et al. (2001).

bility. Home ownership is also correlated with higher levels of family health. Assets have been shown to lead to greater economic security and to decreases in domestic violence (Page-Adams et al. 2001). Assets and homeownership benefit children through better educational outcomes and lower levels of teen pregnancy (Shobe 2002). Saving on the part of the poor can also lead to a number of positive psychological effects. These include feeling more confident about the future and more economically secure. Financial assets also appear to create the future orientation that Sherraden hypothesized, with low-income savers in a recent demonstration project reporting making plans for future education and for retirement (Moore et al. 2001). Together, this body of literature suggests both individual and neighborhood-level benefits to asset-holding.

This chapter surveys a wide range of material, providing data on saving activities, summarizing theories of saving, and hypothesizing why financial institutions have little interest in low-income families. However, our ultimate goal is to be prescriptive. In the financial sector, financial innovation has been a powerful engine of change and growth (Merton 1992). Many financial innovations—in both policy and business practice—primarily serve more well-to-do families. We discuss a number of innovations or practices that might be re-adapted to support asset building by low-income families. Thus, whereas the financial service sector has been enamored with the "truly affluent" and recently dubbed the "mass affluent," we seek to address the real mass of society: the less affluent who make up most American families.

BASIC SAVING FACTS

The two primary measures used in discussions of asset building are new saving, as a percentage of income, and total wealth, as dollars saved. New saving represents the flow of money that accumulates to create the stock of total wealth. Wealth, or net worth, is the difference between assets (financial plus nonfinancial assets) and liabilities (debt).

To begin this discussion, we ask three basic questions about savings and assets. Who saves and holds assets? In what form do people save and hold assets? How do U.S. saving rates and wealth holdings compare internationally?

Saving Outcomes: Who Saves? Who Holds Wealth?

Over the past fifty years, researchers have developed a relatively large literature on the determinants of saving and asset holdings. This body of work examines the demographic and financial characteristics of savers and those who have wealth.

Income, perhaps more than any other factor, has been shown to determine both saving and asset holdings. Early work by Irwin Friend and Stanley Schor (1959) and Dorothy Projector (1968) documents a link between a household's saving rate and current income. Later studies (Avery and Kennickell 1991, Browning and Lusardi 1996; Hugget and Ventura 2000) confirm this association. Projector and Gertrude Weiss (1966) find a similar association between income and asset holdings, showing that households with higher income levels accumulated more wealth. Eric Hurst and his colleagues (1998) also detail the wealth-income association using data from the 1990s.

The 2004 wave of the Survey of Consumer Finances provides additional evidence of these relationships through basic bivariate comparisons between income and saving rates and asset holdings. Families in the lowest income quintile, with average income of $11,000, were far less likely to save at all than families in higher income brackets. Only 34 percent of families in the lowest income bracket, and only 44 percent of families in the second-lowest bracket, saved at all, as opposed to 81 percent of the highest income families (Bucks, Kennickell, and Moore 2006). However, though the correlation between saving rates and income is fairly clear in the literature, this is not to say that low-income families cannot save. Recent evidence from the American Dream Demonstration project shows that low-income families, particularly when given incentives and provided with financial education, can save (Schreiner, Clancy, and Sherraden 2002; Mills et al. 2004).

This saving gap is accompanied by a gap in asset ownership. Families in the three highest income quintiles were 33 percent more likely to hold any kind of financial asset than those in the lowest quintile. Higher-income families were also more likely to hold nonfinancial assets. Those in the top two quintiles were more than twice as likely to own their own home and were also more likely to hold other real estate equity, own a car, or have equity in a business.

Household income can be dynamic, shifting as household members age and change jobs, and a number of studies have attempted to take this into account by substituting current income with proxies for permanent income. Karen Dynan, Jonathan Skinner, and Stephen Zeldes (2004), find that higher levels of permanent income, derived using education, consumption, and past and future earnings, were also associated with higher rates of saving. Francine Blau and John Graham (1990) also proxy for permanent income and find a similar relationship between income and asset holdings. Measured on its own and not as a proxy, education also has an effect on saving rates (Bernheim and Scholz 1993; Attanasio 1994) and on wealth (Keister 2004) with higher levels of education associated with larger amounts of wealth and higher rates of savings.

Age also exerts a significant effect on savings and wealth. Older households tend to have more assets (Hurst et al. 1998; Blau and Graham 1990), though only to a point, because in retirement households begin to spend down their assets (Friend and Schor 1959). Older households save at higher rates as well, though this relationship also follows a hump-backed curve, with saving rates lowest for the youngest and oldest households (Attanasio 1994; Bosworth, Burtless, and Sabelhaus 1991).

Although there is an intuitive relationship between income and age and saving and asset-holding that is bolstered by the literature, other factors also influence wealth and savings rates. Melvin Oliver and Thomas Shapiro (1997) discuss the role of race in asset holdings, pointing to 1988 data from the Survey of Income and Program Participation (SIPP) on the substantial gap between the net worth of African American and white families. This gap persists. Data from the 2004 SCF places median white net worth at $140,700, versus only $20,400 for black families (Bucks, Kennickell, and Moore 2006). The literature on the effects of race on saving and asset holding suggests that, though income has some explanatory effect (Barsky et al. 2002), black households have less wealth, even when controlling for other demographic and financial variables (Blau and Graham 1990; Oliver and Shapiro 1997; Hurst et al. 1998; Chiteji and Hamilton 2005). Earlier studies (Galenson 1972) found that black households did not necessarily have lower saving rates than white households of the same income. Orazio Attanasio (1994) finds continued support for this position.

Oliver and Shapiro (1997) offer one explanation for this disjuncture between unequal asset holdings and similar saving rates. It is attributable, they suggest, in part to other demographic differences between whites and blacks—income, occupation, and education—but in part also to a history of restricted access to home ownership for blacks and the limited degree to which blacks have been able to transfer wealth to succeeding generations. We will more fully examine the extent to which government has differentially helped some to build assets later in this chapter. Although the various studies on race and wealth are generally not at odds, this area is quite complicated. John Scholz and Kara Levine (2002) are right to conclude that "there is no consensus on this issue" (p. 6).

Household structure has also been identified as a determinant of saving and wealth. James Smith and James Lupton (2003) and Ngina Chiteji and Darrick Hamilton (2005) found that married couples had more assets than individuals living in other types of households, even when controlling for the income and wealth aggregation effects of marriage. Barry Bosworth, Gary Burtless, and John Sabelhaus (1991) found that married couples also saved at higher rates. Although most studies confine their analysis to the household unit, Chiteji and Hamilton (2005) took a broader perspective and found that having members of one's extended family living in poverty had a negative impact on the wealth holdings of middle-income households, presumably because better-off family members assisted their poorer relatives. Similarly, Lisa Keister (2004) found that a larger family size and family disruption in childhood through divorce or separation also led to lower wealth holdings in adulthood. Edward Bird and Paul Hagstrom (1999) buttress this finding in part, by arguing that, rather than poor family members directly depleting their relatives' savings, large families function as a form of insurance, decreasing the motive to hold any emergency savings. Social insurance, or public benefits, may also have an effect on savings.

How Do People Save?

When Americans do build wealth, they hold both financial and nonfinancial assets, and homeownership plays an important role. In 2004, 69.1 percent of households owned their own home. In 2001, in the aggregate, home equity made up 27 percent of total assets for all households (Bucks, Kennickell, and Moore 2006; Di 2003). Home equity was particularly important for low-income and minority families. Fewer of these families owned their own homes, but among those that did, home equity made up 77 percent and 55 percent of total household assets respectively (Di 2003). Although home equity is the single largest component of household wealth, checking and savings accounts (91 percent), stocks (21 percent), and retirement accounts (50 percent) are also considerable (Bucks, Kennickell, and Moore 2006). Combined financial assets made up 42 percent of total household assets in 2001 (Di 2003). Ownership of these and other nonfinancial assets was not equal across households of different incomes. Compared with those households in the top decile of income, households in the bottom quintile were far less likely to own stock (5 percent versus 55 percent) retirement accounts (10 percent versus 89 percent), transaction accounts (76 percent versus 100 percent), and vehicles (65 percent versus 93 percent) (Bucks, Kennickell, and Moore 2006). Tables 2.2 and 2.3 present additional data on asset holdings by income quintile.

Americans also hold substantial amounts of debt. Seventy-six percent of all households held some kind of debt in 2004, with roughly equal shares having home equity loans, installment loans, or credit card balances (about 45 percent). The median value of such debt was $55,300, most of which was mortgages and home equity loans. At first glance, low-income families appear less likely to hold debt than families in higher income quintiles, but these figures are slightly misleading (Bucks, Kennickell, and Moore 2006). Although only 30 percent of families in the lowest income quintile had credit card balances, versus nearly 50 percent of those in the 20th to the 90th percentiles, those who had credit cards were much more likely to have outstanding balances. More than two-thirds of families with credit cards and less than $10,000 in income had credit card debt, versus 55 percent of all cardholding families. Low-income families have seen their credit card debt burden rise dramatically over the past fifteen years, up 184 percent since 1989 to $1,837 (Draut and Silva 2003).

Low-income families have also had to contend with a range of debt products that bear very high interest rates and extract high fees from borrowers. These include payday loans, generally with a maturity of two weeks and with effective APRs as high as 390 percent, and refund anticipation loans—short-term, high-fee, loans offered by paid tax preparers that allow tax filers to receive their federal refunds several days faster than the IRS would send it (see Barr 2004a; Berube et al. 2002). Additionally, low-income homebuyers and homeowners face predatory high-rate mortgages that are often targeted at low-income and minority communities (see chapter 8, this volume). One can criticize these products, but their continued success speaks to real and perceived needs for immediate credit by less affluent families.

Economists and businesspeople often focus on net worth or wealth, which is defined as assets less liabilities, to provide the clearest picture of a household's financial health. The specific definition of net worth can vary. Some estimates take all assets and all debts into account, whereas others, which

Table 2.2 Percentage Owning Select Financial Assets, 2004

	Savings Bonds	Certificates of Deposit	Mutual Funds	Stocks	Transaction Accounts	All Financial Assets
Percentile of income						
Less than 20	6.2	5.0	3.6	5.1	75.5	80.1
20 to 39.9	8.8	12.7	7.6	8.2	87.3	91.5
40 to 59.9	15.4	11.8	12.7	16.3	95.9	98.5
60 to 79.9	14.9	14.9	18.6	28.2	98.4	99.1
80 to 89.9	32.3	16.3	26.2	35.8	99.1	99.8
90 to 100	29.9	21.5	39.1	55.0	100.0	100.0
Lowest quintile ownership rate as a percent of top decile ownership rate	20.7	23.3	9.2	9.3	75.5	80.1
Percentile of net worth						
Less than 25	6.2	2.2	2.0	3.6	75.4	79.8
25 to 49.9	13.2	6.5	7.2	9.3	92.0	96.1
50 to 74.9	22.7	16.0	12.5	21.0	98.0	99.4
75 to 89.9	28.5	24.2	32.4	39.1	99.7	100.0
90 to 100	28.1	28.8	47.3	62.9	100.0	100.0
Lowest quintile ownership rate as a percent of top decile ownership rate	22.1	7.6	4.2	5.7	75.4	79.8

Source: Bucks, Kennickell, and Moore (2006).

Table 2.3 Median Value of Select Financial Assets Among Asset Holders, 2004 (in Dollars)

	Savings Bonds	Certificates of Deposit	Mutual Funds	Stocks	Transaction Accounts	All Financial Assets
Percentile of income						
Less than 20	400	10,000	15,300	6,000	600	1,300
20 to 39.9	600	14,000	25,000	8,000	1,500	4,900
40 to 59.9	800	10,000	23,000	12,000	3,000	15,500
60 to 79.9	1,000	18,000	25,500	10,000	6,600	48,500
80 to 89.9	800	20,000	33,500	15,000	11,000	108,200
90 to 100	2,000	33,000	125,000	57,000	28,000	365,100
Percentile of net worth						
Less than 25	300	2,000	2,000	1,900	500	1,000
25 to 49.9	500	5,800	7,400	3,500	2,000	9,900
50 to 74.9	1,000	10,400	16,000	8,000	5,800	47,200
75 to 89.9	2,000	31,000	50,000	20,000	15,800	203,000
90 to 100	2,500	46,000	160,000	110,000	43,000	728,800

Source: Bucks, Kennickell, and Moore (2006).

may be more concerned with the short-term ability of households to survive emergencies, may exclude home equity or other nonliquid assets. Based on the most expansive definition of net worth, there is substantial inequality between households by income, age, race, education, and homeownership status.

Families in the lowest quintile of income had a median net worth of $7,500 in 2004, compared to more than $900,000 for those in the top decile (Bucks, Kennickell, and Moore 2006). Older families also tended to have higher net worth, as did homeowners and families where the head of household had higher levels of education. White non-Hispanic families had a median net worth of more than $140,000, whereas nonwhite families had median net worth of only $24,800. The 25 percent of families with the lowest net worth had a median net worth of only $1,700 and a mean net worth of zero (Bucks, Kennickell, and Moore 2006). During the 1980s and 1990s, the top 20 percent of households by net worth posted the most substantial gains (mean net worth increased by 71 percent), and households in the bottom 40 percent experienced losses, with mean net worth declining 44 percent (Wolff 2006).

U.S. Savings in the International Context

Compared to other nations, U.S. households save less and hold fewer assets. The household savings rate (measured as a percentage of disposable household income) was 2.1 percent in 2003, well below that of other industrialized countries, such as Japan (6.4 percent), Italy (15 percent), the Netherlands (11.2 percent), Germany (10.8 percent), and the United Kingdom (5.7 percent) (OECD 2004). See table 2.4 for additional cross-national savings data. Axel Borsch-Supan and Ana Lusardi (2003) find similar disparities using earlier OECD data. This is not a wholly new phenomenon. The U.S. saving rate was below that of Japan, Germany, and Italy through the 1970s and 1990s but has only recently dropped below that of the United Kingdom (Porteba 1994). As a percentage of disposable income, in 2003, U.S. households had lower levels of net worth than households in Japan, German, Italy, and the United Kingdom. U.S. households also had the lowest levels of nonfinancial assets relative to disposable income, but one of the highest ratios of financial wealth to disposable income, second only to Japan (OECD 2004). This difference may be attributable to home ownership patterns. In the UK, homeownership rates are higher than in the United States, particularly among younger households, leading to greater nonfinancial asset holdings (Banks and Rohwedder 2003). On a per capita basis, these general trends hold. In 2001, U.S. per capita financial assets were higher than those of Japan, Germany, Italy, the UK, and France but per capita residential property assets were the lowest of the six countries (Babeau and Sbano 2002).

Table 2.4   Household Savings as a Percent of Disposable Income

	1999	2000	2001	2002	2003
Canada	4.0	4.6	4.5	4.2	2.0
France	10.4	11.0	11.5	12.1	11.1
Germany	9.8	9.8	10.3	10.6	10.8
Japan	10.7	9.5	6.6	6.4	6.4
Netherlands	9.6	6.8	9.0	8.6	11.2
United States	2.4	2.3	1.7	2.3	2.1
Belgium	14.1	13.1	13.8	15.1	14.3
Italy	15.2	14.6	15.8	16.0	15.0
Sweden	2.0	2.9	8.3	9.7	8.0
Switzerland	10.0	11.7	11.6	11.6	11.6
United Kingdom	5.3	5.5	6.7	5.5	5.7

Source: Adapted from OECD Economic Outlook (2004).
Note: Data measurement varies across countries to some degree, see OECD Economic Outlook (2004) for a detailed explanation.

There is more scattered data available on the saving behavior and asset holdings of the poor in these countries. In Germany, low-income families in the bottom quartile of income tend to have much lower saving rates, between 0 percent and 5 percent over much of the life cycle, versus the higher than 20 percent among families with incomes in the top quartile (Borsch-Supan, Reil-Held, and Schnabel 2003). In Japan, low-income households also have lower savings rates, a difference that manifests itself most clearly in the rates among the elderly. Whereas Japanese households over the age of fifty-five with incomes in the top three income quintiles continue to save at positive rates through old age, low-income households do not (Kitamura, Takayama, and Arita 2003).

Edward Wolff (2002) tracks wealth inequality in the United States, the UK, and Sweden and finds that the share of wealth held by the top 1 percent has been increasing since the 1970s in the United States but declining fairly steadily in the UK and Sweden. He also calculates measures of wealth inequality in the United States, France, Canada, Germany, Japan, and Sweden for the 1980s and finds that the United States has (by any measure) a greater degree of wealth inequality than the other countries in his sample.

ADEQUACY OF SAVINGS AT MACRO AND MICRO LEVELS

Macroeconomists measure aggregate savings levels for the entire economy while others focus primarily on households as the unit of analysis. While both are important, one measures the health of the economy and the other the health of individual families. We now address the question of how much wealth is too little and how much is enough through each of these frames.

Macroeconomic Approaches to Wealth and Savings Rates

National saving (the sum of personal, corporate, and government saving) represents the available stocks of capital for investment. That investment will ultimately determine the level of U.S. income. Essentially, one sacrifices today to save in order to consume later.

Although personal saving rates have declined over the past fifteen years, government saving in the form of surpluses compensated through the late 1990s. However, over the last several years, governmental saving has dropped significantly as federal deficits have risen. Net national saving (national saving less expected depreciation of capital stock) was 1.8 percent of net national income in 2003, a seventy-year low (Orszag 2004). These low levels threaten the nation's ability to provide capital for investment and thus to generate income in the future. Historically, the United States has been able to turn to foreign markets for its capital formation needs. Consequently, since 2000, foreign ownership of the public debt has risen steeply to a forty-year high of 37 percent (Gale 2004). In the second quarter of 2004, foreign capital made up more than 66 percent of net domestic investment, and more than 5 percent of GDP (Cooper and Madigan 2004). Observers in government and business worry that this imbalance is unsustainable and could lead to trouble for the economy, possibly higher interest rates (Greenspan 2004; Roach 2003).

The United States, then, appears to be saving too little from a macroeconomic perspective, but it is possible to save too much. By over-saving, individuals can collectively depress consumption and spending to the point of economic recession. Japan may have run up against this problem in the late 1990s (Goad 1998), but few are worried that the United States faces any real threats from an overly high saving rate.

Equity Approaches to Wealth and Savings

Equity concerns frame a second approach to wealth and saving in the United States. Rather than examine the adequacy of personal savings to meet the requirements of the macroeconomy, this perspective focuses on the distribution of wealth among households, particularly on the inequality of asset ownership between high-income and low-income and between African American and white households. This focus on equity arises from the idea that equal opportunity is tied closely to a diffusion of wealth throughout society. There is substantial wealth inequality among American households, which raises concerns about class mobility and democratic viability (Wolff 2002; Sherraden 1991).

Wolff (2002) tracks the share of total wealth held by the top 1 percent of households between the 1920s and the late 1990s. He finds that whereas the top 1 percent of the population owned 40 percent of U.S. wealth (defined as net worth) in 1922, by the mid-1970s that figure had declined by half. James Smith (1987) finds a similar decline in the share of assets held by the wealthiest 1 percent between 1972 and 1976. However, wealth inequality increased during the 1980s. By 1989, the top 1 percent of households again held nearly 40 percent of the wealth. The degree of inequality is neatly captured by the Gini Coefficient. When all wealth is held equally, the coefficient is equal to 0; the closer to 1, the more unequal the ownership of wealth. During the 1980s, the Gini coefficient rose sharply from 0.80 to 0.84 (Wolff 2002). However, this trend did not continue through the 1990s, when the Gini co-efficient stabilized around 0.83 (Wolff 2006). Although the wealth position of minority households improved relative to white households during that time, by 2001 African Americans still held only 16 percent of the wealth of white households (Kennickell 2003).

Microbenchmarks of Wealth and Savings

A third perspective on asset sufficiency concentrates on microbenchmarks. This literature considers wealth in terms of the amounts necessary to sustain a certain lifestyle. We identify three ways this concept has been applied.

First, a number of studies have generated calculations of how much families need to save for retirement. One common method is to calculate the share of pre-retirement consumption expenses that could be maintained by drawing on assets in retirement. Using this methodology, several studies have documented a general inadequacy in the retirement savings of U.S. households. James Moore and Olivia Mitchell (1997) find that the median household nearing retirement would need to save an additional 16 percent of income to retire at age sixty-two without a drop in consumption and that households in the lowest decile of income would need to save an additional 40 percent of earnings. Two other studies document a similar saving inadequacy and hypothesize that this shortfall is likely due to households not fully understanding their consumption needs in retirement (Banks, Blundell, and Tanner 1998; Bernheim, Skinner, and Weinberg 2001). However, Michael Hurd and Susann Rohwedder (2003) use survey data from the Health and Retirement Study to find that 69 percent of households anticipated decreasing their expenditures in retirement. Mark Waschawsky and John Ameriks (2001) take a different approach in using financial planning software to estimate the share of households that will be able to retire with adequate savings. They find that more than half of middle-income households will not be able to fully fund their retirements. The extent to which households have adequate savings also varies according to which assets are counted (for example, including home equity increases the share that are prepared), and which segments of the population are examined, (for instance, low-income households are much less likely to have adequate savings) (for a recent summary of the literature, see Shackleton 2003).

Second, related to the literature on income poverty, one body of work attempts to define and measure asset poverty. There are essentially two branches to this literature. One incorporates household asset holdings into the measurement of income adequacy in order to gauge poverty. In this approach, assets are generally annuitized and that flow is added to income. J. Murray (1964) and Burton Weisbrod and Lee Hanson (1968) are among the first to adopt this method and both find that this approach decreases the poverty rate but produces a greater inequality between households. More recently, Edward Wolff, Ajit Zacharias, and Asena Caner (2005) undertake similar calculations using data from the 1990s. They, too, find that income adjusted for an annuitized asset stream is more unequally distributed than income alone. Generally, calculations performed using this method find that by including assets, fewer households are classified below the poverty line (Moon 1977; Steuerle and McClung 1977; Wolff 1990). However, several studies, including Daniel Radner and Denton Vaughan (1987) and Wolff (1990), consider both income and assets but do so separately, calculating the share of households falling below either an income or an asset poverty line. This approach tends to increase the share of households in poverty.

This two-part approach is closer to the method Melvin Oliver and Thomas Shapiro (1990) propose, which considers asset poverty independent of income poverty. Using 1988 data, Oliver and Shapiro (1997) find that 44 percent of all households, and 78 percent of African American households, would be unable to survive at the poverty line for three months on their net financial assets alone. Robert Haveman and Wolff (2001) adopt this definition and find that in 1998 more than 25 percent of families would be asset poor based on total household wealth, and that nearly 40 percent would be based on financial wealth. Further, Haveman and Wolff show that the asset-poor percentage of the population increased from the 1980s to the late 1990s. Caner and Wolff (2002) have similar results but also introduce an asset poverty floor of $5,000, regardless of consumption expenses. Employing this minimum, they estimate an asset poverty rate based on financial assets of 46 percent in 1999. This asset-specific approach is perhaps more useful than the combined income asset measures in that it recognizes a unique role for assets as a buffer against emergencies. However, these levels are not individualized to take into account the risks of income and expenditure shocks that particular households face.

Finally, both the popular press and financial education professionals often use "rules of thumb" to determine asset adequacy. Perhaps the most common of these is the maxim that families should keep three to six months' worth of living expenses in reserve in case of emergency (Siskos 2001; Barrett 2002). This rule of thumb is quite similar to the asset-poverty measure that both Oliver and Shapiro (1990) and Haveman and Wolff (2001) use. However, it is both simplified to not require individuals to calculate their monthly expenses at the poverty line and tailored to each family's financial situation.

WHY DO PEOPLE SAVE? WHY IS SAVING IMPORTANT?

In the previous section, we discussed several measures of saving adequacy, with particular focus on emergency and retirement needs. Here, we look more closely at the reasons people save and why saving is important. This classification is descriptive, not prescriptive. Rather than discussing what people should save for, we use survey data, economic models, and empirical studies to establish three primary motivations: emergencies, family development and family support, and retirement and bequests.

Precautionary Motives

Maintaining a stock of assets for use in case of emergency is a key reason for saving. Survey data from the America Saves! Program indicates that having an emergency fund was the leading saving goal among the 15,000 program participants (America Saves 2004a). In a recent study of the savings behavior of low-income tax filers, Sondra Beverly, Daniel Schneider, and Peter Tufano (2006) found that emergency saving is the second most common goal (with only "saving for an unspecified use" named more frequently). The 2004 Survey of Consumer Finances asked respondents their most important reason for saving and found that "liquidity" was the second most frequent response, named by 30 percent of respondents (Bucks, Kennickell, and Moore 2006).

A growing economic literature has attempted to test the extent to which these precautionary saving motives explain wealth accumulation. Martin Browning and Ana Lusardi (1996) review the literature on empirical tests of precautionary saving and find mixed support for its effect on household saving. However, several more recent studies have uncovered stronger evidence. Christopher Carroll and Andrew Samwick (1998) found that precautionary saving motives could explain as much as 45 percent of the wealth of households. Arthur Kennickell and Lusardi (2003) used survey responses to the SCF and found that most households desire precautionary savings and that the amounts desired are roughly 20 percent of financial net worth. However, they found that many households, particularly low-income households, have not reached their stated emergency saving goals.

Although families plan to save for emergencies, and recent studies have documented the role that precautionary saving plays in household asset accumulation, the extent to which this succeeds in helping low-income households deal with emergencies is little studied. However, two papers consider this question and raise doubts. Patricia Ruggles and Roberton Williams (1989) examined poverty spells, measuring the number of families who entered into poverty at least once during the year based on monthly income, even if their total annual income was above the official poverty line. They found that if the families that entered poverty had drawn down their assets during these periods, 40 percent of poverty entries would have been avoided. These findings fit with those of Haveman and Wolff (2001) and Caner and Wolff (2002) showing low levels of asset holdings among much of the population, as well as with those of Kennickell and Lusardi (2003), who found that many households have not achieved their emergency saving goals.

Asset Development and Family Support

In addition to emergency saving, large numbers of Americans name saving goals such as education (12 percent), home purchase (5 percent), and saving for their family (5 percent) (Bucks, Kennickell, and Moore 2006). Any saving is an asset, of course, but investments in education, home purchase, or small business development have been distinguished in the small, but growing, literature on asset-building for their potential to create additional assets and other personal advantages (see Sherraden 1991; Page-Adams et al. 2001).

Life-Cycle Theories of Savings

Finally, SCF respondents most frequently cite retirement as their primary reason for saving (35 percent) (Bucks, Kennickell, and Moore 2006). We have already considered a number of studies on the adequacy of retirement savings; next we briefly discuss the economic literature on retirement and bequest motives. Beginning with Franco Modigliani and Richard Brumberg (1954), economic theories of saving have been modeled around retirement as the primary saving motive. This theory, the life cycle hypothesis, holds that individuals will seek to smooth expenditure over time, with younger households compensating for low levels of current income by taking debt and then increasing saving through middle age before finally spending down savings at retirement. Milton Friedman's (1957) permanent income hypothesis is predicated on a similar set of assumptions. He argues that individuals will consume based on their permanent income, the income they can expect to have over their lifetime, as opposed to their current income, which may fluctuate over time (for a detailed explanation of the life cycle and permanent income hypotheses, see Browning and Lusardi 1996).

WHY DON'T PEOPLE SAVE?

Despite financial planners' advice, economic models, and their own good sense, many people, particularly many with low incomes, don't save. There are a number of possible explanations for this behavior, and it seems likely that they work in concert.

Can't Save

Intuitively, the simplest explanation for low or no saving is that many households find such behavior beyond their means. Low-income households in particular may encounter a structural imbalance between basic consumption needs and income that leaves little room for savings.

The clearest evidence for this explanation is found in census poverty data. In 2003, 12.5 percent of the population, more than 7 million families, lived in poverty; for a four-person household, this meant less than $18,700 in annual income (DeNavas-Walt, Proctor, and Mills 2003; U.S. Census 2004). Further, it is often held that the current poverty measure underestimates the income required to meet basic consumption needs (Ruggles 1990). It seems unrealistic to expect that families living in poverty would have much left over for saving. Sondra Beverly (1997) reviews several studies on the difficulties low-income families face in trying to save while struggling to meet basic consumption requirements. Beverly and her colleagues Jennifer Tescher and Jennifer Romich (2004) hypothesize that subsistence needs will take precedence over saving for very low-income households. Essentially, this perspective suggests that for the poorest families, the phenomenon of low or nonexistent saving is primarily a problem of low incomes versus subsistence needs.

Won't Save

A second approach takes the view that low saving is the result of a strong preference for current consumption. David Laibson (1997) argues that consumers are impatient, would rather consume in the present than save for the future. This suggests that saving is primarily a consumption problem, perhaps exacerbated by business and cultural forces that encourage greater consumption (Holt and Schorr 2000). There is evidence of this to the extent that saving is low even among higher-income families and credit card debt is significant across most income groups (Bucks, Kennickell, and Moore 2006).

In this scenario, households do not plan ahead and set saving targets. Rather, consumers decide on short-run expenditures and, if there is excess income, hold it briefly as savings. If consumption exceeds income, consumers rely on credit. This behavior is akin to the pecking order theory in corporate finance, under which firms do not plan their level of debt financing, but instead undertake external borrowing when internal reserves are not adequate. For households and firms, saving and credit serve as the temporary "plug" in the budget.

Richard Thaler and Hersh Shefrin (1981) and Shefrin and Thaler (1988) place this pattern of spending temptations and ad hoc savings decisions in a behavioral economic framework: families have trouble saving, but can build assets when given the tools to do so. The authors articulate mechanisms that individuals use to resist spending temptations, principally self-control and mental accounting. In discussing self-control, the authors describe a set of rules, both external (such as restricted withdrawal accounts) and internal (such as personal prohibitions on borrowing). Regarding mental accounts, they proffer that individuals conceptually code (or frame) various types of income, considering large bonuses as assets and smaller regular amounts as income.

The Role of Incentives

The federal government provides substantial incentives for wealthier families to save and invest, but fails to do so for low-income families. It was not always this way. There is in fact a long history of government involvement in encouraging saving and investing among all Americans. The passage of the Homestead Act in 1862, for example, allowed hundreds of thousands of Americans to acquire land. Fees were minimal, and the only substantial financial barrier was having enough capital to last until the homestead was self-sustaining. Trina Williams (2005) estimates that tens of millions of Americans have benefited from the assets created through the Homestead Act.

Soldiers returning from World War II were the recipients of an asset-building program on a similar scale. More than 2 million veterans took advantage of the G.I. bill to pursue higher education (Olson 1973). The bill also helped millions of veterans buy homes, building on changes in the structure of residential mortgages that had begun during the 1930s (Boshara 2001). Before the Great Depression, home mortgages were generally short term, required large down payments, and imposed substantial balloon payments at maturity. However, in the 1930s, the federal government's Home Owner's Loan Corporation (HOLC) began to offer longer-term mortgages (Bartelt 1993). This policy continued under the Federal Housing Administration (FHA) which "by changing the terms of mortgages, helped a great many people to become home owners" (Katz 1993, 461). However, though the FHA and HOLC brought home ownership opportunities to many families, they purposefully excluded millions by using strict criteria that disallowed mortgages in poor and minority areas, "redlining" whole neighborhoods (Sugrue 1993).

The federal government continues to promote asset building. A recent report by Lillian Woo, William Schweke, and David Buchholz (2004) concluded that in 2003 the government provided incentives worth some $335 billion dollars to encourage Americans to save. Of this, approximately one-third was spent on home ownership programs, including tax deductions for mortgage interest and property taxes, an additional third on retirement programs, including the tax-privileged status granted to 401(k) and IRA plans, and a final third on policies to encourage saving and investment, including tax exemptions granted on capital gains. The large majority of these expenditures accrued to middle- and upper-middle-income families. The authors estimated that the bottom 60 percent of households by income received only 5 percent of these benefits.

Affirmative federal financial support for asset building by low-income families is weak, and in fact, federal policy often undermines whatever asset building low-income families might undertake on their own. First, a number of government programs appear to make personal saving less important. Several studies have examined the relationship between public assistance and saving and wealth. Glenn Hubbard, Jonathan Skinner, and Stephen Zeldes (1995) argue that public assistance decreases the motive for households to build precautionary savings. Eric Engen and Jonathan Gruber (2001) find that unemployment insurance reduces individual saving. Bird and Hagstrom (1999) show that wealth can be predicted in part by the amount of benefits a household could expect to receive given a shock to income.

Second, many income support programs have an asset test that limits eligibility to those households holding less than a specified amount of wealth. Advocates of asset building for low-income families have argued that these tests unfairly penalize and depress saving by poor households (Sherraden 1991) and a number of studies give credence to those claims. Gruber and Aaron Yelowitz (1999) find that asset tests for public health insurance discourages asset building. Elizabeth Powers (1998) finds a similar effect for AFDC asset limits. James Ziliak (2003) finds evidence that public assistance receipt depresses wealth holdings with or without an asset test. However, a more recent study by Eric Hurst and Ziliak (2006) finds no connection between welfare asset limits and low saving among the poor.

Finally, the unintended consequences of some federal policy may actively discourage the poor from saving. One recent example is the the United States savings bond program, originally conceived in 1935 as a way "to promote nationwide thrift by providing small savers with a safe, liquid, and attractive investment." (U.S. Treasury 1955, 28). Alterations to the program, however, effectively undercut its ability to meet this goal. In 2003, Congress eliminated the entire advertising budget for the program, ending a nearly seventy-year history of encouraging so-called small savers to invest. Additionally, the required minimum holding period for savings bonds was raised from six months to one year (Tufano and Schneider 2005). By further restricting liquidity, the government has imposed a heavy burden on low-income families who would like to save but might need their reserves in the event of an emergency. The Treasury has also begun moving toward an online-based purchasing system that would require the buyer to have Internet access and a bank account.

Beverly and Sherraden (1999) place the saving situation of low-income people in an institutional context, arguing that saving is facilitated by formal saving plans, incentives, education, and pre-commitment, and that the poor have limited access to these supports. Sherraden and Michael Barr (2005) add access, expectations, restrictions, and security. In the case of savings bonds, low-income families are losing one of the few institutional mechanisms they have to save. By cutting marketing, the Treasury decreases awareness and lowers expectations. By increasing the holding period, the Treasury makes it infeasible for many low-income families to take advantage of institutional mechanisms such as the savings bond payroll deduction. By moving purchasing online, the Treasury restricts access to savings bonds, potentially depriving the millions of Americans without bank accounts or on the wrong side of the digital divide, of the ability to buy bonds.

Financial Literacy

Recent survey results testing the financial knowledge of American youth and adults show a general lack of financial competence. A series of studies of the financial literacy of young adults, including high school and college students, finds notably low levels of financial knowledge (JumpStart 2002; Chen and Volpe 1998; Markovich and DeVaney 1997). Studies commissioned by the SEC, Vanguard, and the Investor Protection Trust find similarly low levels of financial literacy among adult investors (Alexander, Jones, and Nigro 1997; Princeton Survey Research Associates 1996; Vanguard 2002). Finally, surveys of adults have also uncovered a more general lack of financial knowledge with only 25 percent of adults scoring a grade of B or higher on a Bankrate.com test of financial literacy (Bankrate.com 2003).

Evaluations of financial education programs suggest that this paucity of financial knowledge may depress savings. Patrick Bayer, Douglas Bernheim, and John Scholz (1996) find that employees who received financial education were more likely to participate in a company pension plan and generally contributed a larger share of their salaries. Lusardi (2002) finds a similar effect with financial education seminar attendance boosting financial wealth and total net worth for those in the bottom quartile of wealth. Douglas Bernheim, Daniel Garrett, and Dean Maki (2001) find that some high school financial education leads to increased personal saving rates and net worth.

THE ROLE OF FINANCIAL SERVICE FIRMS

The preceding discussion focuses primarily on household decisions and government incentives. Financial institutions, however, surely play a critical role in saving activities. Delegated asset management takes place within a host of organizations, including banks, mutual funds, hedge funds, trust companies, insurance firms, brokerage firms, and securities exchanges. These institutions not only hold and invest savings, but also provide advice, education, record keeping, and other services. Furthermore, to thrive, they must also perform the function of marketing. Our simple thesis is that the need for these private-sector entities to maintain acceptable levels of profitability leads to their relative disinterest in low-income savers.

At the outset, it is important, but probably obvious, to point out that without the private financial service sector, saving would likely be considerably lower. How much saving would take place without the panoply of products, the almost daily reminders of financial decisions in advertisements and storefronts, the explicit and implicit education provided by financial service firms? In a consumerist world with strong incentives to spend, these firms compete to try to capture some of our dollars as investments. This competition, though, seems less strong for low-income consumers, which may contribute to their lower rate of saving.[1]

On the product side of the ledger, we have witnessed an explosion in the number and type of investment products. Investors can choose not only among stocks, bonds, or bank accounts, but also mutual funds, nonbank saving products, sweep accounts, derivatives—including futures and options, guaranteed investment contracts, annuities, exchange traded funds, venture funds, private equity funds, hedge funds, folio products, structured bonds, and others.[2] There are considerably more financial products to choose from today than there were half a century ago. Furthermore, process innovation has led to dramatically lower costs of operations for financial service firms. Improvements in hardware, software, and communications have dramatically lowered the costs of processing transactions.

In principle, process innovations should make it even cheaper—rather than more expensive—to serve customers with small balances. This should encourage firms to serve the poor. Falling transaction costs would enable families to create highly customized saving programs on their own. Furthermore, the product innovation would seem to make it easier for families to construct an ideal saving vehicle, one more closely tied to their individual needs.

In practice, this optimism might not be so well founded. With respect to product variety, the wide range of choices could lead to decision paralysis as families face too many choices, a phenomenon Alvin Toffler (1970) first named the overchoice problem and one variety of scholars subsequently documented it.[3] This problem might be most severe for those least comfortable in choosing among the many investing alternatives and when products vary along multiple dimensions. In addition, despite the tremendous amount of product innovation, much of it has yielded complex, higher-risk products, such as hedge funds, private equity funds, venture funds, derivatives, or actively managed equity mutual funds. Far fewer new products have been aimed at the needs of investors with a relatively low tolerance for risk and a high potential need for emergency liquidity. The exceptions might include developments of bond and money market funds, principal protected products (popular in Europe), and perhaps Series I savings bonds.

Why aren't financial institutions rushing to develop a stream of products customized to the needs of less affluent savers? More generally, why aren't more financial institutions clamoring to sell savings products to low-income savers? We offer a number of hypotheses, based on observations and limited data.

Historically, there was congruence between institutions that performed payment system functions—demanded by all consumers—and institutions that provided saving products. Depository institutions—banks, thrifts, savings and loans, credit unions—performed both these functions. Increasingly, the link between payment systems and saving has been broken, especially for low-income consumers. For these consumers, payment systems functions are served by check cashing outlets or nonbanks. Millions of consumers consider a check cashing outlet their primary financial institution.[4] Whether this development is good or bad, because these entities are set up as neither brokers nor bank branches, they do not have the authority to sell investments or accept deposits without gaining regulatory approval or working in conjunction with a regulated broker or bank. This breaks the historical link between payment and saving.

More generally, lower-income areas are less blanketed by place-based financial institutions—physical offices of banks and other financial service firms—that receive savings and in turn make investments. Research shows that high-income neighborhoods still have far more commercial banks and savings and loans per 10,000 residents than low-income areas (Avery et al. 1997). With extensive place-based financial institutions, would-be savers are implicitly reminded to save and the process of saving can be made easier. Because of the persistently low number of branches in low-income neighborhoods, their residents are least likely to enjoy these benefits.

The newer institutions that receive savings and make investments, led by mutual funds, are not primarily place based. Direct sellers, such as Vanguard or Fidelity, depend on investors seeking them out, which puts a premium on investor motivation, education, and confidence in decision making. Others, such as Putnam or American Funds, sell their product via compensated sales forces, which have strong reasons to target more affluent customers.

Sales and marketing are expensive activities. We posit that current financial services marketing is geared toward reaching sophisticated consumers with the greatest profit potential and largest balances. Although financial institutions would not be so insensitive as to say they are uninterested in low-end consumers, they make their interest in high-end consumers clear and subtly act to divert marketing attention away from less affluent consumers. Surely, there is a lively battle for affluent, near affluent, and mass affluent consumers as financial service firms aspire to more "upmarket" positions. The battle for the truly affluent is not new, but the emphasis on the battle for the "mass affluent" is, and demarcates the customers that most financial service firms hope to serve. Paul Nunes, Brian Johnson, and Timothy Breene (2004) identify the mass affluent as those earning at least $60,000. Wall Street observers peg this population as having wealth of $100,000 to $1,000,000.[5] Regardless of where the lower limit of this group is, it is considerably in excess of the income or wealth of most Americans.

The mainstream desire to serve the more affluent is not necessarily a sign of discrimination; rather it reflects the costs that financial service firms face. If the cost to acquire and serve two customers is similar, despite the fact that they have very different balances, on the margin it would make sense to pursue the larger balance customer. A broker, trying to decide whether to make a call to someone with a few hundred dollars to invest or a few million to invest, will surely prefer the latter. Although recent data might suggest that income and wealth is increasingly skewed (Piketty and Saez 2003; Wolff 2002), marketers see the aggregate consumption of the mass affluent (and their investments) as representing a meaningful business opportunity, giving rise to a host of products like Swiffers, SpinBrushes, and Whitestrips.

Returning to the functional perspective and financial services, poorer consumers are worse marketing targets because of two related problems: small balances and less information. Acquiring new customers is an expensive proposition, with financial service firms publicly reporting per customer acquisition costs from $109 to $195 and one article citing an industry-wide average of $200 (T. D. Waterhouse 2001; T. Rowe Price 2003; Stone 2004). In contemplating how to direct these activities, a business will naturally consider the profits it can earn from subsequent activities of the new customer, calculating what is sometimes called the lifetime value of a customer (Donkers, Verhoef, and de Jong 2003; Winer 2001; Berger and Nasr 1998). Almost by definition, the lifetime value of a poorer consumer is smaller than that of a more affluent customer: they will surely invest less, may borrow less, write smaller insurance policies, or take out smaller mortgages than more affluent consumers. Furthermore, firms cannot count on a ready stream of cross-sold products from these or any consumers to provide future profits to justify high current acquisition costs. Finally, these customers may be least interested in the most complicated, highest margin products. Facing high costs of customer acquisition, firms find customers with small balances simply less attractive.[6] Financial institutions are not unlike bank robber Willie Sutton, who when asked why he robbed banks is alleged to have replied, "Because that's where the money is."

At *best,* the cost to market to the poor is the same as for more affluent consumers—but in practice, it may be more expensive to market to low-income consumers. Potential low-income financial service consumers may be less informed about the financial service world and its offerings, be less trustful of financial service firms, and require customized advertising and marketing. These efforts might require additional effort and expense on the part of would-be marketers to low-income consumers. Furthermore, the basic marketing research used to identify valuable market segments is less available for low-income families and communities. There are many market research firms that specialize in profiling high-net-worth customers, but a relative dearth of data about low-net-worth customers.[7]

Finally, one has to consider the impact of competition among financial institutions—and regulation. Perhaps the lower profitability of less affluent consumers would give rise to a valuable business opportunity, and we would observe massive competition for low-income consumers. Indeed, we do see extensive competition for low-income payments services in the form of alternative financial service (AFS) firms like check-cashers, as described elsewhere in this volume. AFS providers deliver payment services, but can do so without getting the extensive regulatory clearances or capital requirements faced by banks, brokers, or securities dealers.

Indeed, it might not be an exaggeration to assert that the asset-gathering arms of the financial service sector would be happy to "fire" many low-wealth customers. The concept of firing customers has gained some prominence in the business world (Johnson 2002). Generally, the idea is to rid yourself of unprofitable customers, or to keep them away at the outset, to maximize profitability. Although it is difficult to prove that this attitude characterizes financial service firms, it appears to be well-accepted. In a front-page *Wall Street Journal* story about a retailer firing unprofitable customers, reporter Gary McWilliams took it as a given that financial service firms follow this strategy: "The financial services industry has used a variation of (the fire your customer) approach for years, lavishing attention on its best customers and penalizing its unprofitable customers with fees for using ATMs and tellers or for obtaining bank records" ("Analyzing Customers, Best Buy Decides Not All are Welcome," November 8, 2004). Given the fiduciary duties financial institutions have to their shareholders and other investors, the decision to avoid expensive, money-losing customers is not nefarious, but rather appeals to basic business sense. Would-be low-income savers are fired in a variety of ways:

- By imposing minimum initial investment restrictions at mutual funds. Although certain funds will accept small initial deposits, some of the largest fund sponsors impose substantial minimum initial investment restrictions. In particular, among the top ten mutual funds in the country, eight impose minimum balance restrictions upwards of $250. Among the top 500, only 11 percent had minimum initial purchase requirements of less than $100 (Morningstar 2004). Furthermore, though others may passively accept small accounts, we have seen no evidence that they actively solicit them, either through advertising or direct sales. See table 2.5 for data on minimum initial purchase requirements at various large mutual funds.

- By maintaining fewer physical locations in low-income communities. Robert Avery and his colleagues (1997) find that low-income neighborhoods have the fewest banks per capita. In a study of five large American cities, John Caskey (1994) finds that neighborhoods with large African American or Hispanic populations are less likely to have a bank branch and that in several of the cities, "low-income communities are significantly less likely to have a local bank than are other communities" (Caskey, 1994, p. 618).

Table 2.5   Minimum Initial Purchase Requirements Among Mutual Funds in the United States

	None	≤$100	≤$250
Among all funds listed by Morningstar			
Number allowing	1,292	1,402	1,785
Percent allowing	7.9%	8.6%	11%
Among the top 500 mutual funds by net assets			
Number allowing	49	55	88
Percent allowing	9.8%	11%	17.6%
Among the top 100 index funds by net assets			
Number allowing	30	30	30
Percent allowing	30%	30%	30%
Among the top 100 domestic stock funds by net assets			
Number allowing	11	13	24
Percent allowing	11%	13%	24%

Source: Tufano and Schneider (2005).

- By establishing fees for low-balance accounts (or waiving them for high-balance accounts). Banks routinely set minimum balance requirements or charge fees on low balances, in effect discouraging smaller savers. Nationally, minimum opening balance requirements for statement savings accounts averaged $97 and required a balance of at least $158 to avoid average yearly fees of $26. These fees were equal to 27 percent of the minimum opening balance. Fees were higher in the ten largest metropolitan statistical areas (MSAs), with average minimum opening requirements of $179 and an average minimum balance to avoid fees of $268 (Board of Governors of the Federal Reserve 2003; see table 2.6).

- By having relatively little marketing and sales efforts in low-income communities. While financial service providers may target these communities for advertising relating to sub-prime (and predatory) credit products, there seems less, if any, marketing relating to asset-building products. Unfortunately, we cannot observe these activities easily, so this assertion cannot be directly tested.

- By using credit scoring tools not just to screen out customers who might give rise to credit losses, but also to screen out customers who might merely be unprofitable to serve. ChexSystems, for example, enables

Table 2.6   Average Savings Account Fees and Minimum Balance Requirements 2001

	Minimum to Open	Monthly Fee	Minimum Balance	Annual Fee	Annual Fee as Percent of Min Balance
All respondent banks	$96.9	$2.2	$157.9	$25.8	27%
New York	$266.5	$3.1	$343.1	$37.1	14%
Los Angeles	$295.2	$2.8	$360.2	$33.6	11%
Chicago	$121.8	$3.5	$206.9	$42.5	35%
District of Columbia	$100.1	$3.2	$152.1	$37.8	38%
San Francisco	$274.7	$2.8	$486.3	$33.8	12%
Boston	$44.0	$2.7	$235.2	$32.9	75%
Dallas	$147.4	$3.2	$198.2	$37.8	26%
Average ten largest CMSAs	$178.5	$2.9	$267.5	$35.2	20%

Source: Tufano and Schneider (2005).

banks to screen prospective clients for problems with prior bank accounts and to report current clients who overdraw accounts or engage in fraud. It is not uncommon for banks to deny consumers with poor credit records the right to open even a *savings* account. More than 90 percent of bank branches in the United States use the systems and approximately 7 million people have ChexSystems records (Quinn 2001; Barr 2004a).

- By implicitly redefining their mandates. Most banks define their "low-income" activities in the context of meeting Community Reinvestment Act (CRA) mandates, not as part of the core strategies of their banks. Most credit unions, while ostensibly receiving special tax treatment because of their unique service role, eagerly serve more affluent customers. This tactic may be profitable, but credit unions enjoy their tax-free status by virtue of provisions in the Federal Credit Union Act of 1989, the text of which mandates that credit unions provide credit to "to people of small means." Given this legislative background, it is interesting that the median income of credit union members is approximately $17,000 higher than that of the median income of all Americans (Board of Governors of the Federal Reserve 2004) and that only 10 percent of credit unions classify themselves as low income, defined as half of the members having incomes of less than 80 percent of the area median household income (National Credit Union Association 2004; Tansey 2001).

This litany obviously ignores the important work of some groups, including community development banks and low-income and community development credit unions discussed elsewhere in this volume. It also does not elaborate on the various trickle up and trickle down theories in which, by making financial services (or other products) less expensive for the more well-to-do, there are benefits for others (see Nunes, Johnson, and Breene 2004). It merely expresses a hypothesis that the bulk of the financial service sector would not be troubled if low-income would-be savers and investors were simply not part of the picture. Indeed, for many of these financial institutions they are not. Like the financial services executive cited earlier, many others in the financial services sector would be content to treat pre-investors as someone else's problem.

ADOPTING POLICY AND BUSINESS INNOVATIONS TO INCREASE ASSET BUILDING

Summarizing the "bad news" up to this point, saving by low-income families is inherently difficult, receives relatively little government incentives, and is—at best—tolerated by the financial sector. But there is potentially better news, in the form of various innovations. Policy innovations have begun to recognize the importance of savings among low-income families. Business innovations can make gathering savings more cost effective and may introduce new means to educate and mobilize low-income consumers. The spirit of this approach is captured in the strategy scholar C. K. Prahalad's *The Fortune at the Bottom of the Pyramid,* which argues that business can profit by using innovations to serve poor consumers, the so-called bottom of the pyramid (2004).

We do not presume to identify which of the impediments to saving catalogued thus far are the most important, or even their relative effects. The data and literature do not allow for a specific accounting of the effect on saving from limited financial knowledge, disinterest from financial service firms, or any of the host of factors so far identified. Rather, we think about each of these barriers to saving and various ways to surmount them.

Stepping back, to increase saving and asset building, one can change the ability and willingness of families to save (stimulating demand) and the willingness and interest in financial institutions to acquire and hold savings by the less affluent (stimulating supply). By leveraging innovations developed elsewhere, one can stimulate supply and demand.

In regard to stimulating demand, we have learned from previous government programs that providing families with incentives to save increases saving and thus discuss a variety of programs that can increase motivations to save.[8] In addition, by recognizing the savings potential of tax refunds received by the poor—and implementing long-known maxims of financial planning, we can potentially divert billions from consumption to saving. Finally, we can borrow an innovation from the technology sector to provide new forms of financial education and advice for low-income families.

On the supply side, by asking which organizations already have strong distribution channels among less affluent consumers, we can fashion new methods of reaching these potential savers. One of these, savings bonds, is not new but can be reinvigorated to serve once again as a meaningful saving vehicle for American families. Second, by exploiting known innovations to efficiently pool accounts and the associated information systems infrastructure, we can drive down the cost of serving small-balance accounts. These two ideas are closely related, new pooling vehicles—such as tapping into tax refunds—may create cost-effective ways to acquire customers. An ample body of literature posits that a vibrant financial services sector leads to a stronger economic sector (King and Levine 1993; Levine 1997). Much of that literature is concerned with creating financial institutions that will allow households and businesses to obtain capital. In that spirit, we examine several innovations that could encourage a more vibrant financial services sector with regard to less affluent families. Additionally, following the same logic as the literature, we examine the potential of these innovations to develop saving rather than simply make credit available.

STIMULATING DEMAND: GIVING FAMILIES INCENTIVES TO SAVE

The vast sums spent to encourage savings and investing by more affluent Americans seem to have yielded some increases in savings. Home ownership rates are at historical highs of 68 percent (Bucks, Kennickell, and Moore 2006) and the most affluent members of the baby boom generation are expected to retire with higher levels of savings than the previous generation (Shackleton 2003). More recently, various political initiatives (such as the Clinton administration's plans for universal savings accounts or the Bush administration's ownership society concept) have sought to create even more incentives for saving, though some argue that those the Bush administration proposes will continue to appeal most strongly to the more affluent, given that the incentives come from reductions in taxes. Over the last few years, programs and proposals have begun to target some asset-building incentives directly at low-income families. These include the Savers Credit, the pilots of individual development accounts, and proposals to adapt 529 saving plans to encourage low-income families to save for college and to establish accounts for all children.[9]

USAs, RSAs, and the Saver's Credit

Beginning with universal savings accounts (USAs) in 1999, a number of programs designed to provide more progressive retirement saving incentives have been proposed. Had President Clinton's USA program been enacted, it would have matched contributions to retirement savings for Americans age eighteen to seventy with incomes between $5,000 and $100,000. Low-income account holders were slated to receive an annual automatic contribution from the government worth several hundred dollars, and low- and moderate-income account holders would have benefited from a refundable tax credit that matched personal or employer 401(k) contributions and decreased with income (Perun 1999). However, in 2000, facing opposition from Congress and concerns over the cost of USAs, a revised program based on retirement savings accounts (RSAs) was substituted (Gale, Iwry, and Orszag 2004). RSAs dropped the USA automatic contribution provision and restructured the match as a tax credit refunded to individuals through financial institutions and employers. RSAs were then in turn reworked as a simpler tax credit for contributions to personal retirement accounts, the Saver's Credit (Gale, Iwry, and Orszag 2004).

Passed in 2001 as part of President Bush's tax cuts, the Saver's Credit provides a tax credit to low-income filers who contribute to a personal retirement account. The credit increases in value as income declines and is worth 10 percent, 20 percent, or 50 percent of contributions up to $2,000 for low- and moderate-income individuals (Orszag and Greenstein 2003). However, it is not refundable. Filers without an income tax liability therefore do not receive any match from the Saver's Credit. Essentially, a filer making a $1,000 contribution to a retirement account would be eligible for a $100, $200, or $500 tax credit, depending on filing status and income, that could only be used toward the reduction of a tax burden. A low-income filer who did not owe any tax would not receive the benefit. Peter Orszag and Matthew Hall (2004) find that because it is not refundable, only 20 percent of filers who are eligible for the 50 percent credit would receive any benefit. Legislation sponsored by former Senator John Edwards (D-NC) proposed to extend the savers credit past its current 2006 expiration and make the credit refundable, allowing low-income families without a tax liability to receive the retirement savings incentives (U.S. Congress 2004a).

USAs, RSAs, and the Saver's Credit are all designed to create incentives for low- and middle-income (LMI) families to save for retirement. A second set of proposals introduced over the past five years has focused on creating more incentives for high-income individuals to save more for retirement.

In addition to the Saver's Credit, the 2001 Economic Growth and Tax Relief Reconciliation Act (EGTRRA) included provisions raising maximum allowable contributions to personal savings plans. These accounts—which include 401(k)s, 403(b)s, and IRAs—grant depositors tax deferral benefits on their retirement savings (Burnham 2003). The increases in the allowable contributions are expected to mostly benefit high-income filers. Only 1 percent of 401(k) holders making less than $40,000 contributed the maximum, whereas 40 percent of those making more than $160,000 did so (Orszag and Greenstein 2003). In 2004, the Bush administration proposed three new tax-privileged savings accounts, lifetime savings accounts (LSAs), retirement savings accounts, and employer retirement savings accounts (ERSAs). Len Burman, William Gale, and Orszag (2004) find that the large majority of the tax benefits of these accounts would go to high-income households and potentially reduce government revenue, national saving, and employer contributions to lower-income workers' pensions.

Individual Development Accounts

In 1991, Michael Sherraden proposed a system of individual development accounts (IDAs) designed to offer savings incentives to those with low incomes. IDA programs are matched saving programs, somewhat similar to 401(k) programs, but aimed at pre-retirement savings goals. Over the past fifteen years, IDAs have taken shape to provide for matched contributions to low-income people's deposits into independently administered saving accounts. These funds, deposits plus matches, are available for a number of specific uses, such as buying a home, starting a small business, or seeking additional education or training—in short, for creating more assets. IDAs work by taking an existing financial product, often a savings account, and linking it to new distribution channels, new incentives, and new sources of education. The accounts have primarily been marketed through social service and community-based organizations, drawing in clients by offering matched saving incentives and requiring participants to take part in financial education. In 2003, approximately 250 IDA programs around the United States served more than 20,000 people. Roughly 5,000 participants have already completed an IDA program (Glackin and Mahoney 2002; Corporation for Enterprise Development 2003).

To date, two sets of programs have been studied, the American Dream Demonstration (ADD) project programs, funded by several private foundations, and programs established under the Assets for Independence Act (AFIA), which Congress passed in 1998. The ADD evaluation found that its low-income participants were capable of saving, though success varied. Participants saved an average of $19 per month (median of $10) and had average net deposits (total deposits less unmatched withdrawals) of $528. Of the 32 percent of participants who made a matched withdrawal from the program as of December 2001, the average value of the withdrawal was $2,586 (Schreiner, Clancy, and Sherraden 2002). The most common use of matched withdrawals was to buy a home, 28 percent made one for that purpose, with an average value of $2,416. Judging from this data, ADD posted encouraging, but mixed saving results (Schreiner, Clancy, and Sheridan 2002).

More recently, Abt Associates completed its evaluation of the ADD IDA program run by the Community Action Project of Tulsa County (CAPTC). Unlike the earlier CSD study, Abt Associates used a randomized experimental design to evaluate the effects of the IDA program. The researchers assigned approximately half of the study population to a treatment group and half to a control group. In addition to baseline data, the researchers collected information from members of both groups at eighteen months and forty-eight months (Mills et al. 2004).

Abt Associates reports finding significant effects on homeownership at the forty-eight-month mark, with the homeownership rate 6.2 percentage points higher for the treatment group than for the control, and with the effect particularly pronounced among African Americans. In addition, members of the treatment group were significantly more likely to have sought additional education. Some treatment effects appear only for certain subgroups of participants. African Americans in the treatment group increased their retirement saving by more than $1,000 over members of the control group. Linked to homeownership outcomes, members of several subgroups experienced increases in real assets, decreases in liquid assets, decreases in financial assets, and increases in total liabilities. IDA advocates and researchers have hypothesized that IDAs might also increase business ownership, home repair, and total net worth, but no such effects were detected by the Abt research team (Mills et al. 2004).

The Assets For Independence Act report found that, like the ADD population, most participants were female and low-income and the majority planned to save for home purchase. The study also found that many organizations had difficulty recruiting potential IDA participants, and that participants needed personalized interaction and assistance to be successful savers. In addition, the report argued that the working poor are the most suitable target population for IDA programs, and that those in serious distress are not well situated for involvement (Mills et al. 2000).

Since 1999, IDA advocates have pressed for the passage of legislation to expand the program and make accounts available to hundreds of thousands more low-income families through a tax credit to financial institutions offering the accounts. Despite significant headway and bi-partisan support, the legislation has (so far) been a victim of the political process. If the Savings for Working Families Act were to pass, it would face a set of administrative challenges. To date, IDA programs have been administered to a relatively small number of participants through existing networks of not-for-profit organizations. At scale, the IDA program would be faced with financial education and account administration requirements that could not be handled easily by these organizations. However, it would be possible to address these concerns through "productizing" individual development accounts, which is discussed later.

529s

IDAs are designed to encourage participants to save for three particular uses, homeownership, education, and small business development. Several other saving vehicles are also designed around specific dedicated uses. College saving accounts, or 529s, are a tax-privileged saving vehicle designed to help parents save for their children's education. However, the accounts were not designed to benefit low-income families in particular and often have high management fees, negative effects on college financial aid, and tax benefits that are unlikely to accrue to low-income families (Clancy, Orszag, and Sherraden 2004). Margaret Clancy and Michael Sherraden (2003) recognize these drawbacks but have suggested that the centralized structure and relatively simple design of 529s makes them an appealing base on which to build a system of accounts to help poor families save for college.

Children's Savings Accounts

In 2004, a bipartisan Senate and House group introduced the America Saving for Personal Investment, Retirement, and Education (ASPIRE) Act in the

Congress. The legislation calls for the creation of a system of KIDS Accounts, endowed savings accounts established at birth for all children who are U.S. citizens or legal residents. The federal government would make an initial $500 dollar deposit into each account with a supplemental deposit for low-income children. Family, friends, employers, and the children would be eligible to make subsequent contributions into the account, which would be matched up to $500 per year at a one-to-one rate for children in families making less than 100 percent of the median income level. The funds in KIDS Accounts could be used for paying for higher education at any time, but would only be available for other uses after the account holder turned eighteen. At that time, the private deposits and government matches could be used without penalty for home purchase or retirement (U.S. Congress 2004b).

The KIDS Accounts proposal builds on a number of similar initiatives. Jamie Curley and Michael Sherraden (2000) trace the origins of children's saving account proposals to what are called children's allowances, cash grants provided to families with children by many European countries. Cramer details the legislative history of a number of proposals to establish some form of children's savings accounts (CSAs) in the United States (Cramer 2004). Currently, CFED (Corporation for Enterprise Development), the Center for Social Development at Washington University in Saint Louis, and the University of Kansas are collaborating to run and evaluate the Savings for Education Entrepreneurship and Down-payment (SEED) accounts program. The SEED program provides initial $1,000 dollar deposits for three cohorts of children, one that will receive the initial deposit at birth and be studied to age five, one that will receive the initial deposit at age six and be followed until age eleven, and another that will receive the deposit at age twelve and be followed to age eighteen. In addition to the initial deposit, the program will match subsequent deposits with the goal of building assets for education, retirement, home purchase, or business development (Corporation for Enterprise Development 2004). Internationally, beginning in 2002, the United Kingdom funded accounts at birth for all children, with supplementary deposits for children from low-income families (Cramer 2004). Like IDAs, these accounts aim to encourage asset building by developing new distribution channels, in this case by opening accounts for all children at birth, and new incentives, here through an initial grant and subsequent matches.

Removing Disincentives to Saving

These policies, tax credits for retirement savings, IDAs, 529s, and children's savings accounts all create incentives for low-income families to save. However, to the extent that these families still face disincentives and restrictions on asset accumulation, the effect of these policies is circumscribed. Currently, only one state, Ohio, does not have an asset test for TANF eligibility. Only five states allow assets of up to $5,000 or more. Fewer states limit assets for Medicaid eligibility. Twenty-three states allow Medicaid recipients to hold assets worth $5,000 or more and eighteen have no asset test at all (Corporation for Enterprise Development 2002). To encourage the widest range of low-income families to save, all of these asset tests should be reviewed and eliminated.

STIMULATING DEMAND: MAKING IT EASIER TO SAVE

A variety of innovations make it convenient for more affluent households to invest. One way to simplify saving is to make it automatic. Automatic payroll deductions for 401(k) investments, automatic investment plans and sweep accounts all accomplish this end. Their structure is quite simple, in that the would-be saver pre-commits to divert part of his or her money to saving. This simple innovation can be adapted to be more useful to low-income families.

Harnessing Tax Refunds for Asset Building

Federal tax policy encourages taxpayers to save by allowing them to reduce their tax liability when contributing to or receiving income in certain qualified accounts. Tax policy can also encourage saving among tax refund recipients, a group that includes millions of less affluent Americans.

Federal tax refunds to low-income filers from the Earned Income Tax Credit (EITC), the Child Tax Credit (CTC), and other refunds are a promising source of savable funds. In 2001, households with incomes of less than $30,000 received more than $78 billion in federal tax refunds (Internal Revenue Service 2001). The refunds received by these households were likely the largest single payment they received all year. If these refunds could be converted into savings, it would substantially increase the assets of low-income families. The notion of paying yourself first has been a staple of personal financial planning for at least a century, and applying this to the tax refunds is a promising way to increase saving by the poor. More recent research on behavioral elements of financial decision making can help to sharpen this common wisdom.

Thaler and Shefrin (1981) and Shefrin and Thaler (1988) identify two ways in which individuals can overcome the short-run temptations of spending. First, many people find it easier to save funds that are received as a lump sum and are not part of their regular income flow. This hypothesis has been borne out in the case of tax refunds by findings that large shares of refund recipients plan to use these funds for saving and durable good purchases (Smeeding, Ross, and O'Conner 2000; Barrow and McGranahan 2000). Second, by deciding to save ahead of time and committing to saving before funds are in hand, individuals can also overcome temptations to spend. Thaler and Shlomo Benartzi (2004) have tested this second proposition with the Save More Tomorrow (SMarT) Plan and find that large shares of employees take up the opportunity to save their annual raises in their company's retirement plan. This strategy raised saving rates more than eight percentage points (2004).

Similar mental accounting and pre-commitment tactics have been applied by a number of free tax preparation sites run by community-based organizations. These organizations have offered low-income tax filers the option of opening a savings account onsite and committing to have their entire refund deposited directly into the account. An evaluation of one such program, at the Center for Economic Progress and Shorebank in Chicago, found a take-up rate of 20 percent but that only 14 percent of account openers maintained balances (Beverly, Tescher, Romich 2004). H&R Block, the largest paid retail tax-preparer in the country, offered a similar program in 2003 and opened 400 accounts, representing a 2 percent take-up rate (Tufano and Schneider 2004).

Taking these behavioral elements a bit further, a recent experiment attempted to offer refund recipients the functionality that wage earners enjoy—to pre-commit part, but not all, of their fund inflows to savings. In 2004, a program run by CAPTC and the Doorways to Dreams Fund (D2D) allowed refund recipients to split their refunds, sending one portion to a savings account and receiving the rest as a check. The service, Refunds to Assets (R2A), allowed participants to decide ahead of time how much of their refund they would save and how much they would have to spend, and then pre-commit to that allocation. Approximately 27 percent of filers expecting a refund who were approached wanted to participate in the program. Another 21 percent wanted to split their refunds with the remainder only interested in opening a new account. Participants had average initial savings deposits of approximately $600. Seventy-eight percent of those planning to save had either achieved their savings goal or will still have refund dollars saved three to five months later. Only 36 percent of those in a comparison group had reached their savings goal or still had savings (Beverly, Schneider, and Tufano 2005). Refund splitting—in conjunction with new account opening—is a promising way to jump-start saving by less affluent Americans. However, the future of the refund-splitting program is uncertain. Although additional pilots of refund splitting will be offered for tax season 2005, it is difficult for small community organizations to undertake the administrative and account processing challenges of splitting. Consequently, a coalition of groups, including the New America Foundation, the Retirement Security Project, D2D, and former IRS Commissioner Fred Goldberg worked with the IRS to secure the Service's commitment to offer refund splitting nationally. It now appears that the IRS will introduce this service by the 2007 tax season (Cramer 2005).

STIMULATING DEMAND: INCREASING SAVING AWARENESS AND EDUCATION

Families need a combination of financial education and advice, but the economics of providing these services—even for customers who have seemingly substantial wealth—is unattractive (see chapter 3, this volume). Little data is available on the cost of providing financial education, but an estimated expense of $100 dollars per participant per seminar or class seems reasonable.[10] These costs can prove prohibitive, especially for small community-based organizations. A survey by the Federal Deposit Insurance Corporation (FDIC) of 9,000 organizations that had requested its MoneySmart financial education curricula found that 41 percent of those not using the curricula were unable to do so because of cost concerns (Burhouse, Gambrell, and Harris 2004).

A few business innovations have been adapted—and can be adapted more extensively—to stimulate demand through awareness and education. On the awareness side, a large body of work details which marketing practices tend to be more effective; indeed, the topic is a staple of marketing offerings in MBA programs. One form of marketing is social, that is, it is used not to induce purchasing, but to change individual behavior. Social marketing is used to change attitudes toward health issues (for example, antismoking, antidrug, or seat belt campaigns). Social marketing has also been used to encourage saving. The America Saves campaign, for example, has enrolled over 20,000 people across the country, through both the national office and local campaigns (2004b). Henry Rowen and John Shoven (1993) have pressed for the creation of a national saving campaign, citing the success of energy and water conservation, safe sex, and—a more direct comparison—the World War II savings bond campaigns.

Businesses have found that cheap and powerful computing power has made realistic and powerful simulations possible. Simulation is used in a variety of settings where conducting actual experiments or training can be costly or dangerous, such as testing the reaction of various compounds in chemical processing plants, or training soldiers and pilots. Often, these simulations incorporate decision support tools that assist the participant in making decisions—for example, the avionics that a pilot might use to gauge progress and safety. Simulation combined with decision support tools is available for wealthier savers trying to make asset allocation and portfolio decisions. Firms such as Financial Engines (www.financialengines.com), for example, which Nobel Laureate William Sharpe developed, provide investors with the ability to see the distributions of returns for their portfolio over various time horizons.

Businesses have also found a ready market for very complex simulations cloaked within the guise of computer games. These can simulate very complicated networks of effects, but present information graphically. Some of the most popular games are indeed simulations, led by the Sims, a family of games developed and marketed by Electronic Arts. This game has reportedly sold over 36 million units since 2000 and has generated profits of roughly $498 million.[11] Games are increasingly used not just for enjoyment, but also to train adults—soldiers, academic administrators, and health-care professionals, for example. What is being called a "serious games" initiative is exploring the potential of using gaming technology in education. D2D Fund, a nonprofit product development group aimed at serving low-income financial consumers, is exploring the potential of marrying simulation, decision support tools, and electronic gaming to create a product that could be used to provide low-income families with financial education and decision support tools.

STIMULATING SUPPLY: REINVIGORATING DISTRIBUTION CHANNELS AND PRODUCTS

As we describe early in the chapter, one potential impediment to increasing saving is that some of the institutions with the strongest connections with less affluent families do not offer them saving and investing products. One set of solutions would be to permit them to do so.

Alternative Financial Service Providers

Because AFS providers already have a large base of low-income customers, they do not face customer acquisition costs. The Financial Services Centers of America (FISCA), an industry association for the check-cashing industry, reports approximately 11,000 neighborhood financial service centers across America, compared with the 76,545 bank branches, 13,699 savings and loan branches, and 9,369 credit unions (FDIC 2004; National Credit Union Association 2003). Although there are fewer financial service centers than depository branches, these organizations have strong penetration in low-income communities (Sawyer and Temkin 2004).

Some partnerships have been established between check cashers and banks or credit unions, whereby the check-cashing customer can obtain access to banking products, such as saving products. In some instances, banking entities are combining their physical locations with check cashers or offering payroll card products.[12] If check cashers could systematically offer a low-cost saving product, it might expand the supply of savings products for many low-income families.

In one set of experiments, alternative financial service providers are making stored value cards available to their clients—but ones that apparently earn interest. Stored Value Cards (SVC) are similar to debit cards. Many are branded by Visa or MasterCard and card holders can make ATM and POS transactions using those networks. SVCs differ from a traditional bank debit card in that they are preloaded, either by the card holder or by a third party (such as an employer). These cards have been used mostly for transactions (Jacob 2004). Beginning in 2005, however, Net Spend, a SVC issuer, began offering an SVC with a linked savings account feature. Card holders are able to transfer funds from the card into a savings account, free of charge (Jacob et al. 2005). As of May 2005, the saving account, held by Inter National Bank of Texas, paid 0.75 percent interest (Wisniewski 2005). These cards are functionally similar to banking accounts that are used for both transactions and savings. Industry sources report that consumers with these cards are accumulating balances on their cards, using them as a savings vehicle.

Nonfinancial Service Firms

A number of firms have extensive contact with less affluent consumers through their existing businesses. For example, the estimated 100 million customers that shop at Wal-Mart each week have mean incomes ($40,000) below those of most other chain retailers (Krasney 2003, and Bloomberg News 2004). Almost 40 percent of Wal-Mart customers have household incomes of less than $30,000 (Hale 2004).

Wal-Mart, like many grocery and convenience stores, already provides check-cashing services for many consumers. In principle, facilitating ways for organizations like Wal-Mart to offer saving products to their customers could substantially increase the effort devoted to helping the poor to save. To take a simple example, Wal-Mart could be allowed to offer consumers savings bonds. However, Wal-Mart and other nonfinancial institutions have been unable to obtain licenses to operate as industrial loan companies (ILCs) that function like banks. Strong opposition from a number of groups has apparently prevented these companies from securing this regulatory clearance (Mandaro 2002). Without judging the full merits of this opposition, it may be easier—from the point of view of providing additional services to low-income consumers—to put additional products into a channel that already reaches these families, rather than trying to convince existing financial service firms to serve those consumers they have evidenced relatively little interest in serving.

Social Intermediaries

South Central Los Angeles has a large concentration of low-income families. In 2000, 37 percent of South Central families lived in poverty and nearly 70 percent of these families had incomes that were less than 200 percent of the U.S. Federal poverty line (U.S. Census Bureau 2000). A few years ago, one of us conducted an informal census of the area, which had more than 600,000 residents. South Central had seventeen bank branches,

122 check cashing outlets, and 518 Catholic, Baptist, or Methodist churches. These numbers may have changed over time, but the ratios are probably still about the same, attesting to the relative strength of social intermediaries in low-income communities. Although it would be imprudent to ask too much of these organizations, making it easier for them to make their congregations aware of simple saving products might be quite feasible (for a discussion of how social intermediaries might help to serve the financial needs of their low-income members, see Fondation, Tufano, and Walker 1999).

Tax Preparers

Commercial and volunteer tax preparers have extensive contacts with low-income families. The three largest retail tax preparation companies in the United States—H&R Block, Jackson Hewitt, and Liberty Tax—prepared tax returns for 20 million filers in 2003. Unbranded tax preparers completed more than 50 million returns (Tufano and Schneider 2004). Families trust these preparers with highly confidential information and these tax preparers facilitate the flow of $78 billion in refunds, some of which can be diverted to savings. Commercial preparers are aware of this opportunity. H&R Block is piloting a new product set called Everyday Financial Services, which may connect Block's low-income clients to transaction and saving products with card-based accounts. Block expects to deliver these financial services to low-income clients more cheaply than AFS providers, banks, or credit unions by virtue of its existing tax-preparation-based client relationships, established network of retail locations, and business-wide benefits of client retention flowing from cross-sells (Tufano and Schneider 2004). However, implementing these programs can be difficult for commercial tax preparation firms which have traditionally not delivered extensive financial services.

Organizing these programs, however, is even more difficult for the thousands of volunteer tax sites that served 1.6 million tax filers in 2003 (Internal Revenue Service 2003).[13] Unless they partner with a local financial institution that can open new accounts for refund recipients at the time of tax filing, these volunteer sites cannot assist less affluent families to build assets. To assist these families, a simple mechanism whereby accounts could be opened during, or even after, the time of tax preparation, but before the refunds were received would be useful. This could be achieved with a relatively simple pooling facility, or even more simply by reinventing savings bonds as a saving alternative of last resort.

Reinventing Savings Bonds

In 1935, Secretary of the Treasury Henry Morgenthau introduced the U.S. savings bond, "designed for the small investor—that he may be encouraged to save for the future and receive a fair return on his money" (U.S. Treasury 1935). This bond offering built on a long history of selling U.S. securities with the intention of helping small savers to invest and plan for the future. During World War I, Thrift Stamps were available in amounts as little as ten cents, convertible into $5 bonds (Tufano and Schneider 2005). After the war, the Treasury continued its campaign to help small savers, arguing the importance of making thrift a "happy habit" for all Americans and the benefits of saving in the event of "a rainy day or a sunny opportunity," and as a way to fund education and home ownership (U.S. Treasury 1918).

This goal seems to have fallen by the wayside. As described earlier, the recent actions of Congress and the Treasury Department have resulted in the wholesale dismantling of the savings bond marketing program, making it far more difficult for small savers to build assets by buying these bonds. A recent consulting report on the savings bond program suggests that the distribution channels for bonds are dysfunctional, and our personal experience concurs with this finding, because we were shuttled from bank to bank before someone was able to provide the paperwork necessary to purchase a simple savings bond (James E. Arnold Consultants 1999).

However, we propose that minor modifications to savings bonds policy could have a significant impact on the program. First, the Treasury should reduce the required minimum holding period from one year to allow small withdrawals for emergency purposes. Second, the Treasury should leverage the purchasing power of LMI tax refunds to allow taxpayers to purchase savings bonds directly, at the time of filing, with their federal tax refunds. In simplest terms, the IRS could add a line to the 1040 forms that allows the filer to dedicate part of the refund to purchasing savings bonds. The remainder of the information needed to complete the transaction is contained on the tax form itself, and this would allow all families to divert money into savings. Congress should restore funding for savings bonds marketing and couple the tax-time bond-buy option with a simple social marketing campaign to encourage LMI families to save and purchase savings bonds with their tax refunds. Third, though the ability to purchase bonds at tax time would broaden distribution channels, the Treasury should explore ways to sell bonds through retail outlets such as Wal-Mart or alternative financial service firms that are far more prevalent in LMI communities than depository institutions. Finally, the Treasury should recognize that if low-income families are to purchase savings bonds, these families may reach a time when they feel able to purchase products with higher returns and more risk. The Treasury should plan for this by allowing roll-overs to other investment vehicles (for a more complete discussion of savings bond policy, see Tufano and Schneider 2005).

STIMULATING SUPPLY: LOWERING COSTS TO SERVE LESS AFFLUENT CUSTOMERS

Low-Cost Accounts

Account ownership is highly correlated with saving and asset accumulation (Vermilyea and Wilcox 2002). Holding a transaction account is a valuable entry to traditional financial services, which offer more saving options than alternative financial service (AFS) providers (Boshara 2001). Bank accounts enable low-income families to increase their saving by using direct deposit, which may decrease the temptation to spend (Beverly and Sherraden 1999). However, an estimated 10 million households lack an account with a bank or credit union (Bucks, Kennickell, and Moore 2006). These households generally conduct their financial transactions through high-cost AFS providers such as check cashers. Both public and private sector initiatives have sought to move these unbanked AFS customers to account ownership and lower-cost financial services.

The 1996 Federal Debt Collection Improvement Act mandated that all federal payments, including wages, vendor payments, and monthly public assistance benefits, but excluding tax refunds, be made by electronic funds transfer (EFT) by 1999 (Stegman 1999). The rationale for this policy change was largely economic; by making payments electronically, rather than sending out paper checks, the federal government could create significant cost savings (Stegman 1999). Given at least 10 million unbanked recipients of public assistance, the Treasury was faced with the formidable challenge of finding a cost-effective way to create bank accounts (Stegman 1999). However, the act also created a significant opportunity to help millions of low-income individuals without banking accounts establish relationships with either banks or credit unions.

The Treasury faced two key issues in shaping the specifics of these electronic transfer accounts (ETAs). Financial institutions expressed concern about the profitability of the accounts and wanted to charge fees, limit services, and receive federal subsidies, even as consumer advocates pressed for low fees, multiple account features, and a loosening of the requirement that all recipients of benefits open accounts (Stegman 1999). The result was a set of rules that capped fees at $3 per month, waived minimum balance and ChexSystems requirements, required monthly statements, allowed for multiple free withdrawals and account balance inquiries, and—significantly—provided automatic waivers of the EFT requirement if benefits recipients did not sign up for an account. At the same time, financial institutions were successful in getting permission to close an ETA if fraud was suspected and to refuse to open an ETA if a previous ETA was closed because of fraud or other account problems. Financial institutions also secured a subsidy from the federal government of $12.60 per account opened (Stegman 1999).

This initiative seems to have had some success. In January of 2005, approximately 79 percent of benefits recipients received payments by EFT, up from 56 percent in 1996 and 72 percent in 1999 (U.S. Treasury 2005). Michael Barr reports that 98,000 ETAs had been opened by May of 2004 (Barr 2004b).

The Treasury Department's First Accounts initiative seeks to subsidize organizations bringing low-income unbanked individuals into the financial mainstream. In the late 1990s, the Treasury began researching the size and composition of the unbanked population and found that there was a large unmet demand for low-cost bank accounts. It designed the First Accounts program to encourage financial institutions to open accounts for these individuals. The program was planned to support financial institutions and not-for-profit organizations that worked to open accounts, provide financial education, increase access to financial services in low-income areas, and study new approaches to providing low-cost financial services (Barr 2004b).

In 2002, the Treasury allocated $8 million dollars to fifteen projects across the country with the goal of banking 35,000 people (U.S. Treasury 2004). Recipients included community-based organizations, credit unions, and banks. The grant beneficiaries proposed a range of strategies for opening accounts, including tying account opening to individual development accounts and to tax preparation. A number of the recipient organizations planned to offer financial education in conjunction with the account opening and several intended to use the funds to expand ATM networks (U.S. Treasury 2004).

More than 230 organizations applied for the First Accounts funding, representing approximately $130 million in proposals for the $8 million in available funds. However, despite this unmet demand, the program has not been expanded and no additional funds have been appropriated (U.S. Treasury 2004). Barr (2004a) has detailed a proposed expansion of the First Accounts program, with the Treasury providing a tax credit subsidy to financial institutions opening accounts for low-income unbanked individuals. Barr argues that with funding between $60 and $150 million, accounts could be opened for as many as 3 million unbanked individuals.

Alternative financial service providers' experiments with using stored value transaction/savings products may be an example of a private initiative that demonstrates how to deliver low cost accounts. Ultimately, one needs to analyze the costs of this program—both to consumers and to the firms offering them—as well as how they are used, to understand their promise.

Processing Small Transactions in Big Pools

Although the First Accounts program may subsidize the cost of low-balance accounts, it does not address the inherent problem of diseconomies of small scale when dealing with less affluent consumers. In aggregate they may have substantial resources. Collecting and managing these funds individually, however, is too costly. Fortunately, the financial services industry has found ways to deal with small transactions and accounts. Electronic funds transfer technology enables the economic transfer of extremely small transactions at low costs. Michael Stegman (1999) notes that EFT costs only $0.02 per payment versus $0.43 for a check. Web-based customer service can dramatically lower the cost of transacting by substituting customer labor for paid service labor. Though exact cost estimates vary, Forester Research reports that a self-service web inquiry costs the company just $1.17, significantly below the $32.74 cost for a customer service exchange by phone (Novak 2001).

Finally, the cost of recordkeeping has been driven down by computing technologies, such as those used for 401(k) processors. A 401(k) system will keep track of the records of thousands if not millions of participants, while the asset manager may only see one omnibus account. D2D Fund has integrated these three elements—EFT, web-based service, and 401(k) record-keeping—to demonstrate how financial institutions can offer individual development accounts at a low cost (see www.d2dfund.org). In general, there are many other ways to leverage these technologies to drive down the cost of serving small-balance accounts.

CONCLUSION

Economists often talk of "diminishing marginal returns." From the perspective of a financial service firm, the poor are beyond the profitable edge of these marginal returns. Costs exceed revenue potential for the poor, but not for the rich. From the perspective of society, however, we may have the margin completely backward. The returns of increasing the financial assets of less affluent families must be higher than increasing those of the affluent. Adding $100 or $500 or $1,000 in saving to a low-income family living close to the edge will surely have a greater impact on their lives—and on society—than adding the same amount to a wealthy family's balance sheet.

Unfortunately, helping less affluent families amass financial assets is not a simple problem, nor does it lend itself to a simple set of solutions. Fortunately, many solutions may be close at hand, products of ongoing innovation to serve more affluent customers and make the financial system operate more efficiently. Electronic funds transfers, 401(k) systems, video games, refund splitting, tax preparers, and other elements of the financial system were not designed primarily to help low-income families save. However, once we recognize the potential of these innovations, we can begin to adapt them to serve the masses of Americans who would most benefit from increased saving.

NOTES

1. There is competition among lenders to offer subprime, and predatory, mortgage loans in LMI communities. But these loans may result in asset drain, rather than asset creation.

2. This is not to argue that innovation is a recent phenomenon. See Tufano (1995) for a discussion of the history of financial innovation. Benjamin Graham and David Dodd's (1934) investing classic contains a long list of quite innovative securities from the first part of the twentieth century.

3. Most recently, Sheena Lyenger and Mark Lepper (2000) show that consumers are more likely to make a choice when they are presented with a limited number of options and more likely to defer when faced with many alternatives. Alexander Chernev (2003) finds that having many choices can make decisions harder for consumers, particularly for those who do not begin the selection process with a clear idea of their desired product. Ravi Dhar (1997) argues that consumers have more difficulty deciding and are more likely to defer their choice when the alternatives presented are similar and equally attractive.

4. Estimates of the number of consumers who consider check cashing outlets their primary financial institution vary. Douglas Dylla (2003) suggests that all unbanked households use check cashers as the primary financial service provider, about 10 percent of the population. Barr (2004a) summarizes a number of studies that suggest lower estimates, including one that finds 70 percent and one that finds 17 percent of the unbanked primarily use check cashers, with the numbers varying widely depending on the area studied. Many banked individuals, particularly those with low incomes, also used check cashers as their primary financial institution. Constance Dunham (2001) estimates that as many as one quarter of banked individuals in low-income New York and Los Angeles neighborhoods primarily rely on check cashers.

5. Reaching the mass affluent is the subject of a number of market research studies (for a journalistic review of some of these studies, see Schmerken 2002).

6. This argument does not take into account the level of competition, which would affect the likelihood of acquiring a customer, given a certain level of marketing activity.

7. As examples of the types of market research directed at understanding high-net-worth customers, see http://www.hnw.com, http://www. spectrem.com, and http://www.ixicorp.com. A few recent projects are

attempting to amass new data on low-wealth customers: the Initiative for a Competitive Inner City has a project to provide a picture of low income neighborhoods (http://www.icic.org) and ShoreBank Advisory Service's MetroEdge services provide businesses with market research of under-served communities (http://www.metro-edge.com).

8. Glenn Hubbard and Jonathan Skinner (1996) provide an overview of the literature on the effectiveness of IRA and 401(k) savings incentives. They report evidence that these incentives generate new saving, but also findings that raise doubts about the effectiveness of these policies. Michael Sherraden and Michael Barr (2005) consider these results and argue that incentives targeted at low-income families will be more likely to be successful given the limited likelihood that these wealth-poor households could transfer assets from standard accounts to tax-privileged or otherwise advantaged accounts.

9. We primarily discuss programs that provide incentives for LMI families to build financial assets. In addition, the federal government also encourages low-income families to seek education and homeownership through programs that are not based around personal saving accounts. A number of federal loans and grants, including Perkins and Stafford loans and Pell grants, assist students with educational expenses and educational Savings Bonds and Coverdale Education Savings Accounts are designed to provide tax incentives for saving for pre-college and college expenses (New America Foundation 2004). Support for low-income homeownership is provided through grants for down payment, affordable mortgages with below-market rates, mortgage insurance, and assistance with home-owner expenses (National Low Income Housing Coalition 2004).

10. *Benefit News* quotes Thomas E. Garman, a board member of the InCharge Institute, placing the cost of retirement planning sessions at $150 per year (Elswick 2004). The IDA SWFA legislation provides a $50 tax credit for the cost of providing financial education and account administration (S. 476, 2003).

11. Calculation based on sales of 36 million copies of Sims, estimated retail price of $30, and estimated gross margins for Electronic Arts (the game publisher) and GameStop (the game retailer).

12. See www.fanniemaefoundation.org/programs/bb/v3i3-competition.shtml, visited Oct. 30, 2004, for a discussion of these partnerships.

13. IRS-supported Volunteer Income Tax Assistance (VITA) and Tax Counseling for the Elderly (TCE) free tax preparation sites prepared returns for 1.6 million individuals in 2003. This figure does not include those free tax preparation sites that are not funded through the VITA or TCE programs.

REFERENCES

Alexander, Gordon J., Jonathan D. Jones, and Peter J. Nigro. 1997. "Mutual Fund Shareholders: Characteristics, Investor Knowledge, and Sources of Information." Economics Working Paper 13. Washington, D.C.: Securities and Exchange Commission, The Office of Thrift Supervision, Office of the Comptroller of the Currency. Accessed at http://www.occ.treas.gov/ftp/workpaper/wp97-13.pdf.

America Saves. 2004a. "Who We Are, What We Do." Accessed at http://www.americasaves.org/about/who.asp.

————. 2004b. "Savings Strategies: The Importance of Emergency Savings." http://www.americasaves.org/strategies/emergencies.asp.

Attanasio, Orazio. 1994. "Personal Saving in the United States." In *International Comparisons of Household Saving,* edited by James Poterba. Chicago, Ill.: University of Chicago Press.

Avery, Robert B., and Arthur B. Kennickell. 1991. "Household Saving in the U.S." *Review of Income and Wealth* 37(4): 409–32.

Avery, Robert B., Raphael W. Bostic, Paul S. Calem, and Glenn B. Canner. 1997. "Changes in the Distribution of Banking Offices." *Federal Reserve Bulletin* 43(9): 708–25. http://www.federalreserve.gov/pubs/bulletin/1997/199709LEAD.pdf.

Babeau, Andre, and Teresa Sbano. 2002. "Household Wealth in the National Accounts of Europe, the United States and Japan." Paper presented at OECD Meeting of National Accounts Experts. Château de la Muette, Paris, October 8–12, 2002. Accessed at http://www.oee.fr/pdf/oeefree_pdf/rf7.pdf.

Bankrate.com. 2003. "Bankrate.com Financial Literacy Survey." Bankrate.com and RoperASW. Accessed at http://www.Bankrate.com.

Banks, James, and Susann Rohwedder. 2003. "Pensions and Life-Cycle Savings Profiles in the UK." In *Life-Cycle Savings and Public Policy: A Cross-National Study of Six Countries,* edited by Axel Borsch-Supan. San Diego, Calif.: Elsevier Science.

Banks, James, Richard Blundell, and Sarah Tanner. 1998. "Is There a Retirement-Savings Puzzle?" *American Economic Review* 88(4): 769–88.

Barr, Michael. 2004a. "Banking the Poor" *Yale Journal of Regulation* 21(1): 121–237.

————. 2004b. "Banking the Poor: Policies to Bring Low-Income Americans into the Financial Mainstream." *Brookings Institution* Research Brief. Washington: Brookings Institution Press.

Barrett, Jennifer. 2002. "Learning to Manage Your Debt." *Newsweek Web Exclusive,* March 23, 2002. Accessed at http://global.factiva.com/ene/srch/ss_hl.asp.

Barrow, Lisa, and Leslie M. McGranahan. 2000. "The Effects of the Earned Income Credit on the Seasonality of Household Expenditures." *National Tax Journal* 53(4): 1211–43.

Barsky, Robert, John Bound, Kerwin Charles, and James Lupton. 2002. "Accounting for the Black-White Wealth Gap: A Non-parametric Approach." *Journal of the American Statistical Association* 97(459): 663–73.

Bartelt, David W. 1993. "Housing the Underclass." In *The Underclass Debate: Views from History,* edited by Michael B. Katz. Princeton, N.J.: Princeton University Press.

Bayer, Patrick J., B. Douglas Bernheim, and John Karl Scholz. 1996. "The Effects of Financial Education in the Workplace: Evidence from a Survey of Employers." NBER Working Paper #5655. Cambridge, Mass.: National Bureau of Economic Research. Accessed at http://papers.nber.org/papers/w5655.pdf.

Berger, Paul D., and Nada I. Nasr. 1998. "Customer Lifetime Value: Marketing Models and Applications." *Journal of Interactive Marketing* 12(1): 17–30.

Bernheim, Douglas B., and John Karl Scholz. 1993. "Private Saving and Public Policy" In *Tax Policy and the Economy,* edited by James M. Porteba. Cambridge, Mass.: MIT Press.

Bernheim, Douglas B., Daniel M. Garrett, and Dean M. Maki. 2001. "Education and Saving: The Long-Term Effects of High School Financial Curriculum Mandates." *Journal of Public Economics* 80(3): 435–65.

Bernheim, Douglas B., Jonathan Skinner, and Steven Weinberg. 2001. "What Accounts for the Variation in Retirement Wealth Among U.S. Households?" *American Economic Review* 91(4): 832–57.

Berube, Alan, Anne Kim, Benjamin Foreman, and Megan Burns. 2002. *The Price of Paying Taxes: How Tax Preparation and Refund Loan Fees Erode the Benefits of the EITC.* Living Cities Databook Survey Series. Washington: Brookings Institution Press.

Beverly, Sondra. 1997. "How Can the Poor Save? Theory and Evidence on Saving in Low-Income Households." Working Paper 97-3. St. Louis, Mo.: Center for Social Development, Washington University. Accessed at http://gwbweb.wustl.edu/csd/Publications/1997/wp97-3.pdf.

Beverly, Sondra, and Michael Sherraden. 1999. "Institutional Determinants of Saving: Implications for Low-Income Households and Public Policy." *Journal of Socio-Economics* 28(4): 457–73.

Beverly, Sondra, Daniel Schneider, and Peter Tufano. 2006. "Splitting Tax Refunds and Building Savings: An Empirical Test." In *Tax Policy and the Economy,* edited by James Poterba. Cambridge, Mass.: MIT Press.

Beverly, Sondra, Jennifer Tescher, and Jennifer Romich. 2004. "Linking Tax Refunds and Low-Cost Bank Accounts: Early Lessons for Program Design and Evaluation." *Journal of Consumer Affairs* 38(2): 332–41.

Bird, Edward, and Paul Hagstrom. 1999. "The Wealth Effects of Income Insurance." *Review of Income and Wealth* 45(3): 339–52.

Blau, Francine D., and John W. Graham. 1990. "Black-White Differences in Wealth and Asset Composition." *Quarterly Journal of Economics* 105(2): 321–39.

Bloomberg News. 2004. "Costco, Kerry Backer, Getting a Boost from Bush Tax Cut." *Bloomberg.com*. October 8, 2004. Accessed at http://quote.bloomberg.com/apps/news?pid=10000176&sid=a7zyxR_ENj8k&refer=us_elections.

Board of Governors of the Federal Reserve. 2003. *Annual Report to Congress on Retail Fees and Services of Depository Institutions*. FRBI-100-0603. Washington: Federal Reserve Board. Accessed at http://www.federalreserve.gov/boarddocs/rptcongress/2003fees.pdf.

————. 2004. *2004 Survey of Consumer Finances*. Electronic Data File. Washington: Board of Governors of the Federal Reserve. http://www.federalreserve.gov/pubs/oss/oss2/2004/scf2004home.html.

Borsch-Supan, Axel, and Ana M. Lusardi. 2003. "Saving: A Cross-National Perspective." In *Life-Cycle Savings and Public Policy: A Cross-National Study of Six Countries,* edited by Axel Borsch-Supan. San Diego, Calif.: Elsevier Science.

Borsch-Supan, Axel, Anette Reil-Heid, and Reinhold Schnabel. 2003. "Household Saving in Germany." In *Life-Cycle Savings and Public Policy: A Cross-National Study of Six Countries,* edited by Axel Borsch-Supan. San Diego, Calif.: Elsevier Science.

Boshara, Ray. 2001. "The Rationale for Assets, Asset-Building Policies, and IDAs for the Poor." In *Building Assets: A Report on the Asset-Development and IDA Field,* edited by Ray Boshara. Washington: Corporation for Enterprise Development.

Bosworth, Barry, Gary Burtless, and John Sabelhaus. 1991. "The Decline in Saving: Evidence from Household Surveys." *Brookings Papers on Economic Activity* 1991(1): 183–241.

Browning, Martin, and Ana M. Lusardi. 1996. "Household Saving: Micro Theories and Micro Facts." *Journal of Economic Literature* 34(4): 1797–855.

Bucks, Brian K., Arthur B. Kennickell, and Kevin B. Moore. 2006. "Recent Changes in U.S. Family Finances: Evidence from the 2001 and 2004 Survey of Consumer Finances." *Federal Reserve Bulletin* 92: A1–A38. Accessed at http://federalreserve.gov/pubs/bulletin/2006/financesurvey.pdf.

Burhouse, Susan, Donna Gambrell, and Angelisa Harris. 2004. "Delivery Systems for Financial Education in Theory and Practice." *FYI: An Update on Emerging Issues in Banking*. September 22, 2004. Washington: Federal Deposit Insurance Corporation. Accessed at http://www.fdic.gov/bank/analytical/fyi/2004/092204fyi.html.

Burman, Len, William Gale, and Peter Orszag. 2004. "The Administration's Savings Proposals: Preliminary Analysis." *Tax Break, Tax Notes*. March 3rd, 2003.

Burnham, Paul F. 2003. *Utilization of Tax Incentives for Retirement Savings.* Washington: The Congress of the United States, Congressional Budget Office. Accessed at http://www.cbo.gov/ftpdoc.cfm?index=4490&type=0.

Caner, Asena, and Edward Wolff. 2002. "Asset Poverty in the United States, 1984–1999: Evidence from the Panel Survey of Income Dynamics." *Review of Income and Wealth* 50(4): 493–518.

Carroll, Christopher, and Andrew A. Samwick. 1998. "How Important is Precautionary Saving?" *The Review of Economics and Statistics* 80(3): 410–19.

Caskey, John. 1994. "Bank Representation in Low-Income and Minority Urban Communities." *Urban Affairs Quarterly* 29(4): 617–38.

Chen, Haiyang, and Ronald P. Volpe. 1998. "An Analysis of Personal Financial Literacy Among College Students." *Financial Services Review* 7(2): 107–28.

Chernev, Alexander. 2003. "When More is Less and Less is More: The Role of Ideal Point Availability and Assortment in Consumer Choice." *Journal of Consumer Research* (30): 170–83.

Chiteji, Ngina, and Darrick Hamilton. 2005. "Family Matters: Kin Networks and Asset Accumulation." In *Inclusion in the American Dream: Assets, Poverty, and Public Policy,* edited by Michael Sherraden. Oxford: Oxford University Press.

Clancy, Margaret, and Michael Sherraden. 2003. "The Potential for Inclusion in 529 Savings Plans: Report on a Survey of States." Research Report. St. Louis, Mo.: Center for Social Development, Washington University.

Clancy, Margaret, Peter Orszag, and Michael Sherraden. 2004. "College Savings Plans: A Platform for Inclusive Saving Policy?" *Perspective.* St. Louis, Mo.: Center for Social Development, Washington University.

Cooper, James C., and Kathleen Madigan. 2004. "The National Piggy Bank is Going Hungry, a Low Savings Rate Threatens Boomers' Retirement and Long-Term Growth." *Business Week.* Accessed at http://global.factiva.com/ene/srch/ss_hl.asp.

Corporation for Enterprise Development. 2002. *State Asset Development Report Card: Benchmarking Asset Development in Fighting Poverty.* Washington: Corporation for Enterprise Development. Accessed at http://www.cfed.org/publications/Final%20SADRC%20PDF.pdf.

———. 2003. "IDA Initiatives." Accessed May 14, 2003 at http://www.cfed.org/focus.m?parentid=2&siteid=374&id=374.

———. 2004. "Overview of the SEED Initiative." Accessed at http://seed.cfed.org/.

Cramer, Reid. 2004. "Net Worth at Birth: Creating a National System for Savings and Asset Building with American Stakeholder Accounts." Working Paper. Washington: New American Foundation, Asset Building Program. Accessed at http://www.assetbuilding.org/files/archive/Doc_File_885_1.pdf.

————. 2005. "Splitting Refunds: A Proposal to Leverage the Tax Filing Process to Promote Savings and Asset Building." Working Paper. Washington: New America Foundation, Asset Building Program. Accessed at http://www.assetbuilding.org/files/archive/Doc_File_1363_1.pdf.

Crane, Dwight B., Kenneth A. Froot, Scott P. Mason, Andre F. Perold, Robert C. Merton, Zvi Bodie, Erik R. Sirri, and Peter Tufano. 1995. *The Global Financial System: A Functional Perspective*. Boston, Mass.: Harvard Business School Press.

Curley, Jamie, and Michael Sherraden. 2000. "Policy Lessons from Children's Allowances for Children's Savings Accounts." *Child Welfare* 79(6): 661–87.

DeNavas-Walt, Carmen, Bernadette D. Proctor, and Robert J. Mills. 2003. "Income, Poverty, and Health Insurance Coverage in the United States." *Current Population Reports*, P60-226. Washington: U.S. Government Printing Office for U.S. Census Bureau. Accessed at http://www.census.gov/prod/2004pubs/p60-226.pdf.

Dhar, Ravi. 1997. "Consumer Preference for a No-Choice Option." *Journal of Consumer Research* 24(2): 215–31.

Di, Zhu Xiao. 2003. "Housing Wealth and Household Net Wealth in the United States: Profile Based on the Recently Released 2001 SCF Data." Cambridge, Mass.: Joint Center for Housing Studies, Harvard University. Accessed at http://www.jchs.harvard.edu/publications/finance/w03-8_di.pdf.

Donkers, Bas, Peter C. Verhoef, and Martijn de Jong. 2003. "Predicting Customer Lifetime Value in Multi-Service Industries." ERIM Report Series Research in Management, ERS-2003-038-MKT. Rotterdam: Rotterdam School of Management, Erasmus University.

Draut, Tamara, and Javier Silva. 2003. *Borrowing to Make Ends Meet: The Growth of Credit Card Debt in the '90s*. New York: Demos, A Network for Ideas and Action. Accessed at http://www.demos.org/pubs/borrowing_to_make_ends_meet.pdf.

Dunham, Constance. 2001. "The Role of Banks and Non-Banks in Serving Low- and Moderate-Income Communities." Paper presented to Changing Financial Markets and Community Development: A Federal Reserve System Community Affairs Conference. Washington, D.C., April 5–6, 2001.

Dylla, Douglas. 2003. "NeighborWorks Focuses on Financial Fitness Education." *The Bridge*. Autumn/Winter(2003): 11–13. Accessed at http://www.nw.org/network/newsroom/articles/pdf/financialFitness Article.pdf,

Dynan, Karen, Jonathan Skinner, and Stephen P. Zeldes. 2004. "Do the Rich Save More?" *Journal of Political Economy* 112(2): 397–444.

Elswick, Jill. 2004. "Retirement Education Pays Off for Participants." *Employee Benefit News*. April 15, 2004. Accessed at http://www.benefitnews.com/retire/detail.cfm?id=5835.

Engen, Eric M., and Jonathan Gruber. 2001. "Unemployment Insurance and Precautionary Saving." *Journal of Monetary Economics* 47(3): 545–79.

Federal Credit Union Act. 12 U.S.C. §1786. Accessed at http://www.ncua.gov/RegulationsOpinionsLaws/fcu_act/fcu_act.pdf.

Federal Deposit Insurance Corporation. 2004. "Summary of Deposits Data." Washington: Federal Deposit Insurance Corporation. Accessed at http://www2.fdic.gov/sod/index.asp.

Fondation, Larry, Peter Tufano, and Patricia Walker. 1999. "Collaborating with Congregations: Opportunities for Financial Services in Inner Cities." *Harvard Business Review.* July/August 1999: 57–68.

Friedman, Milton. 1957. *A Theory of the Consumption Function.* Princeton, N.J.: Princeton University Press.

Friend, Irwin, and Stanley Schor. 1959. "Who Saves?" *Review of Economics and Statistics* 41(2): 213–48.

Gale, William G. 2004. "Foreign Holdings of Federal Debt." *Tax Facts.* Washington: Tax Policy Center, Urban Institute, and Brookings Institution. Accessed at http://www.urban.org/UploadedPDF/1000618_TaxFacts_021604.pdf.

Gale, William G., Mark Iwry, and Peter Orszag. 2004. "The Saver's Credit: Issues and Options." *Retirement Security Project.* Washington: The Brookings Institution. Accessed at http://www.brookings.edu/views/papers/gale/20040419.htm.

Galenson, Marjorie. 1972. "Do Blacks Save More?" *American Economic Review* 62(1/2): 211–6.

Glackin, Caroline E. W., and Eliza G. Mahoney. 2002. "Savings and Credit for U.S. Micro-Enterprises: Integrating Individual Development Accounts and Loans for Micro-Enterprise." *The Journal of Microfinance* 4(2): 99.

Goad, Pierre. 1998. "U.S. Economist Says Japan Has Been Bad Model in Asia." *The Asian Wall Street Journal.* October 12, 1998.

Graham, Benjamin, and David Dodd. 1934. *Security Analysis.* New York: McGraw Hill.

Greenspan, Alan. 2004. Remarks at a symposium sponsored by the Federal Reserve Bank of Kansas. Jackson Hole, Wyo., August 27, 2004. Accessed at http://www.federalreserve.gov/boarddocs/speeches/2004/20040827/default.htm.

Gruber, Jonathan, and Aaron Yelowitz. 1999. "Public Health Insurance and Private Savings." *Journal of Political Economy* 107(6): 1249–74.

Hale, Todd. 2004. "Understanding the Wal-Mart Shopper." *Consumer Insight* 6(2)(Spring): 29–34. Accessed at http://www2.acnielsen.com/pubs/documents/2004_q1_ci_walmart.pdf.

Haveman, Robert, and Edward Wolff. 2001. "Who Are the Asset Poor? Levels, Trends, and Composition, 1983–1998." Discussion Paper no. 1227-01. Madison, Wisc.: Institute for Research on Poverty. Accessed at http://www.irp.wisc.edu/publications/dps/pdfs/dp122701.pdf.

Holt, Douglas B., and Juliet B. Schorr, editor. 2000. *The Consumer Society Reader.* New York: New Press.

Hubbard, Glenn R., and Jonathan Skinner. 1996. "Assessing the Effectiveness of Saving Incentives." *Journal of Economic Perspectives* 10(4): 73–90.

Hubbard, Glenn R., Jonathan Skinner, and Stephen P. Zeldes. 1995. "Precautionary Saving and Social Insurance." *Journal of Political Economy* 103(2): 360–99.

Hugget, Mark, and Gustavo Ventura. 2000. "Understanding Why High Income Households Save More Than Low Income Households." *Journal of Monetary Economics* 45(2): 361–97.

Hurd, Michael, and Susann Rohwedder. 2003. "The Retirement-Consumption Puzzle: Anticipated and Actual Declines in Spending at Retirement." NBER Working Paper #9586. Cambridge, Mass.: National Bureau of Economic Research. Accessed at http://www.nber.org/papers/w9586.

Hurst, Eric, and James P. Ziliak. 2006. "Do Welfare Asset Limits Affect Household Saving? Evidence from Welfare Reform." *Journal of Human Resources* 41(1): 46–71.

Hurst, Eric, Ming Ching Luoh, Frank P. Stafford, and William G. Gale. 1998. "The Wealth Dynamics of American Families, 1984–1994." *Brookings Papers on Economic Activity* 1998(1): 267–337.

Internal Revenue Service Statistics of Income. 2001. *Individual Income Tax Statistics—2001, Table 3.3—2001 Individual Income Tax, All Returns: Tax Liability, Tax Credits, Tax Payments, By Size of Adjusted Gross Income.* Washington: U.S. Department of the Treasury. Accessed at http://www.irs.gov/pub/irs-soi/01in33ar.xls.

————. 2003. *2003 Data Book: Table 23, Internal Revenue Service Taxpayer Assistance and Education Programs, by Type of Assistance or Program, Fiscal Year 2003.* Washington: U.S. Department of the Treasury. Accessed at http://www.irs.gov/pub/irs-soi/03db23ap.xls.

Jacob, Katy. 2004. *Stored Value Cards: A Scan of Current Trends and Future Opportunities.* Chicago, Ill.: Center for Financial Services Innovation. Accessed at http://www.cfsinnovation.com/managed_documents/storedvalue card_report.pdf.

Jacob, Katy, Sabrina Su, Sherrie Rhine, and Jennifer Tescher. 2005. *Stored Value Cards: Challenges and Opportunities for Reaching Emerging Markets.* Chicago, Ill.: Center for Financial Services Innovation. Accessed at http://www.cfsinnovation.com/managed_documents/svcpaper2.pdf.

James E. Arnold Consultants. 1999. *Marketing Strategy Development for the Retail Securities Programs of the Bureau of Public Debt.* Report to the Bureau of Public Debt. Unpublished manuscript. On file with the authors.

Johnson, Lauren K. 2002. "The Real Value of Customer Loyalty." *MIT Sloan Management Review* 43(20): 14, 17.

JumpStart Coalition. 2002. *Personal Financial Survey of High School Seniors: Executive Summary and Questionnaire.* Washington: Jump$tart Coalition for

Personal Financial Literacy. Accessed at http://www.jumpstartcoalition.com/upload/SurveyResultsApril2002.doc.

Katz, Michael B. 1993. "The Urban 'Underclass' as a Metaphor of Social Transformation." In *The Underclass Debate: Views from History,* edited by Michael B. Katz. Princeton, N.J.: Princeton University Press.

———. 1993. "Reframing the Underclass." In *The Underclass Debate: Views from History,* edited by Michael B. Katz. Princeton, N.J.: Princeton University Press.

Keister, Lisa A. 2004. "Family Structure, Race, and Wealth Ownership: A Longitudinal Exploration of Wealth Accumulation Processes." *Sociological Perspectives* 47(2): 161–87.

Kennickell, Arthur B. 2003. "A Rolling Tide: Changes in the Distribution of Wealth in the U.S., 1989–2001." Working Paper. Washington: Federal Reserve Board. Accessed at http://www.federalreserve.gov/pubs/oss/oss2/papers/concentration.2001.10.pdf.

Kennickell, Arthur B., and Ana M. Lusardi. 2003. "Wealth Accumulation and the Importance of Precautionary Saving." Working Paper. Dartmouth, N.H.: Dartmouth College.

King, Robert, and Ross Levine. 1993. "Finance and Growth: Schumpeter Might Be Right." *Quarterly Journal of Economics* 108(3): 717–38.

Kitamura, Yukinobu, Noriyuki Takayama, and Fumiko Arita. 2003. "Household Savings and Wealth Distribution in Japan." In *Life-Cycle Savings and Public Policy: A Cross-National Study of Six Countries,* edited by Axel Börsch-Supan. San Diego, Calif.: Elsevier Science.

Krasney, David. 2003. "Wal-Mart Dumps Cold Water on U.S. Economic Bulls." *Reuters.* November 13, 2003. Accessed at http://www.forbes.com/markets/economy/newswire/2003/11/13/rtr1147178.html.

Laibson, David. 1997. "Golden Eggs and Hyperbolic Discounting." *The Quarterly Journal of Economics* 112(2): 443–77.

Levine, Ross. 1997. "Financial Development and Economic Growth: Views and Agenda." *Journal of Economic Literature* 35(2): 688–726.

Lusardi, Ana M. 2002. "Planning and the Effectiveness of Retirement Seminars." Department of Economics Working Paper. Dartmouth, N.H.: Dartmouth College.

Lyenger, Sheena S., and Mark R. Lepper. 2000. "When Choice is Demotivating: Can One Desire Too Much of a Good Thing?" *Journal of Personality and Social Psychology* 79(6): 995–1006.

Mandaro, Laura. 2002. "Toyota Sizes up Nevada for Thrift Charter." *American Banker* 167(221): 1.

Markovich, Carl A., and Sharon A. DeVaney. 1997. "College Seniors' Personal Finance Knowledge and Practices." *Journal of Family and Consumer Sciences* 89(1): 61–65.

Merton, Robert C. 1992. "Financial Innovation and Economic Performance." *Journal of Applied Corporate Finance* 4(4): 12–22.

Mills, Gregory, Geraldine Campos, Michelle Ciurea, Donna DeMarco, Naomi Michlin, and Douglas Welch. 2000. *Evaluation of Asset Accumulation Initiatives: Final Report.* Cambridge, Mass.: Abt Associates.

Mills, Gregory, Rhiannon Patterson, Larry Orr, and Donna DeMarco. 2004. *Evaluation of the American Dream Demonstration: Final Evaluation Report.* Cambridge, Mass.: Abt Associates.

Modigliani, Franco, and Richard Brumberg. 1954. "Utility Analysis and the Consumption Function: An Interpretation of the Cross-Section Data." In *Post Keynesian Economics,* edited by Kenneth Kurihara. New Brunswick, N.J.: Rutgers University Press.

Moon, Marilyn. 1977. "The Economic Welfare of the Aged and Income Security Programs." In *Improving Measures of Economic Welfare,* edited by Marilyn Moon and Eugene Smolensky. New York: Academic Press.

Moore, Amanda, Sondra Beverly, Mark Schreiner, Michael Sherraden, Margaret Lombe, Esther Y. N. Cho, Lissa Johnson, and Rebecca Vonderlack. 2001. *Saving, IDA Programs, and Effects of IDAs: A Survey of Participants.* St. Louis, Mo.: Center for Social Development, Washington University. Accessed at http://gwbweb.wustl.edu/csd/Publications/2001/shortsurveyreport.pdf.

Moore, James P., and Olivia S. Mitchell. 1997. "Projected Retirement Wealth and Savings Adequacy in the Health and Retirement Study." NBER Working Paper #6240. Cambridge, Mass.: National Bureau of Economic Research. Accessed at http://www.nber.org/papers/w6240.

Morningstar Principia Mutual Funds Advanced. 2004. CD-ROM Data File. Chicago, Ill.: Morningstar Inc.

Murray, Janet. 1964. "Potential Income from Assets: Findings of the 1963 Survey of the Aged." *Social Security Bulletin* 27(12): 3–11.

National Credit Union Administration. 2003. *NCUA 2003 Annual Report.* Alexandria, Va.: National Credit Union Administration. Accessed at http://www.ncua.gov/ReportsAndPlans/annualrpt/2003AR.pdf.

———. 2004. *NCUA Individual Credit Union Data.* Alexandria, Va.: National Credit Union Administration. Accessed at http://www.ncua.gov/index data.html.

National Low Income Housing Coalition. 2004. *Advocates' Guide to Housing & Community Development Policy.* Washington: National Low Income Housing Coalition. Accessed at http://www.nlihc.org.

New America Foundation. 2004. *Existing Federal Policies.* Assetbuilding.org Project. Washington: The New America Foundation. Accessed at http://www.assetbuilding.org.

Novak, Lynn. 2001. "Self-Support: The Evolving Support Portal." *IT Support News* 21(7): 19–20.

Nunes, Paul, Brian Johnson, and Timothy Breene. 2004. "Selling to the Moneyed Masses." *Harvard Business Review* 82(7/8)(July–August): 94–104.

Oliver, Melvin L., and Thomas M. Shapiro. 1990. "Wealth of a Nation: At Least One Third of Households Are Asset-Poor." *The American Journal of Economics and Sociology* 49(2): 129–50.

———. 1997. *Black Wealth/White Wealth.* New York: Routledge.

Olson, Keith W. 1973. "The G.I. Bill and Higher Education: Success and Surprise." *American Quarterly* 25(5): 596–610.

Organization for Economic Cooperation and Development. 2004. *OECD Economic Outlook* 75(1).

Orszag, Peter, and Robert Greenstein. 2003. "Progressivity and Government Incentives to Save." Paper presented at the Building Assets, Building Credit conference. Kennedy School of Government, Harvard University. Boston, Mass., November 18–19, 2003. Accessed at http://www.brook.edu/views/papers/orszag/20031124.htm.

Orszag, Peter, and Matthew G. Hall. 2004. "The Saver's Credit." *Tax Facts.* Washington: Tax Policy Center, Urban Institute, and Brookings Institution. Accessed at http://www.urbaninstitute.org/UploadedPDF/1000498_TaxFacts_060903.pdf.

Page-Adams, Deborah P., Edward Scanlon, Sondra Beverly, and Tom McDonald. 2001. "Assets, Health, and Well-being: Neighborhoods, Families, Children and Youth." Background Paper 01-9. St. Louis, Mo.: Center for Social Development, Washington University. Accessed at http://gwbweb.wustl.edu/csd/publications/2001/ResearchBackground_01-9.pdf.

Perun, Pamela. 1999. "Matching Private Saving with Federal Dollars: USA Accounts and Other Subsidies for Saving." *The Retirement Project* Brief Series no. 8. Washington: The Urban Institute. Accessed at http://www.urban.org/url.cfm?ID=309272/

Piketty, Thomas, and Emmanuel Saez. 2003. "Income Inequality in the United States, 1913–1998." *Quarterly Journal of Economics* 118(1): 1–39.

Porteba, James M. 1994. *International Comparisons of Household Savings.* Chicago, Ill.: University of Chicago Press.

Powers, Elizabeth. 1998. "Does Means-Testing Welfare Discourage Saving? Evidence from a Change in AFDC Policy in the United States." *Journal of Public Economics* 68(1): 5–21.

Prahalad, C. K. 2004. *The Fortune at the Bottom of the Pyramid: Eradicating Poverty Through Profits.* Upper Saddle River, N.J.: Wharton School Publishing.

Princeton Survey Research Associates. 1996. *The Investor Protection Trust Investor Knowledge Survey: A Report on the Findings.* Princeton, N.J.: Princeton Survey Research Associates for The Investor Protection Trust.

Projector, Dorothy. 1968. *Survey of Changes in Family Finances.* Washington: Board of Governors of the Federal Reserve System.

Projector, Dorothy, and Gertrude Weiss. 1966. "Survey of Financial Characteristics of Consumers." Federal Reserve Technical Papers. Washington: Board of Governors of the Federal Reserve System.

Quinn, Jane B. 2001. "Checking Error Could Land You on Blacklist." *Washington Post.* September 30, 2001, p. H2.

Radner, Daniel B., and Denton R. Vaughan. 1987. "Wealth, Income, and the Economic Status of Aged Households." In *International Comparisons of the Distribution of Household Wealth,* edited by Edward Wolff. New York: Clarendon Press.

Roach, Stephen. 2003. "Global: Policy Blunder." Morgan Stanley, Global Economic Forum. April 25, 2003. Accessed at http://www.morganstanley.com/GEFdata/digests/20030425-fri.html.

Rowen, Henry, and John Shoven. 1993. "Let's Have a National Savings Campaign." *The Wall Street Journal,* January 5, 1993.

Ruggles, Patricia. 1990. *Drawing the Line: Alternative Poverty Measures and Their Implications for Public Policy.* Washington: Urban Institute Press.

Ruggles, Patricia, and Roberton Williams. 1989. "Longitudinal Measures of Poverty: Accounting for Income and Assets Over Time." *Review of Income and Wealth* 35(3): 225–44.

Sawyer, Noah, and Kenneth Temkin. 2004. *Analysis of Alternative Financial Service Providers.* Washington: Fannie Mae Foundation and Urban Institute Press. Accessed at http://www.urban.org/url.cfm?ID=410935.

Schmerken, Ivy. 2002. "Wealth Management: The Race to Serve the Mass Affluent." *Wall Street + Technology.* February 1, 2002, p. 1. Accessed at http://www.wallstreetandtech.com/story/mag/WST20020107S0001.

Scholz, John Karl, and Kara Levine. 2002. "U.S. Black-White Wealth Inequality: A Survey." Working Paper. Madison, Wisc.: Department of Economics and Institute for Research on Poverty.

Schreiner, Mark, Margaret Clancy, and Michael Sherraden. 2002. *Saving Performance in the American Dream Demonstration, A National Demonstration of Individual Development Accounts.* St. Louis, Mo.: Center for Social Development, Washington University. Accessed at http://gwbweb.wustl.edu/csd/Publications/2002/ADDreport2002.pdf.

Shackleton, Robert. 2003. *Baby Boomer's Retirement Prospects: An Overview.* A CBO Study. Washington: The Congress of the United States, Congressional Budget Office. Accessed at http://www.cbo.gov/ftpdocs/48xx/doc4863/11-26-BabyBoomers.pdf.

Shefrin, Hersh M., and Richard H. Thaler. 1988. "The Behavioral Life-Cycle Hypothesis." *Economic Inquiry* 26(4): 609–43.

Sherraden, Michael. 1991. *Assets and the Poor: A New American Welfare Policy.* Armonk, N.Y.: M. E. Sharpe.

Sherraden, Michael, and Michael Barr. 2005. "Institutions and Inclusion in Saving Policy." In *Building Assets, Building Credit: Creating Wealth in Low-Income Communities,* edited by Niclas P. Restinas and Eric S. Belsky. Washington: Brookings Institution Press.

Shobe, Marcia A. 2002. "The Future in Anti-Poverty Strategies." *Journal of Children & Poverty Strategies* 8(1): 35–49.

Siskos, Catherine. 2001. "Cash in a Crunch–Emergency Fund as Savings Priority." *Kiplinger's Personal Finance Magazine* 55(2): 94.

Smeeding, Timothy M., Katherine Ross, and Michael O'Conner. 2000. "The EITC: Expectation, Knowledge, Use, and Economic and Social Mobility." *National Tax Journal* 53(4): 1187–209.

Smith, James. 1987. "Recent Trends in the Distribution of Wealth in the US: Data, Research Problems, and Prospects." In *International Comparisons of the Distribution of Household Wealth,* edited by Edward Wolff. Oxford: Clarendon Press.

Smith, James, and James P. Lupton. 2003. "Marriage, Assets, and Savings." In *Marriage and the Economy,* edited by Shoshanna A. Grossbard-Shechtman. Cambridge: Cambridge University Press.

Stegman, Michael. 1999. *Savings for the Poor: The Hidden Benefits of Electronic Banking.* Washington: Brookings Institution Press.

Steuerle, Eugene, and Nelson McClung. 1977. "The Measure of Poverty." Technical Paper IV, *Wealth and the Accounting Period in the Measurement of Means.* Washington: U.S. Department of Health, Education, and Welfare.

Stone, Adam. 2004. "After Some Well-Placed Deposits in Media, Bank Campaign Shows Positive Returns." *PR News,* March 1, 2004.

Sugrue, Thomas J. 1993. "The Structures of Urban Poverty: The Reorganization of Space and Work in Three Periods of American History." In *The Underclass Debate: Views from History,* edited by Michael B. Katz. Princeton, N.J.: Princeton University Press.

T. Rowe Price. 2003. *T. Rowe Price 2003 Annual Report: Elements of Our Success.* Baltimore, Md.: T. Rowe Price Group, Inc. Accessed at http://www.troweprice.com.

T. D. Waterhouse. 2001. "TD Waterhouse Group, Inc. Reports Cash Earnings of $.01 per Share for the Fiscal Quarter Ended October 31, 2001." Toronto, Ontario: T. D. Waterhouse. Accessed at http://www.tdwaterhouse.com.

Tansey, Charles D. 2001. "Community Development Credit Unions: An Emerging Player in Low Income Communities." *Capital Xchange,* September. Washington: Brookings Institution.

Thaler, Richard H., and Shlomo Benartzi. 2004. "Save More Tomorrow(TM): Using Behavioral Economics to Increase Employee Saving." *The Journal of Political Economy* 112(1): 164–87.

Thaler, Richard H., and Hersh M. Shefrin. 1981. "An Economic Theory of Self-Control." *The Journal of Political Economy* 89(2): 392–406.

Toffler, Alvin. 1970. *Future Shock.* New York: Random House.

Tufano, Peter. 1995. "Securities Innovations: A Historical and Functional Perspective." *Journal of Applied Corporate Finance* 7(4): 90–113.

Tufano, Peter, and Daniel Schneider. 2004. *H&R Block and "Everyday Financial Services."* HBS Case No. 205-013. Boston, Mass.: Harvard Business School Publishing.

———. 2005. "Reinventing Savings Bonds." *Tax Notes* October 31, 2005.

U.S. Census Bureau. 2000. *Poverty Status of Individuals and Age and Sex of Individuals.* Washington: U.S. Census Bureau, Population Division. Accessed November 3, 2004 at http://factfinder.census.gov/servlet/SAFFPeople?_sse=on ().

———. 2004. *Annual Estimates of the Population by Sex and Five-Year Age Groups for the United States, 2000–2003, Table 1 and Table 2.* Washington: U.S. Census Bureau, Population Division. Accessed at http://www.census.gov/popest/national/asrh/NC-EST2003-as.html.

U.S. Congress. Senate. 2004a. *A Better Future for American Families Act,* S. 2303, 108th Cong. 2nd session. Accessed at http://thomas.loc.gov/cgi-bin/bdquery/z?d108:SN02303:@@@Thttp://www.govtrack.us/congress/billtext.xpd?bill=s108-2303.

———. 2004b. *America Saving for Personal Investment, Retirement, and Education Act,* S2791, 108th Cong., 2nd session. Accessed at http://www.centristpolicynetwork.org/legislative_updates/files_2004/santorum_corzine_aspire.pdf.

U.S. Department of the Treasury. 1918. *To Make Thrift a Happy Habit.* Washington: U.S. Department of the Treasury.

———. 1935. *United States Savings Bonds.* Washington: U.S. Department of the Treasury.

———. 1955. *Annual Report of the Secretary of the Treasury.* Washington: U.S. Department of the Treasury.

———. 1956. *Annual Report of the Secretary of the Treasury.* Washington: U.S. Department of the Treasury.

———. 2004. *First Accounts Program.* Accessed at http://www.treas.gov/offices/domestic-finance/financial-institution/fin-education/firstaccounts/.

———. 2005. *Electronic Funds Transfer, Reports and Statistics, Payment Volume Charts 1996–2005.* Accessed at http://fms.treas.gov/eft/reports.html.

Vanguard. 2002. "Investors Need to Bone Up On Bonds and Costs, According to Vanguard/MONEY Investor Literacy Test." Vanguard Press Release. September 25, 2002. Accessed at http://www.vanguard.com.

Vermilyea, Todd, and James A. Wilcox. 2002. "Who is Unbanked and Why: Results From a Large, New Survey of Low-and-Moderate Income Adults." Paper presented at Federal Reserve Bank of Chicago, Conference on Bank Structure and Competition, Chicago, Ill. May 8–10, 2002. Accessed at http://www.chicagofed.org/news_and_conferences/conferences_and_events/files/2002_bank_structure_who_is_unbanked_and_why.pdf.

Waschawsky, Mark J., and John Ameriks. 2001. "What Does Financial Planning Software Say About American's Preparedness for Retirement?"

Journal of Retirement Planning May/June, 27–37: 51. Accessed at www.tiaa-crefinstitute.org/Publications/pubarts/pa04-01.htm.

Weisbrod, Burton A., and W. Lee Hanson. 1968. "An Income-Net Worth Approach to Measuring Economic Welfare." *The American Economic Review* 58(5): 1315–29.

Williams, Trina. 2005. "The Homestead Act: A Major Asset-building Policy in American History." In *Inclusion in the American Dream: Assets, Poverty, and Public Policy,* edited by Michael Sherraden. Oxford: Oxford University Press.

Winer, Russell S. 2001. "A Framework for Customer Relationship Management." *California Management Review,* Summer 2001.

Wisniewski, Mary. 2005. "Company Lets People Use Card as a Saving Vehicle." *The Chicago Sun Times.* May 6, 2005. Accessed at http://www.suntimes.com/output/business/cst-fin-currency06.html.

Wolff, Edward. 1990. "Wealth Holdings and Poverty Status in the United States." *Review of Income and Wealth* 36(2): 143–65.

———. 2002. *Top Heavy: The Increasing Inequality of Wealth in America and What Can Be Done About It.* New York: The New Press.

———. 2006. "Changes in Household Wealth in the 1980s and 1990s in the US." In *International Perspectives on Household Wealth,* edited by Edward Wolff. Cheltenham, U.K.: Elgar Publishing.

Wolff, Edward, Ajit Zacharias, and Asena Caner. 2005. "Household Wealth, Public Consumption and Economic Well-Being in the United States." *Cambridge Journal of Economics* 29: 1073–90.

Woo, Lillian, F. William Schweke, and David E. Buchholz. 2004. *Hidden in Plain Sight: A Look at the $335 Billion Federal Asset-Building Budget.* Washington: Corporation for Enterprise Development.

Ziliak, James. 2003. "Income Transfers and Assets of the Poor." *Review of Economics and Statistics* 85(1): 63–76.

CHAPTER THREE

Financial Education and Community Economic Development

Jeanne M. Hogarth, Jane Kolodinsky, and Marianne A. Hilgert

OVER THE LAST several years, the issue of financial literacy and financial education has risen on the agenda of educators, community groups, businesses, government agencies, organizations, and policy makers. It seems that nearly everyone is talking about it. For example, in November 2004 the GAO released the highlights of a forum on the federal government's role in improving financial literacy (2004). And it's not just happening in the United States—the United Kingdom, the EU, the OECD, and Japan all have substantial initiatives targeted toward financial education (see, for example, Organization for Economic Cooperation and Development 2005).

Many have written on the topic, either from a policy perspective (Bayer, Bernheim, and Scholz 1996; Bernheim 1998; Braunstein and Welch 2002; Caskey 2001) or a pragmatic one (Bowen 1996; Garman 1998; Hogarth and Swanson 1993; Montalto 2000; Perry and Ards 2001; Toussaint-Comeau and Rhine 2000). The goal of this paper is to provide a snapshot of the current state of financial education in the United States as it relates to community development. In the process, we will look at a variety of issues: Why is financial education important? What is financial education? What financial education initiatives are underway? Are they working? If so, how do we know? Finally, we will consider the role that financial education plays in community economic development, using a case study from a community development credit union.

WHY IS FINANCIAL EDUCATION IMPORTANT?

Well-informed, well-educated consumers should make better decisions for their families, increasing their economic security and well being. Secure families also should be better able to contribute to vital, thriving communities, further fostering community economic development. Thus, being financially literate is not only important to the individual household and family, it's also important to communities.

The need for financial literacy has always been important, but more recent market and policy developments have raised the saliency and relevance of financial education. Two examples may help illustrate the point. First, complex global financial markets make the twenty-first century different from previous eras. There are more financial products from which to choose among with a wider array of features—the thirty-year fixed-rate mortgage is no longer standard and checking accounts require considerably more choice than what the color of the checks will be. Second, the burden for financial security in later life has shifted from employers to employees, increasing the level of individual responsibility for retirement savings (Copeland 2002). This shift also is seen in the public policy arena in the discussions on private accounts within social security.[1]

Since the early 1990s numerous studies have reported low levels of consumer literacy and financial literacy. The Consumer Federation of America and American Express, for example, conducted a series of "consumer literacy" tests, and found that high school students scored lower than college students and adults (1990, 1991, 1993). The Jump$tart Coalition for Personal Financial Literacy conducts biannual financial literacy tests of high school seniors. In 2004, students answered 52.3 percent of the questions correctly, down from the 56.9 percent in 1997, but up from the 50.2 percent in 2002 (Jump$tart 2004). The American Savings Education Council (ASEC 1999) found that 15 percent of students said they understood financial matters very well, 67 percent said fairly well, and 18 percent said they did not understand them at all. Similarly, 18 percent thought they did a very good job of managing their money, 38 percent said they did a good job, 37 percent said an average job, and 7 percent said a poor job. The Consumer Federation of America and the Cooperative Extension System joined with the Consumer Literacy Consortium to quiz 1,700 adults nationwide on a set of consumer skills; the average score was 75 percent correct (CFA 1998). This quiz covered more "buymanship" than financial management topics, and points toward the range of issues that consumers misunderstand. The Retirement Confidence Survey, conducted by the Employee Benefit Research Institute, found that one-third of workers have a "high" level of financial knowledge, 55 percent have a moderate level, and 11 percent have a "very low" level of knowledge (Yakoboski and Schiffenbauer 1997).

Generally, the importance of financial education is given weight by citing what can happen in its absence. For example, some researchers and educators cite mounting levels of consumer debt—be it credit card debt or the growth in home equity lending—and bankruptcy as what tends to happen without financial education. Others cite low participation and contribution rates for retirement savings as demonstrating a lack of financial education. Although few research studies indicate a correlation between level of financial education and financial management behaviors, Douglas Bernheim, Daniel Garrett, and Dean Maki (2001) showed that consumers who graduated from high schools in states with mandated financial education were more likely to have higher savings rates and higher net worth.

WHAT IS A FINANCIALLY EDUCATED PERSON?

Personal financial education means different things to different people. For some, it is quite broad, encompassing an understanding of economics and how household decisions are affected by economic conditions and circumstances. For others, it focuses quite narrowly on basic money management—budgeting, saving, investing, and insuring. Still others include a set of consumer and buy-manship skills within a financial education framework. In reality, financial education probably can and does include all of these topics.

The consistent themes running through various definitions of financial education include: being knowledgeable, educated, and informed on the issues of managing money and assets, banking, investments, credit, insurance, and taxes; understanding the basic concepts underlying the management of money and assets (for example, the time value of money in investments and the pooling of risks in insurance); and using that knowledge and understanding to plan, implement, and evaluate financial decisions.

This definition implies that the outcome of financial education—that is, what a financially educated person does—includes behaviors such as paying bills on time, having manageable levels of credit, setting financial goals and having a way of achieving those goals through saving and investing, spending wisely, and so on. The specific implementation of these behaviors may vary by income, family circumstance, and asset level, however. For example, we want all households to set financial goals; for some, the goal may be having $200 in an emergency fund, but for others it may be having $20,000 for a down payment on a house.

Less visible, but nonetheless important, are how these themes can be expanded to include community development. Having one's financial house in order can lead to stability in housing and family life, which can contribute to stable educational situations for children, and more involvement of families in their community, including participation in civic activities that range from a parent-teacher organization to neighborhood planning board and beyond. In most cases, we assume these farther-reaching benefits of financial literacy.

WHAT FINANCIAL EDUCATION INITIATIVES ARE UNDER WAY?

In the 1990s it would have been relatively easy to provide a list of financial education initiatives; today, however, it is virtually impossible because new programs and players could be added on a daily basis. There seems to be an abundance of activity on the financial literacy front. Some researchers (Vitt et al. 2000, 2005; Jacob, Hudson, and Bush 2000) have surveyed a variety of educational community-based organizations to determine the availability and extent of initiatives. Lois Vitt and her colleagues (2000) identify ninety-one programs that schools, cooperative extension programs, colleges (including community colleges), the military, faith-based organizations, community groups, employers and others offer. Katy Jacob, Sharyl Hudson, and Malcolm Bush (2000) catalog school and cooperative extension programs as well as those offered by credit counseling agencies, employers and financial institutions, with a special focus on programs targeted to low-income audiences. The Jump$tart Coalition has more than 560 resources in its financial education database. The National Endowment for Financial Education lists more than 150 educational resources and curricula from a wide range of agencies, organizations, and firms in its Economic Independence Clearinghouse database; many of these materials are available in multiple languages (National Endowment for Financial Education 2001). The Federal Reserve Bank of San Francisco includes fifty-six programs and resources in its *Guide to Financial Literacy Resources* (Robinson 2002).

Legislative and public policy initiatives are also driving and developing financial literacy efforts. Financial education is an important part of individual development accounts (IDAs), a policy initiative launched in the late 1990s to help low-income households build assets (see chapter 2 of this volume). The Savings Are Vital for Everyone's Retirement (SAVER) Act included a substantial retirement savings education program (Saving Matters) and Saver Summits held in 1998, 2002, and 2006 (U.S. Department of Labor 2000). For the transition to an "all-electronic Treasury," the Treasury Department included a consumer education program in their EFT'99 initiative (2000). Although not required by recent welfare reform legislation (the Personal Responsibility and Work Opportunity Act), most welfare-to-work programs include some money management information as part of participant training; New Hampshire's Lifeskills for Employment, Achievement and Purpose (LEAP) initiative is one example (University of New Hampshire Cooperative Extension 2004).

Title 5 of the Fair and Accurate Credit Transactions (FACT) Act created the Financial Literacy and Education Commission, involving twenty federal government agencies with some involvement in financial education. The commission was charged with developing a web portal for financial education resources (www.mymoney.gov), to support a toll-free service that links consumers to financial education resources (1-888-my-money), and to develop a national strategy to help educate and inform consumers about financial management matters.

Most financial literacy initiatives have very specific target audiences. But just as there are numerous initiatives, so too are there numerous target audiences. Youth, military personnel (especially young, enlisted personnel), low-income families, first-time homebuyers, employees, church members, and women are all targets of one program or another. Since the welfare reform legislation of the mid-1990s, welfare-to-work programs have also incorporated financial education. Programs are targeted to various ethnic groups (for example, initiatives for Native Americans), various situational groups (including prerelease prisoners), and various demographic groups (such as new parents or preretirees). The National Endowment for Financial Education has collaborated with more than sixty "national nonprofit organizations to create publications for separate, unique constituencies" (2004). In essence, it would be difficult for a U.S. consumer to not be part of a target audience for at least one financial literacy initiative. However, a few target audiences bear special mention.

Because home ownership is both a major investment and a major asset for families, first-time homebuyers are a key audience for many financial literacy programs. These initiatives often target low- to moderate-income families (see, for example, Neighborhood Reinvestment Corporation 2000; National Community Reinvestment Coalition 1998). Some programs cover both prepurchase and postpurchase topics, working with families over several years to clean up their credit records, find affordable housing, and prevent delinquency and default (see, for example, Freddie Mac 2007).

A program housed within the Federal Deposit Insurance Corporation, Money Smart, seeks to "help adults outside the financial mainstream enhance their money skills and create positive banking relationships" (2006). The goal of the program is to provide financial stability for individuals and families as well as communities.

As evident from some of the survey data, youth also are an important audience for financial literacy initiatives. Clearly, the advantage to educating youth is that they then grow up into financially literate adults. The Jump$tart Coalition for Personal Financial Literacy, a broad-based coalition of more than 170 agencies, organizations, and firms, encourages "curriculum enrichment to insure that basic personal financial management skills are attained during the K-12 educational experience" (2001). Recently, Jump$tart expanded its target audience to include college students.

Although most literacy initiatives function in a preventive mode (that is, trying to prevent people from getting into problems), some offer curative programs for consumers with credit problems (National Foundation for Credit

Counseling 2001; InCharge Education Foundation 2004). For many, this is a highly teachable moment in their financial lives. Recent bankruptcy reform legislation includes a provision for debtor education as part of Chapter 13 filings (Braucher 2001). Generally, these programs start off with a counseling format, customized to the consumers' needs; but most organizations involved in credit counseling also offer basic financial education.

DESIGNING FINANCIAL EDUCATION PROGRAMS

To design a learner-centered financial education program requires that planners take into account at least four distinct elements:

- The topics—does the learner need information and education about general cash flow management, credit, saving, investment, retirement planning, estate planning, or some combination of those topics?

- The audience—is the program targeted to the general public, youth, low-income, first-time home buyers, pre-retirees, employees of a particular firm, or someone else?

- Learning styles—is the pedagogy set up for visual, auditory, and kinetic learners?

- Behavior stage—what is the learner's current stage of behavior change? Are most target learners in the precontemplation, contemplation, preparation, action, or maintenance states? (see Prochaska, DiClemente, and Norcross 1992, 1994; Xiao et al. 2004).

Overlaying these elements are the levels of expertise sought or needed in financial education. Here, a medical model may be apt—some consumers in crisis need the equivalent of a financial emergency room to forestall repossession, foreclosure, or utility shut-off. For many financial management issues, consumers can be "self-medicating"—they can take care of themselves with the right financial tools and products and some level of knowledge about when and where to use these. Other financial management issues require the assistance of a financial services general practitioner—someone who can offer broad, basic guidance and access to prescription financial products such as stocks, bonds, and insurance products. Finally, there are those financial issues that require the expertise of a specialist—an attorney or an accountant to deal with the intricacies of tax and estate laws.

With such granularity in the possible combinations of these elements, it is no wonder that there are so many players in the financial education arena. In a review of press releases on economic and financial education from the fall of 2005 through the fall of 2006, we tabulated roughly half as related to general financial education topics and roughly a quarter as related to debt and credit management. Another one in seven focused on retirement and one in ten on home buying. Two-thirds of the releases discussed programs that targeted youth. About two-fifths were issued by nonprofit organizations, another two-fifths by commercial firms, and the remaining fifth by or on behalf of schools.

LINKING FINANCIAL KNOWLEDGE WITH FINANCIAL BEHAVIORS

Many if not most of these programs operate under the implicit assumption that increases in information and knowledge will lead to changes in financial management practices and behaviors. Jean Hogarth, Marianne Hilgert, and Jane Schuchardt (2002) demonstrated that the higher a consumer's financial knowledge (based on a quiz score), the higher the probability that the consumer undertook more positive financial management behaviors and used more financial products and services. For example, consumers scoring 80 percent on the quiz had a 0.37 probability of being "active and engaged" in financial management (that is, they undertook more financial behaviors and used more financial products and services), whereas consumers scoring 50 percent had only a 0.14 probability.

Knowledge and learning preferences seem to be associated with more specific financial behaviors. Persons who were more knowledgeable (again, measured as a quiz score) were more likely to engage in more cash-flow management, saving, and investment behaviors, holding other variables constant (Hogarth, Beverly, and Hilgert 2003). In this study, financial knowledge and learning experiences were the only variables consistently associated with more positive financial behaviors related to cash-flow management, saving, and investing.

Financial knowledge can be statistically linked to credit-related practices as well (Hilgert, Hogarth, and Beverly 2003). In addition, learning experiences—in particular, from family, friends, and personal experiences—were associated with engaging in more financial management behaviors related to all four areas. "This pattern may indicate that increases in knowledge and experience can lead to improvements in financial practices, although the causality could flow in the other direction—or even both ways" (Hilgert, Hogarth, and Beverly 2003, 321).

Are Financial Education Initiatives Working— and How Do We Know?

Perhaps the greatest challenge in financial education is measuring the efficacy of the program. Getting one's financial house in order can take time, and longitudinal studies to prove that a particular program is effective are costly. However, a few longer-term impact and evaluation studies show that financial education can make a difference.

The NEFE High School Financial Planning Program, which has educated more than 2 million high school students in basic personal finance concepts, has had a strong postprogram impact on students (Danes and Boyce 2004). An evaluation of 483 teachers and 5,329 students across the country revealed that participating teens maintained increases in financial knowledge and skills for three months after having taken the course. In addition, increases in knowledge and sound financial behavior led to increased confidence in managing money. Nearly two-fifths (59 percent) understood the costs of buying on credit and more than half (53 percent) knew about investments. Connecting increased knowledge to behavior, the study found that more than half of the teens (53 percent) improved skills for tracking spending and two-fifths (60 percent) reported a change in their saving patterns. On completion, nearly four-fifths (78 percent) reported feeling more confident about managing their money.

Money 2000, a Cooperative Extension System program that focuses on participant debt reduction and savings accumulation, includes an extended-period behavioral monitoring program (O'Neill 1997). Emphasis is placed on achieving specific measurable goals that enrollees set individually. Eight out of ten respondents (80.4 percent) affirmed that the program improved their financial situation. As of the end of 2000, more than 13,000 participants in twenty-two states reported a cumulative increased savings of $10,618,271 and a cumulative decrease in consumer debt of $8,247,219, for a total effect of $18,865,490.[2]

Douglas Bernheim, Daniel Garrett, and Dean Maki studied the relationship between high school financial curriculum mandates and adult savings patterns and net worth. Mandates were found to increase exposure to financial education, and financial education is associated with higher savings rates and higher net worth. "Education," they conclude, "may be a powerful tool for stimulating personal saving" (2001, 426).

Individual development accounts are a relatively new policy initiative designed to help low-income families build wealth by accumulating assets (see chapter 2). IDAs are meant to improve access to savings institutions for the poor by providing matching funds for savings toward home ownership, higher education, and microenterprise. The American Dream Demonstration (ADD) project evaluated preliminary data on IDAs of 2,378 participants (Schreiner, Clancy, and Sherraden 2002). The data showed that average monthly net deposits per participant were $25.42. On average, participants saved 67 percent of their monthly savings target. The average match rate was two to one, and participants accumulated about $900 per year. Financial education is part of the IDA initiative; the ADD data show that average monthly net deposits "increased sharply as hours of general financial [education] attendance increased from zero to 12, after which it leveled off" (Schreiner et al. 2001, 115). This finding seems to confirm the Bernheim finding that education is a powerful tool for stimulating savings, including among lower-income individuals.

Abdighani Hirad and Peter Zorn (2001) examined the effectiveness of a different type of financial education on financial behavior. More specifically, they studied the effects of prepurchase homeownership counseling on reducing ninety-day delinquency rates. Counseling was defined as "specific and tailored to the particular needs of the individual, while education typically is administered in a generic program" (Hirad and Zorn 2001, 5). Only consumers with at least eighteen months of data were included in the study. Data on almost 40,000 mortgages revealed that borrowers receiving counseling had a 19 percent lower ninety-day delinquency rate than those without counseling. Moreover, borrowers receiving counseling through individual programs experienced a significantly greater reduction in delinquency rates, 34 percent compared to 26 percent reductions for those receiving classroom counseling, and 21 percent for those receiving home-study counseling.

These examples plus others, summarized briefly in table 3.1, provide some concrete evidence that financial education—in various forms—can work to improve the economic status of families. There is, however, some limited evidence that education may not always work. In a study of Chapter 13 debtors, Jean Braucher (2001) found that, controlling for some other factors, consumers who attended debtor education were about 12 percent less likely to complete their repayment programs. One possible explanation for this counterintuitive result is that education may be a proxy for other unmeasured variables not included in the study, such as income level, level of debt, and format of the educational program.

The studies cited all focus specifically on evaluating the impacts of financial education. Numerous other studies also incorporate financial education as one of the components, often in combination with financial experiences. For example, Vanessa Perry and Susan Ards (2001) find that childhood financial experiences as well as formal financial education are significant predictors of financial knowledge across the population as a whole, whereas informal, word-of-mouth sources have a significant additional impact on financial knowledge among African American consumers.

Although financial education programs are showing generally positive impacts at the micro level, we still see evidence of problems with credit and bankruptcy and with a lack of planning and participation in retirement savings at the macro level. In the credit arena, delinquency rates on consumer loans and credit cards are 3 and 4 percent, respectively, and have held constant across ten years (the time when financial education has been gaining momentum). Charge-off rates on consumer loans and credit card balances have also remained constant, at 2 and 4 percent, respectively (Federal Reserve Board 2007). Bankruptcy filings more than doubled in the years between 1995 and 2005, though the numbers for 2006 are down considerably, possibly due to bankruptcy reform that was implemented in the fall of 2005) (American Bankruptcy Institute 2006). In the retirement arena, 63 percent of workers

Table 3.1 Summary of Financial Education Impact Evaluations

Authors	Date	Audience-Program	Content
Shelton and Hill	1995	Low- to moderate-income first-time home buyers	Connection between financial education and participants' effective budgeting behavior and home-ownership preparedness
DeVaney, Gorham, Bechman, and Haldeman	1996	Women's financial management	Participants changed attitudes and selected financial management behaviors
O'Neill	1997	Money 2000	Improved financial situation; self-anchoring goals achieved (debts reduced, savings increased)
Boyce and Danes	1998	NEFE High School Financial Planning Program	Teens maintained increases in knowledge and skills; increased confidence in managing money
Garman, Kim, Kratzer, Brunson, and Joo	1999	Employees	Workplace financial education improves financial decision making and increases confidence in investment decisions
O'Neill, Xiao, Bristow, Brennan, and Kerbel	2000	Money 2000	Changes for fifteen financial behaviors and attitudes
Bernheim, Garrett, and Maki	2001	Students in states with financial education mandates	Mandates increase exposure to financial education; financial education associated with higher saving rates and higher net worth
Clancy, Grinstein-Weiss, and Schreiner	2001	IDA participants	Variations in content materials, quality of teaching, teacher/student ratio affect program evaluation; differentiate financial education in general vs. financial education as delivered by a specific program
Braucher	2001	Bankruptcy clients	Those attending debtor education were less likely to complete repayment programs

(continued)

Table 3.1 Continued

Authors	Date	Audience-Program	Content
Hirad and Zorn	2001	Home buyers	Among a variety of pre-purchase educational tactics, counseling was associated with lower rates of ninety-day delinquencies
Kim, Kratzer, and Leech	2001	Employees	Workplace financial education increases participation in 401k plans
Schreiner, Sherraden, Clancy, Johnson, Curley, Grinstein-Weiss, Zhan, and Beverly	2001	IDAs and American Dream Demonstration	Monthly net deposits per participant increased as hours of financial education increased from zero to twelve
Elliehausen, Lindquist, and Staten	2002	Credit counseling program	Those going through one-on-one counseling had higher credit scores and better credit management practices.
Brobeck, Clarke, Wooten, and Wilkening	2003	America Saves	Participants increased interest more than confidence and confidence more than knowledge in saving and wealth-building; motivation alone is not enough to make informed decisions and institute behavioral changes
Lyons and Scherpf	2003	Money Smart	Increased financial knowledge, better able to manage finances
Anderson, Zhan, and Scott	2004	Low-income families	Incentives an important factor when designing financial education programs
Benartzi and Thaler	2004	Save More Tomorrow; workers	Increases in 401(k) savings out of future raises; increased participation rates and increased contribution rates

Table 3.1 Continued

Authors	Date	Audience-Program	Content
Danes	2004	NEFE High School Financial Planning Program	Teens increased knowledge, skills, and confidence in managing money, and maintained these increases over a three-month period
Lusardi	2004	Health & Retirement Study	Financial education (attending retirement seminar and asking for Social Security estimate) associated with increases in financial net worth and total net worth
Rand	2004	Welfare recipients and low income workers	Knowledge gains across several categories of financial management; increases or improvements in several financial management behaviors
Rupured	2004	Consumer Financial Literacy Program, University of Georgia	Better account management, increased savings
Hira and Loible	2005	Employees of an insurance company	Better understanding of personal finances and future impacts; gains in confidence in future financial situation and increase company loyalty
Lyons, Palmer, Jayaratne, and Scherpf	2006	Financial education providers (community educators & others)	A review of the evaluation capacity of community educators and others delivering financial education programs
Lyons, Chang, and Scherpf	2006	Low-income program participants	Behavior changes related to both education and level of experience; those with less experience reported greater behavior changes

Source: Author's compilation.

were eligible for an employer's retirement plan in 2005, but only about 55 percent actually participated—and this is the lowest participation rate in the data series, which began in 1987 (Copeland 2006).

In these examples, defining the problem as lack of financial education may not always be appropriate. Understanding the underlying causes for delinquency, default, bankruptcy, or not participating in a retirement plan is essential to solving the problem. Additionally, though financial education may be part of the solution, it may not be the only—or the best—response to these issues. In the case of bankruptcy, for example, medical insurance programs may help to play a role in reducing bankruptcy rates. Also, opt-out, rather than opt-in, policies for retirement programs may do more to increase participation than financial education programs. Nonetheless, there is still room for improvement in the financial literacy levels of U.S. households, and financial education can be an important complement to other programs and policies.

Difficulties in Measuring the Effectiveness of Financial Education

Although it is clear that financial education is beneficial and has a positive impact on the lives of consumers, what kind of an impact and to what degree are often difficult to measure. Researchers and practitioners continue to debate the rigor of various evaluation techniques and the measures to use (Lyons 2005). Knowledge, attitudes, behaviors, and outcomes (dollars saved or debt reduced) are all current metrics in the field, but researchers and program evaluators are beginning to agree that outcome measures are desirable. Increased knowledge does not necessarily change behavior. In addition, the wide variety of financial education objectives makes measuring changes in behavior difficult. A study evaluating the impact of mortgage counseling on first-time home buyers would have to be conducted differently than one measuring the change in financial knowledge of high school students as the result of financial education being introduced into the curriculum.

Evaluation frameworks need to be tailored to fit the program and individual objectives. Jennefer Sebstad, Monique Cohen, and Kathleen Stack (2006) lay out a framework for evaluating financial education programs and state that "Any evaluation strategy needs to start by defining a specific set of questions, relevant levels of analysis, and measurable indicators. The choice will depend on the purpose of the assessment, the audience, and resources available. It also will depend on what reasonably can be expected to change as a result of the program within the time frame of the study" (Sebstad, Cohen and Stack 2006, 4).

Although the studies listed in table 3.1 point toward the efficacy of financial education, some methodological shortcomings remain. One of the most-often cited is the inherent selection bias in program participants. Because participants were not randomly sampled and placed in these financial education programs and because there is no control group, it is difficult to know how the program would affect a more general population. Most of the studies listed report on the impacts of a single program but could not generalize to other audiences or curriculums. Few of the studies are longitudinal. Most are at a single point in time, reporting only on expected behavior changes or potential outcomes.

As of this writing, several other evaluations of financial education programs are under way or about to get started. The Consumer Federation of America is leading a longitudinal project to evaluate the impacts of credit counseling, including a variety of counseling delivery formats such as in-person, web-based, and over the telephone (see Staten and Barron 2006). The America Saves program is doing a multilevel evaluation of Cleveland Saves, exploring changes at the household and organizational levels. The Philadelphia Federal Reserve Bank is engaged in an evaluation of homeowner counseling programs. Finally, the Federal Reserve Board has undertaken a project with the Department of Defense and a U.S. Army post for a longitudinal evaluation of a financial education program that includes a control group. Thus, in several years, we may know much more about the outcomes and impacts that financial education has on individuals and their communities.

FINANCIAL EDUCATION AND COMMUNITY ECONOMIC DEVELOPMENT?

Evidence that financial education makes a difference in consumers' attitudes and behaviors is increasing, but most such studies have focused on household-level behaviors. Credit has been reduced, savings have been increased, assets have been built up—but virtually none of these outcomes has been related to neighborhoods, communities, or economic development more generally. It may seem logical that these behaviors, in the aggregate, should lead to community improvements, but we really have little data to validate them.

One example of the potential impact comes from the Opportunities Credit Union. Opportunities Credit Union is one of about 300 community development credit unions with a social mission to provide fair and affordable financial services to underserved populations. It provides counseling-based lending and financial services to a predominantly low-income membership of 13,000 Vermonters in 210 towns.

Jane Kolodinsky, Caryl Stewart, and Antonia Bullard (2004, 2006) surveyed OCU members and provide some evidence of a connection between participating in activities in a community development credit union and civic and social engagement. The researchers posited a model in which credit union members were more engaged not only in their near environments (family finances) but also in their social environments (involvement in neighborhood and community).

A follow-up survey revealed additional evidence that the financial education efforts of the credit union staff resulted in community impacts. Participants who reported that the educational programs were important to them were more likely to say that their family financial situation improved, that their community situation improved (in terms of more job and housing opportunities), and that their involvement in the community increased (Hogarth, Hilgert, and Kolodinsky 2004).

CONCLUSIONS

We began this chapter with the goal of providing a snapshot of the current state of financial education in the United States as it relates to community development. We documented an ample number of financial education programs and resources, and touched on a number of evaluative efforts that document the effects of these initiatives in terms of increased knowledge and improved financial management behaviors, at least at the household level.

It is important to keep in mind that knowing and doing may be two different things. Financial education, often associated with increasing knowledge, may incorporate a combination of information, skill building, and motivation to make the desired changes in behavior. The distinction between information and education is an especially important point for policy makers and program leaders making decisions about the allocation of resources. Financial education and awareness campaigns and learning tools, such as Web sites or brochures, all-important in their own right, may need to be coupled with audience-targeted motivational strategies to elicit the desired behavioral changes in financial management practices.

As a corollary, well-educated consumers are a necessary, but not adequate, requirement for an efficient financial marketplace, for several reasons. First, the products in the financial marketplace have become even more complex—a payment option mortgage with the potential for negative amortization is just one example—so that even well-educated consumers may not understand the choices and consequences facing them. In addition, when it come to longer-term products, such as retirement investments, it is unclear that basic financial education can effectively help people to choose among a wide array of investment and insurance products with complicated and nontransparent cost structures and fees. Finally, in many cases, substantive consumer protection laws and regulations are also necessary. Financial education should not be considered a substitute for consumer protection laws and regulations, but as a complement to them, allowing them to work more effectively and efficiently.

It also is important to keep in mind that financial education is only one part of a community economic development strategy. Financial education can serve to complement other policies that enable financial access, provide for substantive protection in the financial marketplace, and offer mechanisms for redress. Also, it is necessary to note that education may need to be accompanied by advising—though general education and financial education courses can be helpful, consumers need to apply what they learn to their families and their situations. In the end, personal finance is, after all, personal.

Making the link between financial education and community development outcomes is a bit thornier. Logically, financially educated consumers should make better decisions for their families, increasing their economic security and well being. Secure families are better able to contribute to vital, thriving communities, further fostering community economic development. Identifying and documenting those links is difficult, however. Data from a community development credit union hint at the potential relationships between financial education and community involvement and give us some hope that financial education programs really are making a difference in communities, and that we will some day be able to document those differences more robustly.

The analysis, comments and conclusions set forth in this chapter represent the work of the authors and do not indicate concurrence of the Federal Reserve Board, the Federal Reserve Banks, or their staff. Mention or display of a trademark, proprietary product, or firm in the presentation by the author or focus group participants does not constitute an endorsement or criticism by the Federal Reserve System and does not imply approval to the exclusion of other suitable products or firms.

NOTES

1. As the social security example demonstrates, the increased salience of financial education also reflects an ideological shift that favors moving responsibility and risk from government to individuals. This, in turn, is manifested in diverse beliefs regarding the appropriate role of financial education. Most consumer and community educators see financial education as a complement to public policy, enforcement mechanisms, and industry self-regulation in making financial markets more transparent and "leveling the playing field" for consumers. Others see financial education as a substitute for various forms of government action. In current discussions of the wage stagnation facing middle- and lower-income households, for example, the latter argue that the real problem is not lower wages but that consumers are spending more than ever. The solution thus becomes financial education rather than higher wages and government intervention to help with medical costs, insurance against the unexpected, and so forth.

2. "Impact Data and Research Results," http://www.money2000.org/prac/impact.htm (site now discontinued).

REFERENCES

American Bankruptcy Institute. 2006. "Annual Business and Non-business Filings by Year (1980–2005)." Accessed at http://www.abiworld.org/AM/AMTemplate.cfm?Section=Home&TEMPLATE=/CM/ContentDisplay.cfm&CONTENTID=46621.

American Savings Education Council (ASEC). 1999. *Youth and Money.* Washington: American Savings Education Council. Accessed at http://www.choosetosave.org

Anderson, Steven G., Min Zhan, and Jeff Scott. 2004. "Targeting Financial Management Training at Low-Income Audiences." *Journal of Consumer Affairs* 38(1): 167–77.

Bayer, Patrick, B. Douglas Bernheim, and John K. Scholz. 1996. "The Effects of Financial Education in the Workplace: Evidence from a Survey of Employers." NBER Working Paper 5655. Cambridge, Mass.: National Bureau of Economic Research.

Bernheim, B. Douglas. 1998. "Financial Illiteracy, Education, and Retirement Saving." In *Living with Defined Contribution Pensions,* edited by Olivia S. Mitchell and Sylvester J. Schieber. Philadelphia, Pa.: University of Pennsylvania Press.

Bernheim, B. Douglas, Daniel M. Garrett, and Dean M. Maki. 2001. "Education and Saving: The Long-Term Effects of High School Financial Curriculum Mandates." *Journal of Public Economics* 80: 435–65.

Benartzi, Shlomo, and Richard H. Thaler. 2004. "Save More Tomorrow: Using Behavioral Economics to Increase Employee Savings." *Journal of Political Economy* 112(1): 164–87.

Bowen, Cathy F. 1996. "Informal Money Management Education: Perceptions of Teens and Parents." In *Consumer Interests Annual 42.* Columbia, Mo.: American Council on Consumer Interests.

Boyce, Laurie, and Sharon M. Danes. 1998. *Evaluation of the NEFE High School Financial Planning Program.* Denver, Colo.: National Endowment for Financial Education. Accessed at http://www.nefe.org.

Braucher, Jean. 2001. *Report on a Study of Debtor Education in Bankruptcy.* Alexandria, Va.: American Bankruptcy Institute. Accessed at http://www.abiworld.org/research/braucher.pdf.

Braunstein, Sandra, and Carolyn Welch. 2002. "Financial Literacy: An Overview of Practice, Research, and Policy." *Federal Reserve Bulletin* 88(11): 445–57. Accessed at http://www.federalreserve.gov/pubs/bulletin/2002/1102lead.pdf.

Brobeck, Stephen, Sommer Clarke, Christina Wooten and Bonnie Wilkening. 2003. *Cleveland/America Saves Evaluation: Saver Survey* (September). Washington: Consumer Federation of America.

Caskey, John P. 2001. "Can Lower Income Households Increase Savings With Financial-Management Education?" *Cascade: A Community Development Publication of the Federal Reserve Bank of Philadelphia* 46 (Summer/Fall).

Clancy, Margaret, Michal Grinstein-Weiss, and Mark Schreiner. 2001. "Financial Education and Savings Outcomes in Individual Development Accounts." Center for Social Development Working Paper 01-2. St. Louis, Mo.: George Warren Brown School of Social Work, Washington University. Accessed at http://gwbweb.wustl.edu/csd/Publications/2001/wp01-2.pdf.

Consumer Federation of America (CFA). 1990. *U.S. Consumer Knowledge: The Results of a Nationwide Test.* Washington: Consumer Federation of America.

————. 1991. *High School Student Consumer Knowledge: A Nationwide Test.* Washington: Consumer Federation of America.

————. 1993. *College Student Consumer Knowledge: The Results of a Nationwide Test.* Washington: Consumer Federation of America.

————. 1998. "American Consumers Get Mixed Grades on Consumer Literacy Quiz." Press release. Accessed at http://consumerinterests.org/files/public/FinancialLiteracy-02.pdf.

Copeland, Craig. 2002. "An Analysis of the Retirement and Pension Plan Coverage Topical Module of SIPP." *Employee Benefit Research Institute Issue Brief,* Number 245. Accessed at http://www.ebri.org/pdf/briefspdf/0502ib.pdf.

————. 2006. "Retirement Plan Participation and Retirees' Perception of Their Standard of Living." *Employee Benefit Research Institute Issue Brief,* Number 289. Accessed at http://www.ebri.org/pdf/briefspdf/EBRI_IB_01-20061.pdf.

Danes, Sharon, and Laurie Boyce. 2004. *Evaluation of the NEFE High School Financial Planning Program, 2003–2004.* Greenwood Village, Colo.: National Endowment for Financial Education. Accessed at http://www.kdcms.com/nefe/company1/content/273/2003-2004%20nefe%20hsfpp%20evaluation.pdf.

DeVaney, Sharon A., Elizabeth E. Gorham, Janet C. Bechman, and Virginia A. Haldeman. 1996. "Cash Flow Management and Credit Use: Effect of a Financial Information Program." *Financial Counseling and Planning* 7(1): 81–80.

Elliehausen, Gregory E., Erica C. Lindquist, and Michael E. Staten. 2003. "The Impact of Credit Counseling on Subsequent Borrower Credit Usage and Payment Behavior." Paper presented at the 2003 Federal Reserve System Community Affairs Research Conference. Washington, D.C., July 23, 2003. Accessed at http://www.chicagofed.org/cedric/files/2003_conf_paper_session1_staten.pdf.

Employee Benefit Research Institute (EBRI). 2001. *The 2001 Retirement Confidence Survey: Summary of Findings*. Washington: Employee Benefit Research Institute. Accessed at http://www.ebri.org/pdf/surveys/rcs/2001/01rcses.pdf.

Federal Reserve Board. 2007. "Charge-Off and Delinquency Rates on Loans and Leases at Commercial Banks." Accessed at http://www.federalreserve.gov/releases/chargeoff/chgallsa.htm.

Freddie Mac. 2007. "Buying and Owning a Home." Accessed at http://www.freddiemac.com/corporate/buying_and_owning.html.

Garman, Eric T. 1998. "Consumer Educators, Now Is the Time for a Paradigm Shift Toward Employee Financial Education." *Consumer Interest Annual* 14: 48–53.

Garman, Eric T., Jinhee Kim, Constance Y. Kratzer, Bruce H. Brunson, and So-Hyun Joo. 1999. "Workplace Financial Education Improves Personal Financial Wellness." *Financial Counseling and Planning* 10(1): 79–88.

Government Accountability Office (GAO). 2004. *Highlights of a GAO Forum: The Federal Government's Role In Improving Financial Literacy*. Publication no. GAO-05-93SP. Washington: Government Printing Office.

Hira, Tahira K., and Cazilia Loible 2005. "Understanding the Impact of Employer-Provided Financial Education on Workplace Satisfaction." *Journal of Consumer Affairs* 39(1): 173–94.

Hirad, Abdighani, and Peter M. Zorn. 2001. "A Little Knowledge Is a Good Thing: Empirical Evidence of the Effectiveness of Pre-Purchase Homeownership Counseling." Working Paper. McLean, Va.: Freddie Mac.

Hilgert, Marianne A., Jeanne M. Hogarth, and Sandra G. Beverly. 2003. "Household Financial Management: The Connection Between Knowledge and Behavior." *Federal Reserve Bulletin* 89(7): 309–22.

Hogarth, Jeanne M., and Josephine A. Swanson. 1993. "Voices of Experience: Limited Resource Families and Financial Management." In *American Home Economics Association: Family Economics & Management Conference Proceedings,* 13–28. Alexandria, Va: American Home Economics Association.

Hogarth, Jeanne M., Sandra G. Beverly, and Marianne A. Hilgert. 2003. "Patterns of Financial Behaviors: Implications for Community Educators and Policymakers." Paper presented at the 2003 Federal Reserve System Community Affairs Research Conference. Washington, D.C., July 23, 2003. Accessed at http://www.chicagofed.org/cedric/files/2003_conf_paper_session1_hogarth.pdf.

Hogarth, Jeanne M., Marianne A. Hilgert, and Jane Kolodinsky. 2004. "Financial Education and Community Development Finance." Paper prepared for Community Development Finance Research Conference, Federal Reserve Banks of New York and Philadelphia.

Hogarth, Jeanne M., Marianne A. Hilgert, and Jane Schuchardt. 2002. "Money Managers: The Good, the Bad, and the Lost." In *Proceedings of the Association for Financial Counseling and Planning Education,* 12–23. Columbus, Oh.: Association for Financial Counseling and Planning Education.

InCharge Education Foundation. 2004. Accessed at http://education. incharge.org.

Jacob, Katy, Sharyl Hudson, and Malcolm Bush. 2000. *Tools for Survival: An Analysis of Financial Literacy Programs for Lower-Income Families.* Chicago, Ill.: Woodstock Institute.

Jump$tart Coalition. 2001. "Statement of Purpose." Accessed at http:// www.jumpstart.org/.

———. 2004. "2004 Personal Financial Survey of High School Seniors." Accessed at http://www.jumpstartcoalition.com/upload/Executive% 20Summary.doc.

Kim, Jinhee, Constance Y. Kratzer, and Irene E. Leech. 2001. "Impacts of Workplace Financial Education on Retirement Plans." In *Proceedings of the Association for Financial Counseling and Planning Education,* 28. Columbus, Oh.: Association for Financial Counseling and Planning Education.

Kolodinsky Jane, Caryl Stewart, and Antonia Bullard. 2004. "Vermont Development Credit Union: Building Healthy Financial Lives—and More." Paper presented at the NEFE Think Tank on Motivating Americans to Develop Constructive Financial Behaviors. Denver, Colo., May 11– 13, 2004.

———. 2006. "Measuring Economic and Social Impacts of Membership in a Community Development Financial Institution." *Journal of Family and Economic Issues* 27(1): 27–47.

Lusardi, Annamaria 2004. "Saving and the Effectiveness of Financial Education." In *Pension Design and Structure: New Lessons from Behavioral Finance,* edited by Olivia S. Mitchell and Stephen P. Utkus. Oxford: Oxford University Press.

Lyons, Angela C. 2005. "Financial Education and Program Evaluation: Challenges and Potentials for Financial Professionals." *Journal of Personal Finance* 4(4): 56–68.

Lyons, Angela C., and Erik M. Scherpf. 2004. *An Evaluation of the FDIC's Financial Literacy Program Money Smart.* Report to the Women's Bureau, U.S. Department of Labor. Urbana, Ill.: University of Illinois.

Lyons, Angela C., Y. Regina Chang, and Erik M. Scherpf. 2006. "Translating Financial Education Into Behavior Change for Low-Income Populations." *Financial Counseling and Planning* 17(2): 27–45.

Lyons, Angela C., Lance Palmer, Koralalage S. U. Jayaratne, and Erik M. Scherpf. 2006. "Are We Making the Grade? A National Overview of Financial Education and Program Evaluation." *Journal of Consumer Affairs* 40(2): 208–35.

MoneySmart. 2006. "An Adult Education Program." Federal Deposit Insurance Corporation. Accessed at http://www.fdic.gov/consumers/ consumer/moneysmart/overview.html.

Montalto, Catherine. 2000. "New Study: More Than Half of Americans Behind In Saving for Retirement." Press Release. April 20, 2000. Washington: Consumer Federation of America. Accessed at http://www.consumerfed.org/nrl5.pdf.

National Community Reinvestment Coalition (NCRC). 1998. *Financial Literacy Manual.* Washington: National Community Reinvestment Coalition.

National Endowment for Financial Education (NEFE). 2001. "Financial Education Clearinghouse." Accessed at http://www.nefe.org/amexeconfund/index.html.

———. 2004. "Collaborative Programs." Accessed at http://www.nefe.org/pages/collaborative.html.

National Foundation for Credit Counseling (NFCC). 2001. "How We Can Help." Accessed at http://www.nfcc.org/canhelp.cfm.

Neighborhood Reinvestment Corporation (NRC). 2000. "Annotated Reference Guide to the Campaign for Home Ownership." Accessed at http://www.nw.org/NWIS/nw/network/strategies/campaign/publications/pdf/Annotated%20Reference%20Guide%2002-01.pdf.

O'Neill, Barbara 1997. "Money 2000: A Model for Personal Finance Employee Education." *Personal Finances and Worker Productivity* 1(1): 76–80.

O'Neill, Barbara, Jing J. Xiao, Barbara Bristow, Patricia Brennan, and Claudia M. Kerbel. 2000. "Successful Financial Goal Attainment: Perceived Resources and Obstacles." *Financial Counseling and Planning* 11(1): 1–12.

Organization for Economic Cooperation and Development (OECD). 2005. *Improving Financial Literacy: Analysis of Issues and Policies.* Paris: OECD Publications.

Perry, Vanessa G., and Susan Ards. 2001. "The Freddie Mac Consumer Credit Initiative: How Consumers Learn About Credit and Implications for Consumer Education and Policy." Working paper. McLean, Va.: Freddie Mac.

Prochaska, James O., Carlo C. DiClemente, and John C. Norcross. 1992. "In Search of How People Change: Applications to Addictive Behaviors." *American Psychologist* 47(9): 1102–14.

———. 1994. *Changing for Good.* New York: Avon Books.

Rand, Dory. 2004. "Financial Education and Asset Building Programs for Welfare Recipients and Low Income Workers: The Illinois Experience." Washington: Brookings Institution Center on Urban and Metropolitan Policy. Accessed at http://www.brookings.edu/urban/pubs/20040413_doryrand.pdf.

Robinson, Lyn, editor. 2002. *Guide to Financial Literacy Resources.* San Francisco: Federal Reserve Bank of San Francisco. Accessed at http://www.frbsf.org/community/webresources/bankersguide.pdf.

Rupured, Michael 2004. "Consumer Financial Literacy Program: The First Two Years." Unpublished manuscript. Athens, Ga.: University of Georgia Cooperative Extension.

Schreiner, Mark, Margaret Clancy, and Michael Sherraden. 2002. *Saving Performance in the American Dream Demonstration*. St. Louis, Mo.: Center for Social Development, George Warren Brown School of Social Work, Washington University.

Schreiner, Mark, Michael Sherraden, Margaret Clancy, Lissa Johnson, Jami Curley, Michal Grinstein-Weiss, Min Zhan, and Sandra Beverly. 2001. *Savings and Asset Accumulation in Individual Development Accounts*. St. Louis, Mo.: Center for Social Development, George Warren Brown School of Social Work, Washington University.

Sebstad, Jennefer, Monique Cohen, and Kathleen Stack. 2006. "Assessing the Outcomes of Financial Education." Working Paper #3. Washington: Microfinance Opportunities. Accessed at http://www.microfinance opportunities.org/docs/Assessing%20the%20Outcomes%20of%20Finan cial%20Education.pdf.

Shelton, Gladys G., and Octavia L. Hill. 1995. "First-Time Home Buyers Programs as an Impetus for Change in Budget Behavior." *Financial Counseling and Planning* 6: 83–91.

Staten, Michael E., and John M. Barron. 2006. "Evaluating the Effectiveness of Credit Counseling—Phase One: The Impact of Delivery Channels for Credit Counseling Services." Washington, D.C.: George Washington University School of Business Financial Services Research Program. Accessed at http://www.consumerfed.org/pdfs/Credit_Counseling_Report061206.pdf.

Toussaint-Comeau, Maude, and Sherrie L. W. Rhine. 2000. "Delivery of Financial Literacy Programs." *Consumer Issues Research Series* #2000-7. Chicago: Federal Reserve Bank of Chicago. Accessed at http://www.chicagofed.org/publications/publicpolicystudies/ccapolicystudy/pdf/cca-2000-7.pdf.

University of New Hampshire Cooperative Extension. 2004. "Family Life Skills Program." Accessed at http://ceinfo.unh.edu/family/Documents/monymang.htm#FA_Flp.

U.S. Department of Labor. 2000. "Retirement Savings Education Campaign." Accessed at http://www.dol.gov/dol/pwba/public/pubs/introprg.htm.

U.S. Department of the Treasury. 2000. "Helping People in Your Community Understand Basic Financial Services." Accessed at http://www.fms.treas.gov/eft/educ/helping.html.

Vitt, Lois A., Carol Anderson, Jamie Kent, Deanna M. Lyter, Jurg K. Siegenthaler, and Jeremy Ward. 2000. *Personal Finance and the Rush to Competence: Financial Literacy Education in the U.S.* Middleburg, Va.: Institute for Socio-Financial Studies.

Vitt, Lois A., Gwen M. Reichbach, Jamie L. Kent, and Jurg K. Siegenthaler. 2005. *Goodbye to Complacency: Financial Literacy Education in the U.S. 2000–2005*. Washington: AARP. Accessed at http://www.isfs.org/Goodbye toComplacency.pdf.

Xiao, Jing J., Barbara M. Newman, Janice M. Prochaska, Berta Leon, Robert L. Bassett, and Janet L. Johnson. 2004. "Applying the Transtheoretical Model of Change to Consumer Debt Behavior." *Financial Counseling and Planning* 15(2): 89–100.

Yakoboski, Paul, and Allen Schiffenbauer. 1997. "The Reality of Retirement Today: Lessons in Planning for Tomorrow." *EBRI* Issue Brief 181. Washington: Employee Benefit Research Institute.

CHAPTER FOUR

Making U.S. Microenterprise Work:
Recommendations for Policy
Makers and the Field

Lisa Servon

MICROENTERPRISE DEVELOPMENT is a relatively broad term that refers to the activity of supporting very small businesses through training, counseling, small loans, or some combination of these. Microfinance and microcredit, as the terms imply, are more focused on the credit aspect of supporting small business.[1]

Initiated in the mid-1980s, the U.S. microenterprise development industry is now approximately twenty years old. With more than 550 programs, the field has grown substantially since its inception. With this growth have come significant achievements and vexing challenges.

At the same time, the policy environment for microenterprise development has shifted in important ways. Programs that provide funding for microentrepreneurs, including the U.S. Small Business Administration (SBA) PRIME and Microloan programs, and the Community Development Financial Institutions (CDFI) Fund of the U.S. Treasury Department, have suffered dramatic funding cuts during the Bush administration.

This chapter assesses the current state of the U.S. microenterprise development field, laying out the challenges in order to make recommendations for the future. I argue that both internal and external changes are needed to enable the field to realize its potential. The term internal here refers to changes that must be made within the field. External changes are those that are needed in the policy environment in order to make entrepreneurship an attractive and viable option, particularly for lower-income Americans.[2]

John Else (2001) cites five movements or activities that fed the emergence of the U.S. microenterprise development field: women's economic development, developing country programs, community development corporations, community action agencies, and strategies linked to unemployment. These factors led pioneers of the U.S. microenterprise development movement to begin to experiment with the strategy. According to Elaine Edgcomb and Joyce Klein (2005), the strategy remains relevant today because of the following key characteristics of the context in which U.S. microenterprise development organizations (MDOs) operate: loss of secure, well-paid, middle-class jobs; downsizing and outsourcing trends; parents' need to balance working and caregiving roles; aging of the population; growth in immigration; changes in the safety net; decline of many rural economies; and emergence of niche markets.

COMPARING PROGRAMS

As mentioned, developing country programs are one of the influences on U.S. programs. However, microfinance is practiced at a much larger scale in less developed countries (LDCs) than in the United States because the contexts differ so greatly. According to Lisa Servon, "starting a microenterprise program in a developed country is much different—and in many ways more difficult—than making it work in a less developed country" (1999, 18). She expounds on the following distinctions between the two contexts: the prevalence and strength of the informal economy in less developed countries, the need for U.S. entrepreneurs to be financially literate to deal with the complex regulatory environment surrounding business ownership, the more established culture of entrepreneurship in many LDCs, and support for LDC-based programs from large national and international organizations. Servon also argues that a lack of understanding of the differences between the U.S. and developing world contexts has led to inappropriate expectations for U.S. programs.

Programs in LDCs are often lauded because of their scale and because they more closely approach self-sufficiency than U.S. programs, which tend to be more highly subsidized. Andrew Vinelli (2002) examines empirical data from twenty-four microfinance organizations in developing countries, concluding that there may be a trade-off between financial sustainability and other goals, such as outreach to women. The policy message from this work is to recognize the potential effects of focusing too heavily on self-sufficiency.

Credit Versus Training

One of the characteristics that distinguishes the U.S. microenterprise development field from its counterparts in the developing world is the extent to which the former focuses on training as opposed to lending. U.S. MDOs are neither pure financial services providers nor are they pure social services entities (Servon 1997; Sherraden, Sanders, and Sherraden 2004). However, they do much more training than programs in LDCs do. In fact, of the 554 MDOs listed in the 2002 Directory of U.S. Microenterprise Programs, 191 engage in lending (Walker and Blair 2002). Of these, 167 program representatives responded to questions regarding the magnitude of their lending programs. Of these, thirteen programs loaned more than half of all the dollars loaned in 2000.[3] Ninety-eight of the 191 programs that do lending had fewer than twenty-five borrowers in 2000.[4]

U.S. programs focus more on training because of the belief that U.S. microentrepreneurs require more and different skills than their developing country counterparts to operate in the complex legal and regulatory environment. Recently, some research has questioned whether training dollars could be better allocated (Servon 2006).

Poverty Alleviation Versus Economic Development

Individual MDOs sit at various places along a spectrum anchored by different definitions of success and different models. Even if a program is clear about its mission, it may sell itself to a funder as being more of an economic development entity or more of a social services entity, depending on the funder's agenda. Economic development and poverty alleviation have very different objectives. Those who are interested in economic development tend to look at outcomes such as job creation, tax base enhancement, and business growth (in terms of revenues and employees, for example).[5] Those who concern themselves with poverty alleviation, on the other hand, are more interested in changes in individual and household income, the acquisition of particular skills (education and soft skills), and issues such as health insurance.[6] The microenterprise field has historically sold itself as both and, indeed, many programs sit in the middle of that spectrum (Servon 1997). This lack of a clear identity for the field as a whole has made it difficult to arrive at definitions of success, standards, and performance measures that can be embraced across the field. According to J. D. Von Pischke (2002), this distinction holds in developing countries as well. He classifies microfinance institutions as either Type 1s, which have commercial approaches and objectives, or Type 2s, which are more concerned with poverty alleviation.

Does It Work?

The lack of a clear identity for MDOs makes it difficult to evaluate their effectiveness. To answer the question of whether the microenterprise development strategy works, it is first necessary to define success. As discussed, different programs define success differently. That difficulty aside, there has only been one study in the United States that uses an experimental design

(Benus et al. 1995). None of the others can claim that outcomes reported were caused by participation in an MDO. The studies that do exist vary widely in terms of their scope and conclusions.[7]

Most studies rely on data from a very small number of programs that often do not represent the field. For example, MicroTest, an initiative of the FIELD program of the Aspen Institute, which provides annual data on the micro-enterprise industry, noted in their first report that the program "manifests the experience and energies of some of the more experienced practitioners in the United States. . . . Because it has attracted programs committed to meas-uring their performance and striving to improve it, MicroTest contains a number of the field's leaders in scale, portfolio quality and training effec-tiveness" (Black et al. 2003, 9).[8] Comparing the programs that submitted performance data in the last round of MicroTest data collection with the larger field shows that those that submitted data are indeed higher-capacity programs than the average.[9] Servon (2006) shows that the MicroTest pro-grams are older, had a larger loan capital fund, made more loans and had more participants and clients than did the average program. We must be careful then, not to generalize from these data to the field.[10]

Whether microenterprise development is cost-effective as an economic development strategy is the subject of debate. Some research supports this notion. Servon and Jeffrey Doshna (2000), for example, cite figures that compare the cost per job created in a small number of MDOs with jobs cre-ated using more traditional economic development strategies and show that MDOs compare favorably. Edgcomb and Klein (2005), on the other hand, cite several other studies suggesting that the benefits of MDOs outweigh their costs.

Studies also disagree as to how effective microenterprise development is as a strategy to alleviate poverty. Using data on 133 low-income microentrepre-neurs from seven MDOs, Margaret Sherraden, Cynthia Sanders, and Michael Sherraden (2004) found that though these organizations "provided vital finan-cial resources, training, and technical support to help them get their businesses off the ground, it was not enough to provide a solid foundation for continued business growth and development" (87). Using the same data, Peggy Clark and Amy Kays (1999) paint a rosier picture. They report increased household income and reduced reliance on public assistance for five years.

Most research supports the notion that the majority of microentrepreneurs engage in "income-patching" or "income-packaging" (Clark and Kays 1999). In other words, self-employment alone is unlikely to provide low-income people with adequate income. Roberta Spalter-Roth, Enrique Soto, and Lily Zandniapour (1994) found that most microentrepreneurs engage in self-employment in combination with other wage and salary jobs or a second self-employment job, and their self-employment activity provides smaller annual earnings than does their wage or salary work.

LARGER INDUSTRY ISSUES

A relatively recent body of research examines issues within the microenterprise development field itself—how it is structured, for example, and how programs operate. The findings in this area have not been encouraging overall. Drawing on a review of existing studies and in-depth analysis of two mature MDOs in California, Bhatt and Tang (2001) maintain that, because some U.S. MDOs have "encountered major challenges in social, financial, and administrative intermediation," they have "been ineffective in recruiting clients and in helping them build appropriate human capital, some have failed to manage risks and transaction costs, and some have been plagued with administrative difficulties" (239). In their study of twenty-seven California-based alternative loan programs, Nitin Bhatt, Gary Painter, and Shui-Yan Tang (2002) found that most served a limited number of people, and had a particularly difficult time serving low-income people. They also found that MDOs serving the poor face high loan-loss risks and transaction costs, and are not sustainable because of operational inefficiencies.

An Association for Enterprise Opportunity (AEO) report puts the situation this way: "If the microenterprise development industry was a single business, then it could be characterized as having low market penetration, high costs, increasing competition, inadequate expenditures in R and D and technology, and promising but insufficient returns on investment" (2002, 10). Timothy Bates (1996) maintains that adequate capitalization is an important issue for many small businesses, particularly those owned by African Americans, and that many MDOs undercapitalize the businesses they serve.

This literature review helps to illuminate both the potential and limitations of the U.S. microenterprise development strategy. To realize its potential and minimize its limitations, the field must confront internal problems. At the same time, it also must lobby for external changes in the policy environment.

INTERNAL CHALLENGES

Among the internal challenges the U.S. microenterprise development faces are fragmentation, insufficient data, lack of accreditation and regulation, narrow product lines, and inconsistent or unreliable funding streams.

Fragmentation

Microenterprise development as a field remains fragmented, consisting primarily of many small programs without the capacity to do all of what they try to do well. The flip side of the intense customization that U.S. microenterprise programs provide is the inefficiency and high unit cost that result from widespread duplication of services. Most of these programs have developed their own curricula, their own systems for tracking data, and their own loan documentation. This vertical integration, though perhaps necessary during the initial phase of the microenterprise movement, is no longer functional.[11] In some cases, it can cost up to $4 for a program to lend $1 (Edgcomb and Klein 2005). The field is now characterized by inefficiency resulting from a large number of organizations needing relatively high capacity to make a very small number of loans. This makes sustainability difficult. Furthermore, fragmentation and lack of standardization have resulted in enormous duplication of effort and no benefits from economies of scale. Although large areas of the country are not served by MDOs, some cities—Philadelphia and San Francisco, for example—house two or more programs, vying for the same funding dollars and the same clientele.

Insufficient Data

Standardized data is particularly important in a field as small and fragmented as U.S. microenterprise because aggregate data is needed to assess the costs and benefits of the intervention, to access capital, and to convince funders and policy makers of their worth. The microenterprise field has made important progress in terms of data collection in recent years, but it is still a long way from where it needs to be.

The MicroTest Web site, for example, documents that seventy-seven programs currently participate in MicroTest.[12] Although MicroTest collects performance and outcomes data on an annual basis,[13] not all of these programs participate in the performance or outcomes process each year. Getting seventy-seven programs to participate in MicroTest is an impressive accomplishment. However, this number represents only 14 percent of the 554 practitioner agencies listed in the 2002 Directory of U.S. Microenterprise Programs (Walker and Blair 2002). Sixty-one programs (11 percent) contributed performance data in the last round of data collection in the spring of 2003, but only seventeen (3 percent) contributed outcomes data.[14] None of these groups is a random sample, and it is unlikely that they represent the broader field.

The other major data collection effort in the community development finance field is the Community Development Financial Institutions Data Project (CDP). CDP brings together several of the key trade associations representing the different categories of CDFIs, an important accomplishment. The Opportunity Finance Network, a CDFI trade association that coordinates the CDP data collection effort, estimates that approximately 1,000 CDFIs currently operate in the United States. The latest CDP data set, for the 2005 fiscal year, includes 496 CDFIs, 151 of which are loan funds. Fifty-three of these are exclusively or primarily microlenders.[15] An additional forty-one make some microloans but focus primarily on larger loans.[16] The fifty-three primarily microlenders in the CDP data set overlap substantially with the MDOs profiled by MicroTest.

Despite the tremendous advances that these two data collection efforts represent, data in the community development finance field is woefully inadequate. Given the lack of representativeness of the MDOs profiled in these data sets, they have the potential to oversell the field. The data being collected also is not consistent with what might be needed to create relationships with mainstream financial institutions and other investors (Moy and Okagaki 2001).

Lack of Accreditation

Lack of accreditation, regulation, or both make the microenterprise development field opaque and less likely to attract funding and investment. Funders and investors cannot be sure what they are getting when they choose to put their money into a microenterprise development program. The issue of accreditation also addresses standardization; accreditation processes can create incentives for programs to conform to field standards.

There has in fact been some movement in the microenterprise field toward accreditation. AEO recently initiated its National Microenterprise Standards and Accreditation Project (MSAP), which "proposes minimally acceptable numerical performance standards drawing on data available from the MicroTest project" (2006). Adopting a strict set of standards would potentially motivate a necessary winnowing of the field and provide funders with greater confidence that remaining programs were worthy of investment.

Narrow Product Lines

Despite the need for a wide range of financial services in the communities and among the groups that MDOs target, program product lines tend to be very narrow. According to the AEO, "many microenterprise programs do not substantively research clients' or potential clients' needs or diversify products to attract and retain customers" (2002, 9). On the training side, programs tend to offer one curriculum to serve clients ranging from those who have only an idea for a business to those who have been in business for several years.

Inconsistent or Unreliable Funding Streams

Given their high cost of operations and low rates of sustainability, the vast majority of U.S. MDOs depend heavily on subsidies from government and philanthropic institutions. Public funding from some key sources, such as the Program for Investment in Microentrepreneurs (PRIME) has declined in recent years, and some philanthropic funding agencies that historically funded microenterprise programs, such as the Ford Foundation, are eliminating these programs. On the positive side, some state microenterprise associations and state microenterprise intermediaries are helping increase the funding pool for programs in the states where they exist, while boosting the legitimacy and visibility of local and state programs.[17] At least three states have appropriations from their general funds targeted to include microenterprise development: Nebraska, North Carolina, and Colorado (personal communication with Eugene Severens and Michelle Levy-Benitez, November 8, 2004). Overall, however, few MDO programs have devised ways to cover their costs of doing business in a significant way. Their resulting reliance on external subsidies makes them vulnerable to shifts in funder preferences and policy priorities.

OVERCOMING INTERNAL CHALLENGES

How should the microenterprise field confront these challenges? The recommendations that follow are made with three criteria derived from the interviews and literature review. First, they focus on creating new and leveraging existing infrastructure, both within and outside the field. Second, they are framed with the goal of creating an appropriate incentive environment for programs. Third, they aim to help the field benefit from a business mentality while maintaining concern for social services outcomes.

Restructure the Field

The following suggestions for restructuring the field follow trends in the for-profit sector, shifting from vertical integration to a more horizontal industry structure and pursuing greater economies of scale.

Mergers and Partnerships

Mergers between organizations conducting similar or complementary activities make a great deal of sense in the current environment. Although mergers do not necessarily address the fundamental economic challenge of microenterprise finance, that is, the high administrative costs of making small loans and providing technical assistance, they can allow for some economies of scale through greater efficiency (for example, one executive director, not two) and greater reach. ACCION, for example, recently merged with Working Capital, expanding its presence in Massachusetts. In addition, where two or more organizations are operating in the same market, mergers can reduce competition for resources.

There also are disincentives to merging. Directors of programs do not want to lose their jobs. Some of them, furthermore, were the founders of their organizations and may fear that their vision would be lost if they were to merge.

The experience of MicroBusiness Development Corporation (MBDC) of Colorado demonstrates some of the benefits of mergers. MBDC has undergone two mergers in recent years and is considering a third. In one instance, the organization with which it merged had just been turned down for a key grant and was on the brink of closing down its operations. According to MBDC's executive director, the mergers did several things for the organization. First, they enabled MBDC to offer a much wider range of services and products— loans up to $60 thousand and peer lending, for example. Second, they lessened competition for funding. Third, they allowed the organization to work more innovatively, attracting a broader client base.

By way of illustration, the executive director said, "if all we were doing was serving the refugee population, or the disabled, we'd be dead. But they are very valuable groups within the context of the organization. We can serve them better because we are a bigger organization" (Personal communication, October 2004). MBDC's size and product range also enables the organization to provide funders and policy makers with concrete evidence of outcomes, something many smaller providers cannot do.

Separate Training from Lending

The many programs that are essentially training programs with a small amount of lending should stop lending and instead originate loans and provide the necessary follow-up and technical assistance throughout the life of the loan, but outsource lending operations. The idea is to divorce any part of the transaction that is not about the relationship between borrower and lender from the MDO.[18] Although separating training from lending would not address the expense associated with providing technical assistance, it would reduce costs by eliminating the need to maintain an expensive in-house lending staff to service a small number of financial transactions.

This type of restructuring can be achieved by using regional lenders, either CDFIs or mainstream financial institutions, or providers of "back office" services. Regional lenders could be established to handle all of the loans for the MDOs in a particular region. The MDOs themselves could provide training, technical assistance, and loan origination. They would pay the lender, who would handle all of the technical aspects of processing the loan.

This is essentially the situation that is beginning to evolve in Atlanta, where the Atlanta Loan Fund (ALF) has handled the loans of two local women's business development programs. More recently, ALF has entered into a more formal arrangement with two other programs that want to provide access to capital to their clients but do not want to handle the details. These arrangements are too new to have exhibited the kind of results necessary to judge the workability of this option.

Separating training from lending would allow organizations to specialize in what they do best. An AEO staff member also sees the importance of training-led organizations expanding their services—eliminating lending would give them greater latitude to do this.[19] MDOs could be doing much more to support businesses after participants graduate from formal classes, supporting them with more individualized technical assistance, for example.[20] Specializing in training would also allow these organizations to serve larger and more stable businesses, thereby helping to achieve the economic development goals of the MDO strategy.

Another way to essentially separate training from lending is for programs to continue to offer access to financing, but to outsource the aspects of the transaction that are not oriented to the relationship by purchasing services from a back office provider. MicroBusiness Development Corporation currently provides back office services to six other organizations in the state and collects data from them using the MicroTest system.

Innovate

It is important that MDOs innovate, particularly given the generally tight funding environment in which they operate. Three ways that they can do so are to expand their product lines, employ technology, and standardize and accredit.

Expanding Product Lines

To approach sustainability and do a better job of serving their target markets, U.S. MDOs must continually experiment with, test, and introduce new products. Gregory Ratliff and Kirsten Moy (2004) present case studies from both the private for-profit and nonprofit sectors to illustrate the stages through which an idea or set of institutions must move to achieve scale. Moving through these stages takes considerable time and is more likely to happen in organizations with the capacity to devote adequate research and development dollars, staff time, and expertise to the process.

Some organizations have begun to experiment with new products. For example, ACCION USA currently is piloting a credit builder loan to be available to anyone who does not have a credit rating. Some MDOs are experimenting with equity investments in client businesses. The Montana CDC, for example, has a patient capital fund. Other programs have begun to offer savings vehicles such as individual development accounts (IDAs), which provide a match for participants' savings. Generally, accounts must be used for one of three purposes: home ownership, education, or business (for a discussion of individual development accounts, see chapter 2). The business option clearly works well with microprogram missions.

Employment of Technology

In business, strategic deployment of technology is often the key to greater efficiency and systemic innovation. In the financial services industry, one of the greatest innovations involving technology in recent years is credit scoring. Credit scoring,[21] which is generally automated, lets a financial institution know almost immediately whether a potential borrower fits the institution's risk profile. Charles Tansey of Neighbor Works has proposed an idea that builds on mainstream financial institutions' current use of credit scoring. In Tansey's automated sourcing scheme, mainstream financial institutions would identify loan requests that do not meet their risk requirements but do fall into the range deemed acceptable by MDOs. The banks would refer these clients to MDOs, potentially substantially increasing the deal flow to MDOs.

Count Me In, the nation's first online microlender, employs a unique credit scoring system to make loans of $500 to $10,000 available to women across the United States. ACCION USA is also working on a rapid decision matrix that will enable lending via the Internet. Many in the community development finance field cringe at the thought of using credit scoring. Count Me In's chief credit officer explains: "Credit scoring is so often seen as evil, when really it's just a tool that can be used well or poorly." The key is to determine whether it is possible to tweak traditional credit scoring models in such a way that the mission of microcredit programs—to finance businesses that mainstream financial institutions will not finance—will not be compromised. Clearly, credit scoring will not work for all businesses, such as those to immigrants or others with little to no credit histories, but may make lending to many businesses more efficient.

Both Count Me In and Circle Lending are experimenting with the automation of some training aspects of microenterprise development by moving materials online. MicroMentor, an online mentoring system that matches microentrepreneurs with mentors, is also attempting to use technology to extend the technical assistance and support available to microentrepreneurs. In all three of these cases, it remains to be seen whether online support and materials are effective for the populations U.S. MDOs tend to target.

Standardize and Accredit

To begin to approach sustainability, U.S. microenterprise development must develop specific standards and adopt an accreditation strategy. Without pushing ahead on these issues, the field will neither have the ability to demonstrate results nor establish the legitimacy it needs to secure more consistent streams of funding and create the kind of innovative partnerships that will move the field forward.

It will be impossible to achieve scale without greater standardization than currently characterizes the field (Ratliff and Moy 2004; Bhatt and Tang 2001). The first area in which movement toward standardization should be made is data collection. As discussed, the MicroTest initiative and CDFI data project are important steps in this direction. However, participation in these efforts currently is much too low.

Standardization in other areas could also assist the field. It could occur in loan documentation, screening procedures, aspects of curriculum, and pre- and post-testing of areas in which the field claims to affect positive change, such as self-esteem. Moy and Alan Okagaki (2001) concisely lay out the trade-offs involved between standardization and customization:

The argument for accreditation is that the field has now matured to a point that we have a solid sense of what reasonable performance standards look like. In addition, endorsing an accreditation framework is one step that could move it to industry status. Writing more generally about the CDFI industry, of which microlending organizations are a part, Moy and Okagaki argue that the field should continue to "professionalize itself as an industry with the mainstream financial services industry as a model . . . copy[ing] specific tools and techniques from the mainstream capital markets to access larger amounts of capital" (2001, 16).

The Association for Enterprise Opportunity had members vote on a set of proposed standards, with the intention of engaging a third party to ensure compliance with such standards and grant accreditation. Although members approved the standards, no accreditation process has yet been put in place and no incentives exist for members to conform to the standards. One inter- viewee who thought the trade association should take a stronger stand expressed concern that the standards and accreditation were "getting watered down by the membership." AEO must be careful not to compromise stan- dards so much that they do not hold up to outside scrutiny.

EXTERNAL CHALLENGES

In addition to the internal challenges already laid out, microenterprise devel- opment in the United States faces external challenges that stem in large part from the policy environment in which it operates. The following recom- mendations address the issues related to the current policy context. Some must be tested and worked through before they are rolled out on a grand scale. This section presents creative, feasible ideas that respond to some of the obstacles that small business owners, particularly those at the low end of the socioeconomic spectrum, face.

Better Information and Tools

Filing taxes is a key formalizing event in the life of a business. Moving businesses from the informal to the formal economy could provide incentives for small business owners to invest more in their businesses, and enable these entrepreneurs to access tax-favored asset building features that are only available through filing. We know little, however, about the costs and benefits of filing for entrepreneurs and their businesses.[22]

The tax code already delivers important but poorly understood benefits to low-income self-employed households, many of which claim EITC benefits that can, in part, offset liabilities of the self-employment tax. An income-tested credit that specifically negates the tax could enhance the benefits of filing taxes for this population. It also could function as an asset-building strategy to enhance self-employment as a tool for improving household assets and income.

In filing taxes, entrepreneurs could better understand the business's actual costs and have a benchmark for multiyear business comparisons. Filing would also provide them the essential business skill of navigating tax laws and access to faster growth by opening up the business to the "above ground" markets. The documentation from tax returns would allow them to verify the business's profitability. Compared to wage-earners, self-employed individuals have added hurdles to establishing credit or applying for a mortgage. As mentioned, filing also could improve proprietors' household finances through tax-favored asset building programs. Finally, these small business owners would benefit from the satisfaction of "getting their business right"—knowing their business is "legal" and that they have accepted their share of citizen responsibility.

Filing taxes for the first time formalizes a business and, in most situations, if the business sees a profit, exposes it to significant tax liabilities. We know very little about why or when in the business start-up process a new business chooses to file for the first time. We do know that filing can have a significant, if uncertain, impact on the business's future and that there are few sources of information to help new filers balance and sort out their options. Anecdotal evidence from microenterprise development providers suggests that new businesses do not have a sound understanding of the tax system and how it might affect their businesses. A new, high profile business and tax literacy campaign could inform new sole proprietors about business taxation and asset-building options so that they can make better decisions about filing. The value of such a campaign could be tested through a pilot project. A business literacy campaign could operate in conjunction with this idea. Such a campaign would operate primarily at the state level and be led by appropriate microenterprise training programs or state microenterprise associations, or both. Allying this campaign with the IRS VITA (Volunteer Income Tax Assistance program) tax preparation sites also should be explored.[23]

Creating Incentives for Saving

Individual retirement accounts—IRAs—are an important asset-building tool. IRAs currently allow several preretirement uses that promote asset building and retirement security, including first-time home purchase and postsecondary education. However, penalty-free withdrawals from IRAs for small business start-up costs are not permitted, nor can individuals borrow against these assets to capitalize their businesses. Expanding these uses to small business capitalization makes sense, as doing so could provide another incentive for people to save and accrue assets.

Amending the tax code to allow for penalty-free withdrawals would not be particularly complicated. It would in fact require only adding "business start-up expenses" to the section of the code that lays out the exceptions to the 10 percent penalty tax on early distributions from IRAs. Lawmakers have already introduced several bills over the years that would have done exactly this.

Providing a match would give low-income people an incentive to save, and make the benefit of IRAs meaningful to this population. Studies of individual development accounts (IDAs) show that such matches are an effective way to motivate people to save for specific purposes (CFED 2001).

Structuring funding as loans rather than as straight distributions would partially mitigate against the concern that low-income savers might dissipate their hard-earned assets on ill-conceived or risky ventures and thereby lose funds they could have used for education, a home, or retirement. It would not, however, prevent the loss of IRA assets should the business fail.

If loans against IRA plans rather than distributions from the plans were used to fund small business start-ups, then private lenders or the SBA could underwrite the loans and evaluate the merits of the proposed business plans, helping to prevent ill-conceived plans from going forward. To avoid perfunctory underwriting procedures arising from the secured nature of the loans, minimum underwriting standards and procedures could be prescribed. More important, only partial security for the loan could be permitted, with the lending institution thereby assuming the risk of the loan balance. Because underwriting such small loans is expensive, a subsidy of some form would need to be offered, to make it an attractive proposition for lenders.

Removing Obstacles to Self-Employment

The current policy environment includes significant obstacles that remove self-employment from the range of viable options available to low-income people. These obstacles include a lack of affordable health insurance and, in some states, TANF requirements that inhibit entrepreneurship.

Lack of Affordable Health Insurance

Lack of affordable health care is one of the biggest issues facing the self-employed and small business owners. According to the U.S. Chamber of Commerce, "small business owners have faced five successive years of double-digit increases in health-care premiums, which have eroded their ability to attract and keep qualified workers, decreased their international competitiveness, and limited their ability to grow and expand domestically" (2004, 1). Not surprisingly, an estimated 40 percent of small-business owners do without insurance, according to the Insurance Information Institute Web site, because they believe they cannot afford it. On average, a worker in a firm with fewer than 10 employees pays 18 percent more for health insurance than a worker in a firm with 200 or more employees (see http://www.iii.org).

Health insurance is a particularly vexing problem for low-income entrepreneurs. A five-year study of microentrepreneurs conducted between 1991 and 1997 found that only 57 percent had health insurance; among the low-income group, fully half did not (Clark and Kays 1999). Most low-income entrepreneurs—67 percent—received their health insurance from government sources; the current time limits imposed on welfare recipients mean that many of these have likely moved into the ranks of the uninsured. For those who do not get benefits through a spouse or a government program, the choice is to purchase individual insurance at prohibitively high rates, or remain uninsured (Black 2005).

To be able to afford health insurance, low-income entrepreneurs need subsidies, an avenue to purchase health insurance that affords them access to administrative economies of scale and broad risk pooling and, in the long run, broader health system reform that will lower the trajectory of health-care cost growth relative to wages, prices, and incomes (Personal correspondence with Len Nichols, June 1, 2005). Association health plans (AHPs) are the most likely vehicles for fulfilling these needs. The Department of Labor, for example, advocates AHPs as a solution for insuring small businesses (2005).

Encourage Development with TANF

The National Survey of America's Families (NSAF) found that in both 1997 and 1999, 6.8 percent of working TANF leavers were self-employed, a figure that equals the national rate of self-employment (Edgcomb and Klein 2005). When the Personal Responsibility and Work Opportunity Reconciliation Act (PRWORA) took effect in 1996, replacing Aid for Families with Dependent Children (AFDC) with Temporary Assistance for Needy Families (TANF), better known as welfare reform, responsibility for moving people off welfare and into work devolved to the states. Under this new law, different states treat self-employment differently. The strong "work first" philosophy undergirding welfare reform has created a situation wherein many states do not consider self-employment as a viable option. For some welfare recipients—typically those who are more educated—self-employment income can, by itself or in combination with wages from work, help lift families above the poverty line. In the current environment of time limits, it is critical that all viable options be made available to those who can benefit from them. Specifically, the following changes in this area may be beneficial. These proposed changes would neither restrict existing state flexibility nor impose new federal costs.[24]

- Clarify that self-employment can count as employment in the list of TANF work activities.

- Clarify that self-employment preparation, which includes activities aimed at equipping an individual to engage in or expand existing levels of self-employment, can count toward satisfying TANF participation requirements, within the limits that apply to vocational training.

- Clarify that the job search period that can count toward TANF work requirements also includes the time spent in active exploration of self-employment potential.

- Add language to the TANF state plan requirements specifying that a state's TANF plan must describe the state's approach to encouraging and supporting self-employment when feasible for parents receiving assistance, including a description of when participation in self-employment preparation activities will count in satisfying work requirements, and a description of income and asset rules applicable to self-employed individuals.

Help SBA Better Serve Very Small Businesses

The mission of the Small Business Administration SBA, as it explains on its Web site, is to "maintain and strengthen the nation's economy by aiding, counseling, assisting, and protecting the interests of small businesses and by helping families and businesses recover from national disasters" (http://www.sba.gov). However, it defines a small business as one that has 500 or fewer employees. The microbusinesses that are the focus of this chapter have five or fewer employees, very different from most of the businesses that the SBA defines as small, and as a result all but overlooked by most of the SBA's programs.

The SBA does have two programs that specifically target microbusinesses—the SBA Microloan program and the 7(a) program. Both of these programs could be greatly improved in order better to address the needs of very small businesses.

The SBA Microloan Program provides loans and grants to nonprofit intermediary lenders. It is the largest federal program solely dedicated to supporting the credit needs of disadvantaged microentrepreneurs and is unique among SBA lending programs in that it combines training and technical assistance with loan capital under the assumption that training will improve chances of business success and aid in loan repayment.[25] The technical assistance microentrepreneurs receive through the program is intensive, starting before the loan is made and lasting through the life of the loan (up to six years).

Detractors insist that the program is not necessary because private sector banks already make loans to microentrepreneurs the program currently serves (personal interviews 2004). They also argue that the SBA 7(a) Community Express Program can serve the Microloan market better (personal interviews 2004). Neither hard data nor the experiences of entrepreneurs support this contention. The Microloan and 7(a) programs serve different markets, and there is a role for each.

Banks do serve very small businesses, but, unlike most MDOs, most do not serve start-up businesses. Banks define start-ups as businesses with less than two years of history and records whereas MDOs define them as businesses that have not yet made a sale.

Most banks also offer very small businesses consumer rather than business loans, based on the entrepreneur's credit score. These are significantly less time consuming and expensive for banks to administer because they do not require an analysis of the business plan and assets of the business. However, they are also more expensive for the entrepreneurs, often carrying higher interest rates. Thus, they create an additional barrier to success for microentrepreneurs. Even the smallest entrepreneurs should have access to business loans to finance their businesses. In addition to being less expensive, business loans also help businesses establish creditworthiness and help entrepreneurs separate their business and personal finances.

The SBA 7(a) programs do offer several loan products geared to small businesses.[26] They are, however, different from the Microloan program in important ways. For example, though both Community Express and Microloan provide technical assistance (TA), the banks that participate in the Community Express program partner with other organizations that provide the technical assistance, whereas the MDOs provide the technical assistance themselves. Community Express businesses also tend to be larger—the maximum loan size is $250,000—and require less technical assistance than do those entrepreneurs who use MDOs. An additional concern is that 7(a) programs have historically been "underfunded[,] resulting in severe restrictions that deny entrepreneurs access to the funds needed to start, grow, and expand their businesses" (U.S. Chamber of Commerce 2004, 12).

Maintain Programs that Assist Microentrepreneurs

Currently, several valuable policies and programs do help create a more hospitable environment for low-income entrepreneurs, among them the Program for Investment in Microentrepreneurs and the Community Development Financial Institutions Fund. Funding for these programs, as well as the SBA

Figure 4.1   Federal Funding for CDFI Fund and SBA's Microloan and Prime Program

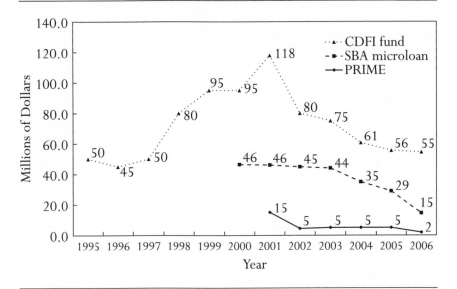

Source: Author's compilation.
Note: Data for the SBA Microloan program includes technical assistance funding and program-level funding.

Microloan Program, however, has been declining since 2001 (see figure 4.1). In addition to generating new, creative ideas to maximize the potential of entrepreneurial energy among low-income groups, it is important to retain and improve these existing programs.

The Program for Investment in Microentrepreneurs Act of 1999, or PRIME Act, authorized the U.S. Small Business Administration to establish a microenterprise technical assistance and capacity building program. SBA PRIME is the first federal program to focus on providing training and business assistance to low- and very-low-income entrepreneurs, regardless of whether they seek loan capital. Microentrepreneurs need training and technical assistance in areas such as financial management, bookkeeping, and marketing. PRIME addresses the funding gap between credit and training and ensures that adequate resources are targeted to very low-income entrepreneurs and the microenterprise organizations that serve them.

Community Development Financial Institutions (CDFIs) work in market niches not adequately served by traditional financial institutions. CDFIs include community development banks, community development venture capital funds, community development loan funds (a category that includes MDOs), and community development credit unions (for more on community development financial institutions see chapters 1, 5, and 6). CDFIs provide a wide range of financial products and services, including commercial loans and investments to start or expand small businesses. They also provide services that help ensure that credit is used effectively, such as technical assistance to small businesses and credit counseling to consumers (Benjamin, Rubin, and Zielenbach 2004).

Minorities are underrepresented in the business community, and CDFIs help these groups to start, stabilize, and grow small businesses. Although only 2 to 3 percent of Small Business Investment Company funds go to minority businesses, 48 percent of CDFI business financing does so (U.S. Chamber of Commerce 2004).

The Community Development Financial Institutions Fund of the U.S. Department of the Treasury provides capital to CDFIs to build the capacity of individual institutions and bolster their ability to start, expand and improve their programs. CDFIs can use this assistance to support an array of community development activities, including housing for low-income people, businesses owned by low-income people, basic financial services, commercial facilities that promote job creation or retention, and technical assistance. The CDFI Fund's activities strengthen and expand the national network of CDFIs, and therefore should be preserved.

CONCLUSION

This chapter makes a wide range of suggestions to improve the effectiveness and efficiency of the microenterprise development field. Certainly, the internal issues that microenterprise development organizations in the United States now face are not unique. They are shared by many nonprofits, particularly those in the field of community development finance. To date, each group has confronted these issues largely in its own silo.[27] Much could be gained from a joint conversation, particularly given that many of these entities are targeting the same population with different products and services. There clearly is room for greater coordination within the community development finance field.

If undertaken, many of the suggestions made here will lead to a winnowing of the field, as weaker and less efficient programs close their doors and stronger ones survive. It is time for this kind of reorganization to take place so that dollars can be redirected to more efficient and effective programs. The field will be smaller but stronger as a result, and this small, strong base can be the foundation for a truly effective industry.

On the external side, windows of opportunity also exist. Despite the central role of very small businesses in our economy, and the opportunities these businesses provide for individual asset-building among low-income people, they are not well served or supported by either government or the private sector. Some of the recommendations made here to address the external challenges could have a powerful impact and are actually quite doable. Others require larger changes but could also create profound positive change. Some will create broader efficiencies. Policy in key areas should be promoted in order to enable these low-income entrepreneurs to get the training, capital, and health care they need to succeed. The legislative changes laid out in this chapter could go a long way toward putting these businesses on a sound footing, and enabling them to contribute to the economy to their fullest potential.

NOTES

1. Many community development loan funds provide microloans. This chapter focuses on those entities that work primarily or exclusively with microbusinesses. Chapter 5 discusses CD lenders that make larger loans.

2. Research for this chapter included a wide-ranging literature review, not only in the area of microenterprise development, but also in the areas of community development banking and finance. In addition, I conducted thirty-five interviews with the following categories of individuals: thirteen practitioners; five funders; five people who work in or lead community development financial institutions' trade associations; three researchers; and nine other field experts. Many of these people agreed to be interviewed only with the assurance that their comments would be kept confidential because they perceive that their own views run counter to the direction the field is moving. I developed protocols for each category of interviewee. In selecting interviewees, I began with practitioners considered to be leaders in the field (for example, board members of the Association for Enterprise Opportunity (AEO), the field trade association), longtime funders of the movement, and those who have conducted research on, advocated for U.S. microenterprise development or both. I then employed the "snowball method," asking each of these interviewees for names of other practitioners and field experts. Twenty-four interviews were conducted by telephone and eight were done in person. Given the stature of the interviewees and the kind of information I sought, I conducted the interviews as "guided conversations," using the interviewees' responses to direct the flow of the interview (Rubin and Rubin 2004). I analyzed the text of my interview notes to discern trends and to ensure that quotes used to illustrate points typified interviewees' comments. I also analyzed data from the Aspen Institute's *2002 Directory of US Microenterprise Programs* (Walker and Blair 2002) categorizing pro-

grams according to particular characteristics such as size, age, primary activities (lending or training) and geographic scope. I analyzed data from the Community Development Financial Institutions Data Project (CDP) to: compare microenterprise programs from this data set to those found in the Aspen directory; and compare the CDP microenterprise programs with other categories of community development financial institutions (CDFIs). CDP data is available for purchase from the National Community Capital Association. MicroTest is an effort spearheaded by the Aspen Institutes Fund for Innovation, Evaluation, Learning and Dissemination (FIELD) to standardize data collection among U.S. microenterprise programs. Although I was unable to obtain MicroTest data in order to conduct my own analysis, I did review the data collection forms and used statistics from this data set that were available from other documents. Strengths and weaknesses of the data sets used will be provided below, in the section on insufficient data.

3. Eleven programs that are not listed as doing any individual lending or group lending (which is how we have counted the number of programs doing any lending) are listed as having disbursed some loans. We have not included these programs in the 167 respondents figure.

4. This statistic is based on 158 respondents out of those that said they engaged in individual or group lending. Twenty-two programs provided data for number of borrowers but were not categorized as engaging in any lending.

5. The contribution of microenterprises to local economies has been widely debated. See Bates (1996), Servon (1997), Servon and Doshna (1998).

6. There have been continued debates about the effectiveness of microenterprise development as a poverty alleviation strategy. See especially Bates (1995), Clark et al (1999), Klein, Alisultanov, and Blair (2003), Schreiner (1998), Servon and Bates (1998), Spalter-Roth, Soto, and Zandniapour (1994).

7. The Benus study, which consisted of tracking unemployment insurance recipients in Massachusetts and Washington State—some of whom received microenterprise training and some of whom did not (the control group)—found that those who received services from a microenterprise program had a higher rate of business ownership than those who did not.

8. Emphasis added. MicroTest is a management tool designed to gauge and improve the performance of individual microenterprise programs and the outcomes of their clients. The MicroTest framework has been developed through a collaborative effort with industry practitioners since 1997.

9.   Although sixty-one programs submitted data, twelve were not included in the *2002 Directory of U.S. Microenterprise Programs*. Therefore, this analysis is based on the forty-nine programs that submitted MicroTest data and were included in the Directory. Further, only those organizations that provided data for the specified fields in the attached tables were used while comparing the two data sets (see the column "count" to note the number of organizations that provided data for any particular field).

10.   In a report on MicroTest data, Jeremy Black and his colleagues claim that theirs is "a large and representative sample of U.S. microenterprise programs" (2003, 6). Even the subtitle of this publication, which is "Performance of the US Microenterprise Industry" implies that the findings within are representative of the field. Other publications have made similar leaps. For example, in a publication based on Self-Employment Learning Project (SELP) data, Peggy Clark and her colleagues say, "While the field of microenterprise programs has grown exponentially since SELP's inception to over 200 programs today, we believe that the [seven] SELP programs are representative of the field of microenterprise assistance as a whole" (1999, 9). However, they have not conducted the basic comparative analysis such as that done in this article to verify this assertion.

11.   Corporate America has lessons here for the nonprofit sector, as we have witnessed the evolution of many industries from using a Fordist mode of production to one more greatly characterized by flexible specialization (Piore and Sabel 1986). Technology, which is insufficiently utilized by U.S. microenterprise programs, has aided this evolution.

12.   See http://fieldus.org/li/microtest for more information.

13.   2003 was the first year for which outcomes data were collected.

14.   Email correspondence with Joyce Klein, October 28, 2004, and November 3, 2004. Twenty-one programs actually submitted data; four of these programs were excluded because they did not meet one or both of the following criteria: they had to draw a random sample of their overall client base, and MicroTest analysis had to show that there was no significant bias in terms of those who responded.

15.   Defined as having more than 50 percent of all financing outstanding through the end of fiscal year 2005 in the form of loans of $35,000 and less.

16.   Microloans represented only 1 percent of the dollars outstanding for these forty-one organizations.

17.   State Microenterprise Associations provide their member organizations with technical assistance, training, a network for peer exchange,

and help in identifying and securing resources. State Microenterprise Intermediaries are financial intermediaries whose primary objective is to raise funds for redistribution to the microenterprise practitioners that provide services in the state.

18. This idea originally came from an interview with an AEO staff member, September 10, 2004.

19. Lichtenstein and Lyons (2001) present some ideas for how entrepreneurial training could be expanded and enhanced.

20. Interview with Jason Friedman, September 10, 2004, and email exchange January 18, 2005. An AEO staff member also suggests that organizations specializing in training increase their breadth by providing financial education training, offering free tax preparation, and other services to increase the economic security of low-income people. Training-oriented programs can also "go deeper" by teaching e-commerce skills, offering specialized industry consultants and the like.

21. Credit scoring is a technique used by creditors to determine to whom they should give credit. Information about a potential borrower's credit history is entered into a statistical program that compares this information with the credit performance of consumers with similar profiles. A total number of points (the credit score) helps to predict the likelihood that the borrower can make payments on time and repay the loan.

22. Eugene Severens, director of the National Fund for Enterprise Development (NFED), has pioneered thinking in this area and the ideas that structure this recommendation. CFED, which houses NFED, received a grant in from the Annie E. Casey Foundation to explore these ideas further.

23. IRS VITA volunteers are not trained to do tax preparations that include Schedule C income, even if the taxpayer is EITC-eligible.

24. These recommendations are derived largely from FIELD, 2002.

25. The SBA 7(a) Community Express program also provides technical assistance, but to a much more limited extent.

26. The 7(a) program, the most basic and used type of SBA loan, is intended to reduce the risk to lenders when they provide financing to qualified small businesses that would not otherwise be able to secure a loan. All 7(a) loans are provided by lenders who agree to structure them to SBA requirements in exchange for a SBA guaranty on a portion of the loan. The maximum loan amount is $2 million. The SBA

will guaranty up to 75 percent of the loan. LowDoc refers to low documentations requirements on loan up to $150,000, for individuals with a good credit history. The SBA will guaranty up to 80 percent of such loans that are for $100,000 or less. The Community Express program refers to revolving loans of up to $250,000 and is restricted to low and moderate income communities. Recipients also must receive pre and post loan technical and management assistance. The SBA Express program provides SBA guarantees up to 50 percent of the value of loans as great as $350,000. These revolving loans usually are used for working capital.

27.   There are some important exceptions to this statement. For example, the CDFI Data Project is led by Opportunity Finance Network and enjoys the participation of the microenterprise field along with other key actors in the community development finance field.

REFERENCES

Association for Enterprise Opportunity. 2002. National Microenterprise Strategy: Capturing the Promise Of Microenterprise Development In The United States. Arlington, Va.: Association for Enterprise Opportunity.
————. 2006. "Draft Numerical Performance Standards for the Microenterprise Industry." Accessed at http://www.microenterprise works.org/projects/msap/draft-standards.htm.
Bates, Timothy. 1995. "Why Do Minority Business Development Programs Generate So Little Minority Business Development?" Economic Development Quarterly 9(1): 3–14.
————. 1996. "The Financial Capital Needs of Black-Owned Businesses." Journal of Developmental Entrepreneurship 1(1): 1–15.
Benjamin, Lehn, Julia Sass Rubin, and Sean Zielenbach. 2004. "Community Development Financial Institutions: Current Issues and Future Prospects." Journal of Urban Affairs 26(2): 177–95.
Benus, Jacob M., Terry R. Johnson, Michelle Wood, Neelima Grover, and Theodore Shen. 1995. "Self-Employment Programs: A New Re-Employment Strategy, Final Report from The UI Self-Employment Demonstration." Unemployment Insurance Occasional Paper 95-4 Washington: US Department of Labor.
Bhatt, Nitin and Shui-Yan Tang. 2001. "Making Microcredit Work in the United States: Social, Financial, and Administrative Decisions." Economic Development Quarterly 15(3): 229–41.
Bhatt, Nitin, Gary Painter, and Shui-Yan Tang. 2002. "The Challenges of Outreach and Sustainability for US Microcredit Programs." In Replicating Microfinance in the United States, edited by James H. Carr and Zhong Yi Tong. Washington: Woodrow Wilson Center Press.

Black, Jeremy. 2005. *Health Insurance for the Self-Employed: Summary Analysis of Health Insurance Gaps, Policies, and Promising Strategies.* Washington: The Aspen Institute.

Black, Jeremy, Elaine Edgcomb, Joyce Klein, Tamra Thetford, and Laura Casoni. 2003. *A Measure of the Microenterprise Industry: A Report from MicroTest.* Washington: The Aspen Institute.

Clark, Peggy, and Amy Kays. 1999. *Microenterprise and the Poor: Findings From the Self-Employment Learning Project Five Year Study of Microentrepreneurs.* Washington: The Aspen Institute, Economic Opportunities Program.

Clark, Peggy, Amy Kays, Lily Zandniapour, Enrique Soto, and Karen Doyle. 1999. *Microenterprise and the Poor: Findings from the Self-Employment Learning Project.* Washington: Aspen Institute.

Corporation for Enterprise Development (CFED). 2001. *Building Assets: A Report on the Asset Development and IDA Field.* Washington: Corporation for Enterprise Development.

Edgcomb, Elaine, and Joyce Klein. 2005. *Opening Opportunities, Building Ownership: Fulfilling the Promise of Microenterprise in the United States.* Washington: FIELD.

Else, John. 2001. *Microenterprise Development in the U.S.: Is There a Case for Public Support?* Geneva: International Labour Organization.

Klein, Joyce, Ilgar Alisultanov, and Amy Blair. 2003. *Microenterprise As a Welfare to Work Strategy: Two-Year Findings.* Washington: The Aspen Institute.

Lichtenstein, Gregg A., and Thomas S. Lyons. 2001. "The Entrepreneurial Development System: Transforming Business Talent and Community Economies." *Economic Development Quarterly* 15(1): 3–20.

Moy, Kirsten, and Alan Okagaki. 2001. *Changing Capital Markets and their Implications for Community Development Finance.* Washington: Brookings Institution.

Piore, Michael J., and Charles F. Sabel. 1986. *The Second Industrial Divide: Possibilities for Prosperity.* New York: Basic Books.

Ratliff, Gregory A., and Kirsten S. Moy with Laura Casoni, Steve Davidson, Cathie Mahon, and Fred Mendez. 2004. "New Pathways to Scale for Community Development Finance." *Profitwise News and Views,* December 2004.

Rubin, Herbert, and Irene Rubin. 2004. *Qualitative Interviewing: The Art of Hearing Data.* Newbury Park, Calif.: Sage Publications.

Schreiner, Mark. 1998. "Self-Employment, Microenterprise, and the Poorest." *Social Service Review* 73(4): 496–523.

Servon, Lisa J. 1997. "Microenterprise Programs in U.S. Inner Cities: Economic Development or Social Welfare?" *Economic Development Quarterly* 11(2): 166–80.

———. 1999. *Boostrap Capital: Microenterprises and the American Poor.* Washington: Brookings Institution.

———. 2006. "Microenterprise Development in the United States: Current Challenges and New Developments." *Economic Development Quarterly* 20(4): 391–3.

Servon, Lisa J., and Timothy Bates. 1998. "Microenterprise as an Exit Route from Poverty: Recommendations for Programs and Policy Makers." *Journal of Urban Affairs* 20(4): 419–41.

———. 1999. *Bootstrap Capital: Microenterprises and the Poor.* New York: Brookings Institute.

Servon, Lisa J., and Jeffrey Doshna. 1998. *Microenterprise as an Economic Adjustment Strategy.* Washington: U.S. Department of Commerce, Economic Development Administration.

Sherraden, Margaret S., Cynthia K. Sanders, and Michael Sherraden. 2004. *Kitchen Capitalism: Microenterprise in Low-Income Households.* Albany, N.Y.: State University of New York Press.

Spalter-Roth, Roberta, Enrique Soto, and Lily Zandniapour. 1994. *Microenterprise and Women: The Viability of Self-Employment as a Strategy for Alleviating Poverty.* Washington: Institute for Women's Policy Research.

U.S. Chamber of Commerce. 2004. *Small Business Platform: Recommendations to the Parties.* Washington: U.S. Chamber of Commerce.

U.S. Department of Labor. 2005. *Association Health Plans: Improving Access to Affordable Quality Health Care for Small Businesses.* Washington: U.S. Government Printing Office.

Vinelli, Andrew. 2002. "Financial Sustainability in U.S. Microfinance Organizations: Lessons from Developing Countries." In *Replicating Microfinance in the United States,* edited by James H. Carr and Zhong Yi Tong. Washington: Woodrow Wilson Center Press.

Von Pischke, J. D. 2002. "Current Foundations of Microfinance Best Practices in Developing Countries." In *Replicating Microfinance in the United States,* edited by James H. Carr and Zhong Yi Tong. Washington: Woodrow Wilson Center Press.

Walker, Britton A., and Amy K. Blair. 2002. *2002 Directory of U.S. Microenterprise Programs.* Washington, D.C.: The Aspen Institute.

PART II

Building Institutions

CHAPTER FIVE

Financing Organizations with Debt and Equity: The Role of Community Development Loan and Venture Capital Funds

Julia Sass Rubin

COMMUNITY DEVELOPMENT financial institutions (CDFIs) are intermediaries that help redress the financial exclusion of low-income communities. CDFIs consist of community development loan funds (CDLFs), community development venture capital funds (CDVCs), community development banks, and community development credit unions. This chapter focuses on community development loan and venture capital funds. Chapter 6 reviews community development banks and credit unions.[1]

CDLFs and CDVCs provide debt and equity capital for transactions that conventional capital sources consider too risky. They primarily fund organizations, including businesses, housing and real estate developers, and nonprofit community groups that need facility or operating loans, with the objective of furthering economic development of distressed communities by creating the high-quality jobs and infrastructure necessary for their residents.

Although all community development financial institutions serve low-income communities, and there is some overlap in the services that each provides, there also are important differences among them. Unlike community development banks and credit unions, community development loan and venture capital funds are unregulated financial institutions that cannot rely on federally insured deposits for their capital. They also, however, are not subject to the financial rules and audits that apply to regulated institutions, enabling them to take more risks and potentially to be more innovative.

The late 1990s was a hospitable economic and political environment for community development financial institutions (Benjamin, Rubin, and Zielenbach 2004). Like all CDFIs, CDLFs and CDVCs grew significantly both in absolute numbers and in capitalization levels. However, the environment has changed dramatically since 2000, leaving many community development loan and venture capital funds struggling to stay alive, as the subsidized capital necessary to fund their operations largely has evaporated. This environmental change has sparked a conversation within the industry and among its supporters regarding what the future business and industry models should be for CDLFs and CDVCs.

This chapter provides an overview of community development loan and venture capital funds, including the challenges they face going forward. It is based on analysis of data from the 2005 CDFI Data Project, as well as extensive interviews with practitioners, funders, and policy makers involved with the field.[2]

COMMUNITY DEVELOPMENT LOAN FUNDS

Community Development Loan Funds (CDLFs) lend capital to businesses, for-profit and nonprofit real estate and housing developers, various types of nonprofit organizations looking for facility or operating capital, and increasingly individuals looking for financing to purchase or rehabilitate their homes. Most of the organizations and people that are financed by CDLFs are not able to obtain capital from more traditional sources, or cannot obtain it on terms that they can afford.[3] CDLF financings are intended to further various social goals, such as creating low-income housing, furthering economic growth and job creation in low-income areas, stabilizing population declines in distressed communities, improving the availability and quality of community facilities in underserved markets, increasing the number of businesses owned by women and ethnic minorities, and promoting the growth of businesses that do not harm the environment (Caskey and Hollister 2001).

As of 2005, there were approximately 500 community development loan funds in existence in the United States, with more than \$3.5 billion in assets.[4] CDLFs financed more than \$2.6 billion of activities that year, with more than \$2.3 billion in additional financings outstanding. These figures are somewhat misleading, however, as a few large organizations accounted for most of this activity. The five largest CDLFs, for example, accounted for 52 percent of total loan fund capital and 58 percent of all direct financing outstanding. The top twenty CDLFs held 77 percent of all capital and were responsible for 79 percent of all financing outstanding. Most CDLFs are relatively small, with median capital of \$8.9 million as of 2005 (CDFI Data Project 2007a).

The community development loan fund model emerged from a variety of origins, including efforts in the late 1960s and 1970s, by a few community development corporations and a group of revolving loan funds, to make loans to businesses in order to promote economic development (Grossman, Levere and Marcoux 1998; Rubin 1998). In addition to business lending, many of the early CDLFs focused on financing construction of low-income housing in response to the lack of alternative sources of capital for such projects.

Although housing and business loans still make up the bulk of CDLF financing activities, accounting for 66 percent and 17 percent of all CDLF dollars outstanding, many CDLFs have diversified their offerings, moving into the provision of operating and facility construction loans to nonprofits, such as charter schools, child-care centers, health-care facilities, social services agencies, and arts organizations (CDFI Data Project 2007a). As with their business and housing finance activities, CDLFs began providing capital to nonprofits because more traditional capital sources viewed the nonprofits' revenue streams as too unpredictable to make them good credit risks.

The newest area of CDLF activity is providing home loans to individuals. As of 2005, twenty-two CDLFs reported providing housing loans directly to individuals and this type of financing is continuing to increase (CDFI Data Project 2007a). Self-Help, a North Carolina CDFI, has gone further in its efforts to promote home ownership for individuals who cannot obtain financing from a bank or conventional lender because of credit or other problems and those who traditionally have been underserved by banks, such as female-headed households, minority households, rural families, and low-income households. In 1994, Self-Help began buying such nonconforming mortgage loans from area banks. In 1998, the organization joined forces with Fannie Mae and the Ford Foundation to offer the national secondary market for affordable home loans. Under this partnership, the Ford Foundation awarded Self-Help a $50 million grant. Self-Help has used it as a loss reserve to enable it to acquire many more nonconforming loans, made by conventional lenders, to free up capital that the lenders could use to make additional loans to underserved customers. Self-Help credit enhances the mortgages and sells them to Fannie Mae (Ford Foundation 1998).

CDLFs, which are primarily nonprofit in legal structure, have relied on a combination of grants and below-market-rate loans to capitalize their activities.[5] CDLFs re-lend this capital at market or near-market rates, using the spread—or difference—to help finance their operations.

Most CDLF capital is in the form of debt, which accounted for 68 percent of all capital as of 2005.[6] CDLFs raised the bulk of their debt capital from banks and thrifts (49.6 percent). The remaining identified sources came from foundations (16.3 percent); federal (9.5 percent) state and local (4.6 percent) governments; religious institutions (6.4 percent); non-depository financial institutions—such as pension funds (4.0 percent); individual investors (2.9 percent); national intermediaries—such as Opportunity Finance Network (2.5 percent); and corporations (2.5 percent).[7] Most CDLFs also must raise ongoing operating subsidies to pay for the technical assistance they provide to borrowers, for the high cost predevelopment and microloans, and for other aspects of their operations that the spread on lending does not cover.[8]

CDLFs lend both independently and in conjunction with conventional lenders. When lending in partnership with more conventional institutions, CDLFs generally take a subordinate position, absorbing most or all of the risk. Because most CDLF loans are riskier than those made by banks, and at times are unsecured, CDLFs also provide extensive pre- and post-investment technical assistance to their portfolio companies. The technical assistance is used both to help potential borrowers qualify for capital and to assist them with various aspects of operations after they have received that capital. The type of assistance provided includes help with writing business plans, putting together marketing strategies, and developing financial systems.

An aspect of CDLF activity that has received little attention is the role CDLFs play in demonstrating the financial viability of low-income communities to traditional financial institutions. In small business lending, for example, both through successful solo lending and by taking the higher risk portions of joint deals, CDLFs have encouraged banks to lend to small business customers in low-income markets, a group that banks had previously rejected (Rubin and Stankiewicz 2001).

In multifamily housing, CDLFs have helped bring banks into projects and demonstrated that such deals could be successfully and profitably underwritten. CDLFs also have helped banks understand how to lend within those communities. Banks now consider lending to multifamily development projects reasonably safe because of the underlying physical collateral; the presence of subordinate, risk-alleviating financing such as CDLF loans, Low Income Housing Tax Credit equity, and public loans; and the extensive organizational and project-based counseling and technical assistance that the CDLFs provide to the borrowers (Zielenbach 2006).

As a result, conventional financial institutions have become much more involved in projects previously financed primarily or exclusively by CDLFs. Construction and permanent financing now comes quite frequently from banks and less often from CDLFs. In certain markets, CDLFs and their bank supporters find themselves competing for the same multifamily loans.

As banks have moved into markets once served entirely by CDLFs, the latter have had to take on increasingly risky investments (Rubin and Stankiewicz 2001).

In real estate finance, for example, as conventional lenders have become more willing to take on more of a project's financing costs, CDLFs have often been pushed further into making early-stage, higher-risk loans. This heightened risk position, coupled with a lower interest rate spread associated with higher interest rates, has caused many multifamily CDLF lenders to revisit their loan pricing to make it closer to market cost. CDLFs are less willing and able to offer deeply discounted monies and more willing to provide market-rate financing, particularly if their dollars are effectively the only ones available for seed or gap capital (Zielenbach 2006).

Another little-documented area of CDLF activity is the role they have played in shaping policy. CDLFs and other types of CDFIs have influenced government at both the national and state levels. The Clinton administration's creation of the CDFI Fund, the New Markets Tax Credit, and the New Markets Venture Capital programs were all strongly encouraged and shaped by CDFIs and their leaders. CDFI advocacy also played a role in the Clinton administration's 1995 strengthening of the Community Reinvestment Act (Pinsky 2001).

At the state level, CDFIs also have advocated successfully for increased regulation and consumer protection. Such advocacy has included efforts to enact and strengthen state-level community reinvestment act legislation; enact laws to curtail predatory lending and fringe banking; and advocate on numerous local issues, ranging from workforce to environment policies. Some of the largest CDFIs—such as Self-Help, The Reinvestment Fund, and Coastal Enterprises—have created specialized subsidiaries, or have dedicated personnel, to conduct research and influence policy. Self-Help's Center for Responsible Lending, for example, has contributed significantly to knowledge and regulation on the issue of predatory lending, including passage and evaluation of the first state-level anti-predatory-lending legislation. The center works with academics and advocates around the country to conduct research, build coalitions, advocate for anti-predatory-lending policies, and support litigation.[9]

Given the large number of community development loan funds in existence and the high level of diversity among them, it is perhaps not surprising that, beyond the largely descriptive data collected by the CDFI Data Project, little research has been done on the CDLF industry as a whole. There have been, however, several high-quality studies that have examined the social outcomes achieved by some of the largest and most established CDLFs, including Enterprise Corporation of the Delta, Kentucky Highlands Investments Corporation, and Coastal Enterprises (for an analysis, see chapter 9). It is difficult to generalize from these studies to the much smaller loan funds that populate most of the industry.

Beyond the sector's social outcomes, many other questions about CDLFs remain. For example, we have only anecdotal information regarding the activities of CDLFs in financing nonprofit facilities, and we know little about the differences between CDLFs and more conventional financial institutions in terms of their default and delinquency rates or the composition of their customers. We also need to examine the role of CDLFs as innovators— which demonstrate to conventional financial institutions the viability of new products that benefit low-income communities and new markets populated by such communities—and as intermediaries—which enable and support the activities of other organizations that serve low-income communities.

COMMUNITY DEVELOPMENT VENTURE CAPITAL FUNDS

Community development venture capital (CDVC) providers make investments of equity and near-equity in small businesses. An equity investment consists of cash that a company receives in exchange for partial ownership of that company, in the form of preferred or common stock. A near-equity investment consists of a loan with special features, such as warrants, royalties, or participation payments, which enable the lender to participate in the upside if the company receiving the capital is successful. Both equity and near-equity are forms of patient capital, giving young firms the funds they need in their early years without requiring the immediate repayment of those funds, as is the case with most loans.

The earliest CDVC providers were Title VII community development corporations, which in the early 1970s began making equity investments in businesses as part of their economic development work. Other CDVC funds were begun by individual states, intending to stimulate business growth in low-income areas, and by community development loan funds, which expanded into equity provision in order to meet the needs of their debt clients (Rubin 2001).

According to the Community Development Venture Capital Alliance (CDVCA), the industry's trade association, there were eighty-two CDVC providers either active or in formation as of the end of 2004, with $870 million under management (CDVCA 2006). This is a substantive increase from the six providers, with less than $100 million under management that existed just a decade earlier (Rubin 2001). This dramatic growth reflects the overall growth of community development financial institutions during this period, due in large part to the Clinton administration's active support of the industry. In the case of CDVCs, the growth also reflects the overall positive perception of venture capital during the late 1990s, as traditional venture capitalists made record-breaking profits for their investors via a strong economy and an unprecedented public appetite for initial public offerings.

CDVCs differ from traditional private venture capital funds and small business investment companies (SBICs) in a number of ways. Most important, unlike the majority of traditional venture capitalists and SBICs, which have an exclusively financial returns objective, CDVCs invest with both social and financial goals. Thus, before making an investment, they consider both a company's potential to create significant high-quality jobs for low-income individuals as well as its likelihood of rapid economic growth. As a result of this dual-bottom-line, CDVCs are willing to invest in companies in numerous industries, stages of development, and locations. This sets them apart from traditional venture capitalists, which tend to specialize by industry and stage and to invest almost exclusively in a handful of domestic technology corridors, such as California's Silicon Valley and the Boston area's Route 128.

The earliest CDVC funds also differed from traditional venture capital in their legal structures. Unlike traditional venture capital funds, which are for-profit and usually structured as either limited liability companies (LLCs) or limited partnerships (LPs), the early CDVC providers utilized a multitude of nonprofit, for-profit and hybrid legal structures. More recently, however, CDVC providers have begun adopting the more conventional LP and LLC legal structures for their investment activities. This has helped them attract bank investors, who are familiar—and comfortable—with traditional venture capital models (Rubin 2001).

Many of the CDVCs using the LP and LLC models have created nonprofit subsidiaries that have enabled them to raise grant funds to offset operating expenses. CDVCs tend to have higher operating expenses because most of them provide their portfolio companies with technical assistance. The technical assistance is necessary because CDVC funds often have a more limited number of investment prospects, whether due to geographic restrictions or to the social screens some of them impose to meet other objectives (for example, a company's environmental or labor practices). This limited deal flow may require the funds to invest in companies with less experienced management and then advise those companies, either directly through fund staff or indirectly through outside experts, to increase the companies' level of knowledge and market readiness (Rubin 2001).

The most common sources of capital for traditional VC funds are pension funds, foundation endowments, and financial institutions. Financial institutions also have played an increasingly important role in capitalizing the CDVC industry, accounting for more than 40 percent of the industry's overall capital and 90 percent for some of the newer funds (CDFI Data Project 2007b; Rubin 2001). These figures reflect the important role that the investment requirement of the Community Reinvestment Act has played in encouraging banks to invest in equity providers.

The federal government has been another major source of CDVC capital, through both the New Markets Venture Capital program and the CDFI Fund. Government sources account for approximately a quarter of the capital raised by the CDVC industry. Foundations were an important early source of CDVC capital. As of 2005, they accounted for approximately 11 percent of all industry dollars (CDFI Data Project 2007b). Most foundation investments, however, have been in the form of program related investments structured as low-interest debt versus the equity dollars that venture capital investing requires. Furthermore, foundations appear to have moved away from supporting individual CDVC funds, investing in few of the most recently capitalized funds (Rubin 2001). This trend is discussed in more detail in Part II of this chapter.

Like traditional venture capitalists, CDVC providers must exit their investments to make a profit and free up capital for new investments. In general, they tend to hold their investments longer than traditional venture capitalists do, tying up valuable capital and management time and decreasing their financial returns. The longer holding times reflect both the greater difficulty of exiting from the types of companies in which CDVCs invest and the unwillingness of many CDVC managers to force an exit that would be detrimental to a company's overall survival or to the survival of any jobs the company could have created. This longer holding time, combined with the industry's relative youth, has meant that most CDVC funds are still holding the bulk of their investments.

Although the CDVC industry is young, some bifurcation within it has already emerged between those funds that are structured as nonprofits, have smaller capitalizations of one and a half to five million dollars, make investments of $10,000 to $250,000 dollars, and target specific distressed rural and urban geographies consisting of a city, several counties or a state, and the newer CDVC funds that are more likely to be for-profit, have larger capitalizations of $10 to $20 million, target broader geographies such as New England or the entire eastern United States, and make larger investments of $250,000 to $1 million. These two models have attracted different investors and operate under somewhat different sets of economic constraints.

Sometimes, the same parent entity will have two CDVC funds, the older of which will exhibit characteristics of the first model, whereas the newer one will exhibit characteristics of the second. In part, this reflects the challenge of raising a CDVC fund before the mid-1990s, when the concept of community development venture capital was still largely unknown. Many of the early sources of capital were social and imposed specific constraints on the CDVC funds in which they invested, which were designed to maximize the social impact of their investments. These constraints, such as limits on the geographies in which the funds could invest and requirements that the funds create large numbers of jobs for low-income people, along with the marketing approach that the early CDVC funds had to undertake to appeal to socially oriented investors, often made it more difficult for them to raise capital from more profit-oriented sources. Newer CDVC funds, with larger capitalizations, deal sizes and target geographies, have had much greatest success in raising capital because of their ability to attract investments from banks and financial institutions. Even these funds, however, have found this task significantly more difficult recently, for reasons discussed in the next section.

CHALLENGES FACING THE FIELD

Of all the challenges that CDLFs and CDVCs currently face, by far the greatest is raising the capital necessary to fund their operations. The economic and political environment for community development finance has changed dramatically since 2000, making it increasingly difficult for CDLFs and CDVCs to raise capital at subsidized rates, which they require for the high-risk loans and investments, the provision of technical assistance, and the financial experimentation that is their mainstay.

Economic Environment

The economic slowdown that began in the spring of 2001 and the decline in the value of the stock market since the spring of 2000 have had a significant impact on the community development finance industry by limiting disposable capital for many investors. It also dampened conventional financial institutions' enthusiasm both for making direct loans in lower-income markets and for providing subsidized support to CDFIs. At the same time, it increased the need for the services that CDLFs and CDVCs provide. It also made it more difficult for CDVCs to exit the investments they already had made, constraining their profitability and thus limiting their ability to raise new capital.

Although all CDFIs have faced a more challenging fundraising environment since 2000, CDVCs have been particularly affected, for several reasons. First, they have yet to demonstrate the consistent, risk-adjusted rates of financial return that would appeal to traditional investors. The earliest CDVCs, such as Northeast Ventures, projected rates of return of 0 to 5 percent for their primarily foundation and government sources of capital (Jackson and Lerner 1996). Subsequent funds, however, have looked to traditional financial institutions for investment capital and thus have had to target rates of financial return closer to those of conventional venture capital. Most of these funds are too new to have exited the bulk of their investments and calculated a fund-wide internal rate of return (IRR). Given the longer holding times for CDVCs, it is likely to take a few more years before such return figures are available for multiple funds. There have been successful individual exits, but it is not clear yet whether these will translate into sufficiently high portfolio-wide financial returns to attract additional capital from existing investors.[10] Their lack of a successful track record also has made it more difficult for CDVCs to raise money from other sources accessed by traditional venture capital, such as pension funds and endowments.

An additional challenge for CDVC funds has been the difficulty of quantifying the social impact of their investments beyond the widely used outcome measures of jobs created and retained. Even the job-related figures are challenging to aggregate because individual funds use different methodologies to track this information. This lack of consistent, industry-wide outcome data has made it more difficult for the industry to raise capital from more socially oriented sources such as foundations.[11]

Political Environment

The political challenges that CDLFs and CDVCs are facing are greater than the economic ones. The most dramatic increases in financial service provision in lower-income markets occurred during the mid- to late 1990s, during a presidential administration that made a strong commitment to such a goal. Clinton's support of the Community Reinvestment Act and sponsorship of the CDFI Fund was critical to the growth of the CDFI industry and to the expanded efforts by conventional financial institutions to serve historically underserved communities. The G. W. Bush administration has been much less welcoming to community development finance than its predecessor. Evidence of this abounds, particularly in the administration's treatment of the Community Reinvestment Act, the Community Development Financial Institutions Fund, and the New Markets Venture Capital and Rural Business Investment programs.

Community Reinvestment Act

Congress passed the Community Reinvestment Act (CRA) in 1977 to encourage regulated financial institutions to meet their "continuing and affirmative obligations to help meet the credit needs of the local communities in which they are chartered" (NCRC 2005, 1) The act is enforced by four agencies— the Federal Office of Thrift Supervision (FOTS), which examines savings and loan institutions; the Office of the Comptroller of the Currency (OCC), which examines nationally chartered banks; and the Federal Deposit Insurance Corporation (FDIC) and the Federal Reserve (Fed), both of which examine state-chartered banks (NCRC 2005).

Regulations for the CRA have been revised several times. Most significantly, they were strengthened in 1995 via changes that "focused CRA evaluations on objective performance measures rather than the more subjective and process-oriented factors that regulators previously had used. . . . required banks and thrifts to disclose information about their small-business, small-farm, and community development lending" and instituted tailored examinations for large banks, small banks, and wholesale or limited-purpose institutions that "more closely align[ed]" the CRA examinations of different types of banking institutions with their business strategies (Barr 2005, 112). Large banks, those with assets of $250 million or more, were subsequently evaluated on their lending, investments and services. Smaller banks underwent a streamlined review of their lending activities only.

The 1995 revisions also expressly recognized community development financial institutions as qualifying CRA investments and borrowers, giving commercial banks a significant incentive to financing CDFIs (Pinsky 2001). The 1995 revisions, and the "increasingly intense consolidation in the banking industry, which provided greater opportunities for community organizations and regulators to evaluate bank and thrift performance under CRA in the context of merger applications" (Barr 2005, 113), led to a broadly perceived strengthening of the CRA.

In 2001, the four federal enforcement agencies began a review of the 1995 regulations that resulted in amendments to the act in 2004 and 2005.[12] For the first time in the history of the CRA, they did not issue a consistent set of rules. The Federal Deposit Insurance Corporation (FDIC), Office of the Comptroller of the Currency (OCC), and Federal Reserve (Fed) adopted identical amendments to the CRA regulations. The Office of Thrift Supervision (OTS) issued a different set.

The amendments issued by the FDIC, OCC and Fed created a new category of banks, known as intermediate small banks. This category encompassed institutions with assets of between $250 million and $1 billion. Such institutions were no longer to be evaluated on their investment and service activities. Instead they are evaluated under the small bank lending test and a flexible new community development test. The new rules also exempt the intermediate small banks from CRA loan data collection and reporting obligations for their small-business, small-farm and community development loans. Finally, the new rules dictate that holding company affiliation will no longer be a factor in determining which CRA evaluation standards will apply to a bank. A bank's CRA evaluation therefore will be determined solely by its asset size, regardless of how large its holding company's assets are. The new regulations did not change the evaluations for those banks with assets of more than $1 billion or those banks with assets of less than $250 million (Marsico 2006).

The OTS went a step further than the other three agencies, increasing the asset threshold for small savings associations (which are subject only to the streamlined lending test and have no investment or service requirements), from less than $250 million to less than $1 billion. The OTS also exempted the savings and loans with more than $1 billion in assets from the three-part community development test, replacing it with one requiring 50 percent for lending and any combination of lending, investment, or financial services to satisfy the remaining 50 percent (Marsico 2006). In March 2007, after significant lobbying by CRA supporters, the new director of OTS reversed these changes, aligning the agency's CRA regulations with those of the three federal banking agencies.

Supporters of the Community Reinvestment Act see these actions on the part of regulators as part of an ongoing effort by the law's opponents to "dismantle the act, piece by piece" (Rubin and Rubinger 2004, 1). The National Community Reinvestment Coalition found that as a result of the intermediate small bank category changes "1,508 banks with 13,643 branches and total assets of $679 billion were no longer subject to the more rigorous lending, investment, and service tests for large banks and no longer required to disclose data about their small business, small-farm and community development lending" (Marsico 2006, 540).

The current political environment also makes it highly unlikely that CRA will be expanded to cover other types of financial services providers, such as investment banks, mortgage banks, or insurance companies. Such an expansion had been advocated by CRA supporters, by representatives of populations that lack access to financial services, and by some commercial banks that had argued for it on fairness grounds. With bank deregulation, commercial banks are accounting for an increasingly small portion of all financial services. The diversification and mergers within the industry also mean that more and more commercial banks are part of larger organizations that can minimize CRA scrutiny by moving assets to those operations not covered by the act.

Given the significant role that banks play in providing investment capital for community development loan and venture funds, any weakening of the CRA translates into fewer resources for such activities. CDVCs and CDLFs are particularly hurt by the reduction in the number of banks and savings and loans that must comply with the CRA investment test, which could be met via equity investments in such developmental finance institutions.

Community Development Financial Institutions (CDFI) Fund

The CDFI Fund is one of the few sources of equity capital for community development finance. It has been an increasingly important source of late as CRA regulations have reduced the number of banks that must meet the investment test and foundations have curtailed their grant and equity investments in the field. As table 5.1 demonstrates, under the Bush administration, the CDFI Fund has seen a dramatic reduction in funding from $118 million in 2001, the last budget under President Clinton, to $55 million in 2007. Even this reduced level of support required a significant lobbying effort by the CDFI industry because the administration's proposed 2006 budget called for moving all funding to the Department of Commerce except what was necessary to oversee existing commitments and to administer the New Markets Tax Credit (NMTC) program.[13] The administration's 2007 budget again called for similar consolidation provisions. The 2008 budget, proposed following the election of Democratic majorities in the House and Senate, reversed this strategy and asked for a twenty-nine million dollar allocation for the fund.

In addition to reducing overall funding levels, the administration also has limited the fund's flexibility by pushing it to focus more of its resources on evaluation, and by prioritizing NMTC administration over other spending. For example, the president's 2008 fiscal budget requests $12 million for administering the NMTC, leaving only $17 million to fund technical and financial assistance.

New Markets Venture Capital

The New Markets Venture Capital (NMVC) program—part of the Community Renewal Tax Relief Act of 2000—was designed to increase the supply of

Table 5.1   CDFI Fund Budget, FY 2001 to 2008 (Proposed)

Fiscal Year	Amount
2001	$118 million (Last year of President Clinton's budget)
2002	$80 million
2003	$75 million
2004	$60.6 million
2005	$55.5 million
2006	$54.5 million
2007	$54.5 million
2008	$29 million (proposed)

Source: Author's compilation.

equity and near-equity capital flowing into distressed communities. The program, which is administrated by the Small Business Administration of the U.S. Department of Commerce, was intended to provide ten to twenty new NMVC companies with matching capital—$100 million in debt for making investments ($150 million of debenture guarantees allocated on a discounted basis) and $30 million in grants to offset overhead expenses. The program would have resulted in a significant expansion of the financial resources available to the CDVC industry.

Six NMVC companies were given final approval in the first round of the program. The SBA expected to run a second round of the program starting in the spring of 2003. In March of that year, however, funding for the second round was deleted from the 2003 Fiscal Year Omnibus Appropriations Bill during the budget reconciliation process. Although new legislation has been introduced in both the House and Senate to reauthorize the program, to date, such efforts have not been successful.

Rural Business Investment Program

The Rural Business Investment Program (RBIP) was designed to promote developmental venture capital investments in smaller enterprises in rural areas. It was created by the 2002 Farm Bill and modeled on the NMVC program. The original legislation indicated that the program would make available approximately $280 million of investment dollars as well as operational grants to provide technical assistance to portfolio companies. In 2003, the U.S. Department of Agriculture reached an agreement with the SBA to have the SBA administer the program.

The 2005 budget allocated $10 million for the program, which would have yielded at least $50 million in debentures and up to $3 million in technical assistance grant funds, enough to support two to three rural business investment companies. The SBA conditionally approved three, giving them a year to raise the $10 million in equity capital required to become fully approved. On full approval, each would have been eligible for $20 million of government guaranteed debentures for making investments and a $1 million operational assistance grant for providing technical assistance to the companies that received investments.

Only one of the three, Meretus Ventures, was able to raise the necessary capital and become a rural business investment company. The Budget Reconciliation Act of 2005 subsequently rescinded funds appropriated for the program that were not obligated by October 1, 2006, and repealed the authority to spend funds in the future, ending any future funding for the program.

Other Sources of Support

The decline in federal government support for community development finance has precipitated or coincided with declines in other sources of capital, such as conventional financial institutions and foundations. Early hopes that the New Markets Tax Credit Program would provide capital for non–real estate based business-related financings have also largely been unrealized.

Conventional Financial Institutions

The U.S. financial services sector has gone through significant changes over the last few decades, caused by globalization, domestic deregulation, and technological advances (Avery et al. 1999). One of the most dramatic has been a consolidation of the banking industry through mergers of increasingly large organizations. The ten biggest commercial banks now control 49 percent of all domestic banking assets, a substantial increase from the 29 percent they controlled a decade ago (The Economist 2006).

This consolidation has had both positive and negative affects on the CDFI industry. On the positive side, banks planning to acquire or be acquired have been more likely to be concerned about their CRA rating and thus to make community-development related investments, even unprofitable ones (Bostic et al. 2002; Avery, Bostic, and Canner 2000). This benefit has been watered down somewhat by the recent decrease in large-bank mergers, and the perceived reduction in CRA enforcement.

The negative consequences of consolidation have included a reduction in both home purchase and small business lending by the resulting organization. This is particularly true for larger banks that acquire other larger banks and for markets that experience increased concentration of banking services (Samolyk and Richardson 2003; Avery et al. 1999).

Another related concern is the reduction in absolute sources of capital for community development that occurs when large institutions merge. Anecdotal evidence indicates that the postmerger institutions do not provide as much community development capital as the total of what the two merging entities did separately, resulting in a reduction of overall capital availability. Mergers among larger banks also leave fewer sources of capital for CDFIs to approach, reducing the overall odds of a CDFI being able to obtain a capital commitment.

Bank consolidation also has resulted in an increased emphasis on profitability by the larger banks, which have felt pressure to justify the mergers to their shareholders. This has led them to consolidate activities and cut costs (Tully 2006). It also has encouraged them to focus on their most lucrative activities, such as advising on mergers and acquisitions, at the cost of riskier and less profitable ones, such as commercial lending (Hovanesian 2005).

The increased profitability pressures also have translated into less subsidized capital available for CDFIs as banks increasingly view their CRA-related activities as profit centers. This is made easier by the recent increase in investment options created specifically to provide financial institutions with market-rate or near-market-rate returns yet enable them to receive investment test or similar credit under the CRA. These include mutual funds, such as the Access Capital Community Investment Fund and the CRA Qualified Investment Fund, which invest in economically and geographically targeted fixed income instruments. They also include separately managed accounts that groups such as CRA Fund Advisors can set up to suit the particular investment objectives of banks, pension funds, and foundations.

Even developmental venture capital alternatives have mushroomed. The minority-focused venture capital industry has grown significantly in the last decade (Bates, Bradford, and Rubin 2006), and funds such as UrbanAmerica, LP, the Canyon-Johnson Urban Fund, and the Genesis Family of Funds invest in inner-city real estate with the goal of achieving both market-rate returns and economic development for their underserved residents. These investment options pose challenges for CDLFs and CDVCs, many of which cannot compete on financial returns and have not been able to demonstrate that they produce higher social returns than other community development investment alternatives.

CDLFs and CDVCs seeking bank investments must also contend with higher interest rates, which translate into a higher cost of capital for banks and CDFI borrowers. For those CDLFs reluctant to pass the higher costs on to their borrowers, the higher rates mean a smaller profit margin with which to cover their own expenses.

The losses that many banks experienced from their Small Business Investment Company (SBIC) investments following the market correction of 2001 have also hurt CDVCs' ability to raise capital. Although CDVCs have not pursued the Internet-related investments that led so many SBICs to lose money, they have been hurt by the connection some bankers have made between them and SBICs, as equity investments in both enable banks to meet the CRA investment test.

Foundations

Foundations have been a small but important source of capital for both CDVCs and CDLFs, particularly for operating support and equity dollars, which are always difficult to secure. Over the last decade, a handful of large foundations, including The Ford Foundation, The John D. and Catherine T. MacArthur Foundation, and the F. B. Heron Foundation, have made numerous investments in the field, while others, such as the Rockefeller Foundation, the Fannie Mae Foundation, the Open Society Institute, the Annie E. Casey Foundation and the W. K. Kellogg Foundation have supported specific organizations and/or initiatives.

In the last few years, foundation support for community development finance has declined. This is due partly to the stock market decline that began in 2000, shrank foundation assets, and led to an overall reduction in foundation giving. More significant, however, have been decisions by the most active foundation investors to change the nature of their support for the sector or to withdraw support entirely. Foundations generally view their dollars as seed money, intended to catalyze other sources of capital and ultimately lead to organizational or project sustainability. For CDFIs, this has meant that the subsidized dollars that foundations provided to many organizations in the industry's beginnings have become rare or unavailable.

Some foundations have pulled back entirely, no longer funding CDFIs except when the work of individual organizations overlaps with their other programmatic interests, such as workforce development; health care, education, or child-care initiatives; or efforts to stop predatory lending. Others are focusing their resources on those few organizations or programs perceived to be the most innovative and likely to bring about the next wave of significant development within the industry—such as securitization or ways to use market-rate capital, or policy initiatives that could increase the impact of CDFI activities.

Even those few foundations that have continued to fund individual CDLFs and CDVCs evaluate these investments relative to the range of other community development options available, such as the fixed instrument and equity funds discussed previously. As one foundation official pointed out, "There has been a lot of activity in the last five years and it has reshaped the landscape a lot and signaled to foundations and banks that they can have the same impact with a better return."

Nor do program-related foundation dollars, which by law must annually equal at least 5 percent of a foundation's assets, match the endowment dollars that foundations invest in market-rate instruments. This is true even for those foundations, such as F. B. Heron, which commit a portion of their endowment investments to mission related opportunities. In 2004, for example, the foundation invested $1,500,000 in four CDVC funds through program related investments, and $10,000,000 of endowment funds in six socially oriented market-rate equity funds, such as UrbanAmerica, L.P. (F. B. Heron 2004).

New Markets Tax Credit Program

The NMTC program was designed to combine public and private sector resources in order to bring $15 billion in new investments to impoverished rural and urban communities. The program was enacted as part of the Community Renewal Tax Relief Act of 2000, along with the New Markets Venture Capital program. The last round of the NMTC originally was to take place in 2007. However, in December 2006, the program was extended through 2008, with an additional $3.5 billion credit allocation. A bill to authorize new funding for an additional five years has been introduced in Congress

The CDFI Fund, which administers the NMTC program, allocates a set pool of tax credits to financial intermediaries, called community development entities (CDEs), based on a competitive application process. The CDEs then offer the credits to investors in exchange for equity capital investments. The credit is equal to a 39 percent cumulative tax reduction for the investors and must be used over seven years—allowing for a 5 percent reduction in taxes in each of the first three years, and a 6 percent reduction in each of the remaining four years (CDFI Fund 2005).

The program came into existence with strong encouragement and support from CDFI industry. When the program was being designed, there was great hope that it would be a significant new source of equity capital to fund business lending and investments. Due to several statutory and regulatory provisions, however, the program has so far been used almost exclusively to finance real estate-related transactions. The highly competitive nature of the program and the expense and expertise required to meet its legal and compliance requirements have favored the largest and most sophisticated CDFIs in being able to obtain a NMTC allocation (Rubin and Stankiewicz 2005).

These limitations aside, the NMTC has provided CDFIs with a critical new source of fee-based revenue and an opportunity to expand the size and nature of financing activities at a time when other sources of subsidized capital have become more difficult to obtain. Additionally, some smaller CDFIs have been able to take advantage of the NMTC program by partnering with larger entities, such as Coastal Enterprises, or the Community Reinvestment Fund.

OPPORTUNITIES AND INDUSTRY RESPONSE

In response to the increasingly challenging environment that CDLFs and CDVCs are facing in raising subsidized capital, they have turned their energies toward finding ways to reduce their ongoing reliance on such capital by becoming more sustainable. For many organizations, sustainability is associated with growing in size. Although some small CDLFs and CDVCs can survive due to ongoing local subsidies, overall it is difficult to cover operating expenses with a small capital base. They thus are exploring new sources of subsidized capital, such as state-level initiatives. They also are identifying ways to access new sources of capital that historically have not been significant for community development finance, such as pension funds and individual investors. Finally, they are rethinking the way they do business and repositioning themselves to become more sustainable by cutting costs and by finding new ways to use market rate capital and tap traditional capital markets to fund their operations.

State and Local Governments

Most state governments experienced a significant financial crisis that began in 2001 and lasted through 2004. The crisis was a result primarily of the national economic slowdown, exacerbated by reductions in federal funding to the states. Although state revenues generally have grown rapidly since then, not all states have returned to fiscal solvency. Furthermore, the Center on Budget and Policy Priorities warns that "states risk a rapid return to deficits unless they recognize that some of their current 'surplus' revenues are only temporary and thus should not be used to fund ongoing tax cuts or spending increases" (McNichol and Lay 2006, 1).

Although the variable economic conditions in the states present an uneven playing field for community development finance, overall the states offer a more receptive policy environment than the federal level currently does. Community organizations have a track record of successfully lobbying for state-level CDFI Funds, Community Reinvestment Acts, and tax credits designed to encourage community economic development.[14]

The power of state-level initiatives is best illustrated by California, where public-sector activity over the last decade has encouraged the creation of numerous innovative sources of capital to fund community development finance. In 1996, The Community Organized Investment Network (COIN) was established in the state at the request of the insurance industry as an alternative to state legislation that would have required insurance companies to invest in underserved communities. As of 2003, it had facilitated more than $740 million in insurer investments in affordable housing and economic development projects.

The COIN program also certifies California CDFIs, which then become eligible for investments from the COIN managed pool of capital. Most recently, COIN member insurance companies were responsible for the creation and capitalization of Impact Community Capital, which has been an innovator in securitizing multifamily mortgages in low- and moderate-income communities.

In 1997, California adopted a 20 percent tax credit for qualified deposits of $50,000 or more in CDFIs in the state. In 2001, the program was extended for five more years.

In May 2000, State's Treasurer Philip Angelides launched *The Double Bottom Line: Investing in California's Emerging Markets Initiative,* "to direct investment capital—through state programs and the State's pension and investment funds—to spur economic growth in those California communities left behind during the economic expansion of the past decade" (Angelides 2001, 1). As part of this initiative, Angelides successfully encouraged the boards of two of California's largest public pension funds, on which he serves, to invest in real estate and businesses in the state's poorest communities. The two pension funds, the California Public Employees' Retirement System (CalPERS) and the California State Teachers' Retirement System (CalSTRS), have so far made $4.34 billion in real estate and $1.09 billion in business investments in such communities (Angelides 2005).

One indication of how successful these initiatives have been is a forthcoming report by the Milken Institute that found, contrary to national trends, that developmental finance institutions in the state are not experiencing any shortages of capital (Interview with Betsy Zeidman, June 21, 2006). Not surprisingly, the Bay Area Equity Fund, the largest community development venture capital fund in the country, is based in California.

Pension Funds

U.S. pension funds control over $7 trillion in assets (Anand 1998). This includes public pension funds, which manage the retirement assets of state and local government employees and have more than $2.8 trillion in assets (Moore 2002); Taft-Hartley pension funds, which are managed jointly by labor unions and employer groups and have approximately $420 billion in assets (Heim 2002); and corporate pension funds, which manage the pension assets of corporate employees.

Historically, most pension fund assets have been very conservatively invested, due in large part to the prevailing interpretation of ERISA (the Employee Retirement Income Security Act of 1974), which Congress enacted in response to numerous private sector pension scandals. Before 1994, ERISA was interpreted to mean that investments could only be selected for their economic return and safety. In 1994, the Department of

Labor issued an interpretive bulletin on the subject, stating that economically targeted investments (ETIs), which are "investment programs designed to produce a competitive rate of return as well as create collateral economic benefits for a targeted geographic area, group of people, or sector of the economy" (McNeill and Fullenbaum 1995, 1), were allowable as long as they met the benchmark financial return rate of comparable investments with comparable risks. If the investment could not be expected to meet the risk-adjusted rate of return for the asset class, it was improper, regardless of the social benefits (Logue and Clem 2006).

Some of the public and Taft-Hartley pension funds have incorporated economically targeted investments (ETIs) into their portfolios (for an overview of how public pension funds began making ETI investments, see Democracy Collaborative 2005). Conservative estimates place the ETI commitments of public pension funds at more than $43 million (Democracy Collaborative 2005).

To date, most of the pension fund ETI investments have been in fixed income and real estate. The real estate focus has created an opportunity for CDLFs to access this capital, if they can provide the scale and rate of return that pension funds require. One example of a pension fund investment in a CDLF is the $25 million loan that the New York City Public Pension Funds made to the Community Preservation Corporation's Revolving Construction Loan Fund, which "makes short-term construction loans for affordable housing, mixed-use development and commercial properties in low- and moderate-income areas" (NYC Comptroller 2006, 1). An open-ended request for proposals asking for debt-based ETIs is posted on the Web site of the New York City comptroller, who advises the five New York City Public Pension Funds.

A growing number of pension funds also have included venture capital as an allowable investment. Pension funds now account for more than 50 percent of all the capital placed in venture funds (National Venture Capital Association 2006). Pension funds have been reluctant, however, to make private equity ETI investments, because of both cost and risk. Only a few of the most innovative have done so. The most notable among these is the California Public Employees Retirement System's $500 million California Initiative to target companies in the state's underserved markets (Hess 2006). In 2001, the California Initiative selected ten private equity firms to receive a capital commitment of $475 million (Hess 2006). Pacific Community Ventures, a San Francisco–based CDVC, was among these ten and received a $10 million investment (Pacific Community Ventures 2005).

Although pension investments in CDVCs are still the exception, they are likely to increase if the CDVC funds can demonstrate an appropriate risk-adjusted rate of return and an ability to absorb larger investments. Despite CalPERS' willingness to invest $10 million in Pacific Community Ventures, pension funds generally prefer to make larger investments because the costs of due diligence are the same regardless of investment size.

More pension funds are adding private equity to their ETI portfolios, including NYCERS (the New York City Employees' Retirement System), which set out a policy in August of 2005 to move into private equity investments and to target low-moderate income areas in the five boroughs of New York City (Hess and Hagerman 2005). Given the geographic nature of most public pension fund ETI investments, developmental venture capital funds that invest in states whose public pension funds are willing to make private equity ETI investments have a much greater chance of attracting pension fund capital.

Individual Investors

Individuals have been a source of capital for community development finance from the field's beginnings. The first community development loan funds relied on individual contributions through below-market rate loans that the loan funds could use to fund their own lending activities. Likewise, Shorebank, the first community development bank, originated the idea of using individual deposits that paid a lower-than-market rate of return in exchange for the social benefits that result from the bank's activities.

At present, community development banks and credit unions rely on individual investments for approximately three-quarters of their capital (CDFI Data Project 2007a). Much of this is in the form of government-insured certificates of deposit (Phillips 2006). For nondepository CDFIs, however, socially responsible investors make up a fairly small percentage of all capital sources. In 2005, for example, community development loan funds received only 3 percent of their investment capital from individuals (CDFI Data Project 2007a). Although there is anecdotal indication that some CDVC funds recently have been able to attract larger investments from individuals, they accounted for only 6 percent of all CDVC investments as of 2000, the last year for which this data is available for the entire industry.

Community development loan and venture funds face a number of challenges in attracting individual investors. First, unlike banks and credit unions, they cannot offer insured deposits. Their products also are more diverse and difficult to explain to investors, making them more challenging to sell than conventional offerings. Additional challenges include a perception by investors that community investments are higher risk, and the fact that CDFIs offer lower broker commissions, which can translate into reduced incentives for brokers to offer community investment products (Kanders 2002). As the field of social investing continues to evolve, however, CDLFs and CDVCs increasingly are looking at individuals as a potentially important source of future capital.

Individuals can invest in specific CDFIs directly through an equity investment in a CDVC or a loan to a CDLF. Most CDVC funds will accept equity investments of $50,000 or more from individuals, primarily as part of limited partnerships and limited liability corporations (MacDonald 2005). SJF Ventures, a fund that invests in companies whose competitive advantages include environmental or workforce innovation, has found individual investors increasing receptive to investing in its funds. Many of these individuals have experience as angel investors and have found it easier and safer to invest with a CDVC. Although their investments are generally smaller than those of commercial banks, such individuals are high value-added investors because they provide additional due diligence on individual deals and refer potential portfolio companies to the fund.

CDLFs, which are primarily nonprofit and thus unable to accept equity investments except as grants, generally structure their investments from individuals as low-interest loans. The Reinvestment Fund (TRF), a CDFI headquartered in Philadelphia, offers individuals the option of investing as little as $1,000 for a period of three to ten years. TRF admits that the financial return on such loans is "modest," but argues that the social return "is enormous" (2006a, 4).

Individuals also can invest in CDFIs via intermediaries, which aggregate the capital and provide due diligence on different CDFIs. Intermediaries include socially responsible investment organizations such as the Calvert Foundation, Trillium Asset Management, and Domini Social Investments, which offer community investments as a specialized asset class or as part of bond and money market funds. The minimum investment sizes vary. Calvert's community investment notes, which had raised $100 million as of June 2006, has a minimum investment of $1,000 and Trillium will not accept any individual clients with less than $1 million (Calvert Foundation 2006; Trillium Asset Management 2006). Some CDFI trade associations also serve as investment intermediaries for both large and small individual investors. The Community Development Venture Capital Alliance (CDVCA), for example, has a central fund that accepts individual loans of as little as $10,000 for ten years.

CDFIs also are borrowing from the higher education and foundation models and encouraging investors to dedicate the proceeds of a trust to them or include them in their estate planning. TRF's investment application, for example, asks investors if, in the event of their deaths, they want to donate any outstanding principal from their loans to the organization (2006b).

The Social Investment Forum, an organization of socially conscious asset managers, estimated that by 2003, $14 billion dollars had been allocated to community investments. Most of this capital, however, has come from institutional investors rather than individuals. To attract more investors, the Social Investment Forum established the 1 percent or more in Community Campaign—to encourage individuals to allocate 1 percent of their investment portfolios to community investments. The campaign's current goal is to "grow the community investing industry to more than $25 billion in assets in 2007" (Community Investing Center 2006, 1).

Accessing Market-Rate Capital: Securitization and Structured Financings

Given the decreasing availability of subsidized capital, significant energy is being focused on finding ways to fund CDFI activities via market-rate capital and the traditional capital markets. Two possibilities that have proven effective for CDLFs are the use of structured financings and securitization. Structured financings enable certain assets with more or less predictable cash flows to be isolated from the originator and used to mitigate risks, and thus secure a credit (Hew 2000). One type of such structured financing is a pool of capital that includes a loan from conventional investors secured by a grant, program related investment, or guarantee from a foundation or government entity. This is the model used in raising a fund to finance community child-care center facility development and renewal in low-income communities in California, which resulted from a partnership between the Low-Income Investment Fund (LIIF), a national CDLF; Impact Community Capital, a consortium of insurance companies; and the Packard Foundation. The insurance company investors provided $10 million in long-term capital, the Packard Foundation provided a $1 million first-loss guarantee and $3 million for "technical assistance, systems building and infrastructure improvements," and LIIF provides origination, underwriting and servicing expertise (Dunlap, Okagaki and Seidman 2005, 7).

Another type of structured financing is a pool of loans that includes senior and subordinate tranches. The senior tranche is sold to private investors, and the subordinate tranche is held by the CDFI and secured by grants. An example of this type of transaction is the National Cooperative Bank Development Corporation's (NCBDC) Enhancement Fund for Charter Schools, which is using "an $8 million grant from the U.S. Department of Education (DOE) to leverage $80 million in private sector financing for charter school facilities development in four states" (Dunlap, Okagaki and Seidman 2005, 8).[15] NCBDC, a national CDFI, sells the A tranche to investors and uses the DOE grant as a first loss reserve to back the subordinate B tranche, which it holds (Dunlap, Okagaki and Seidman 2005; NCB 2005).

Securitization consists of aggregating loans with similar characteristics and selling them to investors. It revolutionized the mortgage finance industry in the 1970s, dramatically increasing the supply of available capital and enabling millions more people to purchase a home. It also holds the promise of significantly increased liquidity for CDFIs that have loaned out most or all of their available funds (Stanton 2003).

Selling loans to free up capital is not a new concept for CDFIs, many of which have sold their loans to commercial banks and to the Community Reinvestment Fund (CRF), a national nonprofit headquartered in Minneapolis, which since 1989 has operated a secondary market for CED loans. Historically, however, these loan purchases were made by a socially motivated and thus limited pool of investors.[16] Furthermore, despite their historically low loss rates, CDFIs have had to discount their loans in order to make them attractive to banks and to the Community Reinvestment Fund, reducing the amount of capital produced by such transactions.

The industry needed to bring non–socially motivated investors to the table and to make them comfortable with the CED loan product, which they perceived as performing less well than loans from conventional financial institutions. To make their loans a viable option for institutional investors, the industry also had to offer a product that was at a scale of $50 million and above, the size necessary to make a public placement cost efficient (Dunlap, Okagaki and Seidman 2005). The solution was to combine loans from multiple organizations and to have them rated by a Wall Street rating agency, making the investment attractive to mutual funds, insurance companies, and pension funds.

This happened for the first time in 1999 when the Neighborhood Housing Services of America "obtained an "AA" rating from Standard and Poor's for a $75 million issue of non-conventional, affordable residential mortgages (Moy and Okagaki 2001). It happened again in 2002 when Impact Community Capital LLC obtained Standard & Poor's rating on a pool of low- and moderate-income multifamily housing loans. Almost 90 percent of the pool, worth approximately $145 million, was rated, with 90 percent of that receiving a rating of AAA. The loans in the pool came primarily from Bank of America, with an additional 10 percent originated by the California Community Reinvestment Corporation, a nonprofit multibank lending consortium (Moriarty and Fitzpatrick 2002).

A third milestone occurred in 2004 when the Community Reinvestment Fund obtained Standard & Poor's rating on a $46 million pool of community development loans originated by various CDLFs, CDCs, and government lenders. Fifty-seven percent of the pool obtained a rating of AAA (Swack 2004). In both Impact's and CRF's transactions, the highest risk portion of the loans was not rated and was held by the aggregators, with the support of subsidized capital from socially oriented sources. In 2006, CRF obtained a Standard & Poor's rating on a second pool of loans. Both of CRFs offerings were oversubscribed, attracting a number of new insurance, banking, and pension fund investors to community development finance (for a case study of CRF's first rated transactions, see Swack 2004).

Although these examples demonstrate that the traditional capital markets can be used to bring new investors to community development finance, there still are obstacles to making this an ongoing source of capital for more CDFIs. The most significant is a lack of standardization in loan performance data, documentation, and underwriting procedures. Each CDFI handles these functions its own way, which complicates the securitization process and is perceived by investors as increasing risk (GAO 2003).

A second major barrier is the lack of infrastructure to support these types of transactions. To make securitization a viable alternative for more lenders, there need to be consistent ways for lenders to sell loans to aggregators and for aggregators to achieve the volume of loans needed for a securitization. There also needs to be a way of ensuring quality control throughout the process (GAO 2003).

Another stumbling block is the lack of mechanists for forecasting future borrower demand for community development loans, which leaves open the possibility of low future demand, which could reduce loan volume and hamper securitization. Others include lack of capacity on the part of some community development lenders and the belief on the part of many lenders that their loans will be substantially discounted in the securitization process (GAO 2003).

Several initiatives are under way to overcome the remaining barriers and make securitization a viable, ongoing way for CDLFs to access capital. Already, Frank Altman, CRF's president and CEO, notes that CED lenders' knowledge of and comfort level with securitization has grown. "When CRF first began operating, many lenders only sold loans on an as-needed basis. Increasingly, CED lenders are selling loans before they run out of loan capital. 'That has led many groups to be repeat sellers,' says Altman. 'They've developed a schedule' " (Pohlman 2004, 4).

Securitization may also hold the promise of increased liquidity for CDVCs. Elyse Cherry, CEO of the Boston Community Capital, a CDFI with two community development venture funds in its portfolio, has been working on a model for a viable secondary market for CDVC investments and those in small to medium-sized companies made by more traditional venture capital funds. Cherry envisions the creation of an entity that could help these funds exit their investments and gain liquidity by purchasing from them their ownership in small companies that are performing well enough to generate a healthy profit (for example, 10 to 15 percent annually), but do not have the growth projections likely to generate an exit through an external purchase or an IPO. The entity would securitize these investments and sell them on the secondary market to investors interested in a stable, ongoing stream of income.

Repositioning and Rethinking

In addition to identifying innovative ways to attract capital to make growth possible, CDLFs and CDVCs are rethinking their business models to become more sustainable and less reliant on subsidized capital. Toward that end, many of them have undertaken strategic planning processes to determine how to reach this objective (Dunlap, Okagaki and Seidman 2005). For CDLFs, the resulting innovations have included:

- Identifying and focusing on the most lucrative and socially meaningful activities, while outsourcing others, such as loan processing and back office operations, to cut expenses.

- Finding ways to use market rate capital by drawing on in-depth knowledge of local markets to create products that conventional financial institutions consider too high risk.

- Forming partnerships and networks to cut costs.

- Tying access to capital to other priorities (for example, workforce development, education, sufficiency of housing, continuation of welfare reform) to build new coalitions and attract new sources of philanthropic dollars that share those programmatic objectives.

As discussed previously, CDLFs also have diversified their base of borrowers and their mix of products. Entities that used to be focused principally on serving community development corporations now include public housing authorities, private developers, and other community organizations among their borrowers. Business and multifamily housing lenders now finance a range of community facilities as well.

CDVCs also are considering alternatives that would enable them to access new sources of capital. However, the industry is divided as to how to proceed. Many current and potential investors associate CDVCs with smaller capitalization levels, tightly drawn geographic target areas, small deals, and low financial returns. Those CDVC funds that have moved away from this model want to broaden the field to change perceptions of the industry to make it possible to raise more capital. They point to other examples of socially oriented venture capital that CDVCs could incorporate, such as minority and female-focused funds or funds that invest in clean technology. Despite having both social and financial objectives, these kinds of venture funds market themselves as able to deliver competitive financial returns and have attracted billions of dollars from traditional investors.

Other CDVC managers advocate that the industry include funds that make double-bottom line equity investments in real estate, such as the UrbanAmerica and Genesis funds, which have been able to raise hundreds of millions of dollars. Still others suggest that CDVCs reposition themselves to fill the void of equity investments of under $5 million in geographies not served by traditional venture capital. They argue that this could become especially attractive as the number of SBIC funds making equity investments shrinks in response to the elimination of SBA leverage for participating security SBICs.[17] Individual funds have pursued some of these ideas, but the industry as a whole has yet to embrace them.

CONCLUSIONS

Community development loan and venture funds are at a critical junction. The economic and political environment of the late 1990s, which facilitated their growth in numbers and size of assets, is unlikely to return. The last five years have also brought increased competition for capital in the form of new financial products that promise both community impact and market-rate returns. To be able to access new capital in this environment, they need better to understand and document the social and financial outcomes of their work. This includes their role as policy advocates on behalf of low-income communities, as innovators that demonstrate to conventional financial institutions the viability of this market, as intermediaries that bring together other sources of capital to make projects and programs possible, and as direct providers of financial products, services, and education. Foundations and universities should make available the financial and academic resources necessary to make these evaluations both rigorous and effective.

Given the limited pool of social capital, CDLFs and CDVCs must find new ways of using market-rate capital, and of accessing new sources of capital, such as pension funds and broad-based securitization, in order to continue growing and serving the needs of low- and moderate-income communities. However, funders should not lose sight of the field's ongoing need for subsidy. Subsidy is necessary to finance the technical assistance and smaller investment sizes that are at the heart of the CDVC model. Subsidy also is necessary to finance the continual innovation and risk-taking that have enabled CDLFs to demonstrate repeatedly the viability of new products; to maintain an in-depth knowledge of the low- and moderate-income communities that they serve; and to provide extensive technical assistance, microloans, nonprofit operating loans, and predevelopment financing, which are generally not cost efficient. Without ongoing subsidies, the ability of both CDLFs and CDVCs to serve low-income communities would be greatly diminished.

The federal government played a critical role in the formation of community development financial institutions, most recently with the Community Reinvestment Act and the CDFI Fund. In the face of shrinking federal support, however, CDLFs also should look to individual states. California provides an excellent model for how states can make capital available for community economic development and of the important role that public policy plays in spurring private investment.

The low- and moderate-income communities that CDLFs serve are facing an increasingly difficult environment. The U.S. poverty rate has grown since 2000, whereas funding of services for the country's neediest has shrunk. The products, services, and knowledge that CDLFs and CDVCs provide are needed more than ever. These organizations serve a critical public good and should not be allowed to fail.

NOTES

1. For clarity, this chapter treats CDLFs and CDVCs as distinct entities. However, it is not at all uncommon for CDLFs to make equity investments out of their loan fund capital or for CDVCs to make loans. CDFIs are becoming increasingly more complex in their organizational structures, and many of the larger CDFIs include both loan and venture fund subsidiaries, with some also including a depository institution such as a community development bank or credit union, in the mix.

2. Since 2001, annual data about a larger number of community development loan funds has become available via the CDFI Data project (CDP), an industry collaborative comprised primarily of membership organizations representing the various CDFI institutional types, and a group of project funders. CDP data is self-reported by the participating organizations. For more information on the CDP see http://www.communitycapital.org/community_development/finance/cdfi_data_project.html.

3. Some CDLFs require that potential borrowers first apply to a conventional lender, and will only accept applicants who have been rejected once or twice by banks and traditional financial institutions.

4. The total number of community development loan funds is an estimate provided by the Opportunity Finance Network. This figure includes microenterprise funds. In 2005, the CDFI Data Project surveyed 151 of the approximately 500 CDLFs in existence. This chapter focuses on a subset of those CDLFs for whom microloans of $35,000 or less, constituted less than 50 percent of their financing activities. There were ninety-eight such organizations in the 2005 CDP sample. The CDLF data presented in this chapter is based on those ninety-eight. Loan funds that primarily or exclusively make microenterprise loans have a different economic model than CDLFs that make larger loans. For more on microenterprise and microfinance, see chapter 4 of this volume.

5. Two of the ninety-eight loan funds in the CDP Data Project data base had a for-profit legal structure.

6. The remaining 32 percent of CDLF capital consisted of equity. Because most CDLFs are nonprofit in legal form, this equity primarily took the form of grants. The debt figure also includes equity equivalent investments (EQ2s), "highly subordinated debt instruments with features such as rolling term and limited right-to-accelerate payments that enable them to function similar to equity. Banks are the primary investors in EQ2s because of the favorable CRA treatment . . . [EQ2s] typically are long-term capital (7–15 years) that allows CDFIs to leverage additional debt" (CDFI Data Project 2006, 38).

7. Percentages based on analysis of ninety of the ninety-eight CDLFs in the 2005 CDFI data project. Analysis excluded six CDLFs that did not provide the relevant information and the two largest CDLFs, Self Help and Local Initiatives Support Corporation (LISC), which had unique funding streams whose size skewed the overall results.

8. Community Development Loan Funds offer a range of financial instruments. Products offered to businesses include senior and subordinate debt, working capital loans, machinery and equipment loans, loans for purchase and renovation of commercial real estate, and loan guarantees. Product offered for housing and facility construction include acquisition and predevelopment loans, financing that enables the project developer or sponsor to gain control of the property in question and cover the pre-construction costs (related to environmental assessments, architectural and legal fees, permitting, for example) associated with development and/or rehabilitation. A variation of this loan is the predevelopment grant, a smaller, zero-interest loan designed specifically to cover the preliminary, nonconstruction costs associated with a project. If the project does not go forward, the CDLF may choose to waive repayment. In either case, the loans tend to feature interest-only payments until maturity, when the borrower repays the entire principal amount. In addition to the early stage financing, CDFIs frequently provide some sort of a short-term construction loan or line of credit. This loan often is repaid by more conventional capital (a bank first mortgage, for example) once construction gets to a certain stage and the project's overall completion risk has diminished accordingly. Some CDFIs offer "mini-perms," mortgages with terms of up to ten years, to higher-risk projects. For the most part, these loans feature regular principal and interest repayments, although amortization schedules may be based on extended (twenty-year, for example) maturities. CDLF loans generally tend to be short- to medium-term in length. Some CDLFs also provide businesses with equity or near-equity capital.

9. See http://www.responsiblelending.org.

10. CDVCA, the industry's trade association, calculated the financial performance of three of the industry's oldest funds. It found that these funds had achieved an internal rate of return of 15.5 percent (Schmitt 2004). However, because these three funds were not structured as limited life, for-profit entities, it was not possible to break out their overhead expenses and factor them into the financial analysis. This severely limited the evaluation of their financial performance, as their overhead costs are substantial and would undoubtedly skew the relevant figures.

11. CDVCA has performed several analyses of social returns using the data available. The first analysis compared the employment figures reported by seventeen CDVC funds that provided data on the number of full-time equivalents their portfolio companies employed at the time of their investment and at the end of 2003. Based on these figures, CDVCA computed a 46 percent change in employment. Nine CDVC funds also tracked whether the jobs created went to low-income individuals. Based on this data, CDVCA projected that most of the job growth in CDVC portfolio companies was among low-income, full-time equivalent employees. The number of such employees increased by 124 percent from the time of first investment until the end of 2003, but non–low-income FTEs increased by only 37 percent. Finally, CDVCA used data from three funds that tracked and reported employment figures at the portfolio company level to create a five-year model portfolio that included thirty-eight companies financed by the three funds. Based on this self-reported fund data, CDVCA found that the thirty-eight companies had added 4,335 jobs (Schmitt 2004).

12. Although the review had been agreed to at the time of the 1995 amendments, the nature of the amendments reflects the political preferences of the Bush administration as the four regulatory bodies are controlled entirely by appointees of the president. The director of the Office of Thrift Supervision and the comptroller of the currency were both appointed by President G. W. Bush. Both the director of the OTS and comptroller of the currency sit on the FDIC board, which also includes two other appointees of President Bush. All seven members of the Federal Reserve Board of Governors, which oversees regulation for the Federal Reserve, were appointed by President Bush.

13. This consolidation was referred to as the Strengthening America's Communities Initiative. In 2006, it called for eliminating eighteen economic and community programs and consolidating their activities into a new program, to be administered by the Department of Commerce. It also called for cutting funding from the $5.6 billion the eighteen pro-

grams received in 2005 to $3.7 billion for the new program. The 2007 version of the Strengthening America's Communities Initiative called for a similar consolidation and funding reduction, but the Community Development Block Grant program and a few smaller programs would remain at the Department of Housing and Urban Development. The consolidation proposals failed, following strong resistance from Congress.

14. States with CDFI Fund-like entities created to support community development finance through grants and investments include California, New York, Illinois, Maryland, Pennsylvania, and New Jersey. In 1998, Massachusetts also legislated the creation of two insurance company investment pools for the purpose of investing funds in community development efforts in the state. Each was capitalized at $100 million. State-level CRAs applicable to state-chartered banks were enacted in New York in 1978 and in Massachusetts in 1997. The Massachusetts regulations are, in many ways, more expansive than the federal ones. Tax credits for which CDFIs are eligible were enacted in California in 1997 and South Carolina in 2000.

15. As of September 2005, NCB had assembled and made available the first $40 million (NCB 2005).

16. Banks purchased CED loans as part of their obligations under the Community Reinvestment Act, whereas the Community Reinvestment Fund used grants and program related investments from foundations and social investors to subsidize the portfolios it sold in private placements to banks, thrifts, insurance companies, pension funds and other qualified institutional investors. Self-Help's program was supported by the Ford grant discussed previously.

17. The U.S. Small Business Administration stopped granting Participating Security leverage commitments on September 30, 2004, and is not licensing any more Participating Security SBICs (Petillon 2005). This occurred after the Office of Management and Budget assessed losses of $2 billion and the Administration decided that the program is not needed as comparable financing was being provided by the SBIC debenture program.

REFERENCES

Anand, Vineeta. 1998. "Market Contributions Boost Pension Assets." *Pensions & Investments,* October 19, 1998.

Angelides, Philip. 2001. "The Double Bottom Line: Investing in California's Emerging Markets." *Ideas to Action.* June. Sacramento, Calif.: California

State Treasurer's Office. Accessed June 15, 2006 at http://www.treasurer.
ca.gov/publications/DBL.htm.

———. 2005. "Double Bottom Line Investment Initiative Five Years Later:
Delivering on Both Bottom Lines." *Ideas to Action.* October. Sacramento,
Calif.: California State Treasurer's Office. Accessed at http://www.
treasurer.ca.gov/publications/dbl/five_years.pdf.

Avery, Robert B., Raphael W. Bostic, and Glenn B. Canner. 2000. *The
Performance and Profitability of CRA-Related Lending.* Washington: Board of
Governors of the Federal Reserve System.

Avery, Robert B., Raphael W. Bostic, Paul S. Calem, and Glenn B. Canner.
1999. "Trends in Home Purchase Lending: Consolidation and the
Community Reinvestment Act." *Federal Reserve Bulletin* 1999(February):
81–102. Accessed at http://federalreserve.gov/pubs/bulletin/1999/
0299lead.pdf.

Barr, Michael S. 2005. "Credit Where it Counts: The Community
Reinvestment Act and Its Critics." *New York University Law Review* 80(2): 513.

Bates, Tim, William Bradford, & Julia Sass Rubin. 2006. "The Viability of
the Minority-Oriented Venture-Capital Industry Under Alternative
Financing Arrangements." *Economic Development Quarterly* 20(2): 178–91.

Benjamin, Lehn, Julia Sass Rubin, and Sean Zielenbach. 2004. "Community
Development Financial Institutions: Current Issues and Future
Prospects." *Journal of Urban Affairs* 26(2): 177–95.

Bostic, Raphael, Hamid Mehran, Anna Paulson, and Marc Saidenberg. 2002.
"Regulatory Incentives and Consolidation: The Case of Commercial Bank
Mergers and the Community Reinvestment Act." *Federal Reserve Bank of
Chicago* Working Paper 2002-06. Washington: Board of Governors of
the Federal Reserve System.

CDFI Data Project. 2006. *Providing Capital, Building Communities, Creating Impact,*
4th ed. Arlington, Va. Accessed at http://www.cdfi.org/cdfiproj.asp.

———. 2007a. Self-reported 2005 information on CDFIs. Available from
Opportunity Finance Network, Philadelphia, Pa.

———. 2007b. *Providing Capital, Building Communities, Creating Impact,* 5th ed.
Arlington, Va. Accessed at http://www.cdfi.org/cdfiproj.asp.

CDFI Fund. 2005. "New Markets Information Session." August 4, 2005.
Accessed June 5, 2006 at http://www.cdfifund.gov/docs/nmtc/2005/
NMTCoutreachPresentation8-4-05.pdf.

CDVCA. 2006. "CDVC Statistics." http://www.cdvca.org. Accessed July 1,
2006 at http://www.cdvca.org/index.cfm?fuseaction=Page.viewPage&
pageID=321.

Calvert Foundation. 2006. "Calvert Community Investment Notes."
Accessed at http://www.calvertfoundation.org/products_and_services/
community_investment_notes/.

Caskey, John P., and Robinson Hollister. 2001. "Business Development Financial Institutions: Theory, Practice, and Impact." *Institute for Research on Poverty* Discussion Paper no. 1240-01. Madison, Wisc.: University of Wisconsin.

Community Investing Center. 2006. "The 1% or More in Community Investing Campaign." Accessed at http://www.communityinvest.org/investors/campaign.cfm.

Democracy Collaborative. 2005. *Building Wealth: The New Asset-Based Approach to Solving Social and Economic Problems.* Washington: The Aspen Institute Nonprofit Sector Research Fund.

Dunlap, Helen, Alan Okagaki, and Ellen Seidman. 2005. *Review of the Current State of Community and Economic Development Finance: A Memo to Funders.* White paper prepared for the John D. and Catherine T. MacArthur Foundation. December 7, 2005.

The Economist. 2006. "Thinking Big." *The Economist* 379(8478): 3–6.

F. B. Heron Foundation. 2004. *F. B. Heron 2004 Annual Report.* New York: The F. B. Heron Foundation. Accessed at http://www.fbheron.org/2004ar.pdf.

Ford Foundation. 1998. "Ford Foundation Grant of $50 Million Will Generate $2 Billion in Affordable Mortgages For 35,000 Low-Wealth Home Buyers." Press Release. Accessed at http://www.fordfound.org/newsroom/view_news_detail.cfm?news_index=7.

Grossman, Brian, Andrea Levere, and Kent Marcoux. 1998. *Counting on Local Capital.* Washington: Corporation for Enterprise Development.

Heim, Steven. 2002. "Workers and Their Capital: Labor Unions as Shareholder Activists." Boston, Mass.: Walden Asset Management. Accessed at http://www.waldenassetmgmt.com/social/action/library/0204li.html.

Hess, Tessa. 2006. "Public Pension Funds and Urban Revitalization." California Case Study A: Private Equity CalPERS' California Initiative. Presented at the Regional Investment Roundtable on Sustainable Job Growth, Pittsburgh, Pa., June 5, 2006. Accessed at http://urban.ouce.ox.ac.uk/network.

Hess, Tessa, and Lisa Hagerman. 2005. "Best Practices in Pension Fund Urban Investments." Paper presented at the Pension Funds and Urban Revitalization seminar. Hartford, Conn., October 25, 2005. Accessed at http://urban.ouce.ox.ac.uk/notes051025.pdf.

Hew, David. 2000. "Structured Finance Deals: How Do They Work and Will They Work?" Presented at High-level Regional Consultative Meeting on Financing for Development Asia and the Pacific. Jakarta, Indonesia, August 2–5, 2000. Accessed at http://www.unescap.org/drpad/projects/fin_dev/hew.ppt.

Hovanesian, Mara Der. 2005. "The New Corporate ATMs." *Business Week Online,* October 10, 2005. Accessed at http://www.businessweek.com/magazine/content/05_44/b3957065.htm.

Jackson, Eric K., and Josh Lerner. 1996. "Northeast Ventures: January 1996." Harvard Business School Case Number 9-296-093. Revised edition. Cambridge, Mass.: Harvard Business School. Accessed at http://harvard businessonline.hbsp.harvard.edu/b02/en/cases/cases_home.jhtml.

Kanders, Kristin. 2002. "Social Investors: New Patrons of Community Development." *Communities & Banking* 18(3)(Summer): 9–12. Accessed at http://www.bos.frb.org/commdev/c&b/2007/summer/summer07.pdf.

Logue, John, and Steve Clem. 2006. "Putting Labor's Capital to Work: Capital Strategies for Ohio Employees." Ohio Employee Ownership Center, Kent State University, May 30, 2006. Accessed at http://dept.kent.edu/oeoc/oeoclibrary/LogueClemLaborCapital.htm.

MacDonald, G. Jeffrey. 2005. "For Investors With a Conscience, Options Grow." *The Christian Science Monitor,* September 19, 2005.

Marsico, Richard D. 2006. "The 2004–2005 Amendments to the Community Reinvestment Act Regulations: For Communities One Step Forward and Three Steps Back." *NYLS Clinical Research Institute* Paper No. 05/06-20. Accessed at http://ssrn.com/abstract=902430

McNeill, Mariana, and Richard Fullenbaum. 1995. *Pension Funds and Small Firm Financing.* Rockville, Md.: M&R Associates. Accessed at http://www.sba.gov/advo/research/rs153.html.

McNichol, Elizabeth C., and Iris J. Lay. 2006. "State Budgets: On the Edge?" Washington: Center on Budget and Policy Priorities. Accessed at http://www.cbpp.org/5-4-06sfp.pdf.

Moore, Richard H. 2002. "State Treasurer Richard Moore Announces Landmark Public Pension Fund Investment Initiative." Press Release. July 1, 2002. Raleigh, N.C.: North Carolina Department of State Treasurer. Accessed at https://www.treasurer.state.nc.us/NR/rdon lyres/AA243C7D-D01B-474A-9BBA-95672BAC2DB2/0/Investment Protection.pdf.

Moriarty, Christopher P., and Ryan Fitzpatrick. 2002. "Impact Community Capital LLC, California: Housing, Affordable Housing." New York: Standard & Poor's. Accessed at http://www.impactcapital.net/research.htm.

Moy, Kirsten, and Alan Okagaki. 2001. *Changing Capital Markets and their Implications for Community Development Finance.* Washington: Brookings Institution.

NCB. 2005. "$40 Million Loan Fund Now Available for Charter Schools in Florida, Georgia, Minnesota & Wisconsin." NCB Development Corporation Communities Enewsletter, September. Accessed at http://www.ncbdc.org/documents/NCBDCCommunities_eNews0905.doc.

NCRC. 2005. "Policy." Accessed at http://www.ncrc.org/policy/cra.

National Venture Capital Association. 2006. "The Venture Capital Industry—An Overview." Accessed at http://www.nvca.org/def.html.

NYC Comptroller. 2006. "Asset Management." Accessed at http://www.comptroller.nyc.gov/bureaus/bam/rfps.shtm.

Pacific Community Ventures. 2005. "About Us: Our Team. Our Commitment to Public/Private Partnerships." Accessed at http://www.pacificcommunityventures.org/aboutus/statementofcommitment.html.

Petillon, Lee R. 2005. "SBIC Program in Transition." Accessed at http://www.abanet.org/buslaw/committees/CL930000pub/newsletter/200507/SBICInTransition.pdf.

Phillips, Ron. 2006. "New Approaches in Social Investing." *Communities & Banking* Winter. Accessed at http://www.community-wealth.org/_pdfs/articles-publications/cdfis/article-phillips.pdf.

Pinsky, Mark. 2001. *Taking Stock: CDFIs Look Ahead After 25 Years of Community Development Finance.* Washington: Brookings Institution. Accessed at http://www.brookings.edu/es/urban/capitalxchange/pinsky.pdf.

Pohlman, Devon. 2004. "With Support, Securitization Could Boost Community Development Industry." *Community Dividend* 2. Accessed at http://www.minneapolisfed.org/pubs/cd/04-2/securitization.cfm.

Rubin, Julia Sass. 1998. "Public Policy and High Growth Firms: The Role of Institutional Forces in the Creation and Growth of Hybrid Social Enterprises." Paper presented at the Babson College-Kauffman Foundation Entrepreneurship research conference. Ghent, Belgium, May 1998.

———. 2001. "Community Development Venture Capital: A Double-Bottom Line Approach to Poverty Alleviation." In *Proceedings of the Changing Financing Markets and Community Development,* Second Federal Reserve System Community Affairs research conference. Washington: Federal Reserve System. Accessed at http://www.chicagofed.org/cedric/files/cfmacd_rubin.pdf

Rubin, Julia Sass and Gregory M. Stankiewicz. 2001. "The Los Angeles Community Development Bank: The Possible Pitfalls of Public-Private Partnerships." *Journal of Urban Affairs* 23(2): 133–53.

———. 2005. "The New Markets Tax Credit Program: A Midcourse Assessment." *Community Development Investment Review.* San Francisco, Calif.: Federal Reserve 1(1): 1–11.

Rubin, Robert E., and Michael Rubinger. 2004. "Don't Let Banks Turn Their Backs on the Poor." *New York Times,* December 4, 2004.

Samolyk, Katherine, and Christopher A. Richardson. 2003. "Bank Consolidation and Small Business Lending within Local Markets." FDIC Working Paper. Accessed at http://www.fdic.gov/bank/analytical/working/wp2003_02/#footnote2.

Schmitt, Brian T. 2004. "CDVCA Report on the Industry 2004." Accessed at http://www.cdca.org.

Stanton, Gregory. 2003. "Unblocking Obstacles to Capital Markets for Community Development Lenders." *Community Economic Development* occasional paper. Manchester: Southern New Hampshire University School of Community Economic Development.

Swack, Michael. 2004. "The Relationships between Community Development Finance and Conventional Capital Markets—Opportunity for Innovation." Paper presented at the Federal Reserve Research Conference on Community Development Finance. New York, December 9, 2004.

TRF. 2006a. "It's Amazing How You Can Transform a Community When You Make the Right Investment." Accessed at http://www.trfund.com/about/pdfs/WhyInvestFINAL.pdf.

———. 2006b. "Investment Application TRF Loan Fund." Accessed at http://www.trfund.com/investors/pdf/APPLICATION.pdf.

Trillium Asset Management. 2006. "Customized Portfolio Management for Individuals & Institutions." Accessed at http://www.trilliuminvest.com/pages/invest/invest_custom.asp.

Tully, Shawn. 2006. "In This Corner! The Contender." Fortune/CNN.com. March 29, 2006. Accessed at http://money.cnn.com/magazines/fortune/fortune_archive/2006/04/03/8373068/index.htm.

U.S. Government Accountability Office (GAO). 2003. *Community and Economic Development Loans: Securitization Faces Significant Barriers.* GAO-04-21. Washington: U.S. Government Printing Office. Accessed at http://www.gao.gov/new.items/d0421.pdf.

Zielenbach, Sean. 2006. Personal correspondence with author.

CHAPTER SIX

The Un-Banks: The Community Development
Role of Alternative Depository Institutions

Marva E. Williams

ONE OF the most important functions of financial institutions is to provide services such as checking and savings accounts. These accounts are the most basic financial assets that most households own (Williams and Hudson 1999) and, when held in insured depository institutions, provide a safe place to keep money, create opportunities to build wealth, and often serve as prerequisites for obtaining other forms of credit. Households without such transaction accounts face a number of financial disadvantages. They typically have to use currency exchanges to cash checks. They also have difficulty establishing the credit history necessary to purchase a home or build other wealth. Overall, low-income households without transaction accounts are 43 percent less likely to have positive holdings of net financial assets, 13 percent less likely to own a home, and 8 percent less likely to own a vehicle than those with such accounts (Carney and Gale 2001). In short, the lack of such services can be a major impediment to asset accumulation and financial security.

Alternative depository institutions, consisting of low-income and community development credit unions and community development banks, play a major role in the United States in addressing the challenges of the unbanked.[1] Their overall objective is to provide low-income individuals and communities with access to financial services as well as to loans for consumers, businesses, and nonprofit organizations that often are neglected by conventional banks. They also enable low-income people to become viable borrowers by providing credit counseling, personal finance management advice, and credit repair programs.

Community development banks provide many of the same services, investments, and loans offered by conventional banks. However, their primary mission is the comprehensive development of lower-income, often minority, communities.

Credit unions are tax-exempt, nonprofit financial cooperatives that provide members with access to affordable savings and checking accounts as well as reasonably priced consumer loans and home mortgages. Membership in a credit union is based on a common bond—referred to as a field of membership. A field of membership may include membership in a church, residence in a community, or employment in a business.

The credit union industry has evolved to include two subsets, low-income credit unions and community development credit unions. Low-income credit union (LICU) is a designation made by the National Credit Union Administration (NCUA), which regulates credit unions, for credit unions that can demonstrate that more than 50 percent of their members have incomes at or below 80 percent of the median income of the community. To support their services to lower-income consumers, low-income credit unions are eligible to receive technical assistance and grants from the NCUA and other sources, and deposits and investments from nonmembers. They also benefit from flexible NCUA fields of membership regulations, allowing them to expand into other communities.

Community development credit unions (CDCUs), or members of the National Federation of Community Development Credit Unions,[2] focus on revitalizing lower-income and minority communities, often in partnership with other community-based organizations (not to be confused with mainstream credit unions with a community field of membership). They play an important role in lower-income communities by providing basic deposit and transaction services and loans, often working in communities that have been abandoned by mainstream financial institutions. In fact, community development credit unions may be the only source of capital in some disadvantaged communities. Many of them focus on youth, offering young people special accounts, leadership training, and opportunities to participate in field trips and conferences.

There is substantial overlap between community development credit unions and low-income credit unions; 86 percent of community development credit unions are also low-income credit unions, and about 25 percent of low-income credit unions are also community development credit unions.

Credit unions and community development banks have advantages over other forms of community development financial institutions (CDFIs).[3] Deposits in banks and credit unions are insured up to $100,000 by the Federal Deposit Insurance Corporation (FDIC), and deposits in credit unions are insured up to $100,000 by the NCUA or private insurance funds. This makes it easier for these institutions to attract funding than it is for community development loan and venture capital funds, which cannot offer a guarantee to their investors.

Deposits in community development banks and credit unions can be used to make loans, which provide revenues to these institutions. Banks and credit unions also benefit from the ability to substantially leverage their equity capital. Banks, for example, often lend out fourteen to twenty times their equity in contrast to a leverage ratio of two to three for nondepository CDFIs (Ellen Seidman Personal correspondence with author, December 5, 2004).

Conversely, unlike community development loan and venture capital funds, community development banks and credit unions are regulated institutions. All community development banks are supervised by one of four federal regulators. State-chartered community development banks also are regulated at the state level. Community development banks must comply with the Community Reinvestment Act (CRA)[4] and the Home Mortgage Disclosure Act (HMDA),[5] which requires them to report their residential lending activity.

Credit unions with national charters are regulated by the National Credit Union Administration and state-chartered credit unions are supervised by state regulators. Additionally, the majority of state-chartered credit unions maintain deposit insurance from the National Credit Union Share Insurance Fund (NCUSIF), which is managed by the NCUA. Therefore, they too are subject to NCUA supervision. Credit unions are not subject to the Community Reinvestment Act. However, credit unions with assets over $33 million are required to file publicly available HMDA reports on their home mortgage applicants and borrowers.[6]

Bank and credit union regulations govern safety and soundness, including capital adequacy, earnings, loan delinquencies, defaults and charge-offs, and management. Safety and soundness regulations can limit the number of "risky" loans a community development bank or credit union can make. These regulations also make it more difficult to organize a new credit union or community development bank. Organizers must raise significant funding or membership pledges and meet other chartering requirements.

Despite these regulations, community development banks and credit unions have developed strategies that allow them to make higher risk loans and not violate safety and soundness regulations. They raise grants from foundations, banks, and others to establish loan-loss reserves so their capital is not at risk. Another strategy is to partner with other community organizations that can guarantee a portion of the loan and to broker and facilitate government loan programs like those of the Small Business Administration.

The next section reviews the industry trends and community development achievements of community development banks, credit unions, low-income credit unions, and community development credit unions.

COMMUNITY DEVELOPMENT BANKS

Community development banks channel deposits, investments, and other funding into loans for affordable housing, commercial development, and other community development projects. As regulated, for-profit financial institutions, community development banks are obligated to operate in a safe and sound manner and bring a return to their investors and shareholders. In fact, community development banks have a double bottom line—they must be financially sustainable and foster community renewal. Their main source of income is the interest earned on deposits and loans from consumers and businesses. They also receive equity from stockholders as well as investments from socially responsible investors. ShoreBank, for example, which is the first and best-known community development bank, has deposits and investments from all fifty states and over seventeen countries (Esty 1995).

Although community development banks remain small relative to their conventional counterparts, with total assets of approximately $11.10 billion and median per-bank assets of $121.59 million (CDFI Data Project 2005), they experienced significant growth in terms of numbers, assets, and deposits since the 1973 founding of ShoreBank. There currently are approximately 100 U.S. banks that have a primary purpose of community development (National Community Investment Fund as cited in the CDFI Data Project 2004). Fifty have been certified as community development financial institutions by the CDFI Fund of the U.S. Department of Treasury, which entitles them to federal funding for developmental activities.

As with all CDFIs, most of the growth among community development banks occurred during the late 1990s (see chapters 1 and 5, this volume). The number of banks with $50 to $100 million in assets doubled from 1996 to 2001 and total deposits increased from $1.72 billion in 1992 to $8.99 billion in 2005 (Bush and Nieman 2002; CDFI Data Project 2005). Community development bank loan volume also grew by more than 250 percent from 1992 to 2001 (Bush and Smith 2003). As of 2005, the fifty-one community development banks surveyed by the CDFI Data Project had $7.23 billion in loans outstanding and $9.97 billion in funds available for lending.

The capitalization levels and profits of community development banks also improved during this period. The median core capital ratio increased from 7 percent in 1992 to 8 percent in 2001, well above the standard of 5 percent for a well-capitalized bank. Return on assets, which assesses a financial institution's profit per dollar of assets, also increased from 0.47 percent in 1992 to 0.63 percent in 2001 (Bush and Nieman 2002). Forty-seven of the fifty-three banks surveyed by the CDFI Data Project in 2004 were profitable, with an average net income of $1.95 million.

Community development banks also appear to have improved their operating efficiency. Operating efficiency ratios measure a bank's operating costs, such as rent and other overhead expenses, as a percentage of total income. A high operating efficiency ratio indicates a lower proportion of funding for services, loans, and programs. Community development banks experienced a declining median efficiency ratio from 1992 to 2001, which indicates better management of operating expenses and improved economies of scale (Bush and Nieman 2002).

Community development banks lend primarily to low-income individuals and to the businesses and nonprofit organizations that serve low-income communities. Forty-nine percent of all community development bank loans went to individuals. These loans were small in size, however, accounting for only 6 percent of all the dollars lent. Small businesses and commercial real estate loans made up only 23 percent of the total number of loans, but 60 percent of the total dollars lent. Housing and agricultural loans accounted for an additional 15 and 9 percent, respectively, of the total dollars lent. The average loan size in 2004 was $69,681.

Whether community development banks operate in rural (30 percent) or in urban (70 percent) environments, their focus consistently is on low-income and minority communities (CDFI Data Project 2005). Approximately 75 percent of community development bank customers are minority and almost 70 percent are lower income (CDFI Data Project 2003). The Woodstock Institute found that community development banks in Chicago made a much higher percentage of their loans to low- and moderate-income (LMI) borrowers than other lenders did (Bush and Nieman 2002). More than half (53 percent) of the single-family residential loans of community development banks were to LMI borrowers, versus 37 percent of the loans of other lenders. Further, more than 70 percent of community development bank single-family residential loans and more than 90 percent of the multifamily loans were made in LMI communities versus 45 percent of the former and 69 percent of the latter made by all other lenders. Community development banks also performed well with minority borrowers and communities. Almost 90 percent of their single-family loans were to minority borrowers and 97 percent of the multifamily loans were in minority communities.

In addition to lending, community development banks also have begun to offer more depository services, to support family asset development, and to provide alternatives to the high cost payday and predatory home mortgage lenders and check cashers that target low- and moderate-income communities. Community development banks offer a wide range of financial services, including direct deposit, electronic funds transfer, money orders, ATMs, and wire transfers (CDFI Data Project 2005). A number of them are experimenting with affordable short-term credit services, including overdraft protection and various alternatives to payday loans (CDFI Data Project 2005). Some offer individual development accounts (IDAs),[7] affordable income tax refund anticipation loans (RALs), and tax preparation counseling.

Community development banks also facilitate innovative financial service partnerships. The Center for Economic Progress (CEP) and ShoreBank launched free tax counseling and preparation assistance to help low-income people file returns for the earned income tax credit (EITC).[8] The Center for Budget and Policy Priorities estimates that taxpayers applying for EITC paid over $1 billion in tax preparation fees and interest on high-cost refund anticipation loans (RALs) in 2001 (Zdenek 2003). The CEP/ShoreBank partnership resulted in 222 new savings accounts with $200,000 in initial deposits in the first two years. By 2003, ShoreBank estimated that it had established about 500 accounts (Fannie Mae Foundation 2003).

Little research has been done examining the overall performance of community development banks, reflecting both the industry's youth and the challenges of evaluating organizations with a double bottom line. Benjamin Esty demonstrated many of these challenges in his 1995 study of Shorebank. He compared housing vacancies, population increases, educational attainment, employment, income, and number of bank branches in the South Shore community, which houses ShoreBank, with those of contiguous communities. His results were mixed. He found that employment rates and condominium vacancies improved in South Shore compared with the other communities. Its performance on other impact factors was worse, however. Esty encountered several methodological challenges when attempting to measure the affect of ShoreBank on the South Shore community. His methodology made it difficult to identify attribution for the changes in the impact factors. Further, he did not measure the affect that ShoreBank may have had in contiguous areas. In addition, the period of the study, from 1970 to 1990, may have been premature (the bank was founded in 1973). As a result, Esty recommended further study to assess the bank's impact.

CREDIT UNIONS

The first credit union in the United States was formed by Alphonse Desjardins in 1909, in response to the high interest rates loan sharks charged working-class consumers (see http://www.ncua.gov/AboutNCUA/historyCU.html). A number of credit unions were formed during the Great Depression, to serve people of modest means who were left out of the mainstream banking system and forced to rely on informal credit from high-cost lenders.

Since its genesis, the credit union movement has expanded appreciably in the United States. By 2002, some 9,688 state- and federal-chartered credit unions held total assets of $557 billion.[9] Credit union membership is also up, increasing from 73.5 million in 1998 to 80.9 million in 2002, a 10 percent rise. Although the industry has grown, it still has a very small market share. As of June 2003, the market penetration of consumer savings accounts by banks and thrifts was 71 percent, versus 10 percent for credit unions (Credit Union National Association 2003).

The guiding principle of credit unions, which are organized as nonprofit cooperatives, is "not for profit, not for charity, but for service." Their governance is also very progressive when compared with other financial institutions. Credit unions are democratically controlled by their members. Further, votes are not commensurate with the amount of deposits. Each member has one voting share. Despite their democratic ethos and nonprofit status, mainstream credit unions have come under increased criticism for not focusing more on low-income or otherwise underserved communities.

Credit unions are not required to collect and disseminate information on the incomes or other characteristics of their members. Using a range of data sources, however, six recent studies have found that mainstream credit unions fail adequately to serve low-income and underserved communities.

In the mid-1990s, the International Labor Organization commissioned a series of studies that assessed the role of credit unions in poverty alleviation. It examined access to financing, outreach to the poor, and the role of partners. The researchers found different degrees of poverty-orientation among credit unions, and that many of those in poor countries, such as those in West Africa, sought to cater to the poor. However, they concluded that though they do not actively exclude poorer members, most credit unions do not specifically seek out the poor. Further, they found that as credit unions grow in size, they have a tendency to serve higher proportions of higher-income consumers (Balkenhol 1999).

Using 1999 data from the Federal Reserve Board's Survey of Consumer Finances, the Filene Institute compared the incomes of households that predominantly[10] use banks or credit unions, with mixed results. The mean household income of consumers that mostly used banks was approximately $63,000, over $3,000 more than those that predominantly used credit unions. The results were somewhat different when examining median household income. The median household income consumers that predominantly used credit unions ($53,000) was $4,000 higher than median household incomes of those that mostly used banks ($49,000). However, consumers that only used banks had median incomes of $30,000, $3,000 more than those who only used credit unions (Lee and Kelly 2001).

The U.S. Treasury surveyed 1,030 of the 1,514 credit unions that had member business loans as of June 1999 (2001). The report found that 13 percent of their outstanding member business loans went to members with household incomes of less than $30,000. Another 20 percent of the loans were to households with incomes between $30,000 and $50,000. However, the Treasury Department believes that these results should be interpreted with caution because of data inaccuracies. First, 80 percent of the credit unions that participated in the survey did not provide any household income data. Treasury reports that these credit unions tended to have the largest member business loan portfolios, and therefore, the household income of borrowers was reported in only 65 percent of all the member business loans. Second, some credit unions may have provided out-of-date household income data that did not reflect the borrower's income at the time of the survey. Treasury's findings must also be regarded within the context of credit union member business lending. In June 2000, only 14 percent of credit unions made member business loans. Further, member business loans, which totaled $4.3 billion, represented only 1.5 percent of the total $287.4 billion loan volume of credit unions in 2000.

In a 2002 report, the Woodstock Institute found that credit unions in the six-county Chicago region serve much higher percentages of middle- and upper-income households than of lower-income households. Only 12 percent of households earning between $10,000 and $20,000 and 23 percent of households earning between $30,000 and $40,000 had a credit union member. By contrast, 40 percent of upper-income households with incomes between $60,000 and $70,000 had a member. The study found that African Americans were slightly more likely to be credit union members. After controlling for income, age, and education level, being African American more than doubled the odds of a person having a credit union account. It also reduced his or her odds of having a bank account by more than half. This finding, the authors argue, is partly explained by the fact that in the Chicago region African Americans may be "overrepresented" in public sector jobs or other highly unionized industries that often sponsor credit unions (Jacob, Bush, and Immergluck 2002).

The Government Accounting Office, renamed the Government Accountability Office in 2004, (GAO) found that a smaller proportion of lower-income consumers used mostly credit unions (36 percent) than banks (42 percent). Households that only or primarily used credit unions were more likely to have moderate to higher incomes than those that only or primarily use banks (2003).

Using 2001 HMDA data, the GAO also identified the income of households that received mortgages from credit unions and banks.[11] It found that credit unions made a lower proportion of mortgage loans to low- and moderate-income households (27 percent) than banks (34 percent). Further, banks appear to serve a larger proportion of consumers at the bottom of the economic ladder. Credit unions made 7 percent of their loans to low-income households, compared with the 12 percent by banks (2003).

In May 2005, the National Community Reinvestment Coalition (NCRC), a coalition of community and consumer organizations that advocate stronger community and consumer protections in the regulations of financial institutions, released a study that compared the lending performance of credit unions and banks over three years, from 2001 to 2003. Using HMDA data, NCRC looked at fourteen measures of fair lending to gauge statewide home purchase, home improvement, and refinance loan patterns of banks and credit unions to minority and lower-income consumers. The study also examined the residential loan trends of credit unions in Massachusetts, the only state with a community reinvestment regulation for state-chartered credit unions.

The NCRC study documented that banks have a better record than credit unions of making loans to lower-income and minority consumers. When all three residential loans are combined, banks outperformed credit unions in thirty-six states. When home purchase lending is analyzed on its own, banks outperformed credit unions in forty states. Further, though credit union performance improved from 2001 to 2003, bank lending still exceeded credit union lending in the great majority of states (National Community Reinvestment Coalition 2005).

NCRC also compared the loan performance of Massachusetts-chartered credit unions, which are subject to a state community reinvestment policy, to federal-chartered credit unions in the state, which are not subject to the law. This analysis documented that credit unions covered by the reinvestment policy outperformed their federal-chartered counterparts 69 percent of the time, leading NCRC to conclude that a federal community reinvestment policy for credit unions could lead to increased loans to underserved consumers.

The credit union industry attacked the NCRC analysis as flawed for several reasons. First, they asserted that credit unions have higher approval rates for mortgage loans for lower-income borrowers than banks. Credit unions approved 72 percent of home mortgages to low-income borrowers, compared with the 48 percent for other lenders in 2003 (Epstein 2005). However, this reasoning may be flawed. The higher denial rate of banks may be due to increased outreach and marketing efforts. Bankers argue that though the number of residential loans to minorities increased significantly as they cast the net more widely, loan applicants became more diverse and included more who do not qualify, resulting in relatively high denial rates. It also is possible that due to the traditional field of memberships associated with employment, applicants for credit union loans may be more qualified.

Second, credit unions also complained about the use of HMDA lending data, asserting that residential lending is a very small portion of credit union loans. They contend that an examination of consumer loan patterns would find different conclusions regarding lending to modest income consumers.

Interestingly, this last concern is shared by community activists. It is true that home mortgages represent a small portion of the loans of credit unions. Further, HMDA is only required for institutions with assets over $33 million, and therefore the lending of smaller institutions is excluded. Unfortunately, HMDA is the only comprehensive, publicly available borrower or customer database for financial institutions. Consumer lending data is not disclosed by banks or credit unions. Further, institutions are not required to disclose data on the race or income of account holders. Community organizations like NCRC and the Woodstock Institute have advocated for additional data disclosures on consumer loans and account holders by credit unions and banks. Financial institutions, including credit unions, have successfully repelled such efforts, complaining that it represents a regulatory burden. This lack of data makes it challenging to assess other loan and financial services market trends, enabling credit unions to reject HMDA analysis and provide anecdotal evidence that they serve low-income and minority borrowers.

Nevertheless, mainstream credit unions are feeling pressure to do more. Community organizations, such as the National Community Reinvestment Corporation and the Woodstock Institute, have developed campaigns intended to improve credit union membership in lower-income communities. These include advocating increased loan and service data disclosures as well as a community reinvestment policy. Further, the Woodstock Institute is working with community organizations to develop partnerships with mainstream credit unions in five cities. The project includes identifying community financial service needs and potential credit union partners, facilitating meetings with credit union managers, negotiating partnership agreements, and monitoring the partnerships.

Credit unions also have been subject to unprecedented levels of pressure from banks that contend that their nonprofit, tax exempt structure allows them unfair advantages when competing for customers by enabling them to provide higher interest payments for accounts, lower rates on loans, and less expensive basic financial services than their banking counterparts. Bank trade associations have advocated that state and federal governments tax credit unions and limit their fields of membership.

Taking a different approach, some academics and community advocates have tried to praise, advise, and persuade credit unions to focus more on low-income communities. Caskey and Humphrey, for example, argue that credit unions are best suited to work with lower-income consumers because of their historical mission to serve individuals with modest incomes and because consumers perceive them as more trustworthy than banks. The authors also contend that increasing services to lower-income consumers can enhance political support for credit unions (Caskey and Humphrey 1999).

The nonprofit status of credit unions is often cited as a reason that they can effectively reach lower-income consumers. Ruth Witzeling cites an example of the establishment of a new credit union branch in a small town in New York that was without financial services for two years. She writes that credit unions, because of their emphasis on service over profit, offer great deals on basic services because, after meeting expense and reserve requirements, they return net earnings to members (1993).

Both Witzeling and Bernd Balkenhol argue that credit unions have a sense of social responsibility that is demonstrated by their willingness to volunteer during emergencies, such as hurricanes, and engage in community efforts like improving literacy, and building playgrounds, and environmental protection projects (Witzeling 1993). Balkenhol maintained that many credit unions in Latin America, Africa, and Asia support microenterprises because their missions are linked to social objectives such as poverty alleviation (Balkenhol 1999).

Several authors have noted that credit union services and delivery systems are tailored to member needs. In addition to basic services, they offer special services and products for distinctive markets, such as youth, college students, or senior programs (Witzeling 1993). Caskey and Humphrey argue that many credit unions offer products and services that are attractive to lower-income consumers. For instance, they allow members to deposit small amounts to accounts, offer higher than normal interest rates, and may also encourage asset development by imposing a financial penalty for early withdrawals and making mortgages to consumers with small down payments (Caskey and Humphrey 1999).

Burger and Zellmer advise credit unions to approach serving lower-income consumers as a business proposition, be willing to innovate with new loan or service products, make saving a key part of the package of services offered, and solicit input from the groups they hope to serve. Member education, they argue, should assume a major role, that credit unions should be prepared for more one-on-one efforts, and that the boards of directors must make a sustained commitment to expand these services (1995). They also provide guidance on program implementation, and suggest that credit unions develop business plans for serving underserved areas and recruit tellers comfortable with a diverse membership (1995).

John Caskey and David Humphrey recommend that those interested in serving more low-income consumers should form partnerships with small credit unions already active in this market, open new branches, add low-income employee groups to their field of membership, and develop new transaction accounts. The authors also suggest that they consider establishing new products, including secured credit cards, low down payment home mortgages, share-secured loans, debt counseling, and savings incentives (1999). Mark Meyer argues that offering check cashing services can also enhance a credit union's suitability for lower-income consumers (2004). Marva Williams advises mainstream credit unions considering a low-income designation to emphasize the provision of financial education and counseling services; establish partnerships with other community organizations or businesses; generate financial support; develop financially sustainable initiatives; and establish effective marketing strategies (2004).

A colloquium organized by the Filene Institute addressed improving services to recent immigrants. They suggested that credit unions desiring to increase the membership of people new to the United States should research the local market, develop services for unbanked immigrants, offer low-cost remittances, provide basic savings products, and explore small loan and mortgage programs. Colloquium presenters also stressed the importance of training staff thoroughly, offering financial literacy education, and establishing special communication programs (Colloquium at the University of California 2003).

Academics and community advocates also have proposed ways that mainstream credit unions can make serving low-income consumers more financially sustainable. Caskey and Humphrey's advice includes developing realistic financial projections and taking steps to ensure that outreach efforts are financially sustainable. They also suggested using the earnings from general membership to support loss-making activities, imposing fees on specific services, lowering service delivery costs by encouraging members to use ATMs and telephone banking, and sharing the cost of services with other partners (1999).

Albert Burger and Mary Zellmer recommended that credit unions can improve their financial sustainability and serve a higher proportion of LMI members by pricing services to reflect costs and risks (1995). James Lambrinos and William Kelly reported that a decrease in the incomes of members did not affect higher loan delinquencies or net charge-offs of the credit unions they studied. They asserted that though the net savings per member did decrease, the credit unions in their sample actually had higher net income as the proportion of lower-income members increased. They suggested that this is due to the fact that the credit unions that participated in their study proceeded with caution and used prudent and tested strategies to reach this population (1996). Developing appropriate loan services can also improve financial sustainability. Burger and Zellmer stressed that credit unions should focus on making loans, not denying them, maintaining credit standards, using credit scoring with caution, tailoring their products to meet members' needs, and building personal relationships with members to encourage their trust and comfort (1995).

Mainstream credit unions are responding in several ways to the negative publicity the studies generated and to the advocacy by banks, community organizations, and academics. The NCUA has given credit unions significant regulatory flexibility to add underserved communities to their fields of membership. As a result, the NCUA reports that from 2000 to 2004, almost 700 federal credit unions adopted 1,215 underserved areas, totaling 92.1 million potential members (NCUA 2005). Unfortunately, the NCUA does not monitor whether these potential members have modest incomes or whether they actually join a credit union.

To serve more low-income individuals, mainstream credit unions also are increasingly establishing geographic fields of membership that allow anyone who lives or works in a community to join, instead of relying primarily on traditional fields of membership associated with an occupation or employer. By doing so, however, they have furthered angered bankers, who charge that adopting such large community fields of membership allows credit unions to compete more effectively for bank customers.

LOW-INCOME CREDIT UNIONS

Low-income credit union is a designation made by the NCUA for credit unions that have documented that the majority of their members have incomes at 80 percent or below the area median. To help support their services to lower-income communities, these organizations are eligible for financial assistance and regulatory flexibility. NCUA allows them to receive deposits from nonmembers. They also are eligible to receive secondary capital investments, which allow them to improve their net worth. Finally, they benefit from additional flexibility in defining their field of membership.

The number of low-income credit unions has grown significantly, from 244 in 1990 to 1,023 in 2004 (see figure 6.1). There are several reasons for the dramatic increase. First, in the early 1990s the NCUA provided additional resources and support for low-income credit unions by expanding the Community Development Revolving Loans Program, which provides low-interest loans and technical assistance grants to low-income designated credit unions. Second, there also was a change in perception by NCUA examiners. Before the 1990s, low-income credit union staff complained that NCUA examiners treated them rudely and were insensitive to or lacked an understanding of community development finance. As a result of advocacy from credit union managers and others, the NCUA established training programs for its examiners on the financial and management challenges of low-income and community-development credit unions. Third, due to pressures on mainstream credit unions to document services to lower-income consumers, CUNA and state credit union leagues have encouraged credit unions to secure low-income designations (Isbister 1994).

Most of the growth in the number of low-income credit unions is in fact directly attributable to this. Only 146 (16 percent) of low-income credit unions in 2002 had low-income designations in 1990. Membership in low-income

Figure 6.1   Number of LICUs, 1990 to 2006

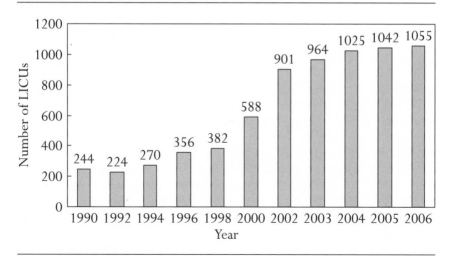

Source: Author's compilation.

credit unions increased by 735 percent over the period, from 343,297 in 1990 to over 2.8 million in 2002. The average number of members per credit union grew by 126 percent, from 1,407 to 3,181. However, membership is still small relative to mainstream credit unions, where the average membership is more than 8,000. Asset size is also on the rise. In 1990, the average low-income credit union had assets of $2.9 million. By 2002, average assets were $14.4 million, an increase of 176 percent (Williams 2004).

Williams found that, as more mainstream credit unions receive a low-income designation, not only is the total number of low-income consumers served increasing, but the re-designated credit unions also appear to serve a higher proportion of modest-income consumers than mainstream credit unions. The average account balance per low-income credit union member was $3,976 in 2002, compared with almost $6,000 for mainstream credit unions. William also found that lending by low-income credit unions to members has grown appreciably, more than 1,700 percent from 1990 to 2002, and that the average loan volume per credit union has increased from $1.9 million in 1990 to $9.4 million in 2002. Despite the increase in loan volume, delinquencies decreased. In 2002, loan delinquencies were 1.7 percent, a decrease of almost 300 points from 1990 (Williams 2004).

COMMUNITY DEVELOPMENT CREDIT UNIONS

Community development credit unions (CDCUs) are credit unions that participate in the National Federation of Community Development Credit Unions. They have a rich history of providing financial services and loans and of participating in community development efforts in lower-income and minority communities.

The oldest community development credit union was chartered in 1930 (CDFI Data Project 2004). Many of the early institutions were formed by African Americans in response to lending discrimination in the South. The number of CDCUs rose dramatically during the civil rights movement, as reflected by their 1967 median date of charter (CDFI Data Project 2004). Others were chartered in the 1980s, in response to community opposition to redlining and bank branch closings. CDCUs currently serve a primarily low- to moderate-income (73 percent), minority (70 percent), and female (59 percent) population. Twenty-nine percent of CDCU members live in rural areas (CDFI Data Project 2005).

CDCUs have grown tremendously in the last few years, due largely to more credit unions self-identifying as community development organizations and joining NFCDCU or becoming certified by the CDFI Fund of the U.S. Treasury. Eighteen new CDCUs also have formed since 2000. Finally, existing CDCUs have grown in members, assets, and loans outstanding (CDFI Data Project 2005).

As of 2005, the 280 CDCUs surveyed by the CDFI Data Project had $5.7 billion in assets and 1.3 million members. These figures were skewed by the eleven largest CDCUs, each of which had assets of $100 million or more. The largest CDCU had assets of more than $1.1 billion. In contrast, the median CDCU had an asset size of $2.4 million and a membership of 1,092 (CDFI Data Project 2005; 2004).

Community development credit unions combine deposits from members and nonmembers with investments and grants from mainstream credit unions, banks, governments, foundations, and corporations, to support lending programs. Member deposits are by far the largest source of CDCU funds, accounting for $4.9 billion (85.7 percent) of the $5.7 billion total, and almost three-quarters of this comes from individuals (CDFI Data Project 2005).

CDCUs also have access to nonmember deposits, from both individuals and organizations. Forty-five percent of all CDCUs took advantage of such deposits, which came primarily from other credit unions (39 percent) and banks (28 percent). CDCUs that have a low-income credit union designation are also allowed by the National Credit Union Administration to raise funds and improve their net worth through secondary capital investments from banks and foundations. These investments are subordinate to all other claims, uninsured, and not redeemable before they mature (CDFI Data Project 2005). Twenty one percent of all CDCUs took advantage of such loans, supplied primarily by CDFI intermediaries (22 percent); non-depository financial institutions (17 percent), and the federal government (12 percent) (CDFI Data Project 2005).

Despite interest income and secondary capital investments, funding deficiencies persist for CDCUs, especially for long-term, subordinated investments. This is often cited as the reason that 50 percent of community development credit unions established in the 1990s failed (Tansey 2001). Other possible factors include the difficulty of sustaining and growing CDCUs due to NCUA restrictions on product offerings (Pinsky 2001), and higher operating costs caused by small scale and higher staff levels relative to assets (Isbister 1994).

Interestingly, higher loan default rates do not appear to be a factor in CDCU failures. Although both Emil Malizia and Virginia Hopley (1997) and John Isbister (1994) documented higher rates of delinquent loans for CDCUs than for mainstream credit unions, Isbister found that charge-off rates were only slightly higher for CDCUs. This seemed to indicate that, though community development credit union borrowers made later loan payments on average, their loans did not go into default.

Lending

Lending is a critical aspect of CDCU operations. As of fiscal year end 2005, CDCUs had 495 thousand loans outstanding totaling $4.2 billion. The median CDCU had 250 loans outstanding, worth $1.5 million (CDFI Data Project

2005). In 2005, CDCUs were able to make loans to more than thirty-seven thousand people who had no credit history. Most CDCU loans are very small, with an average size of $2,178. These "personal development" loans, which account for almost 46 percent of all CDCU loans and 12 percent of all dollars lent, are not for a specific purchase. Rather, they often are intended to allow low- and moderate-income individuals to weather a financial emergency or cover an unanticipated expense.

CDCUs also made 69,980 new auto loans totaling almost $1.03 billion in 2005. These account for approximately 49 percent of all dollars outstanding. Housing is another important area of CDCU lending. In 2005, CDCUs made 10,880 housing loans worth $560 million, including first mortgage loans worth almost $400 million. This accounted for 7 percent of all loans but 30 percent of all loans outstanding (CDFI Data Project 2005).

Several studies have examined the lending performance of community development credit unions. A study analyzing the lending of the Lower East Side People's FCU, a New York City community development credit union chartered in 1986, found that 90 percent of loan applications were approved, primarily for minority and lower-income borrowers. Further, most of the borrowers had no credit record and almost half had no relationship with a mainstream financial institution. The amount of the loans was fairly modest, with a median of $1,700. Most of the loans were for short-term consumer, housing, and small business needs. The loans had a charge-off rate of less than 1 percent (Rosenthal and Schoder 1990).

Similarly, Isbister's examination of the lending performance of seven community development credit unions found that most of the borrowers were lower-income Hispanics, African Americans, and other minorities. Although the loan purposes varied, most loans were for auto purchases or for small personal lines of credit. The interest rate charged on the loans tended to be higher than the rate at mainstream credit unions, and all of the community development credit unions had low or declining delinquency rates (1992).

Jessica Wasilewski (2002) calculated a cost benefit analysis of the Working Wheels program of Opportunities credit union, which makes transportation loans to welfare-to-work clients. Wasilewski used actual program costs to the credit union and taxpayers and projected financial benefits for clients from working versus receiving welfare payments. She found that the program yielded a net benefit in the range of $103,700 to $333,650, which was equivalent to 175 to 560 percent of the program's costs. Wasilewski considered this a conservative estimate, because her analysis did not incorporate other benefits to clients, such as time saved, stronger credit records, or improved quality of life.

Emil Malizia and Virginia Hopley concentrated on examining the commercial lending by community development credit unions (1997). They determined that only 15 percent of the organizations offered business loans, though many reported business loans under other categories, such as unsecured loans or lines of credit. Malizia and Hopley recommended that to make a stronger impact on the economic development of their communities, community development credit unions needed to improve their commercial lending experience and capacity to provide small business counseling (1997).

A 2003 study found that CDCUs at least ten years old had more extensive loan portfolios than newer ones. They also offered more financial service products. Those that served a predominantly rural membership were larger than urban credit unions and had a more varied financial services selection. Further, though rural community development credit unions had higher lending rates, their loan delinquencies and loan loss rates were lower than urban ones. The study also found that faith-based organizations make up approximately one-third of all community development credit unions, and most of them (75 percent) were small, with assets of less than $1 million. Their lending and financial service products, due to their size, are very limited (Gemerer 2003). However, the faith-based community development credit unions serve a higher proportion of minorities than others and are more likely to provide loans for community services.

Other Activities

In addition to financial service provision and lending, CDCUs offer other services, such as financial education, alternatives to payday loans, and individual development accounts (IDAs), all of which are designed to help their members achieve financial security. Some credit unions, such as the Bethex Federal Credit Union of the Bronx, also have adopted innovative ways of delivering services to their members.

Financial education and counseling is an important part of CDCUs member services. In 2005, 82 percent of all CDCUs provided specialized home buyer, consumer credit, or business counseling for more than 105,000 members (CDFI Data Project 2005; see also chapter 3, this volume).

CDCUs' work to combat predatory payday lending consists both of the previously discussed personal development loans, and of lower-cost payday loan alternative programs. Twenty seven percent of all CDCUs offered such programs in 2005, accounting for an estimated 11,401 payday substitute loans worth $7.4 million (CDFI Data Project 2005).

CDCUs also help members build assets through individual development accounts. CDCUs match member deposits into these specialized accounts, the proceeds of which can be used only for wealth-building purposes, such as buying a home or paying for education. As of 2005, 19 percent of CDCUs had such programs, enabling an estimated 2,400 members to accumulate approximately $1.4 million (CDFI Data Project 2005).

The Michigan State University Community and Economic Development Program (CEDP) conducted an assessment of twenty-three CDCU IDA Programs and found that IDAs were being offered with considerable success by community development credit unions. They attribute this to the program's compatibility with other asset-building services being offered, and the ability of community development credit unions to leverage resources through collaborations with other organizations (Michigan State University Community and Economic Development Program n.d.).

The most recent example of CDCUs' innovation is the partnership between Bethex Federal Credit Union and the RiteCheck check cashing firm. The partnership, which was implemented in 2001 after four years of planning, allows credit union members to cash Bethex checks, and make deposits and withdrawals at point of banking (POB) terminals at RiteCheck Cashing stores, at no cost. Bethex pays RiteCheck $1.88 per withdrawal and $.70 per deposit. The partnership also allows Bethex members to cash checks not issued by Bethex for a reduced fee.

The partnership has benefits for Bethex members, the check casher, and the credit union. Bethex members are able to conduct Bethex financial transactions at more locations at no additional cost. The partnership provides fee income for RiteCheck and helps the check cashing industry improve its image. Last, it allows the credit union to expand services to new and existing members without the large investment a new branch would require.[12]

However, Michael Stegman and Jennifer Lobenhofer do identify a number of concerns the partnership raises. First, some advocates worry that alliances with check cashers will damage the credit union industry image. Second, there are legal liability issues in terms of the responsibility for balance discrepancies and the bonding of employees. Stegman and Lobenhofer also note that such partnerships would not have been possible just a few years ago because of limited technology enabling off-site transactions (2002). In May 2002, Actors Federal Credit Union developed a similar program and extensive outreach by check cashers, credit unions, banks, and financial service providers to other credit unions began in November 2003 (Jacob 2004).

Community Development Achievements

Several studies designed to access the overall affects of CDCUs have found strong positive benefits from CDCU membership. Jane Kolodinsky, Caryl Stewart, and Antonia Bullard (2001) investigated whether having a relationship with the Opportunities Credit Union of Vermont changed members' lives. Using both quantitative and qualitative analysis, they found that the answer was yes. In fact, the number of services used showed a clear and consistent positive relationship with client impact. Kolodinsky, Stewart and Bullard also found that membership in the credit union resulted in wealth building for low-income members. Finally, the authors evaluated a number of outputs in relation to the $478,000 in operating grants that Opportunities had received since inception, including cost per dollar provided to low-income borrowers (less than one cent), and cost per changed life ($85.45).

James DeFilippis documented the community economic development achievements of Bethex Federal Credit Union and established that almost 30 percent of the credit union's members were unbanked before joining it. He also documented high levels of satisfaction with the credit union. His review of Bethex loan data determined that most of the approved loans were considered too small or too risky for banks and therefore the credit union provided a strategic service not available in the mainstream market. However, Bethex, like many relatively small community development credit unions, did not provide larger small-business or residential loans (2001).

Marva Williams found that community development credit unions fostered and sustained resident participation in community life and empowered their members by providing an opportunity for them to define their own problems, develop solutions, and establish community networks. However, Williams concluded, several critical challenges remained. Community development credit unions must develop a consistent means to chronicle their community development achievements and the smaller organizations must develop larger economies of scale to be effective and sustainable in the long term (1997).

CONCLUSION

Alternative depository institutions were formed on the premise that all consumers and communities, including those with modest incomes, have the right to safe and affordable financial services and credit. Although many alternative depository institutions have an impressive record of meeting the credit and financial service needs of the communities and consumers they serve, some encounter challenges in providing financial services on a large and comprehensive scale. Community development banks and smaller credit unions may not have the infrastructure necessary to provide services on a competitive basis, and customers may be frustrated with long teller lines, teller turnover, limited products, and slow systems. These institutions may be even further stretched to work with lower-income consumers, who often have low-balance accounts and conduct frequent transactions.

Low-income credit unions provide important basic services and loans. However, their impact on community reinvestment has not been thoroughly documented. Further, regular audits of their files are not conducted by the NCUA to determine whether the designation is still warranted.

Findings of studies by the GAO, Woodstock Institute, and NCRC conclude that the mainstream credit union industry is not effectively serving consumers with modest incomes. Analysis of credit union and bank customer data raises concern that households that primarily or only use credit unions are more likely to have moderate or higher incomes than those that primarily or only use banks. The Woodstock Institute's analysis of Chicago-area consumer data documented that credit unions serve a smaller proportion of lower-income than of higher-income consumers. There is also concern about the home mortgage lending of credit unions. Studies by the GAO and NCRC found that banks have a much better record of making home loans to lower-income consumers than do credit unions. One area that has not been documented as well is small-business lending. A 2001 study by the Treasury Department found that only 13 percent of credit union member business loans went to members with household incomes of less than $30,000. However, further analysis of this type of credit union lending is warranted.

Much more needs to be done. First, the collection of additional loan data, as well as information on the income and race of account holders at credit unions (and banks), is crucial to determining credit union penetration in lower-income and minority communities. Second, adoption of a community reinvestment policy may encourage credit unions to improve their record of serving lower-income consumers.

Research on best practices can provide guidance on how ADIs can reach a larger scale and improve efficiency. There also may be lessons to be learned from community development finance efforts in other countries, particularly in the area of microenterprise finance. In addition, it is important to examine and compare the records of community development banks, credit unions, low-income credit unions, and community development credit unions in serving people and communities of modest means. A rating system, such as the one Justine Evans (2003) proposed for credit unions, could compare these types of institutions on factors measuring economic development impact, including levels of individual and business checking and savings accounts, loan volume, counseling, and participation in other activities, such as the sponsorship of local programs.

Much work has been done by the CDFI industry, including the CDFI Data Project, to measure the outputs and outcomes of community development banks and community development credit unions. However, uniform and consistent disclosure on these measures, and the ability to gather this data for mainstream credit unions, is an enduring challenge.

Last, it is important to remember that mainstream financial institutions, which control the vast majority of the financial services market, have an affirmative obligation to serve people of all incomes in their assessment areas in order to comply with the CRA. Further research on product innovations, marketing and outreach, and the financial sustainability of their loans and services to lower-income consumers should be conducted.[13]

NOTES

1. Although only community development and low-income credit unions expressly serve low-income communities, all credit unions can be thought of as alternative depository institutions. By their nature, credit

unions are cooperative, nonprofit organizations designed to serve communities that banks do not. As discussed in a subsequent part of this chapter, however, the reality of mainstream credit union membership does not reflect this idealism.

2. The federation was formed in 1974 to provide technical and financial support to CDCUs. It also advocates changes in policy and increased resources for CDCUs with the NCUA, the CDFI Fund, and foundations.

3. For more on community development financial institutions, see chapters 1 and 5 in this volume.

4. CRA requires banks to meet the loan, service, and investment needs of all sectors of their assessment area, including lower-income geographies (for more on CRA, see chapter 5, this volume).

5. HMDA was enacted by Congress in 1975 (for more on HMDA, see chapters 7 and 8, this volume).

6. This threshold is adjusted annually.

7. IDAs are legislatively authorized savings accounts for low-income persons, who agree to save for an approved wealth-building asset (such as down payment on a home, starting a micro-business, or investing in education and training) and, upon reaching their savings goal, benefit from "match" funds to assist that purchase (for more on IDAs, see chapter 2, this volume).

8. EITC, which is administered through the Internal Revenue Services, is a refundable tax credit for low-wage workers.

9. Despite the general growth trends, credit unions have recently become more concentrated, due primarily to mergers, with the number of state- and federal-chartered credit unions declining from 11,125 to 9,688 between 1998 and 2002.

10. Households that predominantly use credit unions are households that use both banks and credit unions but have more savings in credit unions. Households that predominantly use banks have most of their savings in banks but also maintain credit union accounts.

11. Using HMDA data to assess the penetration of lower-income communities is of limited value. Only large credit unions are required to submit HMDA data. Consumer lending, which tends to be a relatively large portion of the lending of most credit unions, is not measured.

12. There are some advantages relative to the location of the partnership. New York State has very strict laws governing check casher fees, and due to state laws limiting usury rates, most check cashers do not offer payday loans.

13. Community banks, independent, locally-owned and operated institutions with assets ranging from less that $10 million to several bil-
lion dollars, also are an important element in reaching underserved
consumers and communities. This is particularly true for those community banks that are located in small towns and rural areas, and
focus on consumers, local businesses, and farmers. According to the
Community Bankers Association, there are 8,800 community banks,
including commercial banks and thrifts, with almost 40,000 locations
in the United States.

REFERENCES

Balkenhol, Bernd. 1999. *Credit Unions and the Poverty Challenge*. Geneva:
International Labour Office.

Burger, Albert E., and Mary Zellmer. 1995. *Strategic Opportunities in Serving
Low to Moderate Income Members*. Madison, Wisc.: Center for Credit Union
Research.

Bush, Malcolm, and Kimbra Nieman. 2002. *Doing Well While Doing Good: The
Growth of Community Development Banking, 1992–2001*. Chicago, Ill.:
Woodstock Institute.

Bush, Malcolm, and Geoff Smith. 2003. *Community Development Banks
Substantially Outscore Other Banks in Serving Low-Income and Minority
Communities: Implications for the Federal Budget and the Community
Reinvestment Act*. Chicago, Ill.: Woodstock Institute.

Carney, Stacie and William Gale. 2001. Asset Accumulation in Low-Income
Households. In, *Assets for the Poor: The Benefits of Spreading Asset Ownership*,
edited by Thomas M. Shapiro and Edward Wolff. New York, New York:
Russell Sage Foundation.

Caskey, John P., and David B. Humphrey. 1999. *Credit Unions and Asset
Accumulation by Lower-Income Households*. Madison, Wisc.: Center for
Credit Union Research.

CDFI Data Project 2003. *Providing Capital, Building Communities, Creating
Impact*, 3rd ed. Arlington, Va.: CDFI Coalition. Accessed at http://www.
cdfi.org/Uploader/Files/cdp_finalfy03.pdf

———. 2004. *Providing Capital, Building Communities, Creating Impact*, 4th
ed. Arlington, Va.: CDFI Coalition. Accessed at http://www.cdfi.org/
Uploader/Files/CDP_fy2004_complete.pdf.

———. 2005. *Providing Capital, Building Communities, Creating Impact*, 5th ed.
Arlington, Va.: CDFI Coalition. Accessed at http://www.cdfi.org/
Uploader/Files/cdp_fy_2005_full.pdf.

Colloquium at the University of California, San Diego. 2003. *Serving New
Americans: A Strategic Opportunity for Credit Unions*. Madison, Wisc.: Center
for Credit Union Research.

Credit Union National Association. 2003. *Serving Members of Modest Means: Survey Report*. Madison, Wisc.: CUNA.

DeFilippis, James. 2001. "On Community, Economic Development and Credit Unions: The Case of Bethex FCU and the South Bronx." Paper presented on COMM-ORG: The On-Line Conference on Community Organizing and Development. Accessed at http://comm-org.wisc.edu/papers.htm.

Epstein, Jonathan D. 2005. "Group Says Credit Unions Failing Their Mission." *Buffalo News: Business Today,* May 24, 2005.

Esty, Benjamin. 1995. "South Shore Bank: Is it the Model for Community Development Banks?" *Psychology and Marketing* 12(8): 789–819.

Evans, Justine Scott. 2003. *Community Development Credit Union: Evaluating its Success in Improving the Urban Community.* Knoxville, Tenn.: University of Tennessee Press.

Fannie Mae Foundation. 2003. *Innovations in Personal Finance for the Unbanked: Emerging Practices from the Field: Access and Second Chance Accounts.* Washington: Fannie Mae Foundation.

Gemerer, Greg. 2003. *Financial Trends in Community Development Credit Unions: A Statistical Analysis.* National Federation of Community Development Credit Unions.

Isbister, John. 1992. *Lending Performance of Community Development Credit Unions.* Davis, Calif.: University of California.

———. 1994. *Thin Cats: The Community Development Credit Union Movement in the United States.* Davis, Calif.: University of California.

Jacob, Katy. 2004. *The PayNet Deposit Program: Check Casher-Credit Union Partnerships and the Point of Banking Machine.* Research Series Report #2. Center for Financial Services Innovation. October 2004. Accessed at www.cfsinnovation.com/managed_documents/pobpaper.pdf.

Jacob, Katy, Malcolm Bush, and Dan Immergluck. 2002. *Rhetoric and Reality: An Analysis of Mainstream Credit Unions' Record of Serving Low-Income People.* Chicago, Ill.: Woodstock Institute.

Kolodinsky, Jane, Caryl Stewart, and Antonia Bullard. 2001. "Measuring Impact of Community Development Programs: The Vermont Development Credit Union." *Consumer Interests Annual* Volume 47. Accessed at http://www.consumerinterests.org/i4a/pages/Index.cfm?pageid=3629.

Lambrinos, James, and William A. Kelly, Jr. 1996. *Effects of Member Income Levels on Credit Union Financial Performance.* Madison, Wisc.: Center for Credit Union Research.

Lee, Jinhook, and William A. Kelly, Jr. 2001. *Who Uses Credit Unions.* Madison, Wisc.: Filene Institute.

Lipson, Beth, and Allison Myatt. 2002. *CDFIs Side by Side: A Comparative Guide.* Philadelphia, Penn.: National Community Capital Association.

Malizia, Emil E., and Virginia Hopley. 1997. *Development Banking in Low-Wealth and Minority Communities: The Roles of Community Development Credit Unions with Emphasis on Commercial Lending.* Chapel Hill, N.C.: University of North Carolina at Chapel Hill.

Meyer, Mark C. 2004. *Growth Opportunity for Credit Unions.* Madison, Wisc: Filene Institute.

Michigan State University Community and Economic Development Program. n.d. *Michigan Family Independence Agency-Final Report.* Lansing, Mich.: CEDP.

National Community Reinvestment Coalition. 2005. *Credit Unions: True to Their Mission?* Washington: NCRC.

Pinsky, Mark. 2001. "Taking Stock: CDFIs Look Ahead After 25 Years of Community Development Finance." *Capital Xchange,* December. Washington: Brookings Institution. Accessed at http://www.brook.edu/es/urban/capitalxchange/pinsky.pdf.

Rosenthal, Clifford N., and Joseph Schoder. 1990. *People's Credit: A Study of the Lending of the Lower East Side People's FCU.* New York: National Federation of Community Development Credit Unions.

Stegman, Michael A., and Jennifer S. Lobenhofer. 2002. "Bringing More Affordable Financial Services to the Inner City." *Building Blocks* 3(3). Accessed at http://www.fanniemaefoundation.org/programs/bb/v3i3index.shtml

Tansey, Charles D. 2001. "Community Development Credit Unions: An Emerging Player in Low Income Communities." *Capital Xchange,* September. Washington: Brookings Institution.

U.S. Department of the Treasury. 2001. *Credit Union Member Business Lending.* Washington: U.S. Government Printing Office.

U.S. Government Accounting Office. 2003. *Credit Unions: Financial Condition has Improved, but Opportunities Exist to Enhance Oversight and Share Insurance Management.* Washington: U.S. Government Printing Office.

Wasilewski, Jessica. 2002. "Low-Income Credit Rationing and Social Return on Investment: Welfare-to-Work Car Loans in the State of Vermont." Unpublished paper. Middlebury College.

Williams, Marva. 1997. *Credit to the Community: The Roles of CDCUs in Community Development.* Chicago, Ill.: Woodstock Institute.

———. 2004. *Financial Services for People of Modest Means: Lessons from Low-Income Credit Unions.* Chicago, Ill.: Woodstock Institute.

Williams, Marva E., and Sharyl Hudson. 1999. *Building the Savings and Assets of Lower-Income Consumers Examples from Community Development Credit Unions.* Chicago, Ill.: Woodstock Institute

Witzeling, Ruth. 1993. *People, Not Profit: The Story of the Credit Union Movement.* Dubuque, Ia.: Kendall/Hunt Publishing.

Zdenek, Robert O. 2003. "Building Wealth." *Shelterforce* January/February 2003. Accessed at http://www.nhi.org/online/issues/127/bldgwealth.html.

CHAPTER SEVEN

Financing Production of Low-
and Moderate-Income Housing

Rachel G. Bratt

HOUSING IS a central component of community development. It is critical to neighborhood vitality, to family well-being, and, indeed, to the economy at large.[1] Yet low- and moderate-income households continue to face considerable obstacles locating decent quality housing that they can afford.[2] Consider the following statistics about the various housing challenges these groups encountered in 2003:

- About 5.18 million unassisted renter households with incomes below 50 percent of area median income paid more than half their income for housing or lived in severely substandard housing. This group, according to HUD, had "worst case housing needs" (2005, 1).

- Nearly 70 percent of those in the bottom quartile of the income distribution paid more than 30 percent of their income for housing; the number of those in this income category who paid more than 50 percent for housing increased by 1.5 million from 2000 to 2003, raising the share with such affordability problems to 44 percent (Joint Center for Housing Studies 2005, 24–25).

- There were only 44 units of housing affordable and available for every 100 renters with incomes below 30 percent of area median income and only three-fourths are physically adequate (HUD 2005, 41). This translates into a national shortage of about 5 million units (HUD 2003).

- Over the course of a given year, some 2.5 to 3.5 million people are homeless (Joint Center for Housing Studies 2004, 4).

Public intervention to assist low- and moderate-income households cover their housing costs has attempted, in various ways, to reduce the extent of these problems.[3] Such intervention has been necessary because housing is expensive to build and maintain, and without public assistance, it is not profitable for the private sector to provide housing affordable to these lower-income groups. Acknowledging the economic obstacles to low-income housing production, a report reflecting on the 1990s stated: "The fact that shortages of affordable housing worsened so much during a decade of strong economic growth makes it clear that economic growth alone cannot answer America's low income housing problems" (Nelson, Treskon, and Pelletiere 2004, 1).

Using a framework based on the three essential components of the housing finance process—raising equity; securing debt financing; and, in the case of lower income households, creating mechanisms to maintain the long-term affordability of the units—this chapter discusses how public, private, and nonprofit-oriented programs have attempted to fulfill these three requirements for both traditional homeownership units and multifamily rental dwellings. It provides answers to three questions concerning affordable housing finance:[4] Is finance the key issue in housing production for low-income households? Should homeownership for low-income households be encouraged? What is needed to stimulate the production of rental housing affordable to low-income households?

This inquiry is timely. There is an enduring bipartisan commitment to expand homeownership opportunities for lower-income, particularly non-white households (see HUD 2002d). Finance is obviously a cornerstone of any such discussion. There also appears to be a relatively new consensus that a renewed commitment to supply-side programs to encourage multifamily housing production is required. The debate about whether public subsidies for the production of this housing are needed has, for the most part, been put to rest.[5] Although housing vouchers are acknowledged to be a good policy response under some market conditions, they cannot meet the needs of all households in all market conditions. One recent report noted that: "production subsidies are *relatively* better used in some circumstances than in others" (Khadduri, Burnett and Rodda 2003, 1). Further, "the types of places and people that have low success using vouchers may be reasonable targets for the use of production subsidies (such as) for households with five or more people; for single, non-elderly, non-disabled households; in tight housing markets; and in jurisdictions that do not have laws barring discrimination on the basis of source of income" (29).

Since the 1930s, the federal government as well as the nonprofit and private sectors, have developed an array of programs with a variety of distinct objectives related to promoting homeownership for low- and moderate-income households. The system is far from simple, but compared with multifamily rental housing finance programs, it is, as the saying goes, a breeze.

The story of federal involvement with rental housing is a few years shorter than its efforts to promote homeownership. Since 1937, when the public housing program was created, the way in which multifamily rental housing affordable to low- and moderate-income households is financed has gone through multiple distinct stages and has created a layered, convoluted process.[6] Private entities, particularly the large nonprofit housing intermediaries, have created a number of programs that complement the federal initiatives. Finally, an entire industry of private-sector companies has evolved to promote affordable housing finance.[7] What, then, have we learned from past initiatives aimed at enhancing the financing of housing for low- and moderate-income households and how can these experiences inform future policy?

RAISING EQUITY

Whether equity is in the form of a down payment in the case of homeownership, or the working capital that a developer brings to a rental housing deal, up-front money is generally a necessary component of housing finance.

Homeownership

Studies have revealed that the "lack of necessary down payment presents a greater constraint to home purchase than income requirements" (Quercia, McCarthy, and Wachter 2003, 52).[8] In recognition of this fact, and consistent with bipartisan support for increasing homeownership opportunities, the federal government has created a number of vehicles to assist lower-income households become homeowners by reducing the amount of down payment needed to qualify for a loan and by providing up front grants for down payment assistance.

The Section 235 program, created in 1968, is the largest subsidy program aimed at providing homeownership opportunities for low and moderate-income nonrural households. The program reduced the amount of down payment needed to as little as $200. The federal rural subsidized homeownership program, created in 1949 and still operational today, has no required down payment amount (Housing Assistance Council 2003a). HUD's Nehemiah Housing Opportunity Grant Program, enacted in 1987, the same year in which the Section 235 program was terminated, provided lower-income buyers an opportunity to purchase new or renovated homes in economically depressed areas. Based on an analysis of the program's operation in twelve locales, researchers found that households' cash contributions upon purchase ranged from $200 to $5,800, an average of 4 percent of the price of the home, far less than the typical 20 percent down payment requirement (Phipps, Heintz, and Franke 1994, 4–6).

A number of studies have documented the potentially negative aspects of requiring little or no down payment. In the case of the Section 325 program, the low down payment was found to be problematic because homeowners assumed little financial risk in purchasing their homes. This was cited as one of the factors contributing to a high foreclosure rate.[9] A 2002 HUD report also disclosed a much higher default rate among owners participating in the Nehemiah program that had received down payment assistance, compared with FHA insured mortgagors who did not receive such assistance (2002c, 9).[10] Advocates of Nehemiah and other programs that allow for low down payments have argued that the methodology of the HUD study was flawed, so the loans are not much riskier. In an apparent contradiction, however, they also note that the extra risk is worth it (Lewis 2003).[11]

The HUD data just cited has certainly contributed to the view that loans made without down payments are risky. *The Boston Globe,* for example, noted that "zero-down-payment mortgages are seductive to low-income renters. But the prospective homeowner risks waking up with unmanageable monthly payments and costly mortgage insurance." Citing a study by the Congressional Budget Office, the *Globe* warns that such mortgages could have "the unintended consequence of excessive defaults and foreclosures" ("Unsound Housing Policy," October 11, 2004).[12]

Despite the controversy, there is an increasing trend toward reducing the amount of down payment needed (Barakova et al. 2003; Quercia, McCarthy, and Wachter 2003). In 2003, Congress enacted the American Dream Down-payment Act. This legislation, if fully funded, could provide 80,000 families with an average of $5,000 in down payment assistance.[13] And, in 2004, the Zero Down Payment Act was introduced in Congress, which would have required the FHA to offer federally insured mortgage loans to certain eligible households without a down payment.[14] Although experience with the Section 235 and Nehemiah programs suggests that this approach may be problematic, it is also possible that improved screening and counseling efforts would be able to balance the goal of promoting homeownership among lower-income households while ensuring that new homeowners are fully prepared for the responsibilities and risks of owning a home, even without paying anything up front.

Rental Housing

The need for equity in multifamily housing deals is essential. It is necessary to cover the many costs associated with the early stages of the project, before any rental revenue becomes available. In addition, lenders typically require that developers have a considerable amount of money invested in a deal.

Since the 1960s, private for-profit and nonprofit developers have been the key actors in the production of rental housing. Acknowledging that nonprofit developers are often ill-equipped to cover the various early costs involved in producing housing, intermediaries, such as the Local Initiatives Support Corporation, have created specific programs to meet the expenses of pre-development activities. In addition, nonprofit developers often use their developer's fee, which is an allowed disbursement from the mortgage proceeds, to cover a portion of the equity for a project.

A far greater portion of equity, however, is generated through limited partnerships in which private investors provide the equity capital needed for development, with tax credits and depreciation provisions contained in the Internal Revenue Code providing the incentives for these investments. The opportunity to realize considerable tax savings was, in fact, the primary engine behind the below-market interest rate programs of the 1960s and the Section 8 production programs of 1974. Before 1986, depreciation laws also provided particularly lucrative opportunities for investors in low-income housing (for good summaries of the federal tax incentive programs for privately owned multifamily housing that existed before 1986, see Case 1991; DiPasquale and Cummings 1992).

In 1986, Congress created a new investment vehicle aimed at encouraging equity investments in low-income housing, known as the Low-Income Housing Tax Credit (LIHTC).[15] The LIHTC allows a dollar of tax savings for each dollar of tax credit purchased by the investor. In addition, equity investors in LIHTC deals, as well as other housing, are able to take deductions through the IRS's depreciation laws. The LIHTC program is far from simple and a lack of compliance with stringent rules about income limits of residents jeopardizes an investor's ability to enjoy the benefits of the tax credit.

Despite the availability of tax credits, most sponsors of housing targeted to low-income households require more equity than can be provided through this mechanism alone (Cummings and DiPasquale 1999). Although debt financing may be readily available, the income generated from the development has to be able to cover the debt service. In most deals, there is a gap between proceeds from the sale of tax credits and available debt financing that can be supported by the anticipated rental income, on the one hand, and total development costs of the project on the other. This gap is generally covered through an assortment of public, private, and nonprofit sector grants and deferred payment loans,[16] hence the term *creative finance*. According to Michael Stegman, "born of necessity, creative finance is the piggybacking of several different subsidies in a single project—until they are sufficient to reduce rents to affordable levels" (1991, 361).

The phrase has a somewhat lyrical sound, but there is nothing harmonious about the process that developers using tax credits must undertake. Almost since the program's creation, there has been a debate on whether LIHTC is an efficient tool for raising equity in low- and moderate-income housing developments (see Stegman 1991; Quercia, Rohe, and Levy 2000). In critiquing the LIHTC, Stegman noted that the financing of projects was cumbersome. Of twenty-four developments studied, each project had an average of five financing sources. Moreover, Stegman argued, the tax credit was inefficient because the cost was substantially higher to the federal government in terms of foregone revenues when compared to the amount of equity raised through the sale of the tax credits (see also GAO 1989). In addition, a portion of the money raised from selling tax credits has to cover the costs of syndicating the investment deal and there invariably are other high transaction costs that must be absorbed by the public-private partners engaged in the development (Stegman 1991, 362, 370).[17]

Nearly a decade after Stegman made these observations, a team of researchers examined twenty housing developments that had used creative finance to assess whether they were meeting their goals of providing decent, affordable housing to lower-income households. Roberto Quercia, William Rohe, and Diane Levy (2000) concluded that the developments were, indeed, meeting this overall objective and that to the extent that several were encountering financial difficulties, creative finance, per se, was not the culprit. Rather, they offered that sponsors of such housing would face less precarious finances if, for example, funding for predevelopment activities were made available and Section 8 funding were provided over longer periods than through annual renewals. Moreover, creative finance has some distinct benefits—long-term partnerships are often created through the process, community acceptance of the housing appears to be enhanced, and the development skills of the sponsoring organization may be improved (Quercia, Rohe, and Levy 2000).

Over the past decade, two of the large nonprofit intermediaries have facilitated the ability of sponsors of LIHTC developments to tap into equity markets. The National Equity Fund (NEF), sponsored by the Local Initiatives Support Corporation (LISC) and Enterprise Community Investment, Inc. (ECII) sponsored by Enterprise Community Partners, were both created in 1987 to provide a market for tax credit investments. Both NEF and ECII are tax-credit syndicators, raising money from investors and identifying low-income housing developments in which to invest that capital. NEF, for example, has funded about 1,500 projects in forty-three states, raised $5.5 billion for investment, and helped develop some 80,000 homes. ECII boasts community investments at a rate of nearly $1 a billion year.[18]

Equity for rental housing developments is also raised through real estate investment trusts (REITs). REITs are corporate entities, usually created by a commercial bank, insurance company, or mortgage banker, that enable investors in the trusts to reap the benefits from real estate ownership and sales. Income is passed from the trust to shareholders, and as long as nearly all income is distributed, the trust enjoys a special tax status that provides exemptions from corporate taxation. There are several types of REITs, but Kent Colton reports that as of 1999, equity trusts (trusts set up to raise equity and take an ownership interest in properties) made up 95 percent of the total REIT market (2003, 152).[19]

SECURING DEBT FINANCING

Debt financing generally covers the largest portion of the actual costs involved with producing housing. Unlike conventional homeownership arrangements, in which a borrower goes to a financial institution and, based on underwriting criteria and a property appraisal, the loan may be transacted easily and quickly, the process of financing homeownership and rental housing for lower-income households typically involves more steps and more actors. Indeed, even the conventional mortgage lending process has become considerably more complex since the 1960s as major changes in the secondary mortgage market have occurred.

Homeownership

One of the first federal interventions in housing was also among the most powerful tools used during the New Deal to stimulate a moribund housing industry and an economy that was still in the midst of the Great Depression. By minimizing risk for lenders through mortgage insurance, the Federal Housing Administration (FHA) created a strong incentive to builders. Starting in 1934, and then again after World War II, thousands of modest homes were financed through this vehicle. Although FHA was a major boon to first-time homebuyers during the first several decades of its existence, recent studies have pointed out that it is playing a less important role and that "to the extent that FHA has any influence on home ownership, it is mostly to accelerate home purchase, not to enable it among households that otherwise would never be able to buy" (Goodman and Nichols 1997, 184). The FHA also provided mortgage insurance for multifamily properties, though this was never as dominant as the single-family insurance program, which was the mainstay of the FHA.

FHA came under considerable attack during the late 1960s, when several federal commissions found that the agency had consistently redlined inner-city areas and that FHA personnel had frequently discriminated against non-white home buyers (President's Committee on Urban Housing 1968; National Commission on Urban Problems 1968). In response, Congress enacted a set of legislative initiatives in 1968 aimed at increasing homeownership opportunities for low-income households (Section 235), for households wishing to buy homes in inner-city areas (Section 223(e)), and for households with poor credit histories (Section 237). The programs were poorly implemented, however, and the target of unscrupulous practices both within the government and by private sector entrepreneurs. Although more than 500,000 households achieved homeownership through the Section 235 program, as stated earlier, there was a high rate of foreclosure, and by 1973 it was effectively dead, though it was not officially terminated until 1987 (Hays 1995; Martinez 2000).

The federal government created the FHA to stimulate the provision of credit, but by the 1930s the risks of lender illiquidity were also well understood. During the Great Depression, as borrowers were facing increased difficulties making mortgage payments, lenders were unable to convert mortgage documents into cash unless they foreclosed on the home and then tried to sell the asset. However, with the economy in such a weakened state, the market for foreclosed homes was limited and lender liquidity became an increasingly elusive goal.

The Federal National Mortgage Association was created in 1938 to purchase mortgages from mortgage originators. Little used during the early years of its existence, Fannie Mae, as it is now called, became a privately owned stock corporation in 1968, although it still retains close links to the federal government. Similarly, in 1970, the Federal Home Loan Mortgage Corporation, now known as Freddie Mac, was created to serve as a secondary mortgage market institution for loans originated by thrift institutions. In 1989, with the passage of the Financial Institutions Reform, Recovery, and Enforcement Act (FIRREA),[20] Freddie Mac became very similar to Fannie Mae—a privately owned corporation with private stockholders, set up to purchase mortgage loans from a wide array of financial institutions, with the timely payment of interest and principal on bonds issued by the agency guaranteed by the federal government. Currently, nearly 70 percent of all home mortgages are securitized and sold into the secondary market by Fannie Mae and Freddie Mac. This figure has more than doubled since 1990 (Apgar, Calder and Fauth 2004).[21]

When Fannie Mae was spun off as a private corporation in 1968, Congress simultaneously created the Government National Mortgage Association, or Ginnie Mae, to serve as a purchaser of government subsidized and insured single and multifamily loans or other loans that are perceived by investors to be high risk.[22] Similar to Fannie Mae and Freddie Mac, Ginnie Mae raises funds by issuing securities that are backed by the value of the mortgages it holds, and in turn guarantees the timely payment of principal and interest to investors.

Also supplementing the activities of Fannie Mae and Freddie Mac, the NeighborWorks America network[23] now has its own secondary market that is operated through the Neighborhood Housing Services of America (NHSA). NHSA offers a variety of loan options to member organizations, as well as purchasing loans from network organizations. This enhances the liquidity of local loan funds that network organizations use and promotes a steady stream of capital for revitalization efforts.

Along with the growth of the secondary mortgage market, there also has been a shift in the types of entities originating mortgage loans. During the 1990s, the fraction of originations by savings institutions and independent mortgage companies declined and originations by mortgage company subsidiaries of depository institutions increased. These latter entities "are much larger and operate across larger geographic areas than depositories" and, as a result, they may "have less connection to local communities than depositories and may have less incentive to serve the affordable segment" (Nothaft and Surette 2002, 73–74).

There also has been enormous consolidation in the financial institutions that originate mortgage loans, as evident in the following trend. In 1990, "the top 25 originators accounted for 28.4 percent of an industry total of less than $500 billion in home mortgages. In 2002, the top 25 originators accounted for 78 percent of the $2.5 trillion in loans originated that year. Of these, the top five originators. . . . each made more than $100 billion in mortgages, comprising more than half of all loans" (Apgar, Calder, and Fauth 2004, 11).

The Federal Home Loan Bank system is another part of the affordable housing finance system, sponsoring homeownership as well as multifamily rental assistance programs. Since 1990, Federal Home Loan Banks have been required to contribute 10 percent of their annual net income toward housing for lower-income households through the Affordable Housing Program (AHP). Through this initiative, as well as the Community Investment Program (CIP), member institutions provide direct subsidies and subsidized interest rate advances, which are then made available to qualified homebuyers or to sponsors of rental housing; occupancy is targeted to lower-income households. About one-third of the funds provided through the AHP has supported homeownership; two-thirds have supported rental housing (Federal Home Loan Banks 2004). By mid-2003, AHP subsidies totaled more than $1.6 billion and contributed to the creation of more than 364,000 units of affordable housing. Lending through the CIP program has exceeded $32 billion and has helped finance more than 500,000 housing units and 700 economic development projects (Hunter 2004).

Mortgage revenue bonds also are critical tools in the overall housing finance picture for low- and moderate-income households. First authorized in 1968 by amendments to the Internal Revenue Code, MRBs are tax-exempt securities issued by state housing finance agencies intended to provide lower interest rates to first-time homebuyers within certain income limits. The National Council of State Housing Agencies reports that MRBs have enabled over 2.4 million households to become homeowners; approximately 100,000 homeowners are assisted every year.[24]

Two federal block grant programs, the Community Development Block Grant (CDBG), created in 1974,[25] and the HOME Investment Partnerships program (created in 1990), provide various types of assistance, including both grants and debt financing, for both homeownership and rental housing development. Unlike CDBG, which can fund an array of activities including housing, HOME is the largest direct federal subsidy targeted to the production and preservation of affordable housing. With flexibility provided to states and localities concerning the use of the funds, about 90,000 units have been financed under the HOME program (National Low Income Housing Coalition 2007).

In the late 1970s and early 1980s, three major nonprofit intermediaries were created—the Local Initiatives Support Corporation (LISC), the Enterprise Foundation (now known as Enterprise Community Partners), and the Neighborhood Reinvestment Corporation (now known as NeighborWorks America) to assist nonprofit housing providers.[26] LISC and Enterprise aggregate private funds and channel these monies into a variety of community development activities, particularly affordable housing, both rental and homeownership. NeighborWorks America relies on private funds, as well as annual funding provided by the federal government. In addition to providing loans and grants to nonprofit housing sponsors, these three entities provide a wide range of technical assistance and educational opportunities through workshops and conferences.

Also in the 1970s, activists focused on the provision of credit by private lenders and Congress responded with two significant pieces of legislation—the Home Mortgage Disclosure Act of 1975 (HMDA) and the Community Reinvestment Act of 1977 (CRA). HMDA directed federally regulated depository institutions (above certain asset sizes) to collect information on where in a given geographic area they provide credit and to whom, on the basis of race, gender, and income. CRA went one step further by underscoring that banks have an obligation to meet the credit needs of their service area, with particular consideration to the needs of low- and moderate-income households. It also gave community groups or others wishing to question a bank's practices the opportunity to file critical comments, which could provide grounds for the federal chartering agency to turn down requests by a given financial institution to change its operation, such as opening or closing a branch or merging with another bank.

More recently, community development financial institutions (CDFIs) have evolved to promote access to capital for low-income communities, including the provision of affordable housing. CDFIs include a variety of entities such as community development loan funds, community development banks, community development credit unions, micro enterprise lenders, community development corporations, and community development venture capital funds. These institutions are assisted by the Community Development Financial Institutions Fund of the Treasury Department; the mission of the fund is to increase the number and capacity of CDFIs operating in distressed communities across the nation (see Benjamin, Rubin, and Zielenbach 2004). Authorized through the Community Development Banking and Financial Institutions

Act of 1994, the CDFI Fund assists CDFIs by providing equity investments, capital grants, loans, and technical assistance for both housing and economic development activities.[27]

In recent years, many financial institutions have begun to relax traditional underwriting criteria in an effort to qualify more homeowners for loans. Some of these approaches may have been stimulated by a desire on the part of financial institutions to comply with the Community Reinvestment Act and the liberalization of lending criteria may be a benefit to households with lower incomes or weak credit histories. For example, loan-to-value ratios and debt ratios applied to borrowers' incomes may be eased and, as mentioned earlier, down payments may be reduced and weaknesses in credit reports and employment histories may be accepted (The Enterprise Foundation 1995).[28] There is a downside to these more lenient loan terms, however. Subprime lending can cause problems for borrowers and can be predatory in nature.[29]

Rental Housing

In 1992, Denise DiPasquale and Jean Cummings observed that the mortgage market for single-family homes had been effectively transformed over the previous two decades and that national and international capital markets were efficiently filling local credit needs. However, they continued, "the story is quite different . . . when the lens is focused on multifamily rental housing. Although there is a growing secondary market for mortgages on multifamily housing, the market is in the early stages of development and remains quite small" (77). At the same time, the National Task Force on Financing Affordable Housing was challenged to propose an improved "system of long-term financing for multifamily housing, one that extends to serve affordable—including subsidized— housing," and aims to promote the development of "a secondary market for affordable multifamily mortgages that is efficient and liquid, much like that for single-family mortgages" (1992, 4).

In 1980 and until the middle of that decade, only about 5 percent of the outstanding multifamily mortgage debt was in the hands of Fannie Mae and Freddie Mac. By 1990, their market share had grown to 9 percent, and within the next ten years it nearly doubled, to 17 percent (Schnare 2001, 11). A large part of this change was due to the promulgation of new affordable housing goals that HUD set for government-sponsored enterprises (GSEs), specifically Fannie Mae and Freddie Mac. Authorized by the Federal Housing Enterprise Financial Safety and Soundness Act of 1992, these goals were to be enforced through HUD's new Office of Federal Housing Enterprise Oversight (OFHEO). In addition, OFHEO was given the responsibility of ensuring that Fannie Mae and Freddie Mac were adequately capitalized and operating safely.

Despite the increasing importance of GSEs in the multifamily mortgage market, their role has been described as cautious. Elaborating on this point,

William Segal and Edward Szymanoski note: "There is evidence that the GSEs have continued to concentrate their efforts with respect to affordability in the middle of the multifamily mortgage market. GSEs have reduced their credit risk on multifamily transactions to a degree that many of their loans would have been made by the nonagency sector without GSE participation" (1998, 60).[30] Henry Cisneros and his colleagues have detailed a number of ways in which GSEs can become more responsive to affordable housing goals. One calls for Fannie Mae and Freddie Mac to set aside a percentage of annual net profits or operating budgets as a source of capital for affordable housing (2004, 62).

Non-GSE participation in the secondary mortgage market has also grown considerably over the past decade due, in part, to the Resolution Trust Corporation's disposition of assets acquired from failed and ailing thrift institutions. Privately issued commercial mortgage backed securities (CMBS) became a prime vehicle for disposing of these assets. According to Ann Schnare, "as investors gained familiarity with these securities—and as Wall Street developed a series of complex derivative products tailored to meet a variety of investment needs—the CMBS market exploded" (2001, 12).

Another key change in the federally supported multifamily mortgage market has been the reduced role of FHA. Although multifamily housing was never the chief focus of the agency, it was still a leader in the multifamily market in the post–World War II era. Between 1980 and 1992 its market share declined from 30 percent to about 5 percent (Segal and Szymanoski 1998, 63).

Similar to mortgage revenue bonds, multifamily housing bonds (MHBs) are also issued by state housing finance agencies and are tax-exempt. The proceeds are used to finance multifamily housing where at least 25 percent of the units are set aside for lower-income households. MHBs have provided financing for more than 824,000 apartments affordable to lower-income families (National Council of State Housing Agencies 2004). Typically, these bonds are "credit-enhanced" by a third party, most often Fannie Mae, but also by Freddie Mac, FHA, or a financial surety entity. This mechanism provides a guarantee to the investor that the bonds will generate timely payments of interest and principal.

In addition, funds for housing for lower-income households, as well as other community development activities, are supported through the low-income investment fund (LIIF). A national CDFI founded in 1984, LIIF's financing and technical assistance has totaled over $500 million in twenty-six states across the nation. Through its investments, LIIF has contributed to the development of about 50,000 units of low-income and special needs housing. Overall, it "occupies a very specific niche within the CDFI industry," serving very low-income households, first-time borrowers with unconventional revenue streams, and providing financing for all phases of a development project (including permanent mortgages) as well as operating lines of credit for nonprofit organizations.[31]

PROMOTING LONG-TERM AFFORDABILITY

Equity and debt financing are essential for all housing production, but in order to enable housing to be affordable to lower-income households, subsidies are required. Since the 1930s, the federal government has been involved in reducing the cost of housing through a variety of mechanisms, most of which pertain to rental housing. A few approaches, though, have been targeted to homeownership.

Homeownership

Although the federal rural homeownership program has been the subject of far less study than the federal government's urban-oriented programs, the former has, in fact, been in existence for more than a half century, and it has largely escaped the scandals that plagued the latter. Enacted in 1949, the rural Section 502 homeownership program is currently operated by the Rural Housing Service (formerly the Farmers Home Administration) within the Department of Agriculture and provides direct below-market interest rate loans to households at 80 percent or less of median income. Loan terms are between thirty-three and thirty-eight years (for households earning less than 60 percent of median income). As noted earlier, households can become homeowners with zero down payments and may be eligible for a payment assistance subsidy.

Almost two decades after the Section 502 program, Congress enacted the first major subsidized homeownership program targeted to households in urban areas. However, unlike the rural program, which is still in existence, the Section 235 program, as previously discussed, was short-lived. What is important to acknowledge about both these efforts, however, is that the federal government made a commitment to provide homeownership opportunities to lower-income households.

Another federal initiative to promote homeownership for low-income households comes in the form of Section 8 vouchers. Under the Quality Housing and Work Responsibility Act of 1998, the Section 8 program was expanded for use by income-eligible first-time homebuyers to reduce the cost of their monthly mortgage payments. It is not yet clear the extent to which public housing authorities are using their Section 8 allocations for home-ownership and whether they are able to expand their operations to administer the various aspects of the program, including the requirement that households participate in a counseling program operated by either the housing authority or its designee. Moreover, it appears that there is little financial incentive for public housing authorities to adopt a homeownership program, carved out of its funding for the Section 8 program, because no additional administrative funds are available (National Housing Law Project, 2000).

Certainly, the federal government's most massive vehicle for promoting long-term affordability for homeowners is through the provisions in the Internal

Revenue Code that allow owners to deduct the interest portion of their mortgage payments and the amount paid in property taxes from gross income, when calculating their tax liability. This so-called homeowners' deduction provides a subsidy to all homeowners who itemize their deductions and in the aggregate it cost the federal government over $84 billion in 2004 (Dolbeare, Saraf, and Crowley 2004), more than half of the total amount of federal housing subsidies ($156 billion).[32]

Although the homeowners' deduction has the effect of reducing the cost of homeownership for all households who itemize, the largest benefits are enjoyed by those who need assistance the least. Nearly 60 percent of all federal housing subsidies go to households in the upper two quintiles of the income distribution and nearly 75 percent to households in the upper three quintiles (those earning more than $86,000 and $55,000 per year, respectively), and almost all of this subsidy is in the form of tax deductions (Dolbeare, Saraf, and Crowley 2004).

Despite the strong bipartisan support for homeownership, deep federal subsidies targeted to assist lower-income would-be homebuyers living in non-rural areas are not yet available. A new proposal that is receiving considerable support, however, would involve a homeownership tax credit, to be discussed later in the chapter.

Rental Housing

The public housing program, enacted in 1937, was the federal government's first major initiative aimed at promoting long-term affordability for lower-income groups. The program was enacted as a post–Great Depression recovery measure that, in addition to providing housing, was also framed as a key strategy for alleviating unemployment. Despite the larger economic goals, however, the public housing program encountered considerable opposition, especially from private homebuilding, real estate, and banking interests who were concerned that the new housing would directly compete with the privately owned stock of rental housing. Very little public housing has been built since the early 1980s; federal funds to increase the supply of public housing (as opposed to renovate or replace units) have not been appropriated since 1994. Moreover, federal law has capped the number of public housing units at the number each PHA operated as of October 1, 1999.

Although long-term affordability was an objective of public housing, the original funding formula for the program did not, in fact, guarantee that units would stay permanently affordable. Public housing was funded through federal guarantees of municipally originated bonds and this capital cost write-down was enough to provide a subsidy for the first wave of public housing tenants. But by the time this generation moved out—a group that had not been the very poorest of the population to begin with—operating costs had risen, aging buildings needed repairs and maintenance, and the newer occupants generally had significantly lower incomes than their departing counterparts. The result was that, by the late 1960s, many tenants in many public housing developments were paying 50 percent or more of their income for rent. This stimulated passage of the Brooke Amendments (1969 to 1971), which capped rentals at 25 percent of a tenant's income.[33] Three years later, Congress authorized operating subsidies to compensate for the resulting shortfalls in rental income. For fiscal year 2006, $3.6 billion was appropriated to subsidize public housing operations, a level that, according to one estimate, funds public housing authorities at approximately 86 percent of actual operating needs (National Low Income Housing Coalition 2007). However, a major study of public housing operating costs found that, overall, "total funding is roughly equal to estimated needs" (Byrne, Day, and Stockard 2003, 5).[34]

In addition to public housing, the federal government has created a number of other programs aimed at promoting affordable rental housing to lower-income groups. The second major set of strategies depended on mortgage loan interest rate write-downs. Starting in 1959 with the Section 202 elderly housing program, and continuing in 1961 and 1968 with the Section 221(d)(3) and Section 236 programs, respectively, the federal government promoted the production of housing for low and moderate-income households by reducing the interest rate on long-term loans; private nonprofit and for-profit developers could serve as sponsors of these programs. These initiatives provided apartments that were affordable to low- and moderate-income households, but the below-market interest rate subsidy was not enough to reach the lowest-income groups and the formula did not take into account the possibility that additional funds would be needed to manage the buildings at an appropriate level. In other words, tenant contributions amounting to 30 percent of income proved inadequate to cover all the costs of maintaining the buildings and additional federal subsidies were subsequently pumped into the developments.

There was also, however, another serious problem with the below-market interest rate programs. Although affordability for low- and moderate-income households may have been achieved in the short-term, unlike the public housing program, there was not a federal commitment to guarantee affordability (more or less) in perpetuity. Starting in the 1980s, a new problem surfaced that grew out of the limited period—usually twenty years—that developments were required to stay in the subsidized housing inventory. At the end of the contractual period of these so-called use restrictions, the private owners could prepay the outstanding mortgage debt, which had been written on forty-year terms, and thus be released from their regulatory agreement with HUD. The building owners could then rent to market rate tenants, sell the units as condominiums, or sell the building to a new owner who could, similarly, convert the building to a market-rate rental or for-sale development.

The ensuing "expiring use" crisis received a great deal of public attention because thousands of tenants, many of whom had been living at subsidized rents since the buildings had been constructed twenty years before, began to receive notices of substantial rent increases or evictions. To deal with the growing crisis, a number of federal interventions followed and a series of complex programs were put into place (see Achtenberg 2002). These efforts, however, have not been able to safeguard as affordable housing all the developments that were constructed under the below-market interest rate programs. Since 1997, about 110,000 units (of 560,000 constructed) have been removed from the subsidized stock where the owner has prepaid the mortgage and converted the building into market-rate dwellings (Achtenberg 2006). Thousands of additional units are still at risk.[35]

The below-market interest rate programs were replaced in 1974 by the Section 8 New Construction, Substantial Rehabilitation programs.[36] These initiatives were short-lived and the last of the federal deep subsidy production programs. Section 8 attempted to improve on one of the most glaring defects of its predecessors—the lack of connection between the subsidy and the actual costs involved with maintaining the buildings—while retaining affordability to lower-income households. The funding formula for Section 8 involves HUD's determination of the "fair market rent" for a given area.[37] That figure is then used as the basis for determining the upper limit of the Section 8 subsidy, with tenants paying no more than 30 percent of income.

The Section 8 production programs stimulated the construction of some 851,000 units. Similar to the below-market interest rate programs, however, Section 8 developments also had limited use restrictions, ranging from twenty to forty years, depending on the nature of the project's financing and whether it carried HUD-FHA insurance. As of 2001, about 47,000 units of this stock had been lost, because owners opted out of the Section 8 program by not renewing their Section 8 contracts (Achtenberg 2006).

Another source of grant money for housing is targeted to distressed public housing developments through the HOPE VI program. Funds can be used to cover the costs of renovating existing buildings or demolishing them and constructing or rehabilitating new rental and homeownership units. In addition, funds under this program can be used for other physical improvements and various types of self-sufficiency initiatives. This subsidy, though, is targeted to public housing developments only, and cannot be used for a wider range of development opportunities. Moreover, HOPE VI is constantly under attack: President Bush omitted funding for it from his proposed FY 2005 and 2006 budget requests. Although Congress has consistently funded this program, in the final FY 2006 bill HOPE VI only received $100 million, about 18 percent of the appropriation just five years earlier.[38]

Other than the Low-Income Housing Tax Credit program, no major federal subsidies are targeted specifically to project-based housing in non-rural areas.[39] In its original form, the LIHTC only required that units stay affordable to lower-income groups for fifteen years, but that limit has now been extended to thirty years. Also, according to the National Low Income Housing Coalition, the majority of LIHTC-assisted units are dedicated to low-income use for longer than thirty years, with many developments designed so that units remain affordable in perpetuity (2007).

As with homeownership, the Rural Housing Service also administers a rental interest subsidy program. Through the Section 515 program, the federal government provides thirty-year loans at a 1 percent interest rate to public and nonprofit sponsors of rental housing located in rural areas and aimed at households earning below 80 percent of median income. Long-term affordability for these households is assured through the provision of rental assistance subsidies (Section 521 program), which are similar to Section 8 housing voucher subsidies. However, in the Section 521 program, the amount of the subsidy is based on the actual costs of maintaining the development, which includes the cost of debt service, management, maintenance, long-term maintenance reserves, a percentage for vacancy and nonpayment, and heat and utilities, as opposed to the fair market rent levels set by HUD (Housing Assistance Council 2003b).

RECOMMENDATIONS: FOUR VIEWS, THREE QUESTIONS

Our system for financing affordable homeownership and rental housing is complex; any given deal may involve half a dozen or more public, private, and nonprofit entities. The greater the number of different organizations involved, of course, the greater the difficulty, and hence cost, in orchestrating the various requirements that each places on the project. But beyond the complexity, what is the overall assessment of the housing finance system that has been created? And what should be done to promote decent, affordable homeownership and rental housing opportunities? This final section is presented in two parts. The first presents four overarching views of affordable housing finance. The second part discusses three important questions that emerge from the material presented in this chapter and presents recommendations flowing from this analysis.

Conservative View—Housing Industry

Howard Husock, who is among the most ardent critics of federal intervention in housing, has explained that "devoting government resources to subsidized housing for the poor—whether in the form of public housing or even housing vouchers—is not just unnecessary but counterproductive. It not only derails what the private market can do on its own, but more important, it has profoundly destructive unintended consequences" (2003, 14). Additionally, in discussing the Community Reinvestment Act in particular, he asserts that funds are channeled to community organizations that do not understand marketing or finance, resulting in an "amateur delivery system for investment capital" (67).

A more moderate view acknowledges that, with more than two-thirds of all U.S. households being homeowners, with continued low interest rates, and with problems of uneven credit flows for housing eliminated, there are many good reasons to conclude that the overall health of our housing system is strong. As Kent Colton (former CEO of the National Association of Home Builders) has noted, "by most standards, the United States has the best housing finance system in the world" (2003, 209). Specifically, Colton has under-scored the enormous benefits to consumers of the thirty-year fixed rate mortgage that does not carry prepayment penalties. In representing the views of conservative observers, he offers that "the federal presence in housing finance is too great—that public institutions (such as FHA and VA) should be curtailed and (that) the government sponsored enterprises should be limited in their role or cut loose from their federal financial tie" (211). Nevertheless, Colton is an important member of a growing bipartisan group arguing that direct government funding and support is essential to meet our housing needs (Cisneros et al. 2004).

Liberal Academic View

The liberal academic community emphatically rejects the notion that the private housing market, acting on its own, without government assistance can meet the needs of low-income households. Specifically, it recognizes the enormous advancements in the availability of housing finance and typically credits the role of the federal government in these efforts. Schnare, for example, has noted that "for the most part, broad developments in the multifamily mortgage market appear to have been favorable. The multifamily mortgage market—at least for large multifamily developments—is now fully integrated with national and international capital markets, ensuring a ready supply of mortgage funding and moderating, if not eliminating periodic credit crunches" (2001, 28).

Yet, adherents to this view are typically quick to point out that much more needs to be done and that, moreover, the advancements in our housing finance system have come at a cost. As one of the earliest critics of "creative finance," Michael Stegman has noted that: *It simply doesn't make sense to have a national housing policy in which the deeper the targeting and the lower the income group served, the more complicated and costly it is to arrange the financing*" (1991, 363, emphasis in the original).

Further concerns about our housing finance system have been raised by a team of researchers from Harvard's Joint Center for Housing Studies. First, they acknowledge that "the mortgage market in the United States has evolved into one of the most efficient capital markets in the world" and that new technologies related to underwriting, the growth of mortgage banking organizations, and a much expanded secondary mortgage market have produced what has been called a "revolution in mortgage finance." With the aid of an expanding economy during the 1990s and record low mortgage interest rates, there have been "dramatic increases in lending to low-income people and communities." Yet, they continue, "these same forces have also solidified the operations of what appears to be a dual mortgage market in mortgage finance in which low-income and often minority borrowers are served by different lending organizations using a different mix of loan products than is found in the mainstream market" (Apgar, Calder, and Fauth 2004, 1, 61).

Thus, the liberal academic community sees the housing finance system as both providing real benefits, while also articulating the ways in which the system has created problems and added costs, necessitating further government involvement.

Progressive-Critical View

Similar to the liberal academic community, those adhering to a progressive-critical view of housing issues, in general, and housing finance, in particular, see fundamental contradictions in how our system of housing finance impacts the affordability of housing for lower-income households. Michael Stone agrees with some aspects of the conservative and liberal assessments. He acknowledges that the system has "facilitated the production of vast amounts of housing and provided access to homeownership for over two-thirds of all U.S. households" (2006, 100). In addition, the various changes in mortgage financing have provided a substantial boost to real growth in the economy before and after the recessions in the 1970s, 1980s, and 1990s. In general, mortgage lenders have been able to compete more effectively for funds in the national and international capital markets.

Also, similar to the liberal view, Stone argues that there have been real costs associated with the various changes. He goes further in this critique than most liberal analysts, however, emphasizing the contradictory role of the institutions and mechanisms of mortgage lending. Specifically, "they have been essential to the functioning of the private housing market but have also been primary sources of persistent and pervasive housing affordability problems" (2006, 83). Among the costs associated with the various changes in mortgage financing, he notes that new construction focuses on building larger and more expensive homes; increases in the rate of homeownership may be coming at the expense of higher rates of foreclosure among lower-income borrowers; modest-income borrowers often are carrying significant debt burdens and are experiencing financial stress; and the very size and dominance of the GSEs has led to "institutional arrogance, with great risks for taxpayers and financial markets as well as the institutions themselves" (93).

Building on his argument, Stone presents a surprising excerpt from a 1999 article by David Lereah, who was then chief economist of the Mortgage Bankers Association and until mid 2007 was vice president and chief economist of the National Association of Realtors. In an apparent break from the standard housing industry perspective, Lereah notes:

> the share of loans with loan-to-value ratios greater than 90 percent has risen substantially during the past five years [to about 25 percent]. This places greater burden on the quality of loan portfolios in a period of deteriorating economic performance. And if and when the economy turns down, the first group to be hit with lost jobs and unreliable wages will be the lower-income group. According to recent income and debt data, the debt burdens of low-income households relative to higher-income households is rising. If the economy falters, clearly any households that are at the margin in terms of their abilities to meet their monthly mortgage obligations now will bring delinquency and foreclosure problems for mortgage servicers. Thus, it is the low-income families that are experiencing heavy debt burdens, leaving them more vulnerable to recession and meeting their mortgage obligations, while the higher-income groups are actually reducing their debt burdens [via refinancings and higher wages] and lowering their mortgage obligations. (cited in Stone 2006, 97)

So, though liberals, on the one hand, and progressives, on the other, share some overall assessments of the housing finance system, progressives see problems as much more fundamental to the nature of our political and economic system and, it therefore follows that real solutions are unlikely to emerge without fundamental systemic changes.

View from the Ground—Affordable Housing Developer

Toward the end of working on this chapter, I interviewed a nonprofit developer of affordable housing with more than twenty-five years of experience.[40] I wanted to ascertain her impressions of the system for financing rental housing for low and moderate-income households that has evolved. Beyond the observation that we have created a system that is far from straightforward and far too difficult to use, she highlighted a number of challenges that affordable housing developers encounter as they try to integrate equity requirements, debt financing, and subsidies.

First, the lack of adequate deep subsidies appears to be the most pressing of the many problems. In many locales, the LIHTC alone is not enough to reach households at 40 or 50 percent of median income, let alone at lower income levels. And, as pointed out earlier, there are significant costs, both in terms of time and money, in assembling a large number of funding sources. For example, because all funders are likely to participate in a design review of the development, each will come to the table with his or her own ideas about what constitutes good design. Efforts to accommodate this type of varied input can increase costs considerably.

Second, though financing may be available, the question is what restrictions each financing source will carry—concerning interest rates, long-term afford-ability, and so on—and whether the various restrictions and requirements of each funder will be consistent with each other. If they are not, which is typically the case, will it be possible to persuade the funders to reconcile the differences?

Third, many projects seek a large number of Section 8 vouchers in order to make as many units as affordable as possible. However, HUD's rules regarding deconcentration of low-income households require that no more than 30 percent of units in any given development be occupied by low-income residents, unless a waiver is provided. However, if the development is located in a high-poverty area, such waivers are nearly impossible to obtain.

Fourth, HUD may not allow any vouchers to be linked to a specific project (essentially creating a de facto Section 8 project-based program) if a housing authority has been providing more Section 8 vouchers than its actual alloca-tion. In other words, if a housing authority has 1,000 allocated Section 8s, and 800 certificates are being used, it may provide 300 new certificates, on the assumption that at least one-third of the new certificate holders will not be able to use them. However, if a housing authority is using this strategy, HUD will disallow the use of Section 8s as project-based set-asides.

Fifth, the current structure of public funding may add costs to construc-tion, in terms of the need to comply with Davis-Bacon prevailing wage rates and reporting requirements (for example, the number of minority or female-owned businesses and individuals participating in the construction), as well as the need for performance and payment bonds and extensive documentation required for change orders. Although all these rules may make sense and are in place for good reasons, the result is that development can become both more cumbersome and costly.

In summary, the current housing finance system for affordable multifamily development is complex, costly, and time consuming, and the developer must orchestrate a number of federal, state, and local rules, as well as manage and reconcile the objectives of the numerous participants in any given deal. At least three key questions arise from this inquiry.

Is Finance the Key Issue in Housing Production for Low-Income Households?

The answer, for the most part, appears to be "no." This chapter offers consid-erable detail about the range of mortgage financing sources available for both homeownership and rental housing. "Rather than the limited investor base that historically has characterized multifamily finance," one group of researchers has noted, "today the multifamily market has a plentitude of capital made available by an increasing variety of willing investors" (Bradley, Nothaft, and Freund 1998, 11).

However, in some market areas and for some homebuyers, there are still credit gaps and there is still a need for a vigorously implemented Community Reinvestment Act. "Despite the overall increase in access to mortgage capital, a racial gap persists in the ability of minorities to secure prime loans, even after controlling for income . . . race and ethnicity continue to be an important factor in determining the allocation of prime mortgage credit" (Apgar, Calder, and Fauth 2004, 5, 6).[41] Specifically, as recently as 2005, black and Latino households in Boston received less than their proportionate shares of home purchase loans and were denied loans more often than were white households at comparable income levels. In addition, the lending rate in lower-income neighborhoods was dramatically lower in predominantly black and Latino neighborhoods than in economically comparable white neighborhoods (Campen 2006, 3).

A national study (HUD 2002e) disclosed that one of the results of these credit imbalances has been a growth in subprime lending. Subprime lending refers to mortgage and refinancing transactions in which borrowers who do not meet the credit standards for borrowers in the prime market, are able to obtain loans (see chapter 9 for an extensive discussion of predatory and subprime lending). Borrowers may have various types of problematic credit records, an inadequate credit history, or nontraditional credit sources. Subprime lending fills an important niche, but has a significant downside. Some subprime lending may be predatory and may require homebuyers to pay excessive mortgage fees, interest rates, and penalties or carry prepaid credit life insurance, any of which can raise the cost of home buying by thousands of dollars.

The same HUD report further noted that subprime loans are three times more likely in low-income than in high-income neighborhoods and five times more likely in black than in white neighborhoods. In addition, homeowners in high-income black areas are twice as likely as their counterparts in low-income white areas to have subprime loans (HUD 2002e). Furthermore, part of the reason for the growth in subprime loans might be a lack of competition from lenders in these markets. Overall, black borrowers and their neighborhoods may be comparatively underserved by prime lenders (HUD 2002e).

Consequences for recipients of subprime loans can be serious, including higher costs and a higher likelihood of foreclosure. In 2002, for example, foreclosure or serious delinquency rates (payments at least ninety days late) were twenty times higher for subprime than for prime conventional loans (Apgar, Calder, and Fauth 2004).

Finally, although availability of mortgage finance does not appear to be a central issue, it seems clear that the structure of our housing finance system has become considerably less consumer-friendly over the past four decades. As early as the 1970s, the growing role of mortgage companies in the FHA mortgage market, and the lesser involvement of these mortgagees with borrowers compared with traditional thrift institutions, often created problems for consumers in terms of laxity in mortgage underwriting and in weak adherence to HUD's guidelines concerning mortgagors in default (Bratt 1976). More recently, Apgar, Calder, and Fauth have explored the impacts that changes in our mortgage finance system have created for community-based organizations (CBOs). They have noted that "after decades of success in expanding access to capital to historically underserved communities, CBOs and their funding partners . . . must retool their mortgage lending operations [and] strengthen their capacity to assist borrowers to protect themselves from abusive lending, to mitigate the serious consequences of the rise in foreclosure that threatens to undo decades of community revitalization efforts" (2004, 76).

Should Homeownership for Low-Income Households Be Encouraged?

Survey after survey reveals a strong desire for homeownership among millions of renter households (see, for example, Galster, Aron, and Reeder 1999). Moreover, during the 2000s, the Bush administration and HUD continued to tout homeownership. In June 2002, the president set a new goal: to increase minority homeownership by 5.5 million households by the end of the decade, thereby helping to close the gap between white and minority homeownership (HUD 2002d). Five months later, HUD released two reports to support this agenda (HUD 2002b, 2002a). The first outlined the economic benefits that would be realized if the minority homeownership gap was reduced (HUD 2002b). The second recommended modest increases or new funding for home-ownership education, increasing the supply of affordable homes, providing assistance with down payment and closing costs, and offering financing options, thereby making homeownership more accessible to a wider range of house-holds (HUD 2002a). However, that report did not recommend a new deep subsidy to promote low-income homeownership.

After several years studying a range of issues, the Millennial Housing Commission recommended no more than a new homeownership tax credit aimed at first-time buyers with incomes less than 80 percent of median income. It justified this approach with the lackluster observation that "the advantage of the homeownership tax credit over direct subsidy programs is that it devolves authority to states and relies on private-sector partners to deliver allocated resources" (Millennial Housing Commission 2002, 31).

Based on this analysis, as well as the findings presented in another book chapter (Bratt 2007), I offer a series of observations about what is needed to promote homeownership for lower-income households. The overriding point is very simple: a deep subsidy is the sine qua non of homeownership for low-income households. Subsidies can take the form of front-end grants, "silent" second mortgages, interest rate write-downs, housing vouchers, or donated land, labor, or building materials. However assistance is provided, funds are needed to close the gap between the real costs of owning and maintaining a home and the assets and incomes of lower-income homeowners.

The following recommendations concerning low-income homeownership go far beyond the issue of finance, which, as already noted, does not appear to be the most critical limiting factor. First, homeowners should have an investment in their homes, whether through "sweat equity" or with a cash investment. At least some of the risk involved in homeownership should be borne by the owners, and they should be well prepared for these risks. If another entity assumes the risk, such as HUD or a nonprofit, it should act in concert with consumer interests.

Second, prepurchase counseling is an important component of homeownership programs for low-income households. In the nonprofit-administered Habitat for Humanity program, for example, prospective homeowners are assisted to prepare for homeownership through classes and one-on-one training. The homeownership programs supported by the NeighborWorks America and Enterprise Community Partners also typically stress the importance of counseling. One report noted that, "buyers who understand the homebuying process and who are financially ready to assume home-ownership responsibilities are critical to successful outcomes" (DiPetta et al. 2001, 2–2; see also Rohe, Quercia, and Van Zandt 2002; Werwath 1996).[42] An important component of counseling should involve helping homebuyers find the best mortgage product available and educating them on the importance of shopping for credit, much as they do for other goods and services (Apgar, Calder, and Fauth 2004).

Third, along with prepurchase counseling, high quality postpurchase counseling is extremely important. Once a household has become a homeowner, significant efforts should be made to ensure that ownership is retained, even if financial difficulties arise. Postpurchase counseling is necessary to help homeowners understand their maintenance issues, the impacts of market changes, and opportunities to avoid foreclosure (DiPetta et al. 2001, 5–2; Werwath 1996). The Habitat for Humanity program, for example, works closely "with homebuyers to resolve payment problems before they become severe" (Applied Real Estate Analysis 1998, III-19, VI-3).

Fourth, quick resale of properties with large front-end profits should not be allowed. Careful thought is needed, however, to provide a fair balance between enabling homeowners to accumulate equity as an asset in their homes and preventing them from purchasing below the market and quickly reselling at the highest possible price. The Habitat for Humanity and Nehemiah programs typically require homeowners to remain in their homes for a specified period of time, after which all equity and profits accrue to them. Other affordable homeownership programs structure restrictions on resale prices so that the longer a homeowner stays in a house, the greater amount of equity he or she accumulates. This is an attempt to balance the needs of the original homeowners to build assets, while advancing the goal of preserving affordability of the homes for new buyers, at least for a number of years (see Davis 2006).

Fifth, good quality construction and rehabilitation are obviously central to any homeownership program. For example, a close review of eight Neighbor-Works organizations found that almost all offered inspection services for home buyers or maintained a list of reputable home inspectors in the area. Many also had full-time construction managers who were available to assist owners in dealing with the complexities of home renovation (Rohe, Quercia, and Van Zandt 2002, 42; see also DiPetta et al. 2001, 4–2). Similarly, Enterprise Community Partners encourages affiliates to provide pre-purchase home inspections as well as advice concerning home repairs (Werwath 1996, 3).

Sixth, funds should be available to homeowners in need of home repairs. Low-income owners have proven to be good targets for predatory lenders who take advantage of the inability of these owners to access conventional loans for maintenance and significant upgrading.

Seventh, there should be a watchdog agency involved in low-income home-ownership programs. This entity, most likely a nonprofit organization, would be responsible for selecting builders, arranging financing, and screening ten-ants.[43] A report on NeighborWorks America affiliates provides numerous examples of how key actors have been brought into partnership arrange-ments with the nonprofits operating the homeownership programs. Avoiding adversarial relationships, mortgage lenders and real estate agents join the programs from the outset and assist in a variety of ways, including helping homebuyers find homes, providing first mortgages, creating pools of funds to provide additional financing, making outright contributions to the organ-ization, and participating in counseling programs (DiPetta et al. 2001). The early experiences with the Section 235 program underscored that home-ownership programs for low-income households must pay careful attention to the many possibilities for private-market actors to take advantage of the generally inexperienced homebuyers. Instead of merely trying to serve as watchdogs, however, many of the more recent programs appear to be empha-sizing how these key actors can work in partnership with the organizations and residents.

Eighth, though it may be cost-effective to build homes in weak market locales, caution must be exercised about the potential for neighborhood factors to create problems for the new homeowners.[44] There also is some evidence that homeownership can benefit problem-laden neighborhoods—"the attractive appearance and perceived safety of even a small enclave can offset the otherwise negative neighborhood conditions" (Applied Real Estate Analysis 1998, III-15; see also DiPetta 2001). It is probably unrealistic to expect that any single factor such as a low-income homeownership program can transform a surrounding area, but it can make an important contribution in conjunction with other types of neighborhood-focused initiatives. As for homeowners who purchase homes in severely distressed areas, safeguards should be provided in the event they need to sell their homes and if the market is too weak to ensure a full return on their investment.

Ninth, extreme caution must be exercised in screening would-be home-owners to assess their ability to carry the financial responsibilities of home-ownership, despite their limited family income and resources. All homeowners need to be able to cover the costs of ongoing maintenance, including periodic expensive repairs such as a new roof or furnace. Low-income homeownership programs face a dilemma. On the one hand, there is a desire to make the loan terms as attractive as possible and to set credit limits low enough to qualify as many households as possible. On the other, it is very important that the financial arrangement carry some measure of risk for the homeowner and that realistic credit assessments discourage households from purchasing when they are unlikely to do so successfully.

The challenge of providing homeownership opportunities to lower-income households is formidable and requires extensive support. The desire for homeownership, though, is so strong among so many people, regardless of income, that the quest for optimum programs to serve low-income households continues to move forward.

Clearly, we have learned a great deal about what is needed to promote homeownership for low-income urban households. This collective wisdom has led to scores of excellent programs that do not require or expect purchasers to shoulder all the risks and complexities of ownership on their own. Nevertheless, little federal funding is available to support low-income homeownership in general, but particularly urban homeownership.

In 1976, I noted that homeownership for low-income (nonrural) households had not received a fair test at the national level (Bratt 1976). The conclusion holds true today. The only difference is that we now far better understand what such a program would entail, and have concrete evidence that homeownership programs for low-income households can be successful. To make greater strides in closing the gap between minority and white ownership rates, we need a strong federal role.

What Is Needed to Stimulate the Production of Rental Housing Affordable to Low-Income Households?

Deep subsidies to cover capital costs of construction as well as operating costs must be provided. As discussed in a Brookings Institution and Urban Institute report, "rental assistance programs require deep subsidies if they are to reach the neediest households" (Katz et al. 2003, ix). Furthermore, one of the Millennial Housing Commission's boldest and most important recom-mendations outlined a capital subsidy program to build housing for extremely low-income households. Mirroring the public housing program's funding formula, rents would cover operating expenses, though the commission acknowledged that additional subsidies would be required for the lowest-income households.

The nation's leading low-income housing advocacy organization, the National Low Income Housing Coalition, has been in the forefront of promoting the idea of a new National Housing Trust Fund. This would establish a source of revenue to build and maintain new housing,[45] and preserve or rehabilitate existing housing that is affordable to low-income people, with at least 75 percent of the funds earmarked for rental housing. The goal would be to produce, rehabilitate, and preserve 1.5 million units of housing over the first ten years, with initial sources of funds coming from excess FHA and Ginnie Mae revenues.

A 2004 bipartisan report also explicitly called for the creation of a National Housing Trust Fund. Noting that "the supply of low-cost rental housing has not kept up with need or demand" and that it has been more than two decades since a federal housing production program specifically targeted to extremely low-income households had been operational, Henry Cisneros and his colleagues recommended "a source of capital for the production, preservation, and rehabilitation of housing affordable to low-income households" (2004, 21, 49). Although the authors neither specified where the source of capital would come from nor that this is essentially the same proposal the National Low Income Housing Coalition put forth, it is significant that leading Republicans and Democrats in the housing world have now embraced the idea.

As the consensus grows that deep subsidies are needed to support affordable rental housing, it is worth noting that no one talks about bringing back the subsidy formula of the old public housing program, which provided housing through long-term debt covered by the federal government. Public housing is so fully out-of-favor, however, that no mention of reviving it is ever made. In the process of reflecting on affordable housing finance, and as we conclude this lengthy exploration into the complexities of the system we have created, the question is why not?

I would argue that it is the name of the program—public housing—rather than the form of subsidy provided, that provokes virtually unanimous opposition. Unfortunately, the two are closely linked. Hearkening back to the roots of the public housing program, when it was so vehemently opposed by the private real estate industry, publicly owned and managed housing still does not sit well with the public. Also, the program's image has certainly been adversely affected by its most glaring failures and by the conventional wisdom that says public housing is synonymous with vertical ghettos, poorly designed, and a blight on the neighborhood.[46]

In 1987, at about the time that new production of public housing was terminated, the way in which public housing was subsidized was changed from annual contributions provided by the government, which covered the payment of principal and interest on bonds floated by local housing authorities, to capital grants. In passing the legislation, Congress explicitly recognized that the capital method of financing . . . calls for much less budget authority because [it] provides for federal grants for these units "up front" rather than providing annual direct outlays and tax expenditures over the long period of time needed to retire the tax-exempt bonds. The grant method of financing could also result in savings to the public housing authorities by eliminating the accounting and administrative costs related to servicing the loans and reissuing short term bonds over a 40-year period. (cited in Stone 1993, 259)[47]

Stone further points out that the use of direct capital grants is widely used by the government to finance a whole range of activities, including military housing, housing for the elderly (since 1990), major public works (such as the federal share of interstate highway construction), dams, and toxic waste cleanup (1993, 219). More recently, subsidies to convert public housing to mixed-income developments through the HOPE VI program also rely on direct capital grants and the HOME program is also an up-front block grant program. James Wallace (1995) underscores the overall efficiency of capital grants and suggests that the HOME program could be expanded to provide greater assistance for development.

Clearly, the direct capital grant mechanism could be used in a renamed subsidy program and the type of entity sponsoring the housing could be expanded to include, or even focus on, nonprofit organizations, rather than relying solely on public housing authorities. Community development corporations and the network of regional housing partnerships, as well as other nonprofit organizations, would be in a good position to implement a new deep rental subsidy program. They would also be assisted by the national nonprofit intermediaries created to support and promote the work of the locally based groups.

Beyond the need for deep subsidies, it is also essential to continue discussions about how to revamp the regulatory structure in which housing is built and how to overcome NIMBY (not-in-my-backyard) attitudes. Specifically, we should pay attention to how states can use their powers to override local exclusionary zoning and to stimulate affordable housing construction. Massachusetts has had a zoning override in place since 1969 (Chapter 40B) and, more recently, the state has passed two new initiatives aimed at insulating communities from school costs that exceed the local property tax generated as a result of new housing constructed.[48] First, the Smart Growth Zoning and Housing Production Act (Chapter 40R) authorizes the state to provide cash incentives to towns that develop affordable housing under the terms of the new statute. Second, the Smart Growth School Cost Reimbursement Act (Chapter 40S) authorizes state reimbursements to cities or towns to cover the net cost of educating additional children who move to a community following the development of Smart Growth housing.

FINAL NOTE

After several decades of involvement with studying housing issues facing low-income households, it becomes tedious to keep noting that the resolution to these problems is not a matter of knowledge, but of political will. This is still the case, however. Beyond this essential point, this study of housing and housing finance leads to these final observations:

- Finance *is* generally available for most homebuyers and developers of low and moderate-income housing. Deep subsidies that can make housing affordable to low- and very-low-income residents are scarce, however, so it is quite difficult to make either homeownership or rental opportunities available to people with the greatest financial need.

- There is still a race gap in terms of white and nonwhite homeownership rates and subprime lending is a growing problem.

- Despite the pro-homeownership rhetoric, the federal government has not committed itself to a comprehensive homeownership program for low-income, nonrural households.

- Our housing finance system, particularly for multifamily housing, is complex and convoluted, and creates costs in terms of time and money. In short, some aspects of our housing finance system are not-so-consumer-friendly. For low-income homeownership programs, community-based organizations and other nonprofits are needed to serve as intermediaries between lenders and borrowers and to serve as consumer advocates.

- Many analysts now agree that production programs, particularly for rental housing, are a high priority to meet low-income housing needs.

- We know that such housing can be good quality, non-stigmatizing, and blend in well with existing neighborhoods.

- We also know that subsidized rental housing can be built by nonprofit sponsors, public housing authorities, and for-profit developers. Although my strong preference is to rely most heavily on nonprofit and public entities, along with a significant amount of resident involvement, private for-profit sponsors should also be involved. However, in that case, programs need to be carefully structured so that the profit-motivated goals of private entrepreneurs do not conflict with the public sector's need to maintain long-term affordability. Programs such as the Low-Income Housing Tax Credit have been structured to address these concerns.

- Local resistance to new subsidized housing is often significant, particularly multifamily housing. We need to experiment with different mechanisms, probably through statewide initiatives, to encourage communities to accommodate such housing so that the tangible costs of new development are not borne solely by the community.

- Good housing can make a real difference in the lives of individuals and communities.

- We just don't know how to get the public sector to commit the resources— the development subsidies (preferably in the form of direct capital grants, possibly through a new National Housing Trust Fund), as well as operating subsidies—to make housing problems a thing of the past.

Thanks to Louise Elving, Viva Consulting, for her willingness to share her insights concerning the complexities of affordable housing development. I also am grateful to Julia Sass Rubin, for her overall conceptualization of this project and for her helpful comments on this chapter.

NOTES

1. Concerning the role that housing plays in the overall economy, in 2000, consumption and investment spending on housing amounted to 14 percent of the country's gross domestic product, a figure that has held constant since 1950 (Colton 2003, 264; for a summary of the relationship between housing and family well-being, see Bratt 2002).

2. Low-income households, as defined by HUD, earn no more than 80 percent of area median income; moderate-income households earn between 80 and 95 percent of area median income. When the phrase *lower income* is used in this chapter, these are the groups being referred to. *Affordable* refers to housing that these income groups can afford, paying no more than 30 percent of income ("Glossary of Community Planning and Development Terms," http://www.hud.gov:80/offices/ cpd/library/glossary). Also, very low-income households earn 50 percent or less of area median income; extremely low-income households earn 30 percent or less of area median. It should be pointed out that moderate-income is sometimes referred to as including households between 80 and 120 percent of area median income (HUD 2003).

3. It should also be noted that assisted housing programs have had a number of other goals in addition to addressing low-income needs, such as stimulating employment and alleviating social unrest (Bratt 1976; Marcuse 1986).

4. This chapter only touches on, in the final section, several other key factors that impact housing production, namely regulatory restrictions,

including zoning and NIMBY attitudes (not-in-my-backyard). Another area that is not discussed in detail is the preservation of subsidized housing produced through various federal subsidy programs, dating from the 1960s. Also omitted is a discussion on the extent to which public policies aimed at producing units are also used as vehicles to reduce segregation. Throughout this chapter, the focus is on federal or nationally focused initiatives. Numerous state and local programs have been created to assist with the development of affordable housing, but a discussion of these efforts is beyond the scope of this chapter.

5. Before the recent consensus on the need for production programs, John Weicher (1990) summarized the arguments in favor of vouchers. Noting that the relative merits of voucher vs. production subsidies had been considered seriously since 1968, he argued that production programs are expensive, inequitable, and had failed to lift the poor out of poverty. While acknowledging that no program works well in tight markets and that vouchers will not result in the construction of new housing, he pointed out that vouchers appear to help reduce racial and ethnic segregation, that they contribute to the preservation of existing housing, and that they may be more effective in strengthening low-income neighborhoods.

6. For example, in 1999 Bennett L. Hecht, a vice president at the Enterprise Foundation, produced the second edition of his guide, *Developing Affordable Housing.* Of the 680 pages in this tome, about half are concerned with financing issues.

7. There is even a magazine, *Affordable Housing Finance,* which started publication in 1993. Advertisers include nonprofit entities and scores of private sector providers of capital and services related to affordable housing production and management. The magazine follows and reports on various changes in federal laws, funding levels, and programs that impact private sector participation in developing, financing, and managing affordable housing.

8. Although additional research has shown that wealth constraints have the largest impact in reducing the likelihood of homeownership, this factor declined substantially during the 1990s while credit quality-based constraints became increasingly significant barriers to home-ownership (Barakova et al. 2003, 334).

9. By 1975, more than 90,000 units of Section 235 housing had been foreclosed, representing about 18 percent of the total (Hays 1995, 117). In addition to the very low down payment, there were many other factors that contributed to the problems associated with the Section 235 pro-

gram, as documented by numerous congressional hearings and government inquiries (see, for example, Bratt 1976; Hays 1995).

10. Based on data on 2,261 Nehemiah loans that had been originated in four
cities three to five years prior to February 2002, HUD found that more
than 19 percent of the loans reported at least one incidence of default.
This was double the default rate of 9.7 percent for all non-Nehemiah-
assisted loans originated in the same four cities and during the same
period (HUD 2002c, 8). Although defaults do not automatically translate into foreclosures, it is also of concern that HUD processed foreclosure claims on 7.8 percent of the Nehemiah loans, compared with
3.2 percent of the non-Nehemiah loans (HUD 2002c, 9).

11. In a study of the Nehemiah Down Payment Assistance program,
researchers underscored the positive fiscal impacts of the Nehemiah
program in the form of property tax revenues paid to local communities and the extent to which Nehemiah participants enjoyed increases
in the value of their property and, as a result, overall improvements in
their asset profile (Wong et al. 2004).

12. This is no longer a hypothetical prediction. High foreclosure rates among
mortgages that had been originated with low down payments, in conjunction with relatively high or variable interest mortgages, gained the
spotlight in mid-2007. By the summer of that year, this situation created
enormous dislocations in the national and worldwide financial markets.
As this book is going to press (September 2007), it appears that there will
be a significant tightening of mortgage credit; it is unlikely that no down
payment mortgages will be nearly as available in the foreseeable future.

13. Down payment assistance may not exceed $10,000 or 6 percent of
the purchase price of the home, whichever is greater. In fiscal year
2006, Congress appropriated $25 million for this program, one-eighth
the maximum authorization level (National Low Income Housing
Coalition 2007).

14. This bill, though sponsored by a Republican congressman, caused some
concern among conservative groups such as the Heritage Foundation.
Noting that homeownership is a valuable goal, they argued that pro-
homeownership policies should encourage individuals to save on their
own. Further, they maintained, zero down payment programs are tan-
tamount to handouts and foster dependency, similar to the allegedly
failed programs of the Great Society (Utt 2004). The bill was never
voted on by the full Congress and was introduced in a slightly different
format as the Zero Downpayment Pilot Program of 2006. Although
it passed in the Financial Services Committee, the bill died in the
109th Congress.

15. Since 1976 another tax incentive program, aimed at preserving historic structures, has stimulated the rehabilitation of more than 185,000 housing units and created over 140,000 housing units, of which over 75,000 are targeted to low- and moderate-income households (see National Park Service, "Federal Historic Preservation Tax Incentives," http://www2.cr.nps.gov/tps/tax/tax_p.htm).

16. Each lender typically wants to claim credit for making the deal happen— that without their contribution, it would have fallen through. At the very least, each often claims that their investment is responsible for leveraging other investments.

17. The criticism that too much of the LIHTC subsidy is lost due to administrative and transactional costs appears to be less valid than in the earlier years of the program (McClure 2000). Another criticism of the LIHTC is that the subsidy may not, in fact, increase the supply of units. Instead, the LIHTC may be substituting unsubsidized units that would have been built in its absence (Malpezzi and Vandell 2002).

18. See National Equity Fund, http://www.nefinc.org, and Enterprise Community Investment, http://www.enterprisecommunity.com/home/.

19. The extent to which REITs invest in affordable rental housing is not clear. REITs are typically a source of capital for market rate and sometimes mixed-income rental housing.

20. In addition, Alex Schwartz summarizes the impacts of FIRREA as follows: "It caused thrifts to cut back their loan portfolios and lending activities. It contributed to a severe reduction in the availability of mortgage funds for multifamily housing, and it boosted the already ascending secondary mortgage market" (2006, 56).

21. In 2004 Fannie Mae and Freddie Mac became the subject of considerable concern and scrutiny, as various accounting irregularities were uncovered in both agencies (see, for example, Timothy L. O'Brien, "Mortgage Giant Agrees to Alter Business Ways," *The New York Times,* September 28, 2004). In response, a bill was introduced, but not enacted. The Federal Housing Finance Reform Act of 2005 would have created a new independent regulatory entity to oversee the government-sponsored enterprises. The House version of the bill, which was passed in October 2005, would have created a new fund aimed at increasing homeownership opportunities for extremely low and very low income individuals. This fund would have been capitalized with up to 5 percent of the after tax revenues generated by Fannie Mae and Freddie Mac.

22. Loans on projects located on Indian reservations, for example, may be prime for Ginnie Mae guarantees, because of potential conflicts between tribal and U.S. laws governing ownership and foreclosure (The Enterprise Foundation 1995).

23. The NeighborWorks America network is composed of some 240 non-profit organizations across the country that are committed to providing financial support, training, and technical assistance for community-based revitalization efforts. The lead organization, originally known as the Neighborhood Reinvestment Corporation and now known as NeighborWorks America, was created by Congress in 1978. While traditionally committed to homeownership rehabilitation programs, it has expanded its mission to include a wider range of housing options, including multifamily housing.

24. See "About HFAs—HFA Administered Programs." http://www.ncsha.org/section.cfm/3/34/36.

25. The Bush FY 2006 budget proposed to remove the CDBG program from HUD and to move it to the Department of Commerce, along with a 35 percent reduction in funding (National Low Income Housing Coalition 2007). Although the program will remain at HUD, at least for the time being, funding for the CDBG program has declined from $4.9 billion in fiscal year 2004 to $3.7 billion in fiscal year 2006.

26. The Local Initiatives Support Corporation was created by the Ford Foundation, which provided matching funds for the initial $10 million capitalization. Other funders included a number of other financial entities, corporations, and insurance companies. The Enterprise Foundation was created by real estate developer Jim Rouse, as an outgrowth of a grassroots project with which he had become involved in Washington, D.C., known as Jubilee Housing. The Neighborhood Reinvestment Corporation was created by Congress to sponsor and support what was originally known as Neighborhood Housing Services organizations, now known as NeighborWorks organizations.

27. See Coalition of Community Development Financial Institutions, "About Us," http://www.cdfi.org/aboutus.asp.

28. Often, if any one or more of these conditions prevails, the lender may require that the borrower carry some form of mortgage insurance, either through the FHA or through a private mortgage insurer.

29. In view of the high foreclosure rate among subprime borrowers that became international news in summer 2007, this is something of an understatement. See also note 13.

30. To be sure, the key differences between multifamily and single family loans result in more complexity, uncertainty, and risk when multi-

family loans are sold on the secondary mortgage market (Segal and Szymanoski 1998; for further discussion on the challenges facing the secondary mortgage market in relation to multifamily housing, see Cummings and DiPasquale 1998).

31. See Low Income Investment Fund, "What We Do," http://www.liifund. org/about/index_about.htm.

32. The breakdown of the remaining $72 billion in federal housing subsidies is as follows: other housing-related tax expenditures (including capital gains exemptions and investor-related expenditures, such as preferential treatment of bonds and the LIHTC), $35 billion and housing assistance outlays, $37 billion.

33. The formula for calculating tenant contributions toward rent in subsidized housing remained unchanged until 1981, when the Reagan administration increased tenant contributions for rent to 30 percent of income. This figure became the new standard for affordability and has remained constant for over two decades. Whether 30 percent of income, or indeed 25 percent of income, is the right figure for a lower-income household to pay is open to debate. Probably the most articulate and vociferous opponent to any standard percent of income figure as the basis for determining affordability has been put forward by Michael Stone (1993), who argues that for the lowest-income households any percentage of income required for rent may be too much, not allowing sufficient income to cover other necessities of life. Instead, he offers that a "market basket" approach to determining housing affordability be used, taking into account the real costs a family encounters in meeting the costs of food, clothing, transportation and, of course, housing.

34. On the other hand, the Byrne et al. study also pointed out that the fact that funding is dependent on annual appropriations is problematic and that there are "inequities in the distribution of operating funds." The situation with regard to the physical needs of public housing is of much more concern, with an estimated backlog of between $18 and $22 billion (2003, 1, 2).

35. A proposed program, exit tax relief for owners of privately owned, publicly subsidized developments, is attracting bipartisan support. Through such a program, owners would be encouraged to sell their properties to nonprofit or public sponsors that would commit to long-term affordability provisions (see, for example, Cisneros et al. 2004).

36. At the same time that Congress created these new production programs, a new rental certificate component was also created, also known as Section 8, mentioned earlier. When Section 8 is referred to, it is almost always this component of the program that is being discussed, rather than the production programs.

37.   In 2005 HUD's fair market rents (FMRs) came under extensive attack by housing agencies and advocacy groups when the proposed FMRs were announced. The new FMRs would have produced unusually large changes, compared with rent levels set for 2004, due to the use of 2000 census data for the first time and a change in the methodology used for setting FMRs, such as reducing the rent levels for units with three or more bedrooms. Also important was that HUD proposed to change the geographic area on which FMRs are based, by expanding metropolitan areas with relatively high rents to include formerly rural counties where rents were considerably lower (Fischer and Sard 2004). According to the National Low Income Housing Coalition (2004), the final FMRs for 2005 represent only a "relative improvement" over the proposed figures. But HUD did revert to the definition of metropolitan areas used in 2004.

38.   The FY 2001 appropriation was $574 million. The highest appropriation for HOPE VI was in FY 1999, $625 million; $100 million is the lowest appropriation since the program was created in FY 1993 (see Bratt 2003).

39.   As noted earlier, both CDBG and HOME block grants can be used for a wide array of activities, including project-based housing. These subsidies generally provide only a small portion of the funds needed for a housing development. In addition, though the Section 8 New Construction/Substantial Rehabilitation program was terminated in 1983, public housing authorities may designate up to 20 percent of their voucher fund allocations for project-based assistance, as long as no more than 25 percent of the units in a given development are so designated, unless the units are occupied by elderly or disabled families or families receiving supportive services (Schwartz 2006, 144, n.8).

40.   Interview conducted with Louise Elving, VIVA Consulting. Formerly Vice President of Housing Development, The Community Builders, Boston, Massachusetts. October 2004.

41.   Although minorities accounted for about 32 percent of first-time homebuyers in 2001, an increase from about 19 percent since 1973, there is still a huge gap in white and minority homeownership rates. Three-quarters of all white households own their own homes, compared with 48 percent of black households and 47 percent of Hispanic households (Joint Center for Housing Studies 2004, 35). Analyses of national household surveys from the 1960s, 1970s, and 1980s also revealed that for similar white and minority wealth-constrained households, the former group owned homes at higher rates than apparently comparable minority households. Moreover, racial and ethnic homeownership patterns changed very little between about 1970 and 1990. Finally, minori-

ties are much more likely than whites to own in central city than suburban locations (Gyourko, Linneman, and Wachter 1999; Wachter and Megbolugbe 1992).

42. Since the 1970s, housing counseling has been something of a growth industry (McCarthy and Quercia 2000). The Housing and Community Development Act of 1974 authorized HUD to directly fund housing counseling and funding for this purpose grew from $3 million to $12 million between 1977 and 1993 (Quercia and Wachter 1996, 179), reaching $25 million in 2002 (Collins 2002, 33). Although there still are many unanswered questions about efficacy, "its popularity may continue to grow because of its ability to reach and extend homeownership opportunities to traditionally underserved populations" (McCarthy and Quercia, 2000, 29). The Millennial Housing Commission (2002) recommended an expansion of housing counseling based, in part, on research by Freddie Mac showing that pre-purchase counseling and education had positive impacts on loan performance (Hirad and Zorn 2001). For more on financial education and community development see chapter 3 of this volume.

43. Apgar, Calder, and Fauth cite a Fannie Mae survey that emphasizes "the importance of borrowers having access to a trusted advisor to help guide them through the mortgage process." They further suggest that this is an important role for community-based organizations to play, although they add that "many community groups . . . seem reluctant to fill that role, feeling that such assistance goes against the goal of empowering people to make their own decisions" (2004, 92).

44. The impact of poor neighborhood conditions on homeowners can be substantial. Baltimore homeowners, for example, reported concern about living in an area plagued by drugs, crime, and abandoned structures (Phipps, Heintz, and Franke 1994, 4–13).

45. The Trust Fund would provide operating subsidies for new or rehabilitated units for one year. After that time, the operating subsidy would be provided through Thrifty Vouchers funded and renewed through the Housing Certificate Fund. Thrifty Vouchers would be based on actual operating expenses, rather than prevailing market rents (http://www.nhtf.org/about/proposal.asp).

46. Although there are many seemingly unfair criticisms of public housing, there are a number of ways in which the program has, indeed, been problematic. For example, the extensive regulations, including the need for detailed reporting, put substantial burdens on personnel and likely increase costs. In addition, although maintenance problems often may be traced to inadequate federal funding, the fact remains that many

public housing development have, and do, suffer from serious backlogs of repairs.

47. McClure also notes that a capital grant is "the most efficient mechanism for providing government aid to the development of low-income housing" (2000, 111). However, he adds that he is doubtful that such a program would be adopted.

48. Such incentives and insurance may be necessary to stimulate cities and towns to promote the development of housing. However, there is conflicting evidence about whether housing contributes to an increase in school costs. One study in Massachusetts found that: "In most cases, multifamily developments built since 1990 have not contributed significantly to the rise in school enrollments that occurred in many communities across the state. New single-family homes and in some towns, a high rate of turnover in older single-family homes, generated a majority of the state's school enrollment growth . . . it is very unlikely that new multifamily housing has produced a negative fiscal impact on cities and towns" (Community Opportunities Group Inc. and Connery Associates 2003, 2–1). Another study in Massachusetts concluded that for a typical mixed income multifamily development, there would be a net increase in school costs in only 43 percent of communities and the average amount is estimated to be $320 per apartment. The situation is different for single-family homes, which would increase school costs for a typical community an average of $5,000 per home per year, based on a home with a $250,000 assessed value (Carman, Bluestone, and White 2005).

REFERENCES.

Achtenberg, Emily P. 2002. *Stemming the Tide: A Handbook on Preserving Subsidized Multifamily Housing.* Washington: Local Initiatives Support Corporation.

————. 2006. "Federally-Assisted Housing in Conflict: Privatization or Preservation?" In *A Right to Housing: Foundation for a New Social Agenda,* edited by Rachel G. Bratt, Michael E. Stone, and Chester Hartman. Philadelphia, Pa.: Temple University Press.

Apgar, William C., Allegra Calder, and Gary Fauth. 2004. *Credit, Capital and Communities: The Implications of the Changing Mortgage Banking Industry for Community-Based Organizations.* Cambridge, Mass.: Joint Center for Housing Studies of Harvard University.

Applied Real Estate Analysis, by Maxine Mitchell and S. Paige Warren. 1998. *Making Homeownership a Reality: Survey of Habitat for Humanity (HFHI). Inc. Homeowners and Affiliates.* Washington: U.S. Department of Housing and Urban Development, Office of Policy Development and Research.

Barakova, Irina, Raphael W. Bostic, Paul S. Calem, and Susan M. Wachter. 2003. "Does Credit Quality Matter for Homeownership?" *Journal of Housing Economics* 12(4): 318–36.

Benjamin, Lehn, Julia Sass Rubin, and Sean Zielenbach. 2004. "Community Development Financial Institutions: Current Issues and Future Prospects." *Journal of Urban Affairs* 26(2): 177–95.

Bradley, Donald S., Frank E. Nothaft, and James L. Freund. 1998. "Financing Multifamily Properties: A Play with New Actors and New Lines." *Cityscape: A Journal of Policy Development and Research* 4(1): 5–17.

Bratt, Rachel G. 1976. "Federal Homeownership Policy and Home Finance: A Study of Program Operations and Impacts on the Consumer." Ph.D. dissertation, MIT.

———. 2002. "Housing and Family Well-Being." *Housing Studies* 17(1): 13–26.

———. 2003. "Housing for Very Low-Income Households: The Record of President Clinton, 1993–2000." *Housing Studies* 18(2): 607–35.

———. 2007. "Homeownership for Low-Income Households: A Comparison of the Section 235, Nehemiah and Habitat for Humanity Programs." In *Chasing the American Dream: New Perspectives on Affordable Homeownership*, edited by William Rohe and Harry Watson. Ithaca, N.Y.: Cornell University Press.

Byrne, Gregory A., Kevin Day, and James Stockard. 2003. "Taking Stock of Public Housing." Presented to the Public Housing Authority Directors Association. Graduate School of Design, Harvard University.

Campen, Jim. 2006. *Changing Patterns XIII: Mortgage Lending to Traditionally Underserved Borrowers and Neighborhoods in Boston, Greater Boston and Massachusetts, 1990–2005.* Boston, Mass.: Massachusetts Community & Banking Council.

Carman, Ted, Barry Bluestone, and Eleanor White. 2005. *Chapter 40R School Cost Analysis and Proposed Smart Growth School Cost Insurance Supplement.* Report and Recommendations for the Commonwealth Housing Task Force from the Center for Urban and Regional Policy. Northeastern University, Boston, Mass.

Case, Karl E. 1991. "Investors, Developers, and Supply-Side Subsidies: How Much is Enough?" *Housing Policy Debate* 2(2): 341–56.

Cisneros, Henry G., Nicolas P. Retsinas, Jack F. Kemp, and Kent W. Colton. 2004. "Opportunity and Progress: A Bipartisan Platform for National Housing Policy." Joint Center for Housing Studies, Harvard University.

Collins, Michael. 2002. *Pursuing the American Dream. Homeownership and the Role of Federal Housing Policy.* Washington: Millennial Housing Commission.

Colton, Kent W. 2003. *Housing in the Twenty-First Century: Achieving Common Ground.* Cambridge, Mass.: Harvard University Press, Wertheim Publications Committee.

Community Opportunities Group, Inc., and Connery Associates. 2003. *Housing the Commonwealth's School-Age Children: The Implications of Multi-Family Housing Development for Municipal and School Expenditures.* Boston, Mass.: Citizens' Housing Association.

Cummings, Jean L., and Denise DiPasquale. 1998. "Developing a Secondary Market for Affordable Rental Housing: Lessons from the LIMAC/Freddie Mac and EMI/Fannie Mae Programs." *Cityscape: A Journal of Policy Development and Research* 4(1): 19–41.

———. 1999. "The Low-Income Housing Tax Credit: An Analysis of the First Ten Years." *Housing Policy Debate* 10(2): 251–307.

Davis, John Emmeus. 2006. *Shared Equity Homeownership: The Changing Landscape of Resale-Restricted, Owner-Occupied Housing.* Montclair, N.J.: National Housing Institute.

DiPasquale, Denise, and Jean L. Cummings. 1992. "Financing Multifamily Rental Housing: The Changing Role of Lenders and Investors." *Housing Policy Debate* 3(1): 77–116.

DiPetta, Ann, Eileen Flanagan, Maggie Hamer, Michael Schubert, and Alison Tresher. 2001. *Winning Strategies: Best Practices in the Work of Home-Ownership Promotion.* Washington: Neighborhood Reinvestment Corporation.

Dolbeare, Cushing N., Irene Basloe Saraf, and Sheila Crowley. 2004. *Changing Priorities: The Federal Budget and Housing Assistance 1976–2005.* Washington: National Low Income Housing Coalition.

The Enterprise Foundation. 1995. *Overview of Housing Finance Mechanisms.* Columbia, Md: The Enterprise Foundation.

Federal Home Loan Banks. 2004. "The FHLBank System." Accessed at http://www.fhlbanks.com.

Fischer, W., and Barbara Sard. 2004. *Hasty Changes to HUD's "Fair Market Rents" Would Disrupt Housing Assistance.* Washington: Center on Budget and Policy Priorities.

Galster, George, Laudan Aron, and William Reeder. 1999. "Encouraging Mortgage Lending In 'Underserved' Areas: The Potential for Expanding Home Ownership in the U.S." *Housing Studies* 14(6): 777–810.

Goodman, John L., Jr. and Joseph B. Nichols. 1997. "Does FHA Increase Home Ownership or Just Accelerate It." *Journal of Housing Economics* (6): 184–202.

Gyourko, Joseph, Peter Linneman, and Susan Wachter. 1999. "Analyzing the Relationships Among Race, Wealth, and Home Ownership in America." *Journal of Housing Economics* 8(2): 63–89.

Hays, R. Allen. 1995. *The Federal Government and Urban Housing: Ideology and Change in Public Policy.* Albany, N.Y.: State University of New York Press.

Hecht, Bennett L. 1999. *Developing Affordable Housing: A Practical Guide for Nonprofit Organizations,* 2nd edition. New York: John Wiley & Sons.

Hirad, Abdighani, and Peter M. Zorn. 2001. *A Little Knowledge is a Good Thing: Empirical Evidence of the Effectiveness of Pre-Purchase Homeownership Counseling.* Washington: Freddie Mac.

Housing Assistance Council. 2003a. "About RHS Programs: Homeownership Direct Loan Program (Section 502)." Accessed at http://www.rural home.org/pubs/infoshts/info502.htm.

————. 2003b. "About RHS Programs: Rural Rental Assistance (Section 521)." Accessed at http://www.ruralhome.org/pubs/infoshts/ info521.htm.

Hunter, Cynthia Bartlett. 2004. "FHL Banks Support Affordable Housing Through Member Institutions." In *Affordable Housing Handbook.* San Francisco, Calif.: Alexander & Edwards Publishing.

Husock, Howard. 2003. *America's Trillion-Dollar Housing Mistake: The Failure of American Housing Policy.* Chicago, Ill.: Ivan R. Dee.

Joint Center for Housing Studies. 2004. *The State of the Nation's Housing: 2004.* Cambridge, Mass.: Harvard University.

————. 2005. *The State of the Nation's Housing: 2005.* Cambridge, Mass.: Harvard University.

Katz, Bruce, Margery Austin Turner, Karen Destorel Brown, Mary Cunningham, and Noah Sawyer. 2003. *Rethinking Local Affordable Housing Strategies: Lessons From 70 Years of Policy and Practice.* Washington: The Brookings Institution Center on Urban and Metropolitan Policy and The Urban Institute.

Khadduri, Jill, Kimberly Burnett, and David Rodda. 2003. *Targeting Housing Production Subsidies: Literature Review.* Washington: U.S. Department of Housing and Urban Development, Office of Policy Development and Research.

Lewis, Holden. 2003. "Policymakers Give OK to Down-Payment Gifts." Bankrate.com. Accessed at http://www.bankrate.com/brm/news/ mortgages/20031009a1.asp.

Malpezzi, Stephen, and Kerry Vandell. 2002. "Does the Low-Income Housing Tax Credit Increase the Supply of Housing?" *Journal of Housing Economics* 11(4): 360–80.

Marcuse, Peter. 1986. "Housing Policy and the Myth of the Benevolent State." In *Critical Perspectives on Housing,* edited by Rachel G. Bratt, Chester Hartman, and Ann Meyerson. Philadelphia, Pa.: University of Pennsylvania Press.

Martinez, Sylvia. 2000. "The Housing Act of 1949: Its Place in the Realization of the American Dream of Homeownership." *Housing Policy Debate* 11(2): 467–87.

McCarthy, George W., and Robert G. Quercia. 2000. *Bridging the Gap Between Supply and Demand: The Evolution of the Homeownership, Education and Counseling Industry.* Washington: Research Institute for Housing America.

McClure, Kirk. 2000. "The Low-Income Housing Tax Credit as an Aid to Housing Finance: How Well Has It Worked?" *Housing Policy Debate* 11(1): 91–114.

Millennial Housing Commission. 2002. *Meeting Our Nation's Housing Challenges.* Report of the Bipartisan Millennial Housing Commission. Washington: U.S. Government Printing Office.

National Commission on Urban Problems. 1968. *Building the American City: Report of the National Commission on Urban Problems to the Congress and to the President of the United States.* Washington: U.S. Government Printing Office.

National Council of State Housing Agencies. 2004. "About HFAs—HFA Administered Programs." Accessed at http://www.ncsha.org/section.cfm/3/34/36.

National Housing Law Project. 2000. "HUD Issues Final Rule Implementing The Section 8 Homeownership Program." Oakland, Calif.: National Housing Law Project. Accessed at http://www.nhlp.org/html/sec8/homeownershiprule.htm.

National Low Income Housing Coalition. 2004. "The 2005 Final FMRs: An Introduction." Washington: NLIHC

———. 2006. "FY 2007 Budget Chart for Selected Programs." Washington: NLIHC. Accessed at http://www.nlihc.org/doc/061606chart.pdf.

———. 2007. *2007 Advocates' Guide to Housing and Community Development Policy.* Washington: NLIHC. Accessed at http://www.nlihc.org/template/page.cfm?id=46.

National Task Force on Financing Affordable Housing. 1992. *From the Neighborhoods to the Capital Markets.* Washington: Allstate Insurance Company.

Nelson, Kathryn P., Mark Treskon, and Danilo Pelletiere. 2004. *Losing Ground in the Best of Times: Low Income Renters in the 1990s.* Washington: National Low Income Housing Coalition.

Nothaft, Frank E., and Brian J. Surette. 2002. "The Industrial Structure of Affordable Mortgage Lending." In *Low-Income Homeownership: Examining the Unexamined Goal,* edited by Nicolas P. Retsinas and Eric S. Belsky. Cambridge, Mass. and Washington: Joint Center for Housing Studies and Brookings Institution Press.

Phipps, Antony A., Kathleen Heintz, and Monte Franke. 1994. *Evaluation of the Nehemiah Housing Opportunity Program.* Washington: U.S. Department of Housing and Urban Development Office of Policy Development and Research.

President's Committee on Urban Housing. 1968. *A Decent Home.* Washington: U.S. Government Printing Office.

Quercia, Roberto G., and Susan M. Wachter. 1996. "Homeownership Counseling Performance: How Can it Be Measured?" *Housing Policy Debate* 7(1): 175–99.

Quercia, Roberto G., George W. McCarthy, and Susan M. Wachter. 2003. "The Impacts of Affordable Lending Efforts on Homeownership Rates." *Journal of Housing Economics* 12(1): 29–59.

Quercia, Roberto G., William M. Rohe, and Diane K. Levy. 2000. "A New Look at Creative Finance." *Housing Policy Debate* 11(4): 943–72.

Rohe, William M., Roberto G. Quercia, and Shannon Van Zandt. 2002. *Supporting the American Dream of Homeownership: An Assessment of Neighborhood Reinvestment's Home Ownership Pilot Program.* Chapel Hill, N.C.: Center for Urban and Regional Studies, University of North Carolina. Accessed at http://nw.org/network/pubs/applied/documents/SupportingAmerican Dream2002.pdf.

Schnare, Ann B. 2001. *The Impact of Changes in Multifamily Housing Finance in Older Urban Areas.* Washington and Cambridge, Mass.: The Brookings Institution Center on Urban and Metropolitan Policy and The Joint Center for Housing Studies of Harvard University.

Schwartz, Alex. 2006. *Housing Policy in the United States.* New York: Routledge.

Segal, William and Edward J. Szymanoski. 1998. "Fannie Mae, Freddie Mac, and the Multifamily Mortgage Market." *Cityscape: A Journal of Policy Development and Research* 4(1): 59–91.

Stegman, Michael A. 1991. "The Excessive Costs of Creative Finance: Growing Inefficiencies in the Production of Low-Income Housing." *Housing Policy Debate* 2(2): 357–73.

Stone, Michael E. 1993. *Shelter Poverty: New Ideas on Housing Affordability.* Philadelphia, Pa.: Temple University Press.

———. 2006. "Pernicious Problems of Housing Finance." In *A Right to Housing: Foundation for a New Social Agenda,* edited by Rachel G. Bratt, Michael E. Stone, and Chester Hartman. Philadelphia, Pa.: Temple University Press.

U.S. Department of Housing and Urban Development. 2002a. *Blueprint for the American Dream.* Washington: U.S. Government Printing Office.

———. 2002b. *Economic Benefits of Increasing Minority Homeownership.* Washington: U.S. Government Printing Office.

———. 2002c. "Follow Up of Down Payment Assistance Programs Operated by Private Nonprofit Entities." Office of Inspector General, Office of Audit, Region 10, Seattle, Wash.

———. 2002d. "New HUD Report: Increasing Minority Homeownership Will Spur Economy." News Release, October 15, 2002. Washington: U.S. Government Printing Office. Accessed at http://www.ahfc.state.ak.us/iceimages/news/101502-minority-spur-economy.pdf.

———. 2002e. *Unequal Burden: Income and Racial Disparities in Subprime Lending in America.* Washington: U.S. Government Printing Office.

———. 2003. "Trends in Worst Case Housing Needs for Housing, 1978–1999." Washington: U.S. Government Printing Office. Accessed at http://www.huduser.org/publications/PDF/trends.pdf.

————. 2005. *Affordable Housing Needs: A Report to Congress on the Significant Need for Housing.* Washington: U.S. Government Printing Office.

U.S. General Accounting Office. 1989. *Tax Policy: Costs Associated With Low-Income Housing Tax Credit Partnerships: Fact Sheet for the Chairman, Subcommittee on Select Revenue Measures, Committee on Ways and Means, House of Representatives.* Washington: U.S. Government Printing Office.

Utt, Ronald D. 2004. "Congress' Risky Zero Down Payment Plan Will Undermine FHA's Soundness and Discourage Self-Reliance." WebMemo #529, July 7. Washington: The Heritage Foundation. Accessed at http://www.heritage.org/Research/Budget/wm529.cfm.

Wachter, Susan M. and Isaac F. Megbolugbe. 1992. "Racial and Ethnic Disparities in Homeownership." *Housing Policy Debate* 3(2): 333–70.

Wallace, James E. "Financing Affordable Housing in the United States." 1995. *Housing Policy Debate* 6(4): 785–814.

Weicher, John C. 1990. "The Voucher/Production Debate." In *Building Foundations: Housing and Federal Policy,* edited by Denise DiPasquale and Langley C. Keyes. Philadelphia, Pa.: University of Pennsylvania Press.

Werwath, Peter. 1996. "Helping Families Build Assets: Nonprofit Homeownership Programs." Columbia, Md.: The Enterprise Foundation.

Wong, Perry, Daniela Murphy, Frank Fogelbach, and Rob Koepp. 2004. *Expanding Affordable Homeownership with Private Capital: A Study of the Nehemiah Down Payment Assistance Program.* Santa Monica, Calif.: Milken Institute.

CHAPTER EIGHT

Predatory Lending and Community Development at Loggerheads

Kathleen C. Engel and Patricia A. McCoy

FOR DECADES, cities have invested in decaying neighborhoods, trying to revitalize blighted areas and stimulate economic growth. Where their efforts have been successful, homeowners have experienced appreciation in their homes, safer streets, and improved neighborhoods. Cities, in turn, have benefited from increased affluence and tax revenues. Rising home values, and as a consequence increased homeowner equity, have made these "comeback" neighborhoods prime targets for predatory lenders,[1] who focus on financially unsophisticated homeowners with equity in their homes and no relationships with traditional lenders.

Predatory lenders often make loans on terms that borrowers cannot afford. Some borrowers lose their homes. Others forsake necessities such as heat in the winter, health insurance, or home repairs to avoid default and foreclosure. Neighborhoods that were once stable become littered with abandoned and neglected homes. As people lose their homes, cities experience increases in crime, greater demand for social services, and an array of other costs associated with economic decline (Engel 2006, 357–60). Reduced home values and abandoned homes also lead to a decrease in tax revenues. At the end of the day, predatory lenders extract borrowers' increased equity in their homes and plunder city investments in neighborhoods, leaving abandoned and deteriorated properties in their wake.[2] As predatory lenders exploit the benefits of community development and devastate neighborhoods, the question for policy makers is what can be done. In this chapter, we attempt to address this question.

DEFINING PREDATORY LENDING

Historically, predatory lending loans primarily occurred in the subprime market, which is designed for borrowers who cannot obtain prime loans due to poverty, credit blemishes, spotty documentation, or irregular income (Office of the Comptroller of the Currency et al. 2001, 2; Board of Governors of the Federal Reserve System et al. 1999, 1; U.S. Department of Housing and Urban Development and U.S. Department of Treasury 2000, 28; House Committee on Banking and Financial Services 2000, 308–19). More recently, abusive lending also permeated the market for nontraditional prime loans, with the emergence of hybrid, interest-only, and option payment adjustable rate mortgages (Fishbein and Woodall 2006).

Attempts to define which loans are predatory have proven problematic. Early forays usually resulted in detailed catalogs of individual loan abuses (Sturdevant and Brennan 1999). Although useful, these were conceptually unsatisfactory, because they did not explain why terms or practices were abusive. Eventually, the sheer inability to arrive at a working definition of predatory lending emerged as a major fault line in the public debates. Consumer advocates called for the regulation of predatory loans and skeptics rebuffed them with the retort, "How can you regulate something that can't be defined?"

As current laws demonstrate, it is not necessary to devise a comprehensive statutory definition in order to regulate predatory lending. Anti–predatory lending statutes take two approaches, both focusing on specific abuses. One approach (the more common) is to designate "high-cost loans" as the trigger for statutory protection, define high-cost loans in terms of quantitative interest rate spreads or points and fees, and then prohibit or regulate specific loan terms and practices in high-cost loans. The other approach (sometimes used in tandem with the first) is to identify loan terms or practices that are abusive in all home loans and regulate those abuses across the board (Azmy 2005, 297–300, 361–62).

While a comprehensive statutory definition of predatory lending is not necessary, it is critical to identify problem loan terms and practices that require regulation. That, in turn, requires determining whether specific loan terms or practices are abusive and, if so, why.

An examination of various catalogs of loan abuses reveals seven underlying problems, which form a syndrome of abusive loan terms or practices that together constitute predatory lending (Eggert 2004; Engel and McCoy 2002a, 1258–70; Renuart 2003):

1. loans structured to result in seriously disproportionate net harm to borrowers

2. rent-seeking

3. loans involving unlawful fraud or deception

4. other forms of lack of transparency in loans not actionable as fraud

5. provisions requiring borrowers to waive meaningful legal redress

6. exploitative servicing

7. discrimination

Loans Structured to Cause Seriously Disproportionate Net Harm to Borrowers

The subprime mortgage industry offers more flexible lending criteria than the prime mortgage market. Although some of these can work to the benefit of both borrowers and lenders, others are structured to inflict seriously disproportionate net harm on borrowers. When the harm of subprime loans to borrowers and society at large outweighs the benefits, such practices are predatory. Examples include loans made without regard to the borrowers' ability to repay; loan flipping (frequent, repeated refinancings designed to allow lenders to extract cumulative, costly refinancing fees); shifting unsecured debt into mortgages to tap into the homeowner's equity; insisting on larger loans than customers desire; steering prime-eligible customers into high-cost loans; and refinancing subsidized mortgages (such as no-interest Habitat for Humanity loans) at high interest rates for no good economic reason (Freddie Mac 1996; Murray 2000; Sturdevant and Brennan 1999).

Harmful Rent-Seeking

Subprime loans are high cost, either due to higher interest rates or fees or both. Some subprime loans may reflect legitimate risk-based pricing, that is, prices carefully calibrated to higher probabilities of delinquency, default, and foreclosure (U.S. Department of Housing and Urban Development and U.S. Department of Treasury 2000, 27; Jaffee and Russell 1976; Weicher 1997, 69, 74–88). In addition, origination and servicing costs for risky borrowers may be higher because of the need for more intensive underwriting, lower approval rates, and higher servicing costs (U.S. Department of Housing and Urban Development and U.S. Department of Treasury 2000, 28, 67; Weicher 1997, 56–57, tbl. 4.1, 69–70, 74–88). However, when subprime lenders exert market power to charge higher than competitive rates, they engage in predatory lending. They extract rents by hiking prices above risk-adjusted levels and by steering naive prime-eligible borrowers to subprime loans (Lax et al. 2004; Shroder 2000, 14–15; Sturdevant and Brennan 1999; White 2004). Double billing and fees for phantom services similarly serve to extract rents (Sturdevant and Brennan 1999). Finally, unlike the prime mortgage industry, where any prepayment penalty results in a lower interest rate, the subprime mortgage industry generally assesses prepayment penalties on top of high interest rates (White 2004).

Fraud or Deceptive Practices

Sometimes predatory lending involves classic, illegal fraud or deception. Although loan fraud appears in ever-changing guises, essentially it boils down to deception that aims to mislead borrowers about loan terms and the potential consequences of those terms (Office of the Comptroller of the Currency et al. 2001, 10–11; U.S. Department of Housing and Urban Development and U.S. Department of Treasury 2000, 24, 79–90).

Other Forms of Nontransparency Not Actionable as Fraud

It is possible and all too likely for other home loans that are not technically fraudulent to nevertheless be misleading. That occurs when subprime loans omit information of crucial importance to borrowers. Although in the home loan area, two federal disclosure laws—the Truth in Lending Act (TILA) and the Real Estate Settlement Procedures Act (RESPA)—mandate the disclosure of specific loan terms and costs,[3] these statutes suffer from flaws that severely diminish their utility.

Other subprime pricing practices also hinder transparency. Subprime rate sheets are rarely publicly posted. Even when they are, prices vary according to a plethora of factors including credit scores, making it difficult for borrowers to ascertain the minimum price the lender would charge. The lack of standardized fees further impedes transparency (White 2004; McCoy 2007).

Loans Requiring Borrowers to Waive Meaningful Legal Redress

Frequently, subprime home loans contain mandatory arbitration clauses that require borrowers to waive judicial redress and prohibit class action participation (Smith 2001, 1192–3). Even when subprime home loans allow full judicial redress, they may require borrowers to pay the lenders' attorneys' fees.

Exploitative Servicing

Once a loan has closed, a company known as a servicer collects the loan payments. Some servicers engage in exploitative practices, such as charging unjustified fees, force-placing homeowners insurance without cause, instituting foreclosure improperly, and failing to make property tax payments when due (Eggert 2004).

Discrimination

Lending discrimination is yet another type of predatory lending. Some lenders and brokers target people of color, single women, and senior citizens with abusive loans. This targeting, especially when coupled with the marketing of loans with less burdensome terms to those outside protected classes, violates antidiscrimination laws (Renuart 2003).

THE EMERGENCE OF PREDATORY LENDING

By the 1990s, an array of market and regulatory forces converged to create an environment in which predatory lending could flourish. These forces changed the home mortgage market from one in which the supply of capital was limited and only the most creditworthy borrowers could obtain loans to one that provided a steady flow of mortgage capital to borrowers representing almost every level of credit risk. The same forces enabled lenders to exploit naïve borrowers.

Historically in the United States, the demand for residential mortgages exceeded the supply of credit. In deciding which borrowers deserved credit, lenders were motivated in part by the concern that the most risk-averse and most creditworthy borrowers would leave the market if interest rates were too high. Because of this adverse selection problem, lenders tended to make loans only to borrowers who presented the lowest risk of default (for a full discussion of the pricing of home mortgages, see Engel and McCoy 2002a). As a result, there was a queue of borrowers who desired but could not obtain loans, either because lenders had exhausted their supply of capital or because the borrowers presented unacceptable risks of default (Stiglitz and Weiss 1981, 393). The limited availability of mortgage capital had the greatest consequence for low and moderate income (LMI) borrowers.

Market changes starting in the 1980s spurred a dramatic increase in the availability of money for home mortgages. The government-sponsored enterprises, Fannie Mae and Freddie Mac, as well as private securitizers began bundling and securitizing home mortgages. Investors, looking for new investment vehicles, eagerly bought up securities backed by these bundles of mortgages. Securitization, which by 2005 accounted for approximately 80 percent of subprime home loans (Standard and Poor's 2005, 7; for a full discussion of securitization, see Engel and McCoy 2007) has enabled lenders to make loans and sell them on the secondary market, generating new funds to loan. By providing lenders with greater access to capital, securitization has virtually eliminated the problem of unmet demand.

Just as securitization enabled regulated institutions to increase their lending activities, it also opened the door for thinly capitalized nonbank lenders to enter the lending business. Lenders no longer need to be highly capitalized, regulated financial institutions. Indeed, unregulated mortgage bankers and finance companies have captured a significant portion of the home mortgage market. Like banks, they originate loans, typically using a warehouse line of credit, and then sell the loans on the secondary market (Brendsel 1996, 24).

In the 1990s, simultaneous with mortgage capital becoming increasingly available, many LMI borrowers began to see their wages and their home values rise (Kennickell, Starr-McCluer, and Sundén 1997, 5; Canner, Durkin, and Luckett 1998, 249; Hylton 2000, 205). The increased cash flow and equity of these LMI borrowers bolstered their creditworthiness and made them more attractive to lenders. In the previous decade, Congress had liberalized many restrictions on loan terms. The Depository Institutions Deregulation and Monetary Control Act of 1980 (DIDMCA)[4] granted state banks and thrifts the same favorable variable-rate ceiling enjoyed by national banks and preempted state usury caps for loans secured by first mortgages. As a result, high-cost lenders had added incentives to refinance first mortgages at high APRs in lieu of home equity lines of credit and other junior mortgages governed by state usury laws. The Alternative Mortgage Transactions Parity Act of 1982 (AMTPA)[5] broadened the types of loans regulated institutions could make by permitting adjustable rate mortgages, balloon payments, and interest-only loans.

Other federal regulations and laws created incentives for lenders to market their products to LMI borrowers.[6] The U.S. Department of Housing and Urban Development (HUD) set new lending goals for Freddie Mac and Fannie Mae that included a significant increase in the number of loans the GSEs had to purchase from high minority or low income census tracts. (Fannie Mae 2000, 110). In a parallel development, changes to enforcement of the Community Reinvestment Act (CRA) increased incentives for banks and thrifts to serve LMI neighborhoods (U.S. Department of Housing and Urban Development and U.S. Department of Treasury 2000, 106).

These market and regulatory changes transformed the home mortgage market and inadvertently spawned predatory lending. Predatory lenders initially focused on LMI communities and LMI borrowers, who, because of credit rationing, discrimination, and other forces, are relatively inexperienced in and unsophisticated about credit transactions (Bucks and Pence 2006, 2–1, 20–21). These borrowers and communities often have pent-up demand for home mortgages that securitization, by generating new capital, enabled lenders to meet. The CRA incentives to provide banking services in LMI neighborhoods and HUD's loan purchase goals for the GSEs also made LMI borrowers particularly attractive to lenders. These borrowers also were attractive because rising home values increased homeowners' equity into 2006. LMI borrowers were also attractive targets due to their inexperience. Even today, homeowners who do not understand the home mortgage market remain prey for lenders plying them with complex loan products and false promises. Some of these borrowers actually qualify for prime loans but are not apprised of that fact, while others could not obtain a conventional loan on any terms (Lax et al. 2004, 564–65).

The prevalence of predatory loans reflects inefficiencies in the legitimate home mortgage market, which arise because of information asymmetries that predatory lenders exploit.[7] Lenders have extensive information about loan products and terms that even the most experienced borrowers cannot match. For the typical victim of predatory lending, this information is impenetrable (Block-Lieb and Janger 2006, 1528). Unlike the prime market, where fixed-rate mortgages predominate, subprime and predatory loans include a dizzying array of complex terms, from prepayment penalties and balloon payments to negative amortization and floating rates that are tied to the interest on LIBOR or T-bills. The complexity of terms prevents borrowers from knowing what their loan payments will be in any given month and whether they can afford to make payments under various contingencies that could arise. In this situation, borrowers tend to seize upon the information they can understand: the amount of the monthly payment at the time the loan is consummated. When it comes to the information they cannot comprehend, borrowers rely on lenders' assurances that they can afford the loan and that they are in good hands.[8]

Predatory lenders seek out unsophisticated borrowers who are unlikely to shop for loans. Such lenders do so knowing that many of these borrowers erroneously believe they are ineligible for loans and will jump at the opportunity to borrow regardless of the terms. Abusive lenders pinpoint communities that traditional lenders have not served,[9] typically LMI neighborhoods and neighborhoods with a significant percentage of people of color (Calem, Hershaff, and Wachter 2004; Lax et al. 2004, 548). It is easy for lenders to identify these neighborhoods by using Home Mortgage Disclosure Act data that reveal areas with low levels of lending activity and census data that shed light on the income levels and racial composition of neighborhoods.

Once they have targeted specific areas, predatory lenders identify which homeowners have significant equity in their homes and pressing financial needs. Lenders can readily obtain information on homeowners' equity through public records that document the assessed value of homeowners' property and any outstanding mortgages. In addition, through public agencies, lenders can learn which homeowners have unpaid tax bills or outstanding housing code violations. Some unscrupulous lenders drive through neighborhoods looking for decrepit homes in desperate need of repair.

Rather than adopt the traditional persona of a bank loan officer, predatory lenders attempt to make victims feel comfortable and trusting. Their warmth and compassion for borrowers' financial plights make customers believe that the lenders represent their interests. The lenders also exude an aura of authority, which, together with the intimacy they establish with the borrowers, intimidate borrowers from questioning the loans the lenders are peddling. As a result, the lenders are able to foist loans on the borrowers that are not in the borrowers' best interests.

Information asymmetries are not the sole source of market inefficiencies in the predatory loan market. Marketing strategies and a lack of competition from legitimate lenders also contribute. When predatory lenders offer loans to potential borrowers, frequently they insist that the loans will expire if the borrowers do not commit immediately (U.S. Department of Housing and Urban Development and U.S. Department of Treasury 2000). Thus under the gun, the borrowers hasten to sign the loan applications and pay the application fees, becoming psychologically committed to the loan in the process. Lenders know that borrowers will likely rebuff offers from other lenders who might appear on their doorsteps.

Given the incentives for lenders to reach out to LMI borrowers and the demand for mortgages in LMI neighborhoods, one would expect regulated depository institutions and legitimate unregulated lenders to market their loan products to LMI borrowers. For a number of reasons, most banks and thrifts have not entered the subprime market.[10] Many worry that if they begin serving borrowers with elevated default risks, they will reject more applicants, charge higher interest rates, and foreclose on more properties, all of which could spawn public outcry. Where rejection rates, high interest rates, or foreclosure are positively correlated with the race of borrowers, banks could face lawsuits, regulatory actions, and damage to their reputations (Duca and Rosenthal 1994, 101). In contrast, predatory lenders have reduced concerns about reputation and can readily dissolve and incorporate as new entities if their activities tarnish their reputations. Similarly, lawsuits do not pose a serious threat to undercapitalized predatory lenders who are judgment-proof.

Regulatory controls may create disincentives to subprime lending by banks and thrifts. Regulations require banks to maintain loan loss reserves and sufficient capitalization. The amount of protection against losses that banks must retain depends, in part, on the risk propensity of their loans. Subprime lending by definition entails more risk. Conversely, unregulated nonbank lenders can lend without regard to capitalization or other "safety and soundness" requirements because they are exempt from federal loan loss reserve and capitalization requirements (Office of the Comptroller et al. 2001;

U.S. Department of Housing and Urban Development and U.S. Department of Treasury 2000, 18).

Thus, in contrast to banks and thrifts, abusive lenders are substantially less concerned about the level of risk borrowers present. These lenders sell their loans on the secondary market, after reaping their profits from up-front fees (Engel and McCoy 2007). If their deals with purchasers include recourse provisions and borrowers default, the lenders can take back the loans and foreclose on the properties. If a significant number of loans go into default, triggering recourse provisions and threatening the lenders with insolvency, those lenders can dissolve, and escape legal claims by borrowers and secondary market investors. Nothing prevents them from later resuming lending as new entities.

Regulated lenders also lack the special expertise needed to serve LMI borrowers. Unlike their more affluent counterparts, LMI borrowers do not have credit histories that fit neatly within conventional lenders' underwriting guidelines (Litan et al. 2000, 87–88). Some LMI borrowers function solely in the cash economy, receiving their wages and paying their debts in cash. Others may be self-employed, for example as child-care providers or gardeners, and may not report all their income to the Internal Revenue Service. To assess the creditworthiness of these borrowers, banks would have to retool their underwriting methods and identify alternatives to W-2s, bank statements, and credit reports to verify debt and income. This is an expensive proposition and one that might not reap enough performing loans to justify the expense (Weicher 1997, 34–36; Klausner 1995, 1567–68; Avery, Beeson, and Sniderman 1999). Similarly, banks and thrifts are less likely to have offices in LMI neighborhoods, reducing their access to potential customers and hampering their ability to identify promising borrowers and neighborhoods (Avery et al. 1997, 719; Hylton 2000, 218).

Nonbank lenders are better equipped to evaluate potential borrowers' credit risk. Unlike banks that provide an array of services to diverse individuals and entities, nonbank lenders have only one task: making home mortgage loans to homeowners. They can target one neighborhood and learn about individuals within that neighborhood and the overall economic stability of the area.

Predatory lenders' intense focus on specific neighborhoods and personal contact with potential borrowers makes them unique. Legitimate subprime lenders, in contrast, use the Internet and other mass marketing vehicles to attract borrowers. Arguably, these lenders should be able to undercut predatory lenders' prices and drive them out of business. However, mass marketing techniques work best with borrowers who are actively seeking loans, believe they will qualify for a loan, and are willing to contact a remote lender. These methods often will not catch the eye of potential victims of predatory lending, who may not be actively looking for loans, may falsely believe they are ineligible for credit, and may feel uncomfortable dealing with an anonymous lender. As a consequence, the most sophisticated subprime borrowers obtain favorable subprime rates and the more vulnerable borrowers, who may in fact be eligible for prime loans, fall prey to predatory lenders.

The scant presence of conventional bank lenders and legitimate subprime lenders in LMI communities means that the only significant competition predatory lenders face is from other predatory lenders. Competition among predatory lenders is unique. Rather, they compete on access, not price. Whichever lender gets to homeowners first and induces them to sign loan applications wins. The unsuspecting targets cannot believe their good fortune and sign on the line, worried that their opportunity to borrow will vanish if they hesitate (U.S. Department of Housing and Urban Development and U.S. Department of Treasury 2000, 17–18).

COMBATING PREDATORY LENDING

In the past seven years, the debate over predatory lending and its cure has evolved dramatically. As late as 2000, many lenders continued to deny that predatory lending was a problem. That year, then-Senator Phil Gramm, chairman of the Senate Banking Committee, voiced the subprime industry's view when he asserted: "As the regulators themselves admit, there is no definition of predatory lending. I don't know how we can hope to address the problem before we have decided what it is" (Michele Heller and Rob Garver, "Gramm Takes Stand Against Predator Bills," *The American Banker,* August 24, 2000, 1; see also "News Conference with Senator Phil Gramm," *Federal News Service,* January 22, 2001). Concomitantly, the main focus of consumer advocates was on securing the passage of state and federal legislation to regulate conduct by loan originators and mortgage brokers.

Increasingly, advocates and policy makers began investigating the role the secondary market plays in predatory lending through the financing of subprime loans (Engel and McCoy 2007). The debate surrounding whether and how secondary market actors should be held responsible for abusive lending by originators became robust and is still being played out in state anti-predatory lending legislation.

Over the last few years, many states ushered in significant reforms to address predatory lending, while other states have remained passive in the face of mounting abuses. At the federal level, reforms have been incremental and administrative in nature. The Federal Reserve Board amended its rules implementing the federal anti-predatory lending law, known as the Home Ownership and Equity Protection Act (HOEPA), to expand prohibited subprime practices. Although the rules expanded the number of covered loans, HOEPA still covers at most 5 percent of subprime home loans (Board of Governors of the Federal Reserve System 2001). Over the same period, the

Federal Trade Commission brought a number of high-visibility enforcement actions against abusive mortgage lenders under the Federal Trade Commission Act (2003).

With the election of George W. Bush as president in 2000 and Republican dominance in Congress, strong federal legislation became stymied and reformers turned their focus to the states with increased success. As of January 2007, forty-four states and the District of Columbia had enacted anti-predatory lending laws of varying breadth and strength.[11] Some of these laws predate the public outcry about predatory lending and regulate only prepayment penalties or balloon clauses, whereas others have expansive provisions that build on HOEPA standards. Similarly, some laws contemplate only lender and broker liability and others go further and also impose damages liability on assignees of predatory loans (Bostic et al. 2007).

State anti-predatory lending initiatives have come under fierce assault, both before and after passage. The mortgage lending industry filed lawsuits challenging the legality of numerous laws and lobbied Congress for a federal preemption statute. Standard & Poor's and other rating agencies refused to rate securitized subprime loan pools in a few states whose assignee liability provisions they deemed too harsh. The U.S. Comptroller of the Currency declared all state and local anti-predatory lending laws federally preempted for national banks and their operating subsidiaries.

The efforts to combat predatory lending span many fronts, from consumer education to civil litigation and criminal enforcement. Here, we canvass and appraise these various approaches and propose a new vehicle for redressing predatory lending.

Industry Self-Regulation

Some sectors of the financial services industry—securities and life insurance in particular—have strong industry self-regulation. In the securities industry, self-regulation is mandatory and subject to oversight by the Securities and Exchange Commission.[12] In the life insurance industry, more than half of all life insurers participate in self-regulation on a voluntary basis.[13] Although differences between the two models of self-regulation are significant, both require members to comply with codes of conduct designed to protect consumers and monitor compliance with those codes through outside independent assessments or audits and enforcement mechanisms (see Insurance Marketplace Standards Association, http://www.imsaethics. org; 15 U.S.C. §§ 78b–78c; Loss and Seligman 1990, 2653–57, 2669–73, 2795–836).

In contrast, the subprime mortgage industry has resisted establishing a meaningful mechanism for industry self-policing. The only initiatives to date have been a code of ethics and best practice guidelines adopted by the former

National Home Equity Mortgage Association (NHEMA) and best practices standards adopted by the Mortgage Bankers Association (MBA).

NHEMA, which has since been absorbed by the MBA,[14] billed itself as "the only trade association solely representing the non-prime mortgage lending industry" and boasted membership of "approximately 250 mortgage lenders accounting for 80 percent of outstanding non-prime mortgage loans." Nevertheless, NHEMA's code of ethics and best practice guidelines were solely voluntary. Indeed, the preamble to NHEMA's ethics code and guidelines denied that either had legal effect: "the modification of or failure to adopt one or more of these voluntary guidelines shall not necessarily be taken to indicate that the lender has violated any law, duty or standard of care."

Similarly, compliance by MBA's members with the association's best practices standards is purely voluntary and is not subject to independent outside assessment or enforcement.[15] In a 2003 report on predatory lending enforcement, MBA announced its future plans to fight predatory lending. In that report, MBA stated it planned to promote financial literacy, explore new funding for government enforcement, and commission a study on abusive lending practices.[16] Nowhere in the report, however, did MBA commit to strengthen compliance with and enforcement of its own subprime legislative guidelines. Furthermore, the report recited evidence that industry oversight was ineffectual and confirmed that binding best practices standards were not yet in place.

Consumer Education and Counseling

One common proposal to stop predatory lending—championed by lender trade associations and the Federal Reserve Board—is consumer education and counseling (Federal Reserve Board 2003; Greenspan 2001). Although the terms *education* and *counseling* can have varying meanings, here we use education to refer to general educational programs such as workshops or classes that are not transaction-specific and counseling to refer to sessions that are tailored to a particular home purchase or loan transaction (see Gwatkin and McCarthy 2003).

Mandatory mortgage counseling remains the exception and not the rule. Counseling is mandatory for reverse mortgages supervised by the U.S. Department of Housing and Urban Development under the Home Equity Conversion Mortgage program and for high-cost home loans in certain states. Some other states have optional counseling measures that require lenders to advise loan applicants in writing to seek loan counseling before closing and to provide a list of counselors (Azmy 2005, 356–57, 370–71; Azmy and Reiss 2004, 687; U.S. Department of Housing and Urban Development and U.S. Department of Treasury 2000, 92; Harkness 2000, 39–41). Elsewhere, mandatory counseling proposals have failed, either due to lender opposition or cost. In the private and nonprofit sectors, homeowner counseling programs have generally focused on first-time homebuyers and not on existing homeowners who are refinancing their home loans (Hermanson and Wilden 2003, 1–2).

Nonprofits and government agencies sometimes offer mortgage education and predatory lending awareness programs, but these programs are not statutorily mandated. Examples of such programs include the "Don't Borrow Trouble" campaigns found in several U.S. cities and homeowner education initiatives offered by Freddie Mac, Fannie Mae, the Federal Deposit Insurance Corporation, and the Neighborhood Reinvestment Corporation as part of affordable lending initiatives (Federal Reserve Board 2003; Gwatkin and McCarthy 2003, 5–6; Hermanson and Wilden 2003; McCarthy and Quercia 2000; Freddie Mac 2007).

Whether borrower counseling alone would succeed in combating predatory lending is highly questionable. In an overview of research on the effectiveness of homeownership education and counseling programs, Alan Mallach concluded that the findings were "highly ambiguous" and had "serious limitations [which] severely compromise the value of such findings" (Mallach 2002, 5; Hermanson and Wilden 2003, 3–4). One study did find homeowner counseling effective in the prepurchase context. Abdighani Hirad and Peter Zorn found that prepurchase homeownership counseling required under Freddie Mac's Affordable Gold program reduced sixty-day delinquencies on average by 13 percent. The mode of delivery mattered: borrowers who received classroom instruction and one-on-one counseling were respectively 23 percent and 41 percent less likely to have a sixty-day delinquency. Home study and telephone counseling programs, by contrast, resulted in virtually no improvement (Hirad and Zorn 2001, 1–2).

There are reasons to doubt whether the same results would be obtained in situations involving predatory lending. The borrowers studied by Hirad and Zorn were actively shopping for homes and were required under the Affordable Gold program to obtain homeownership counseling. In contrast, predatory lenders often target their operations at the mortgage refinance market, where they pressure vulnerable victims, who are not in the market for credit, into taking out loans (Engel and McCoy 2002a, 1309–10 and n.235; Hermanson and Wilden 2003, 6). In the absence of mandatory counseling, those people who fall prey to high-pressure sales tactics are also unlikely to take the initiative to consult an independent housing counselor before the loan closing (Government Accounting Office 2004, 13).

Even if borrower counseling had proven effective in the subprime refinance market, prospects for mandatory, universal borrower counseling would still be dim. Kathryn Gwatkin and George McCarthy have noted that homeowner education and financial literacy education generally "can be a costly, labor-intensive, process" (2003, 13). Cash-strapped borrowers may not be able to afford retaining a lawyer or credit counseling service. Government sponsorship of readily available credit counseling would be too costly.

From lenders' perspective, counseling is unnecessary and can be against their best interests. Many subprime lenders actively oppose borrower counseling, arguing that "the development of risk-based pricing techniques has made [financial literacy education] all but obsolete as a risk mitigation tool" (Gwatkin and McCarthy 2003, 14). To the extent that consumer counseling makes borrowers more savvy and more likely to engage in comparison shopping, abusive lenders have a decided disincentive to pay for counseling.

Credit counseling also reflects a public goods problem. Even if some advantages, for example, reduced default rates, accrued to lenders who provided counseling, the benefits of the counseling would extend to external actors, who would not bear the cost of the counseling. For example, if a borrower took information obtained through credit counseling with one lender and used that information to secure a loan on better terms with another lender, the original lender would not benefit from the counseling.

Putting cost considerations aside, there is further reason to doubt that mandatory counseling of subprime refinance applicants would really work, given the flaws in the current system of disclosures. In the ideal situation, loan counselors would be able to advise homeowners to shop for other loans before they sign loan applications and become psychologically committed to the loans. Short of that, at least loan counselors could review the final loan documents and disclosures several days before closing in order to provide meaningful advice. However, currently none of the loan documents except the HUD-1 closing cost disclosure is available before closing (except for HOEPA loans) and at most the HUD-1 is available one day before upon request (Engel and McCoy 2002a, 1269). Even with adequate disclosures, as Alan White and Patricia McCoy have demonstrated, the subprime home loan market structures pricing and advertising to impede comparison shopping (McCoy 2007; White 2004).

At bottom, relying on borrower counseling as a predatory lending stopgap is little more than "borrower beware" in new clothes. Borrower counseling depends on victims to protect themselves, rather than on perpetrators to stop abusive practices. Similarly, borrower counseling does nothing to redress the disparities in bargaining power that fuel predatory lending. For these reasons, borrower counseling may be a desideratum, but it is no panacea.

Community Reinvestment Act Oversight

There are a number of ways that banks can directly or indirectly engage in predatory lending. The most obvious is by brokering and originating predatory loans either through the banks[17] or through affiliates that are relatively shielded from scrutiny. Banks may steer borrowers who are eligible for prime rate loans to subprime products or their subprime affiliates may refuse to inform borrowers that they could obtain more favorable terms if they went to the affiliated bank. Banks also engage in predatory lending when they impose more onerous loan terms on people of color or members of other protected groups.

Banks provide indirect support for predatory lending when they purchase loans or buy securities backed by predatory loans. They enable predatory lenders by providing them with warehouse lines of credit and letters of credit. Likewise, when banks provide services, such as underwriting, and act as trustees, registrars, or agents for loan securitizations involving predatory loans they facilitate predatory lending.

CRA provides a vehicle through which bank regulators can detect and sanction banks and thrifts that are involved in predatory lending. CRA mandates that federal banking regulators "encourage [federally insured depository] institutions to help meet the credit needs of the local communities in which they are chartered consistent with the safe and sound operation of such institutions" (12 U.S.C. § 2901(b)). Regulators review banks' CRA compliance during routine CRA exams and when banks seek to expand their activities.

During routine CRA compliance examinations, for banks of all sizes, regulators review the banks' lending activities ("lending test") to determine whether they are "meeting the credit needs of [their] entire communit[ies], including low-and-moderate-income neighborhoods" (12 U.S.C. § 2903(a)(1)). Regulators scrutinize additional factors when evaluating the community reinvestment performance of intermediate small and large banks. For intermediate small banks, with total assets of $250 million to $1 billion, federal banking regulators also examine their community development activities via a flexible new test implemented in 2005. For large banks—with total assets of more than $1 billion—regulators evaluate their investments in community development with an investment test, and the retail depository services they provide with a service test. Following this review, banks can receive one of four CRA ratings, ranging from outstanding to substantial noncompliance (12 U.S.C. § 2906(b)(2)).

When reviewing bank applications related to depository facilities, bank regulators must consider the banks' CRA performance, including any publicly lodged complaints.[18] If regulators conclude that the institutions have failed to meet their CRA obligations, they can deny or place conditions on approving the institutions' applications. Similarly, when regulated lenders apply to become financial holding companies and when financial holding companies and national banks seek to expand into new financial services, the regulators consider the institutions' CRA ratings and deny the applications if any of the holding company's banks or thrifts have ratings below satisfactory.

When banks participate in and provide support for predatory lending, they are not only failing to "meet the credit needs" of their communities, but are also contributing to the decline of already struggling neighborhoods. The regulatory agencies have begun to recognize the role banks may be playing in predatory lending and, in response, are increasing their scrutiny of banks' lending activities. One of the most important shifts has been including nonbank affiliates in examinations when banks apply for deposit facilities. Historically, subprime affiliates of insured banks were not subject to CRA scrutiny; however, in recent years, the Federal Reserve Bank has required lenders seeking approval for deposit facilities to adopt internal controls to detect and protect against abusive lending, including lending by subprime affiliates (Engel and McCoy 2002b, 1590).

Although the Federal Reserve Board and other bank regulators recognize the problem of predatory lending and have taken some steps to address it, their enforcement has not been uniform or widespread. For example, although the Federal Reserve Board now requires banks that are applying for deposit facilities to review their loan applications for steering of prime borrowers to subprime loans (Engel and McCoy 2002b), there is no parallel requirement that routine CRA examinations include review of loan applications to ensure that banks are not engaged in steering. Similarly, CRA examinations do not scrutinize purchases by banks of interests in predatory loans, regardless of a bank's size.

CRA is a powerful and underutilized vehicle for redressing predatory lending. Regulators should use CRA exams to detect predatory loans and, where there is evidence of predatory lending, issue CRA demerits. Likewise, where banks indirectly support predatory lending through financing and other arrangements without proper due diligence to detect it, they should receive ratings downgrades. Finally, affiliates of banks—without exception—should be subject to CRA examinations.

Criminal Enforcement

Numerous predatory loans are infected with fraud and thus subject, at least in theory, to criminal prosecution. However, fraud prosecutions for mortgage abuses are the exception and not the rule. The relative rarity of criminal fraud cases in the mortgage arena is explained in part by the fact that only affirmative misrepresentations, not misleading omissions, are actionable as common-law fraud (*Restatement (Second) of Torts* §§ 525, 537–45). In addition, criminal fraud charges require proof of knowing or willful intent to deceive beyond a reasonable doubt, which is not necessarily easy to show. The high standard of proof needed for culpability can deter prosecutors from bringing criminal fraud cases.

Other pragmatic concerns hinder vigorous prosecution of predatory lending fraud. District attorneys or state attorneys general must be willing to file charges. State and local prosecutors have been slow to indict predatory lenders for fraud except in the most egregious cases. The model home mortgage antifraud program in the County of Los Angeles has been a notable exception (Potter 2000), but it stands alone. In addition to the exacting proof that is needed to show common-law fraud, predatory lending transactions are often technical and complex, daunting prosecutors who lack financial know-how. The lack of systematic reporting requirements that would flag possible loan abuses for prosecutors is another impediment. Finally, severe budget constraints and other pressing priorities, including violent crime, drug use, and terrorism, cause many state and local prosecutors to place predatory lending fraud on the back burner.

Individual Relief

Borrowers have at their disposal an array of tools for combating predatory lending, each of which has varying degrees of efficiency. Historically, usury laws protected borrowers from abusively high interest rates. These laws, which Congress largely preempted, also restricted many borrowers from access to credit. The most widely used approach to redressing predatory lending entails invoking laws and regulations that predate the emergence of predatory lending. These laws were written without predatory lending in mind, making them imperfect mechanisms for relief. Disclosure laws, some of which explicitly address predatory loan terms, fail to fulfill their promise because they are either too narrow or subject to evasion. Increasingly, municipalities and states are passing laws aimed specifically at predatory lending. The enforceability and effectiveness of these laws depends critically on their specificity, the breadth of practices they cover, and whether they are subject to preemption.

Originators and Brokers

Usury   Historically, usury laws served to curtail abusive lending by setting maximum interest rates. Several decades ago, the United States deregulated limits on mortgage rates, including passage of DIDMCA, which preempted state usury limits on first mortgages. With the advent of predatory lending, some policy makers and consumer advocates have argued to reimpose usury laws. Interest rate restrictions, however, are imperfect methods for deterring predatory lending because they limit the amount of capital available to LMI borrowers and spur credit rationing. When interest rates are capped, lenders charge borrowers more in up-front fees and require larger down payments, both of which adversely affect those with limited resources (Tansey and Tansey 1981). Similarly, limits on non-interest-rate terms, such as restrictions on points and fees, lead lenders to reduce the number of loans they make and require higher down payments, which, like interest rate caps, impede lending to LMI borrowers (Phaup and Hinton 1981, 91).

Fraud, Consumer Protection, and RICO   Borrowers, who have been defrauded by lenders through misrepresentations, can bring claims under state consumer protection statutes and antifraud laws. Common law fraud allows recovery when lenders or brokers make material misrepresentations on which borrowers rely to their detriment. Both federal and state consumer protection laws prohibit unfair and deceptive acts and practices.

Although claims based on misrepresentations hold a great deal of hope for borrowers, a number of forces deter and impede the filing of these types of claims. Fraud claims can be time-consuming and expensive, with minimal returns. As a result, borrowers may find it difficult to secure private representation to pursue these claims. The terms of unfair and deceptive acts and practices (UDAP) statutes often present unique obstacles. Some preclude private lawsuits. Others exempt lending or other credit transactions from their coverage. Still others fail to include attorneys' fee provisions that would be an incentive for lawyers to bring UDAP claims (Engel and McCoy 2002a, 1302–5).

When lenders, by engaging in a pattern of racketeering activity, such as mail or wire fraud, or through collection of an unlawful debt, violate certain laws while conducting or participating in an enterprise affecting interstate commerce, they may be subject to claims under the Racketeer Influenced and Corrupt Organization Act (RICO). RICO claims can be even harder to prove than fraud claims. This is because in addition to proving the underlying fraud, borrowers must prove the other elements that are unique to RICO claims (Engel and McCoy 2002a, 1303 and n.199).

Unconscionability   Contract law enables borrowers to bring claims against lenders for unconscionable loans. Unconscionability claims arise when borrowers are not given any meaningful choice as to the terms of contracts and the terms unreasonably favor the other party (U.C.C. §2–302(1)). Borrowers have met resistance from the courts when pursuing unconscionability claims based on price terms. This is because the aggrieved borrowers are contesting prices they knowingly accepted. In addition, it is difficult for plaintiffs to prove that a price is unfair. It is equally difficult for courts to draw the line between an unreasonably favorable and a reasonably favorable price (Engel and McCoy 2002a, 1299–301). Thus, only those borrowers who contest nonprice terms stand much chance of succeeding in unconscionability claims.

Discrimination   When predatory lenders impose more onerous loan terms on members of protected classes, for example, minorities or seniors, they may be subject to state and federal lending discrimination claims. Lending practices that have a disparate impact on protected classes even in the absence of intent to discriminate can also give rise to discrimination claims (Swire 1995).[19]

Victims of discrimination confront unique hurdles to successful resolution of their claims (Dane 1993, 549). The first hurdle is the difficulty of determining whether a lender engaged in unlawful discrimination. Without knowing the lenders' internal processes, borrowers typically cannot deduce whether a loan rejection or loan terms are based on legitimate reasons or unlawful discrimination. Likewise, the lack of access to lenders' underwriting methods and information on other borrowers precludes borrowers from knowing whether they have claims based on disparate impact. Practical hurdles are as formidable as these informational hurdles. Private attorneys shy away from lending discrimination claims because they are costly to litigate, difficult to prove, and often low in awards (for a fuller discussion of the obstacles to fair lending claims, see Engel and McCoy 2002a; Engel 1999). Enforcement, therefore, frequently depends on governmental agencies and nonprofits that are sorely constrained by limited resources, political constraints, and other more pressing priorities.

Disclosure   Several federal laws require lenders to disclose loan features to borrowers. RESPA[20] mandates the disclosure of real estate closing costs through two different mechanisms. First, lenders must provide loan applicants with a good-faith estimate of settlement costs (GFE) within three days after the loan application. Second, at the closing, the lender must furnish the borrower with a HUD-1 settlement statement listing all final closing costs that the borrower must pay (Board of Governors of the Federal Reserve System and U.S. Department of Housing and Urban Development 1998, Executive Summary II). RESPA's effectiveness is minimal because it does not provide any relief if the lenders made any errors in borrowers' GFEs or final accountings of loan closing costs. As a result, the information borrowers obtain from lenders is often unreliable and typically presented when borrowers are on the verge of signing the mortgage and note and, for a variety of emotional and financial reasons, unable to walk away from the loan.

TILA mandates disclosure of finance charges and annual percentage rates. The finance charge portrays the cost of the loan as a lump-sum dollar figure after taking interest payments, points, origination fees, and private mortgage insurance into account. The APR converts the finance charge into an effective annual interest rate. When lenders violate TILA's provisions, they may be subject to criminal penalties (15 U.S.C. § 1611). On the civil side, borrowers may pursue claims—either as individuals or as members of class actions—for actual damages, statutory damages and attorneys' fees (Renuart and Keest 2003, Ch. 8). In addition, in some situations borrowers have a right to rescind their mortgages for up to three years after closing (National Consumer Law Center 2002, Ch. 5). The goal of TILA was to standardize disclosures so that borrowers could easily compare the total cost of the credit lenders were offering on a timely basis. This standardization has failed because a multitude of closing costs are not included in the TILA calculations, which prevents borrowers from engaging in any meaningful loan comparison and shopping. In addition, for adjustable-rate mortgages, borrowers who lack lock-in commitments generally do not receive binding price quotes until the closing or soon before, impeding comparison shopping (McCoy 2007).

HOEPA, which is a subpart of TILA, mandates additional advance disclosures for loans that meet the statutory definition of a high-cost loan.[21] These disclosures include notice of the annual percentage rate and the dollar amount of the borrowers' loan payments, including any increases that could occur if the loans contain adjustable rates. HOEPA also requires that lenders inform borrowers that they have the right to refuse to enter into the loan agreement up until the time of the closing and that, by assuming the loan obligations, the borrowers could lose their homes (Engel and McCoy 2002a, 1305). Lenders who violate HOEPA, like those who violate TILA, may be subject to criminal penalties (15 U.S.C. § 1611). Civil remedies include all the TILA remedies, expanded rights of rescission, and the amount of all finance charges and fees paid by the borrower (15 U.S.C. §§ 1635 and 1640(a)(4)).

HOEPA suffers from its own limitations. Its application is limited to closed end, nonpurchase loans that contain certain, specific "trigger" terms.[22] Lenders can evade HOEPA by making open-end loans or by setting the loan terms below the HOEPA triggers and compensating for the decreased revenue by increasing the charges that are excluded from the HOEPA points and fees calculation.

Tinkering with the TILA, RESPA, and HOEPA requirements will not solve the problem of predatory lending. As quickly as Congress improves these statutes, abusive lenders will invent new ways to evade them. Furthermore, given that most people do not understand the extant disclosures, crafting new and different disclosures will only add more confusion, especially if the disclosures are presented as part of high-pressure closings.

State and Local Anti-Predatory Lending Laws   In 1999, a sharp rise in predatory lending along with perceived deficiencies in traditional remedies for lending abuses led North Carolina to enact the first comprehensive state anti-predatory lending statute (N.C. Gen. Stat. § 24-1.1E). More than half the states, the District of Columbia, plus assorted counties and municipalities followed suit by enacting a wide assortment of anti-predatory lending laws (Bostic et al. 2007).

Some of the new state laws add relatively little protection, either because they mandate only studies, do not expand HOEPA's triggers to reach more loans, do not afford aggrieved borrowers a private right of action, or severely restrict private relief to individual borrowers. In contrast, other jurisdictions, following North Carolina's lead, enacted statutes that significantly increase state regulation of subprime practices and loan terms.

Vigorous state laws that track North Carolina's vary across a host of dimensions. To begin with, some statutes only regulate lenders and brokers, whereas others regulate both groups plus secondary market assignees of subprime loans. In this section, we discuss state regulation of loan originators; later, we discuss state assignee liability provisions.

Of the vigorous state statutes, some regulate high-cost home loans alone and others regulate both prime and subprime home loans. The laws can therefore be classified according to two different models. The first model tracks and often expands on HOEPA by defining high-cost loans as those with minimum numerical APR or points and fees triggers and regulating specific terms and practices in the resulting group of high-cost loans. The second model regulates terms and practices for home loans across the board, both prime and subprime, without regard to interest rates or points and fees. Some statutes take a hybrid approach, adopting the first model for some loan terms and the second model for others (Azmy 2005, 361–62).

Among state laws that follow the first model, there are further variations. Some states, such as Pennsylvania, Connecticut, and Kentucky, set their numerical triggers at the same high level as HOEPA. A handful of other states, most notably Illinois, the District of Columbia, and New Mexico, lowered their APR triggers below HOEPA's (as low as 5 percent above the rate on comparable Treasury securities). At least fourteen states—including North Carolina, New Jersey, New Mexico, and New York—use lower points and fees triggers than HOEPA. Most of the latter states expand on HOEPA in two further ways: first, by defining points and fees to include added charges and second, by covering purchase mortgages and/or home equity lines of credit in addition to closed-end home refinance loans (Azmy 2005).

The vigorous state statutes, plus some state laws that mimic HOEPA's numerical triggers, prohibit certain types of loan terms or practices. Depending on the state, prohibited terms or practices include negative amortization, acceleration clauses, advance payments, increased interest upon default, financing of single premium credit insurance, and lending without regard to ability to pay. Those same statutes subject other loan terms or practices to strict regulation. Such provisions include, depending on the state, balloon clauses, direct payments to home improvement contractors, prepayment penalties, and loan flipping. Some state statutes mandate additional disclosures to borrowers (Azmy 2005, 366–70). Scattered states cap or prohibit the financing of points and fees or outlaw steering of prime-eligible customers into subprime home loans (Azmy 2005, 370–72).

Remedies among state anti-predatory lending laws vary widely. Virtually all of the states that afford aggrieved borrowers private relief award reasonable attorneys' fees to successful plaintiffs and compensatory and statutory damages. Most of those states allow courts to strike down illegal loan provisions as void and to reform loans so that they comport with law. In those states, predatory lending violations commonly provide defenses to foreclosure. A smaller subset of states permits borrowers to rescind loans that violate their statutes. Some states provide defenses to lenders who cure violations in good faith (Azmy 2005, 373).

Federal Preemption   In January 2004, in one fell swoop, the U.S. Office of the Comptroller of the Currency (OCC), which regulates national banks, made a bold countermove at banks' behest by eviscerating state anti-predatory lending laws as those laws apply to national banks and their mortgage lending operating subsidiaries. The Comptroller accomplished this objective by issuing a final rule preempting all state anti-predatory lending laws to the extent those laws apply to those entities.[23] The only exception is where Congress expressly incorporated state-law standards in federal statutes, or a specific state law only has an "incidental" effect on national banks—that is, is part of "the legal infrastructure that makes it practicable" for national banks to operate and does not "regulate the manner or content of the business of banking authorized for national banks" (Office of the Comptroller of the Currency 2004; Wilmarth 2004). In a companion final rule also issued in January 2004, the Comptroller heavily restricted states' exercise of "visitorial powers" over national banks and their operating subsidiaries.

These two rules excuse national banks and mortgage companies that are operating subsidiaries of national banks from complying with all state anti-predatory lending laws. Victims of predatory lending by those lenders cannot sue the lenders for relief under state anti-predatory lending laws. Nothing in the OCC preemption rule affords a new cause of action to aggrieved borrowers to replace the ones that they have lost. Similarly, the rules bar states from examining national banks or their operating subsidiaries for predatory lending violations, from taking enforcement action against them for such violations, and from suing those entities in court to enforce the state laws. Although the OCC has cautioned the entities it regulates against certain abusive lending practices, for the most part, it has demurred from pronouncing specific practices illegal.

If the two rules are interpreted as a charter bid, they have already been successful. In 2004, J. P. Morgan Chase Bank swapped its New York state charter for a national bank charter to take advantage of the OCC preemption rule. Increasingly, independent subprime mortgage companies are casting their independence aside to become operating subsidiaries of national banks for the same reason. Thus, by unilateral agency fiat, the OCC sought to accomplish what many in the subprime home loan industry desire—the effective repeal of the state anti-predatory lending laws.

Suitability Proposal   Vigorous state anti-predatory lending laws such as North Carolina's have much to recommend them. They require abusive loan originators and mortgage brokers to internalize the cost of harming victims. They make victims whole through a variety of techniques, including damages, reformation of loan terms, and defenses to foreclosure. Attorneys' fee provisions provide incentives to attorneys to bring meritorious claims. Often (but not invariably) the laws define predatory practices according to clear and objective standards. Finally, the wide variation among state laws creates a laboratory of state experimentation that will permit future researchers to evaluate the strengths and any unintended consequences of the various approaches.

These accomplishments are highly significant and should not be underestimated. At the same time, the lack of an effective uniform federal standard relegates injured borrowers in states with no or weak anti-predatory lending laws to more traditional remedies, which experience has proven are generally inadequate. Furthermore, most of the state laws patterned after North Carolina's are static. In other words, the laws do not provide a regulatory mechanism for expanding the list of prohibited and regulated practices as new abuses arise. Federal preemption rulings by the OCC essentially have nullified the state laws, moreover, as those laws apply to national banks and their operating subsidiaries.

We would address these problems through enactment of a federal statute creating a uniform national duty of suitability in subprime mortgage lending. The duty of suitability is rooted in federal securities law, which provides that a salesperson should "recommend only securities that are suitable to the needs of the particular customer" (Loss and Seligman 2001, 1010). In the subprime mortgage context, the statute we propose would enunciate a general duty of suitability and implement that duty by prohibiting or regulating the same practices that the state laws address, plus other emerging problems, such as servicing abuses. In addition, the law would authorize an appropriate federal agency such as the Federal Trade Commission to expand the duty of suitability by rule or adjudication to regulate any new abuses that arise.

The federal statute would set a floor, not a ceiling, thereby allowing states to impose stricter limits on subprime lending abuses. Enforcement mechanisms would include a nonwaivable private right of action for injured borrowers with broad-based remedies, federal prosecution, and agency enforcement. Last, because regulatory federal preemption has limited the relief available to states and consumers, our proposed legislation would prohibit federal preemption of state and local anti-predatory lending laws that are stricter than federal law, unless those provisions substantially impede the ability to comply with federal law. In addition, any agency orders or regulations declaring federal preemption of a state or local anti-predatory lending law would be subject to de novo review in federal district court and de novo review on appeal.

Assignee Liability

Under the Uniform Commercial Code, investors who buy loans on the secondary market can cut off most claims and defenses to collection by borrowers under the holder-in-due-course rule. The rule empowers secondary-market purchasers to defeat "personal" defenses to nonpayment if they satisfy the following requirements for a holder in due course: the purchaser is the holder, of a negotiable note, who took the note for value, in good faith, and without notice of the defenses. Once a purchaser qualifies as a holder in due course, it can cut off the defense of unconscionability, as well as all other personal defenses to the loan agreement[24] (White and Summers 2000 §§ 14-1– 14-7, 14-10).

Today, approximately two-thirds of all subprime home loans are sold in the secondary market through securitization. Thus, unless some other law abrogates the holder-in-due-course rule for subprime home loans, borrowers injured by predatory practices are barred from relief against any investors or securitized trusts who own their loans.

HOEPA was the first specific anti-predatory lending law to repeal the holder-in-due-course rule for subprime home loans, but only for the costliest subprime mortgages (for a discussion of assignee liability provisions under other statutes that are not specific to the subprime mortgage context, see Engel and McCoy 2004, 723–27). Under that law, investors who buy HOEPA loans are subject to all claims and defenses a borrower could assert against the original lender unless the assignee can prove that "a reasonable person exercising due diligence" could not have determined that the loan fell within HOEPA (15 U.S.C. § 1641(d)(1)).

North Carolina did not include an assignee liability provisions in its 1999 anti-predatory lending law. However, some other states that passed legislation modeled after North Carolina's did include assignee liability, including Georgia, New Jersey, New York, and New Mexico.

The earliest state to impose assignee liability was Georgia. Its 2002 statute ignited a firestorm of criticism, with many interpreting the assignee liability provisions as imposing unlimited punitive damages and class action liability. When the specter of uncapped liability caused Standard & Poor's and its sister rating agencies to refuse to rate numerous securitized home loan pools originated in Georgia, the Georgia legislature repealed the original law and replaced it with a weaker assignee liability provision that the rating agencies found acceptable (Azmy 2005, 374–75).

Since then, a number of states, including New Jersey, the District of Columbia, Arkansas, Maine, Illinois, Massachusetts, New Mexico, and New York have enacted assignee liability provisions patterned after the later Georgia law. Colorado and Florida have adopted HOEPA's assignee liability language, with provisions to cap damages liability (Azmy 2005, 375). Standard & Poor's rates securitized subprime loan pools from most of those states, but generally requires higher and in some cases enormous credit enhancements to rate those pools because of assignee liability concerns. As of this writing, Standard & Poor's has refused to rate some or all high-cost home loan pools originated in

Indiana, Massachusetts, and New Jersey on the basis of concerns that the damages risk to assignees cannot be quantified (Abrams et al. 2004).

A federal assignee liability provision is essential, both to afford injured subprime borrowers meaningful relief and to create an incentive for Wall Street to stop funding predatory loans. In crafting such a law, it is critical to strike a balance between devising a cost-effective method for screening out abusive loans from loan pools and maintaining the flow of legitimate mortgage loans to LMI borrowers. To achieve that balance, assignees should be rewarded for implementing adequate controls. Thus, we propose that assignees who fail to adopt adequate controls should be subject to all claims and defenses that borrowers could raise against loan originators with full damages liability, including punitive damages. In contrast, assignees that do institute effective controls would be subject to all claims and defenses that borrowers could bring against originators, but awards would be limited to compensatory damages. Under our proposal, Congress would empower a federal agency to define "adequate controls," on the condition that such controls would include, at a minimum, computerized screening of loan-level data to screen out predatory loans and ongoing monitoring of loan performance (Engel and McCoy 2004, 742–43). Our proposal would provide rating agencies with the certainty they require to adequately assess the risks associated with loan pools as long as the assignees instituted our proposed controls. Thus, our approach rewards assignees that help to police predatory lending and creates a mechanism through which injured borrowers can be made whole, all the while permitting rating agencies to rate securitized loan pools that contain subprime loans.

CONCLUSION

In the past fifteen years, cities have made impressive strides in revitalizing urban centers and helping renters to become homeowners and begin building wealth. Where urban planners tread, however, predatory lenders follow. The surge in home equity values in recent years attracted unscrupulous lenders who scheme to tap out equity by refinancing mortgages with high interest and fees, heedless of the toll to homeowners and the neighborhood from bankruptcies, abandoned houses, and foreclosures.

In combating predatory lending, this country finds itself at a crossroads. In up to 80 percent of subprime mortgage loans, the holder-in-due-course rule bars borrowers from any meaningful relief against the owners of their loans. Even when loan originators continue to hold abusive home loans in portfolio, traditional remedies often fail to afford borrowers adequate relief. Some states have addressed these problems through new anti-predatory lending statutes. The rating agencies and the OCC have undercut these laws however, by respectively declining to rate subprime securitizations in some states and preempting the new state laws for national banks and their operating subsidiaries.

With the implosion of the subprime market in 2007, the predatory lending debate has moved to the federal arena as Congress considers a national anti-predatory lending bill. If Congress acts responsibly, it will prohibit subprime lenders from making unsuitable loans and reward loan assignees for refusing to finance predatory loans with damages caps. If Congress does not, predatory lending will continue to evade meaningful redress. Homeowners—and their communities—stand in the balance.

Our thanks to Julia Sass Rubin and participants at the Federal Reserve Bank of New York Community Development Finance Research Conference for their invaluable comments. We are also grateful to Sumy Rhee for her flawless cite checking of the chapter.

NOTES

1. We use the term predatory lenders to include both mortgage brokers and lenders.

2. Community development groups that seek to rehabilitate these properties encounter an array of obstacles. These obstacles are particularly burdensome when lenders elect not to foreclose on the property. Oftentimes, there is a question of who actually owns the property. Recording errors and uncertain transactions can further cloud titles to property. Many of these problems could be resolved through the foreclosure process; however, the entities in the best position to foreclose on the property—the mortgage holders and the taxing authorities—may lack sufficient incentives to initiate foreclosure proceedings. Mortgagees, once they become owners through foreclosure, incur tax liabilities, are subject to housing code enforcement actions, and may have to defend nuisance claims. Taxing authorities may perceive that the immediate costs of foreclosure outweigh any benefits that could accrue from taking title to the property.

3. For a fuller discussion of these statutes, see the section on disclosure.

4. Pub. L. No. 96-221, 94 Stat. 164 (1980).

5. Pub. L. No. 97-320, 96 Stat. 1469 (1982).

6. Federal Housing Administration (FHA) insurance further reduces the costs associated with high-risk borrowers by reimbursing lenders for many of the expenses they incur when borrowers default. (Clauretie and Jameson 1990, 701–2).

7. Lenders also exploit information asymmetries that exist between them and the various secondary market actors involved with the securitiza-

tion of loans (for a discussion of this phenomenon, see Engel and McCoy 2002a, 2004).

8. When borrowers later default, the lenders reappear on the doorsteps, eager to refinance the loans, which enable the lenders to reap additional fees (U.S. Department of Housing and Urban Development and U.S. Department of Treasury 2000, 74).

9. Some borrowers are vulnerable to predatory lenders for other reasons. For example, people who are infirm may not be able to venture from their homes to apply for loans with conventional lenders.

10. There are banks that do engage in subprime and predatory lending through subsidiaries and affiliates that do not have the same names, which reduces the reputational risk to the banks. (Gilreath 1999, 149; Garver 2001, 4; Litan et al. 2000, 76). Banks and thrifts also are complicit in predatory lending when they buy mortgage-backed securities, the underlying loans of which are predatory.

11. Numerous cities also enacted ordinances banning abusive loan terms. Most of these ordinances were preempted by state legislation or enjoined by courts on the grounds that the cities lacked the power to regulate lenders.

12. The securities industry has a long history of industry self-regulation, dating back to the Maloney Act of 1938. In the Maloney Act, 15 U.S.C. § 78*o*–3(b)(6), Congress directed the Securities and Exchange Commission (SEC) to register national securities associations that among other things promulgated rules "to prevent fraudulent and manipulative acts and practices (and) to promote just and equitable principles of trade." Today, such associations are known in securities parlance as securities regulatory organizations or SROs and include the National Association of Securities Dealers, the New York Stock Exchange, and the other American stock exchanges.

13. Such self-regulation is carried out under the auspices of the Insurance Marketplace Standards Association (IMSA), a voluntary membership organization promoting high ethical standards in the sale of individual life insurance, long-term care insurance and annuity products. Insurers must earn IMSA membership by passing an independent assessment designed to ensure their compliance with IMSA's principles and code of ethical market conduct, which are designed to advance sound market practices. (see Insurance Marketplace Standards Association, http://www.imsaethics.org).

14. See Mortgage Bankers Association, "NHEMA to Merge with MBA," Aug. 23, 2006, http://www.mortgagebankers.org/NewsandMedia/PressCenter/44105.htm.

15. MBA members may, but are not required to, agree to conduct their businesses according to the best practices standards. For the most part, the standards are general in nature and do not address specific predatory lending practices (Mortgage Bankers Association, "MBA Best Practices," http://www.mortgagebankers.org/IndustryResources/StandardsandBestPractices/MBABestPractices.htm).

16. MBA has since taken the 2003 Enforcement Summit report off its website (http://www.mbaa.org).

17. As discussed, there are significant disincentives for banks to engage in predatory lending. The actual rates at which banks directly or indirectly are engaged making these loans is unknown, although anecdotal evidence reveals some banks are involved in abusive lending (Kathleen Day, "A Practice That Lends Itself to Trouble; Superior's Failure Spotlights Banks that Court High-Risk Borrowers," *The Washington Post,* August 21, 2001, p. E01).

18. These can include applications: (a) for a bank charter or deposit insurance; (b) to open or close a branch; (c) to relocate a home office or a branch; (d) for a merger, acquisition or consolidation; (e) to acquire another bank's liabilities; or (f) to acquire an insured bank (12 U.S.C. §§ 2902(2)-(3), 2903(a)(2)).

19. The federal statutes that protect against lending discrimination are the Equal Credit Opportunity Act of 1974 (ECOA) (15 U.S.C. §§ 1601 et seq.), which prohibits lenders from discriminating against applicants for mortgages, and the Fair Housing Act (FHA)(42 U.S.C. §§ 3601–3619), which prohibits discrimination in the financing of residential real estate.

20. Congress vested enforcement of RESPA in nine federal agencies (U.S.C. §§ 1607(a), (c)). Borrowers can only pursue private claims for RESPA violations if the lenders failed to inform them that their loans could be transferred, received kickbacks, or steered them to title companies. (15 U.S.C. §§ 2605(f), 2607, 2608).

21. State attorneys general, the same agencies that have the power to enforce TILA and RESPA, can enforce HOEPA (15 U.S.C. § 1640(e)).

22. The triggers are that the annual percentage rate at consummation exceeds the yield on Treasury securities of comparable maturity plus 8 percent or the total points and fees exceed 8 percent of the total loan amount or $400 (subject to annual indexing), whichever is greater (15 U.S.C. §§ 1602(aa)(1)–(aa)(4)).

23. In 2007, the Supreme Court affirmed the OCC rule in Watters v. Wachovia, N.A., ___ U.S. ___, 127 S. Ct. 1559 (2007). Space does not permit description of the other types of broad-ranging and complex federal preemption of state mortgage laws (for a cogent description, see Keest and Renuart 2000).

24. Personal defenses include failure or lack of consideration, breach of warranty, unconscionability, and fraud in the inducement. Borrowers who are sued by secondary-market purchasers may still raise the "real" defenses of infancy, duress, lack of legal capacity, illegality of the transaction, fraud in the factum (that is, fraud in which the plaintiff signed the wrong document and was not at fault), and discharge of the debtor through insolvency. Furthermore, duress, lack of legal capacity, illegality, and fraud in the factum only constitute real defenses for void contracts, which are extremely rare. Where a contract is simply voidable, not void, the latter four defenses are personal defenses and cannot be raised against holders in due course. The Federal Trade Commission has a rule abrogating the holder-in-due-course rule, but this rule only applies to HOEPA loans and the financing of sales of goods or services secured by home mortgages. (White and Summers 2000; 16 C.F.R. § 433.2).

REFERENCES

15 U.S.C. §§ 78b-78c (Securities Exchange Act of 1934 §§ 19(b)–(c)) (2006).

16 C.F.R. § 433.2 (2007).

Abrams, Natalie, Maureen Coleman, Frank Raiter, Susan E. Barnes, and Scott Mason. 2004. "Anti-Predatory Lending Law Update." New York: Standard & Poor's. Accessed at http://www.alta.org/govt/issues/04/sp_0920.pdf.

Alternative Mortgage Transactions Parity Act of 1982, Pub. L. No. 97-320, 96 Stat. 1469.

Avery, Robert B., Patricia E. Beeson, and Mark S. Sniderman. 1999. "Neighborhood Information and Home Mortgage Lending." *Journal of Urban Economics* 45(2): 287–310.

Avery, Robert B., Raphael W. Bostic, Paul S. Calem, and Glenn B. Canner. 1997. "Changes in the Distribution of Banking Offices." *Federal Reserve Bulletin* 83(9): 707–25. Accessed at http://www.federalreserve.gov/pubs/bulletin/1997/199709lead.pdf.

Azmy, Baher. 2005. "Squaring the Predatory Lending Circle." *Florida Law Review* 57(2): 295–410.

Azmy, Baher, and David Reiss. 2004. "Modeling a Response to Predatory Lending: The New Jersey Home Ownership Security Act of 2002." *Rutgers Law Journal* 35(2): 645–715.

Block-Lieb, Susan, and Edward Janger. 2006. "The Myth of the Rational Borrower: Rationality, Behavioralism, and the Misguided 'Reform' of Bankruptcy Law." *Texas Law Review* 84(5): 1481–565.

Board of Governors of the Federal Reserve System. 2001. "Truth in Lending." *Federal Register* 66(245): 65,604–65,622, codified at 12 C.F.R. § 226.34(a)(3) (2007).

Board of Governors of the Federal Reserve System and U.S. Department of Housing and Urban Development. 1998. Joint Report to Congress Concerning Reform to the Truth in Lending Act and the Real Estate Settlement Procedures Act. Accessed at http://www.federalreserve. gov/boarddocs/rptcongress/tila.pdf.

Board of Governors of the Federal Reserve System, Federal Deposit Insurance Corporation, Office of the Comptroller of the Currency, and Office of Thrift Supervisor. 1999. "Interagency Guidance on Subprime Lending." Washington: Board of Governors of the Federal Reserve System. Accessed at http://www.federalreserve.gov/boarddocs/srletters/1999/ sr9906a1.pdf.

Bostic, Raphael W., Kathleen C. Engel, Patricia A. McCoy, Anthony Pennington-Cross and Susan M. Wachter. 2007. "State and Local Anti-Predatory Lending Laws: The Effect of Legal Enforcement Mechanisms." Working paper. Accessed at http://www.ssrn.com.

Brendsel, Leland C. 1996. "Securitization's Role in Housing Finance: The Special Contributions of the Government-Sponsored Enterprises." In *A Primer on Securitization,* edited by Leon T. Kendall, and Michael J. Fishman. Cambridge, Mass.: MIT Press.

Bucks, Brian, and Karen Pence. 2006. "Do Homeowners Know Their Home Values and Mortgage Terms?" *Federal Reserve Board of Governors* working paper. Washington: Board of Governors of the Federal Reserve System. Accessed at http://www.federalreserve.gov/pubs/feds/2006/200603/ 200603pap.pdf.

Calem, Paul S., Jonathan E. Hershaff, and Susan M. Wachter. 2004. "Neighborhood Patterns of Subprime Lending: Evidence from Disparate Cities." *Housing Policy Debate* 15(3): 603–22. Accessed at http:// www.fanniemaefoundation.com/programs/hpd/pdf/hpd_1503_Calem. pdf.

Canner, Glenn B., Thomas A. Durkin, and Charles A. Luckett. 1998. "Recent Developments in Home Equity Lending." *Federal Reserve Bulletin* 84(4): 241–51. Accessed at http://www.federalreserve.gov/pubs/ bulletin/1998/199804lead.pdf.

Clauretie, Terrence M., and Mel Jameson. 1990. "Interest Rates and the Foreclosure Process: An Agency Problem in FHA Mortgage Insurance." *The Journal of Risk and Insurance* 57(4): 701–11.

Community Reinvestment Act, 12 U.S.C. §§ 2901–2908 (2006).

Dane, Stephen M. 1993. "Eliminating the Labyrinth: A Proposal to Simplify Federal Mortgage Lending Discrimination Laws." *University of Michigan Journal of Law Reform* 26(3): 527–70.

Depository Institutions Deregulation and Monetary Control Act of 1980. Pub. L. No. 96-221, 94 Stat. 164.

Duca, John V., and Stuart S. Rosenthal. 1994. "Do Mortgage Rates Vary Based on Household Default Characteristics? Evidence on Rate Sorting and Credit Rationing." *The Journal of Real Estate Finance and Economics* 8(2), 99–113.

Eggert, Kurt. 2004. "Limiting Abuse and Opportunism by Mortgage Servicers." *Housing Policy Debate* 15(3): 753–84. Accessed at http://www.fanniemaefoundation.org/programs/hpd/pdf/hpd_1503_ Eggert.pdf.

Engel, Kathleen. 1999. "Moving Up the Residential Hierarchy: A New Remedy for an Old Injury Arising from Housing Discrimination." *Washington University Law Quarterly* 77(4): 1153–98.

———. 2006. "Do Cities Have Standing? Redressing the Externalities of Predatory Lending." *Connecticut Law Review* 38(3): 355–91.

Engel, Kathleen C., and Patricia A. McCoy. 2002a. "A Tale of Three Markets: The Law and Economics of Predatory Lending." *Texas Law Review* 80(6): 1255–381.

———. 2002b. "The CRA Implications of Predatory Lending." *Fordham Urban Law Journal* 29(4): 1571–605.

———. 2004. "Predatory Lending: What Does Wall Street Have to Do with It?" *Housing Policy Debate* 15(3): 715–50.

———. 2007. "Turning a Blind Eye: Wall Street Finance of Predatory Lending." *Fordham Law Review* 75(4): 102. Accessed at http://papers.ssrn.com/sol3/papers.cfm?abstract_id=910378.

Equal Credit Opportunity Act, 15 U.S.C. §§ 1691–1691f (2006).

Fair Housing Act, 42 U.S.C. §§ 3601, et seq. (2006).

Fannie Mae. 2000. HUD's Proposed Affordable Housing Goals: Fannie Mae's Comment Letter.

Federal Reserve Board. 2003. "An Update on the Predatory Lending Issue." Remarks by Governor Edward M. Gramlich at the Texas Association of Bank Counsel 27th Annual Convention, South Padre Island, Texas, October 9, 2003. Accessed at http://www.federalreserve.gov/BoardDocs/speeches/2003/20031009/default.htm.

Federal Trade Commission. 2003. "FTC Subprime Lending Cases (since 1998)." Accessed at http://www.ftc.gov/opa/2002/07/subprimelendingcases.htm.

Fishbein, Allen J., and Patrick Woodall. 2006. "Exotic or Toxic? An Examination of the Nontraditional Mortgage Market for Consumers and Lenders." Accessed at http://www.consumerfed.org/pdfs/Exotic_Toxic_Mortgage_Report0506.pdf.

Freddie Mac. 1996. "Automated Underwriting: Making Mortgage Lending Simpler and Fairer for America's Families." Accessed at http://www.freddiemac.com/corporate/reports/moseley/mosehome.htm.

———. 2007. "Welcome to Freddie Mac's Anti-Predatory Lending Site." Accessed at http://www.dontborrowtrouble.com.

Garver, Rob. 2001. "Citi Corroborates Two Allegations." *American Banker,* July 30, 2001.

Gilreath, Evan M. 1999. "The Entrance of Banks into Subprime Lending: First Union and the Money Store." *North Carolina Banking Institute* 3(April): 149–68.

Greenspan, Alan. 2001. "The Importance of Education in Today's Economy." Remarks by Chairman Alan Greenspan at the Federal Reserve System Community Affairs Research Conference. Washington, D.C., April 5–6, 2001. Accessed at http://www.chicagofed.org/cedric/files/cfmacd_greenspan.pdf.

Gwatkin, Kathryn, and George McCarthy. 2003. "A Critical Examination of Financial Literacy Education." Working Paper BABC 04-17. Joint Center for Housing Studies of Harvard University. Accessed at http://www.jchs.harvard.edu/publications/finance/babc/babc_04-17_draft.pdf.

Harkness, Donna S. 2000. "Predatory Lending Prevention Project: Prescribing a Cure for the Home Equity Loss Ailing the Elderly." *Boston University Public Interest Law Journal* 10(1): 1–61.

Hermanson, Sharon, and Robert Wilden. 2003. "Homeownership Education and Counseling (HEC)." Issue Brief 65. Washington, D.C.: AARP Public Policy Institute. Accessed at http://assets.aarp.org/rgcenter/post-import/ib65_hec.pdf.

Hirad, Abdighani, and Peter M. Zorn. 2001. "A Little Knowledge Is a Good Thing: Empirical Evidence of the Effectiveness of Pre-Purchase Homeownership Counseling." Working paper LIHO-01.4. Joint Center for Housing Studies of Harvard University. Accessed at http://www.jchs.harvard.edu/publications/homeownership/liho01-4.pdf.

House Committee on Banking and Financial Services. 2000. "Predatory Lending Practices, Hearing Before the House Committee on Banking and Financial Services, 106th Congress." Washington: U.S. Government Printing Office.

Hylton, Keith N. 2000. "Banks and Inner Cities: Market and Regulatory Obstacles to Development Lending." *Yale Journal on Regulation* 17(2): 197–251.

Jaffee, Dwight M., and Thomas Russell. 1976. "Imperfect Information, Uncertainty, and Credit Rationing." *Quarterly Journal of Economics* 90(4): 651–66.

Keest, Kathleen E., and Elizabeth Renuart. 2000. *The Cost of Credit: Regulation and Legal Challenges,* 2d edition. Boston, Mass.: National Consumer Law Center.

Kennickell, Arthur B., Martha Starr-McCluer, and Annika E. Sundén. 1997. "Family Finances in the U.S.: Recent Evidence from the Survey of Consumer Finances." *Federal Reserve Bulletin* 83(1): 1–24. Accessed at http://www.federalreserve.gov/pubs/bulletin/1997/0197lead.pdf.

Klausner, Michael. 1995. "Market Failure and Community Investment: A Market-Oriented Alternative to the Community Reinvestment Act." *University of Pennsylvania Law Review* 143(5): 1561–93.

Lax, Howard, Michael Manti, Paul Raca, and Peter Zorn. 2004. "Subprime Lending: An Investigation of Economic Efficiency." *Housing Policy Debate* 15(3): 533–71. Accessed at http://www.fanniemaefoundation.org/programs/hpd/pdf/hpd_1503_Lax.pdf.

Litan, Robert E., Nicolas P. Retsinas, Eric S. Belsky, and Susan White Haag. 2000. *The Community Reinvestment Act After Financial Modernization: A Baseline Report.* Washington: U.S. Department of the Treasury. Accessed at http://www.treasury.gov/press/releases/docs/crareport.pdf.

Loss, Louis, and Joel Seligman. 1990. *Securities Regulation VI,* 3rd edition. New York: Aspen Law and Business.

———. 2001. *Fundamentals of Securities Regulation,* 4th edition. New York: Aspen Law and Business.

Mallach, Alan. 2002. *Home Ownership Education and Counseling: Issues in Research and Definition.* Philadelphia, Pa.: Federal Reserve Bank of Philadelphia. Accessed at http://www.philadelphiafed.org/cca/capubs/homeowner.pdf.

Maloney Act of 1938, Pub. L. No. 38-719, 48 Stat. 895 (codified as amended at 15 U.S.C. § 78*o* (2000)).

McCarthy, George W., and Roberto G. Quercia. 2000. "Bridging the Gap Between Supply and Demand: The Evolution of the Homeownership, Education and Counseling Industry." Report 00-01. Washington: The Research Institute for Housing America. Accessed at http://www.housingamerica.org/docs/RIHA00-01.pdf.

McCoy, Patricia A. 2007. "Rethinking Disclosure in a World of Risk-Based Pricing." *Harvard Journal on Legislation* 44(1): 123-66. Accessed at http://www.law.harvard.edu/students/orgs/jol/vol44_1/mccoy.pdf.

Murray, Teresa Dixon. 2000. "Borrower Beware; Predatory Mortgage Brokers Don't Give Terms Promised, Causing Some to Lose Their Homes." *Plain Dealer* [Cleveland, Oh.], August 28, 2000, p. 1C.

National Consumer Law Center. 2002. *Stop Predatory Lending.* Boston, Mass: NCLC. N.C. Gen. Stat. § 24-1.1E (1999).

Office of the Comptroller of the Currency. 2004. "Bank Activities and Operations: Real Estate Lending and Appraisals." *Federal Register* 69(8): 1904–17.

Office of the Comptroller of the Currency, Board of Governors of the Federal Reserve System, Federal Deposit Insurance Corporation, and Office of Thrift Supervision. 2001. *Expanded Interagency Guidance on Subprime Lending.* Washington: Board of Governors of the Federal Reserve. Accessed at http://www.federalreserve.gov/boarddocs/srletters/2001/sr0104a1.pdf.

Phaup, Dwight, and John Hinton. 1981. "The Distributional Effects [of] Usury Laws: Some Empirical Evidence." *Atlantic Economic Journal* 9(3): 91–98.

Potter, Joan. 2000. *Fighting Home Equity Fraud and Predatory Lending: One Community's Solution.* Community Reinvestment Report. Cleveland, Oh.: Federal Reserve Bank of Cleveland. Accessed at http://www.clevelandfed.org/commAffairs/crforum/frmsp00/creport1.pdf.

Racketeer Influenced and Corrupt Organization Act (RICO), 18 U.S.C. §§ 1961–1968 (2006).

Real Estate Settlement Procedures Act, 12 U.S.C. §§ 2601–2617 (2006).

Renuart, Elizabeth. 2003. "Toward One Competitive and Fair Mortgage Market: Suggested Reforms in *A Tale of Three Markets* Point in the Right Direction." *Texas Law Review* 82(2): 421–38.

Renuart, Elizabeth, and Kathleen E. Keest. 2003. *Truth in Lending.* 5th edition. Boston, Mass.: National Consumer Law Center.

Restatement (Second) of Torts. 1977. Philadelphia, Pa.: American Law Institute.

Shroder, Mark. 2000. "The Value of the Sunshine Cure: Efficacy of the RESPA Disclosure Strategy." Working paper. Washington: U.S. Department of Housing and Urban Development.

Smith, Shelly. 2001. "Mandatory Arbitration Clauses in Consumer Contracts: Consumer Protection and the Circumvention of the Judicial System." *DePaul Law Review* 50(4): 1191–251.

Standard & Poor's. 2005. *The Subprime Market.* PowerPoint presentation given at MBA's Nonprime Lending and Alternative Products Conference, Washington, D.C., June 17, 2005. Accessed at http://events.mortgage bankers.org/nonprime2005/signatureconferences/nonprime/images/img/TheSubprimeMarket.pdf.

Stiglitz, Joseph E., and Andrew Weiss. 1981. "Credit Rationing in Markets with Imperfect Information." *American Economic Review* 71(3): 393–410.

Sturdevant, P., and W. Brennan. 1999. "A Catalogue of Predatory Lending Practices." *The Consumer Advocate* 5(5): 3–19.

Swire, Peter P. 1995. "The Persistent Problem of Lending Discrimination: A Law and Economics Analysis." *Texas Law Review* 73(4): 787–869.

Tansey, Michael M., and Patricia H. Tansey. 1981. "An Analysis of the Impact of Usury Ceilings on Conventional Mortgage Loans." *Journal of American Real Estate and Urban Economics Association* 9(3): 265–81.

Truth in Lending Act, 15 U.S.C. §§ 1601–1667 (2006).

U.C.C. § 2-302 (1998).

U.S. Department of Housing and Urban Development and U.S. Department of Treasury. 2000. *Curbing Predatory Home Mortgage Lending.* Washington: U.S. Government Printing Office. Accessed at http://www.huduser.org/Publications/pdf/treasrpt.pdf.

U.S. Government Accounting Office. 2004. *Federal and State Agencies Face Challenges in Combating Predatory Lending.* GAO-03-280. Washington: U.S. Government Printing Office. Accessed at http://www.gao.gov/new.items/d04280.pdf.

Weicher, John C. 1997. *The Home Equity Lending Industry: Refinancing Mortgages for Borrowers with Impaired Credit,* Indianapolis, Ind.: Hudson Institute.

White, Alan M. 2004. "Risk-Based Mortgage Pricing: Present and Future Research." *Housing Policy Debate* 15(3): 503–31. Accessed at http://www.fanniemaefoundation.org/programs/hpd/pdf/hpd_1503_White.pdf.

White, James J., and Robert S. Summers. 2000. *Uniform Commercial Code,* 5th edition. St. Paul, Minn.: West Group.

Wilmarth, Arthur E., Jr. 2004. "The OCC's Preemption Rules Exceed the Agency's Authority and Present a Serious Threat to the Dual Banking System and Consumer Protection." *Annual Review of Banking and Financial Law* 23: 225–364.

PART III

Evaluating Progress

CHAPTER NINE

Measuring the Impact of Community Development Financial Institutions' Activities

Robinson Hollister

THIS CHAPTER reviews both attempts to evaluate the impacts of community development financial institutions (CDFIs) and methods of evaluation. Some may find it highly negative about whether the impact can be measured. I therefore begin by explaining the rationale for presenting the material this way.[1]

It seems that many of those calling for estimates of the impact of CDFIs—primarily funders—have unrealistic expectations about both the magnitude of change CDFIs are likely to be able to achieve with their investment activities and the degree to which reliable estimates can be obtained of those changes that might have occurred. To expect a CDFI to have a measurable, sizable effect on the degree of poverty in a given area is unrealistic. As John Caskey has pointed out, the assets of a CDFI are at most about the size of those of a small community bank, and we would not expect such a bank to have a substantial effect on community poverty (conversation with author).[2] As in many fields, at an early stage, those promoting a concept or program make extravagant claims about the likely or actual effects such activities will generate. This has been the case with CDFIs. A first step in trying to help formulate more realistic expectations about "provable" impacts of CDFIs is to show how these misleading, casual, and extravagant claims are often generated.

Second, the distinction between an outcome and an impact is often not well understood. It seems important that those asking for and getting evaluations of CDFI activities be aware of this distinction so they can properly assess what it is they are getting from the evaluation product.

Third, few realize how very difficult it is to establish causality rigorously. One may be provided what is called an estimate of the impact of a CDFI activity, but to determine rigorously that the CDFI actually caused that configuration of events is a very demanding task that will be achievable only in a very limited set of circumstances.

Given this set of rather discouraging considerations, it is important to recognize that there are still worthwhile things that can be learned from quantitative analysis relating outcomes to particular CDFI activities. Therefore, this chapter suggests when and with what methods evaluation and monitoring might partially fill the void. We hope this will help those posing impact goals for CDFI activities they are funding or programs they are managing to formulate more realistic expectations about what it is that an evaluation could provide them. Further, this discussion will help consumers of CDFI evaluations better assess whether the estimates from an evaluation in fact indicate how close to the goals the CDFI activity has come. These consumers should not be asking programs to prove this when there is not an available method that meets a high proof standard. At the same time, they should not be persuaded by flawed estimates that are offered as proof.

A LITTLE HISTORY: PRIS, CDFIS, AND EVALUATION

One component of the War on Poverty efforts in the 1960s was community action, efforts that focused on the community rather than the individual and were often referred to as place-based strategies. Although some elements of that agenda survived the general discouragement over how effective such efforts were, new place-based efforts in the 1970s took the form of community development corporations (CDCs). Some of the most noticed of these—Bedford-Stuyvesant being one example—mixed attempts to attract industry, and thereby employment, to the communities with infrastructure improvements, most notably housing.[3]

A chronologically parallel development was a provision of the Tax Reform Act of 1969, which allowed foundations to make investments to "support charitable activities that involve the potential return of capital within an established time frame" (The Foundation Center 2005). These are called program related investments (PRI). Some foundations began to mix PRIs with the normal grant programs. Often, however, those making PRI investments were in administrative or finance offices and had limited interaction with grant program officers. These developments brought the perspective of financial analysis and management into the social programming area. Eventually, after some notable misadventures with direct investments in particular enterprises, foundations began to realize that specialized skills were needed to assess potential PRIs; even though a higher risk profile was to be expected in the PRI portfolio, sound assessments of the likelihood that capital would be returned called for different types of analysis. On the one side, finance officers were not adept at assessing program content. On the other, grant officers couldn't handle the financials. In the later 1970s and early 1980s, foundations began to turn to intermediary organizations to develop the investment portfolios for them, investments that would have social objectives but would also have a reasonable chance of financial survival. Eventually the phrase "double bottom line" came to be used to characterize the types of enterprises funded, at least in part, through PRIs.

Another thread of development in the same chronology was the federal government's increased demand for evaluations of the effects of social programs and projects. Before the late 1960s, program evaluations had been largely anecdotal; an "expert" would review the project and perhaps visit a few sites and then pronounce on its effectiveness. With the burgeoning of the Great Society programs, pressure increased at the federal level to develop more quantitative evaluations.

The first quantitative evaluations primarily amounted to counting the inputs and outputs of a given program. Then people began to call for the more formal framework of benefit-cost analysis. The benefit-cost framework was itself an adaptation of investment theory. It was recognized that in the social program realm many of the inputs and outputs would not be, in essence, priced in a market. Indeed, the underlying rational for most programs was that there was, to extend the metaphor, a market failure that the program effort was supposed to try to correct. Methods had to be developed to estimate shadow prices for both inputs and outputs not normally priced in a market.

In the late 1960s and early 1970s, the evaluations standard began to be further elevated when demands were made—largely at the federal level but also among some academics—that evaluators "show that the outcome observed was in fact caused by the program."[4] It was soon realized that to establish that a program led to a given outcome, one needed to estimate what would have happened to those who participated had they not done so. This has come to be called the need for a counterfactual.

Initially, evaluators resorted to before-and-after estimates. For example, had those unemployed before the program become employed after the program? Such a change, however, could occur for many reasons besides exposure to a given program. Using the same example, the unemployment rate within a given group could change simply because there is a natural process of people moving from unemployment to employement over time. If at one point in time the program selected a high proportion of unemployed to be in the program—a typical program eligibility criterion—in subsequent periods the proportion of unemployed in the group would fall just by normal processes, even if the program had no effect, a phenomenon often referred to as regression to the mean. The movement might also have occurred simply because the conditions in the local labor market improved over the period in question, and opportunities improving for everyone.

Recognizing these limitations, evaluators turned to constructing comparison groups to provide a counterfactual. The idea was to find a group of individuals as similar as possible to program participants (also referred to as the treatment group), then to follow both groups over time, and finally to measure the outcome of interest for both at a given time after the program ended. The difference was taken to be an estimate of the impact of the program. In some cases, the unit was not individuals but a wider aggregate, such as classrooms or neighborhoods. The methods, though, were essentially the same—a comparison group of similar units matched as closely as possible to the treatment units.

A variety of methods were attempted to define and match such groups. For example, some studies used the pool of individuals who had applied for the program but not entered—either because there were not enough spaces or because they did not show up. Others turned to data sources that gave detailed information on both the characteristics of individuals (or whatever was the unit of treatment) and the outcome measures of interest, such as employment status. An often-used source was the Current Population Survey, a monthly survey of households the U.S. Bureau of the Census carries out to, among other things, estimate unemployment rates. Beginning in the late 1960s, two major longitudinal surveys interviewed a given set of families—drawn to be representative of the U.S. population or some subgroup—every year or two years.[5] These included measures of individual characteristics and outcomes of interest that could be used to match against the treatment group.

While evaluations using such constructed comparison groups were used throughout the 1970s and 1980s, in the later 1960s the first efforts to use an even more rigorous method for obtaining the counterfactual was used in the first major *social experiments* called the Negative Income Tax Experiments. The central feature of this method is the *random assignment* of units to the "treatment group" or to a "control group." Both groups are followed over time and the impact of the program is estimated as the difference in the average of the outcome measure for the treatment group and that for the control group. The importance of the process is that once a reasonably large sample has been randomly assigned, the probability that the mean of any characteristic will be the same for both groups is high. The motivation for resorting to this method is that without random assignment the distribution of characteristics—for example employment status, education levels, family structure—may be different between the treatment group and the comparison group. The effect of such differences has come to be called selection bias. This is particularly important for unmeasured, or unmeasurable, characteristics. The usual example is motivation. If the treatment group has a higher proportion of motivated individuals and if motivation leads to better employment outcomes, then the estimate of the impact will include a positive effect that is due not to the program but instead to a concentration of more highly motivated individuals. To a degree, it may be possible to statistically correct for the effects of differences, but the effects of the unmeasured characteristics remain and thus give rise to selection bias in the estimate of program impacts.

In the 1970s, the random assignment method was limited to a small number of programs (or demonstrations). Momentum for this method grew, however, and by the end of the 1990s had come to be regarded as the gold standard for program evaluation.

GROWTH IN DEMAND: WHO CARES AND WHAT DO THEY CARE ABOUT?

The demands for formal evaluations have come from many different sources. It is important to differentiate among those who appear to be asking for evaluations and the nature of what they seem to be expecting. All refer to measuring impact, but conceptions of what impact should be measured, how it should be measured, and why appear to be very different.

Foundations

I speculate that foundations that have made PRIs and grants to CDFIs have increased their demands for evaluations for several reasons. The special dispensation in the 1968 Tax Reform Act that allowed foundations to make PRIs was contingent on their being able to demonstrate that the PRI was in conformity with the charitable activities constraint on foundation spending. In other words, they couldn't simply make any type of loan or equity investment, there had to be some dimension of the investment or loan that was similar to activities charities typically engaged in. Thus, foundations may have felt that they had to demonstrate that their investments in CDFIs had a social impact. In addition, as outlined, with evaluation activity increasing in the public sector, at least at the federal level, foundation boards and program officers felt that they needed to keep pace and show that they were having an impact on the populations and places that had become targets of interest for public social policy. Increasingly, foundations began specifying the social goals—for example, create 5,000 jobs—that the funded CDFIs had to meet, and did so at the outset rather than after the fact.

Initially, as in the public sector, the standards for demonstration of impact that would satisfy foundation demands were relatively loose. But as standards of rigor began to rise in the public sector, foundations seemed to follow and raise their standards—though with a considerable lag.

Government

The outline of public sector evaluation activity and how it has evolved was sketched out previously. This type of activity was initially largely confined to areas such as welfare, employment and training, some aspects of health, and housing. In 1994, with the creation of the CDFI Fund within the Treasury Department, it became inevitable that some form of CDFI performance accountability would be called for, given that it had increasingly been demanded in other sectors.[6] As described on their website "The CDFI Fund provides relatively small infusions of capital to institutions that *serve distressed communities and low-income individuals*" [emphasis added], so it is not surprising that, in the application phase and now in the operational phase, the fund seeks demonstration of impacts on distressed communities and low-income individuals.[7]

Private Investors

CDFIs historically have had some private investors, but this component has become increasingly important in step with the increase in the community development venture capital (CDVC) form of CDFIs. Banks and other private financial institutions are a primary source of capital for CDVCs. Such investors are demanding and accustomed to receiving regular reports on which to evaluate the performance of their investments. Investors in community development venture capital, however, buy into some sort of community development outcome as a complement to the financial returns—often as an offset to lower rates of financial return than typical of traditional venture capital funds. This creates special pressure on CDVCs to demonstrate that community development or social impacts are in fact being achieved. This has come to be called the double bottom line perspective—the usual one of profitability and a second of social return on investment.

Managers of Firms or Programs

Most firms financed by CDFIs are largely focused on traditional business objectives—market share, profitability, and above all survival. In recent years, however, some firms have sought market niches that have broader "socially desirable" attributes, such as environmentally friendly products and production processes. CDFIs, and other socially oriented investors have sought out entrepreneurs who express an interest in social objectives beyond sheer profitability. In addition, CDFIs have used their financial leverage to entice the firms in which they invest to pay attention to certain social outcomes. For these reasons, managers of firms and programs can become interested in, or enticed to try and measure, the social dimensions of their operations.

PROBLEMS IN APPLYING IMPACT EVALUATION METHODS TO CDFIS

In reviewing the evolution of program evaluation efforts, I quickly sketched a few alternative methods that have been used and some problems with them. I now explore this in more depth and indicate particularly how the character of CDFIs presents problems in attempts to use these methods.[8]

The Unit of Analysis

One needs to be clear at the outset in specifying the unit of analysis for measuring impact. For CDFIs, it might be individuals (employees), firms, industries, structures (housing or facilities), or geographic areas. The strategy of measurement and the feasibility—and credibility—of alternative methods will vary according to the target unit of analysis. Data availability or costs of original data collection will often constrain the choice of unit of analysis. For example, many data sources are geocoded using census tract designations, but if the target is a neighborhood that does not fit easily in tract patterns, such data may not be satisfactory.

Finding a Counterfactual

If one is going to estimate the impact of CDFI activity on an outcome measure, the central problem is to define what would have happened to that outcome measure had that activity not been undertaken. This is the question of establishing the counterfactual, the heart of distinguishing between an outcome and an impact and the parallel distinction between a performance measure and an impact measure.

Further, it is important to distinguish reliable counterfactuals from vulnerable counterfactuals. It is always easy to conjecture what would have happened in the absence of an intervention—for example, "I believe there would have been no job growth in this community"—but such conjectures are highly subjective and can often be shown to have been unreliable. In many cases, as I will argue, it is possible to indicate the kind of risk to which a given method of estimating a counterfactual is subject. Methods that face a high degree of risk generate vulnerable counterfactuals.

To those not steeped in evaluation, obtaining reliable counterfactuals appears at first a trivial problem. They suggest simple straightforward methods, such as the comparison community or the before-and-after evaluation.[9] I believe that these two approaches yield vulnerable counterfactuals, because individuals and communities are changing all the time with respect to the measured outcomes even in the absence of any intentional intervention. Individuals and communities that match on a given variable at one point in time will, as part of normal processes, diverge over time and thus not provide reliable counterfactuals.

It is generally acknowledged that experimental, random assignment designs—where feasible—will provide a reliable counterfactual. I previously sketched out the rationale for this conclusion but repeat it in slightly different form here because it defines the highest standard for what is needed to attribute causality, that is, the estimated impact was in fact caused by (not just correlated with) the intervention. Under this approach, one establishes the counterfactual by randomly assigning applicants either to the treatment group that receives the program intervention services or to a control group that does not.

The important feature of a random assignment study is that, when the number of units randomly assigned gets reasonably large, the probability that any characteristic of units that may be causally related to the outcome being measured will be overrepresented among the treatment group members is quite low. If there were such overrepresentation, the danger is that effects on the outcome that are in fact caused by that particular characteristic will be erroneously attributed to the treatment. This includes both characteristics that have been or could be measured and, more important, such characteristics that are unobservable—motivation, for example.

In addition, the random assignment design ensures that when both the treatment and control group are later measured for the outcome, they will have been equally exposed to any changes in the context that may have occurred over time. For example, if the labor market softened and unemployment rose, both treatment and control group members would have experienced the softer labor market. The control group really does demonstrate what would have happened to the members of the treatment group had they not had the opportunity provided by the treatment intervention—it provides a reliable counterfactual.

When one considers trying to use an experimental design to estimate the impact of a CDFI activity, one faces a number of possible problems. First, although theoretically the random assignment could be at the level of the region, the firm, or the individual worker, for CDFIs not all these levels are feasible. To do a random assignment at a region level, using communities as the unit, one would have to have a very large set of communities (probably about sixty, with thirty in the treatment group and thirty in the control group).[10] All these communities would have to be at about the same level of eagerness to establish a CDFI or the specific CDFI supported activity. Even if this set of potential communities could be identified, it is highly likely that the control group would become contaminated because, once the level of eagerness to create a CDFI has been established, some of the communities would go ahead and create one—funding it from other sources—even if they had been assigned to the control group.

At the corporate level, random assignment is somewhat more feasible, but still very unlikely.[11] Such a design would call for a large set of applicant firms, more than the CDFI could fund with available capital. Among a set of firms eligible for CDFI assistance, some would receive the assistance and others would be turned down. The researcher could then, over time, follow the employment (or other outcome) patterns at a large number of both the assisted firms and the firms denied assistance. The difference between these two groups is the measured impact of the CDFI activity. From my observations to date, no CDFI has a pool of likely eligible applicants that greatly exceeds its ability for funding. Most CDFIs complain about the difficulty of generating quality "deal flow."

An experimental design at the firm level might well be feasible, however, to test certain components of a CDFI's program. For example, some CDFIs have been engaged in a strategy to induce firms they fund to hire and train disadvantaged workers. With a large enough group of firms being funded, it might well be possible to randomly assign a number of firms to receive the incentives for hiring disadvantaged workers and others to a control group that will not. There have been numerous random assignment studies of job training programs, so we know that this type of design is feasible. Still, the sample size requirements of more than sixty firms to be randomly assigned make it very challenging.

Random assignment at the individual level may be feasible in testing specific aspects of CDFI activities. For example, it might be used to establish the relative efficacy of intermediary services provided by some CDFIs to prepare workers for jobs or assist them with services that will help them retain the jobs once they are hired. Individual workers might be randomly assigned to different packages of intermediary services. Individual random assignment would also be feasible if there were a single source from which CDFI financed firms drew their workers. A subset of the pool of potential workers might be assigned to have the opportunity to be hired by CDFI-financed firms and the others to the control group, free to find jobs in whatever fashion they usually would.[12]

Pitfalls of Before-and-After Designs

The most commonly suggested method for establishing impacts, a simple before-and-after study is one in which the status—usually a measure of the outcome variable on which the program seeks to have an impact—before the intervention is implicitly used as the counterfactual against which to assess a change. Depending on the development goal of the CDFI and other practical considerations, the before-and-after study could be done at the level of the individual worker or firm, or at the level of a region.

Consider the case of a CDFI seeking to increase employment levels in a region to reduce unemployment. One might examine employment levels at a set of firms before the CDFI began to work with them and again some time after the CDFI provided them with assistance. The change in employment is attributed to the intervention of the CDFI. Similarly, one could examine unemployment levels in the region before the CDFI began to operate and again several years after it began its operations. The change in unemployment is used as a measure of the impact of the CDFI.

The advantage to a simple before-and-after study is that it is intuitively appealing. Moreover, depending on what one wishes to measure, it may be simpler to implement than other methods. However, there can be—indeed are likely to be—several disadvantages:

- We do not expect a CDFI to have an instantaneous effect on the outcome of interest. Therefore, one would need a substantial gap in time between the periods in which the before and the after measurements are made. Over time, a variety of factors affect unemployment and wages in a region and the longer the period, the greater the extent of naturally occurring change is likely to be. It is impossible to isolate the effect of the CDFI from the general noise created by natural change. Impact of CDFI assistance occurs slowly over time, and many other factors affect the firm over time. Firms may have found other sources of financing or survived or even thrived without external financing. Notice that the bias generated by this unreliable counterfactual could go either way. Firms might have thrived in spite of the CDFI and thus using the before status would attribute a greater impact to the CDFI than it actually had. On the other hand, firms might have declined sharply had the CDFI not intervened, in which case the before status would have missed the stabilizing effect of the CDFI and underestimated its impact.

- Because data on such variables as unemployment and wages are, at best, regularly available only for relatively large geographic regions, one is driven to measure the before-and-after status using broad regional data (for a discussion of problems of small area data, see Coulton and Hollister 1998). However, a CDFI is likely to be too small to have a noticeable impact at the region level. This argues for doing such studies at the organizational level. However, it should be recognized that in a competitive industry, job creation at one firm may destroy jobs in another. For example, a CDFI-assisted producer of hotel furniture may grab the contract for supplying a given hotel site from an existing producer, perhaps even one in the same area, so that what at the CDFI firm appears to be a gain in employment may be no gain in the industry or area. This is sometimes referred to as the substitution effect or displacement effect.

- In some cases, a CDFI loan might enable a firm to grow or stabilize for a year or two before failing as a result of continuing poor management practices or a shift in product demand. Clearly, it would be a mistake to conclude that any jobs created or retained a year or two after a CDFI's initial assistance are permanent. This is, of course, a problem that plagues any evaluation measurement that occurs at a fixed point in time. It is necessary to extrapolate beyond the period of observation and always difficult to find a reasonable way to do so.

- Even if the CDFI seems, using a before-and-after method, to have created jobs, one needs to know the net benefit to the people who get these jobs.

What are the characteristics of these people? What alternative opportunities have they forgone in taking these jobs? This is, again, where a reliable counterfactual is important. Some of those who were unemployed or had low-paying jobs in the before period would have found jobs, or jobs paying better than their before period job even in the absence of the CDFI-created job. Alternatively, some who were employed or well paid in the before period would have lost jobs or had a loss in pay in the absence of the CDFI-created job. To get the net benefits of the CDFI jobs for these people one needs a counterfactual indicating the proportions who would have gained or lost in the absence of the CDFI-created jobs.

Quasi-Experimental Designs

A third strategy for attempting to establish the counterfactual is to compare the performance of a CDFI-assisted community, firm, or group of employees to a comparable group of communities, firms, or employees that did not receive CDFI assistance.

As I noted earlier, using comparison communities to establish the counterfactual is a strategy often advocated by those with little experience with evaluation—it just seems to have face plausibility. The idea is simply to match communities by finding ones where the intervention is not occurring and choose those that match the CDFI communities on given characteristics. In practice, however, it has proved very difficult to create a reliable counterfactual from other communities not experiencing the intervention.

1. First, as noted, there is the problem of the availability of regularly collected small area data that measures the sort of outcomes a CDFI is meant to effect.

2. One needs not only to match the levels of the outcome variable at the start of the evaluation period, but also to match those other variables likely to affect the outcome over the longer term. For example, whereas at the outset communities may match on the level of unemployment, one may have employment concentrated in one industry, say steel production, and the other in another industry, say insurance. These different industry structures are likely to evolve differently over time, say the steel industry collapsing and the insurance industry growing. One evaluation of a very large-scale national employment opportunity program that began in the 1970s and continued into the early 1980s was based on a comparison community design for obtaining counterfactuals. One of the matched comparison sites, Toledo, which had major automobile supplies manufacturers, was subject to a sharp downturn in that industry. In addition, out of ten sites, one had a major hurricane, a second had a substantial flood, and a third had a huge unanticipated volcanic eruption.

3. At the firm level, the comparison group again needs to be matched on many relevant dimensions. The array of comparison firms should be in the same line of business as the array of CDFI-financed ones. They should be of approximately the same size at the outset—because we know from economic research that substantial differentials in wages, benefits, and employment patterns are associated with firm size and tend to persist over time. Given that CDFI clients are presumed to be "unbankable" the comparison firms should be in a similar status. Because the degree of unbankableness is likely to be associated with the structure of financial services in the region, the firms should probably be in similar regions. Even if one could locate apparently similar firms on measured characteristics, there are many differences across firms that are difficult to observe and quantify, such as managerial talent. If a CDFI's clients grow more rapidly than the comparison group, it could be simply because the CDFI's risk-screening process eliminated the worst managed firms from the pool of clients. The list of salient characteristics to be matched could go on and on. Realization of these demanding requirements again points up the virtues of random assignment where feasible. When sample size is large enough, a similar array of characteristics, both measurable and unmeasurable, will end up in both the treatment group and the control group.

4. Constructing comparison samples at the level of individual employees, as a method, has received considerable attention in evaluations of employment and training programs (Friedlander and Robins 1995). Again, the problem is first to find a data source with adequate information on the outcome variables of interest and on the characteristics of the individual that might affect that outcome. Such data are needed both for a baseline period before the CDFI opportunity and for the follow-up point at which the impact of the CDFI treatment is to be assessed.

Once the pool from which potential comparison group members are to be drawn has been identified, then selection from the pool is done by seeking to match characteristics of members of the pool with the characteristics of the individuals in the CDFI treatment group. A variety of matching procedures have been tried.

A series of studies has sought to determine how well the comparison groups' members do by comparing the impact estimates obtained from comparison groups to the "true impact" as estimated from a random assignment evaluation. This is done by using the same members of the treatment group as in the random assignment study but using a constructed comparison group rather than the true control group from the random assignment study. Then one takes the mean value of outcomes for a given set of individuals who have been given the treatment and subtract the mean value of the outcomes for the matched comparison group to get a non-experimental impact estimate. We then compare that non-experimental impact estimate to the experimental impact estimate obtained by subtracting the mean outcome variables for the random assignment control group from those same mean outcomes for the members of the treatment group. The results of these tests have in general shown that the comparison group based, non-experimental estimates of the impact are very unreliable indicators of what the true experimental impact was.

Notwithstanding the conclusions just stated, there have been further attempts to come up with better performing matching procedures. One recent study used a method called "propensity score matching" and again, comparing the impact estimates from the matched comparison group procedure to the estimates from the experiment, claimed to come much closer to the true experimental impacts than had been the case in the earlier studies (Dehejia and Wahba 1999). This study drew the attention of many researchers and policymakers because they thought perhaps a quasi-experimental procedure had been discovered that would allow them to avoid what they saw to be the burdens of carrying out a random assignment study. In Appendix the steps taken in developing a propensity score matching study sketch out so that those who wish to do so can get the flavor of the complexity of the procedures.

Since then, a flurry of papers have attempted similar propensity-score estimates and compared them with the true experimental estimates (Agodini and Dynarski 2004; Michalopoulos, Bloom and Hill 2004; and Wilde and Hollister 2007). Conclusions were remarkably similar even though the studies used widely different types of data: propensity-score results are not consistently close to those from random assignment experiments. The problem always remains that one can match only on measurable and measured characteristics. If unobserved or unobservable characteristics strongly affect the outcomes, then the comparison group outcomes will not give reliable counterfactuals.[13]

Econometric Simulation of the Counterfactual

In all of these procedures, given adequate data, one can try to establish the counterfactual by econometric simulation.[14] That is, one uses time series data before the CDFI intervention to fit an econometric model with the outcome of interest as the dependent variable, and all the variables that may affect that outcome (for which one has substantial time series data) as independent variables. One then uses the estimated parameters and the time series variables, measured during the period for which the CDFI impact is to be estimated, to simulate what would have happened to the community, firm, or employees had there been no CDFI. The estimated outcomes from the model are then subtracted from the outcomes observed during the evaluation period and the difference is attributed to the CDFI. Essentially, this approach is similar to developing a forecasting or projection model. Unfortunately, the record with forecasting model performance for economic outcomes is not very good (on the reliability of macroeconomic forecasts, see McNess 1995).

As an example, attempts were made to project what the welfare caseload would have been for the state of New Jersey to see whether the welfare reform introduced did, in fact, lower the caseload (Garasky and Barnow 1992). The effects of changes in the low-wage labor market appeared to have swamped any predicted changes in welfare caseload, leading to implausible estimates. The model was unable to capture the way in which the low-wage labor markets affected welfare caseloads.

A different formulation of an econometric model would be essentially an extension of the quasi-experimental approach just outlined, but without explicit matching. One would need extensive data on a large number of firms that received varying amounts of CDFI assistance, preferably including many that received no CDFI funding. The data should include information on all of the other factors that could cause changes in employment at the firms. In theory, a multivariate regression would then have the outcome as a dependent variable. There also would be variables both for all the other factors that could affect the outcome and for the extent of CDFI funding and services provided. In theory, if the specification were correct and all relevant variables had been measured and entered into the model, the coefficients for the CDFI variables would reflect the independent impact of the CDFI assistance on employment levels.

There are several problems with the modeling approaches:

- One is unlikely to have adequate previous data on communities, firms, and employees to estimate a reliable model. An unreliable model means that the simulated counterfactual is not likely to be the true counterfactual, so one will misestimate the impact of the CDFI.

- Even with excellent data, one will be uncertain of the proper specification of the model. There is a large literature on the problems of selection bias that would apply particularly to the second formulation of the econometric modeling approach. If an unobserved or unobservable factor, such as entrepreneurial skill, is correlated with the CDFI variables, the effects of those skills would be erroneously attributed to the CDFI impact. Again, note that this bias could go in either direction; there might be more entrepreneurial skill in firms that receive high levels of CDFI funds and services leading to an overestimate of the true impact of the CDFI, or less in firms that receive high levels of CDFI funds and services leading to an underestimate of the true impact of the CDFI. Although procedures for correcting for such selection bias have been suggested, they are complex and the requirements for them to work reliably are quite high and seldom satisfied to a convincing degree.

Logic Models, Theory of Change Evaluations, Balanced Score Cards

A set of procedures for determining impacts has been proposed as distinct but share certain features, so I discuss them as a group. These are logic models, theory of change evaluations, and balanced score cards.

Logic Models

In high quality proposals for a research demonstration program, or for an evaluation of such a program, it has become common practice to specify a logic model. Here is a rough description:

> Basically, a logic model is a systematic and visual way to present and share your understanding of the relationships among the resources you have to operate your program, the activities you plan, and the changes or results you hope to achieve.
>
> The most basic logic model is a picture of how you believe your program will work. It uses words and/or pictures to describe the sequence of activities thought to bring about change and how these activities are linked to the results the program is expected to achieve. The Basic Logic Model components shown in Figure [9.1] above are defined below. These components illustrate the connection between *your planned work* and *your intended results*. They are depicted numerically by steps 1 through 5.
>
> **YOUR PLANNED WORK** describes what resources you think you need to implement your program and what you intend to do.
>
> 1. **Resources** include the human, financial, organizational, and community resources a program has available to direct toward doing the work. Sometimes this component is referred to as ***Inputs.***
> 2. **Program Activities** are what the program does with the resources. **Activities** are the processes, tools, events, technology, and actions that are an intentional part of the program implementation. These interventions are used to bring about the intended program changes or results.
>
> **YOUR INTENDED RESULTS** include all of the program's desired results (outputs, outcomes, and impact).
>
> 3. **Outputs** are the direct products of program activities and may include types, levels and targets of services to be delivered by the program.
> 4. **Outcomes** are the specific changes in program participants' behavior, knowledge, skills, status and level of functioning. Short-term outcomes should be attainable within 1 to 3 years, while longer-term outcomes should be achievable within a 4 to 6 year timeframe. The logical

Figure 9.1   The Basic Logic Model

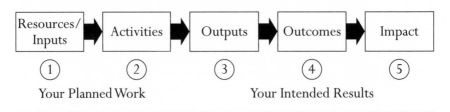

Source: W. K. Kellogg Foundation (2004).

progression from short-term to long-term outcomes should be reflected in impact occurring within about 7 to 10 years.

5. **Impact** is the fundamental intended or unintended change occurring in organizations, communities or systems as a result of program activities within 7 to 10 years. In the current model of WKKF grantmaking and evaluation, impact often occurs after the conclusion of project funding.

The term *logic model* is frequently used interchangeably with the term *program theory* in the evaluation field. Logic models can alternatively be referred to as *theory* because they describe how a program works and to what end (definitions for each employed by leading evaluation experts are included in the Resources Appendix).

(W. K. Kellogg Foundation Logic Model Development Guide, January 2004, 1)

Theory of Change Evaluation

Theory of change is developed much like the logic model. The Aspen Institute offers one description:

As we define it, a Theory of Change defines all building blocks required to bring about a given long-term goal. This set of connected building blocks—interchangeably referred to as outcomes, results, accomplishments, or preconditions—is depicted on a map known as a pathway of change/change framework, which is a graphic representation of the change process. Built around the pathway of change, a Theory of Change describes the types of interventions (a single program or a comprehensive community initiative) that bring about the outcomes depicted in the pathway of a change map. Each outcome in the pathway of change is tied to an intervention, revealing the often complex web of activity that is required to bring about change. (2006)

Recent impetus to the use of this approach derived from an essay by Carol Weiss (1995) For an interesting essay on attempts to apply the theory of change approach, see Connell and Kubisch (1998).

> Weiss popularized the term "Theory of Change" as a way to describe the set of assumptions that explain both the mini-steps that lead to the long-term goal of interest and the connections between program activities and outcomes that occur at each step of the way. She challenged designers of complex community-based initiatives to be specific about the theories of change guiding their work and suggested that doing so would improve their overall evaluation plans and would strengthen their ability to claim credit for outcomes that were predicted in their theory. She called for the use of an approach that at first blush seems like common sense: lay out the sequence of outcomes that are expected to occur as the result of an intervention, and plan an evaluation strategy around tracking whether these expected outcomes are actually produced. Her stature in the field, and the apparent promise of this idea motivated a number of foundations to support the use of this technique—later termed "the Theory of Change approach"—in the evaluations of early CCI efforts. In the years that followed, a number of evaluations were developed around this approach, fueling more interest in the field about its value. (Aspen Institute 2006)

Balanced Score Card

The balanced score card was developed primarily as a management tool for strategic planning but some have proposed it as a tool that includes evaluation of impacts (Arveson 1998).

> The balanced scorecard is a management system (not only a measurement system) that enables organizations to clarify their vision and strategy and translate them into action. It provides feedback around both the internal business processes and external outcomes in order to continuously improve strategic performance and results. When fully deployed, the balanced scorecard transforms strategic planning from an academic exercise into the nerve center of an enterprise. . . .
>
> The balanced scorecard suggests that we view the organization from four perspectives, and to develop metrics, collect data and analyze it relative to each of these perspectives:
>
> The Learning and Growth Perspective
> The Business Process Perspective
> The Customer Perspective
> The Financial Perspective

A scorecard as a matrix of objectives and measures is developed for each perspective.

These three approaches—logic models, theory of change, and balanced score cards—all have as building blocks some measure of inputs, some measure of activities, some measure of outcomes and some measure of impacts. They try to force the clarification of assumptions about how inputs will be configured in the sequence of activities, how the sequence of activities will generate specified outcomes and, finally, what impacts, going beyond the specific outcomes, will follow. The specification of linkages and their chronology is called for, sometimes in general terms and sometimes in very detailed steps.

The theory of change and the balanced score card approaches emphasize the importance of specifying the model of the process from multiple perspectives—or multiple stakeholder viewpoints. The theory of change has often been put forward as a process that will generate an evaluation of the impact of an activity, something that will show whether the activity actually worked and generated the hypothesized impact. It was suggested that benchmark measures be defined for both intermediate and final outcomes and that the impact would be assessed by the degree to which the benchmarks were achieved.

Balanced score card approaches call for benchmark measures and dynamic feedback from those measures. They do not seem to be emphasized as tools for overall evaluation of an activity. Logic models are usually specified at the outset of a project but not necessarily referred to later as a tool for overall evaluations.

All of these approaches call for impact to be measured, but do not seem to address the concept that has been stressed in this chapter: change of an outcome measure from what it would have been in the absence of the activity.

They discuss measures of factors beyond the outcomes directly attributable to the activity (e.g., some measures in the community, changes in the use of tax-supported activities by employees), but they contain little discussion of even some of the flawed measures of *change from what would have happened* that have been discussed above.

Although these methods do not directly address the issue of obtaining reliable estimates of impact, they are nevertheless important tools. As indicated earlier, the logic model is usually called for at the outset of a CDFI activity, for example, in an application for funding. Such a call forces its proposers to be more specific about expected connections between how the resources called for are to be used and the final outcomes that are the objective of the activity; it represents an attempt to make tighter connections between theory and practice.

The theory of change approach is similar in forcing explicit articulation between the resource inputs and the various activities and how they are envisioned to unfold over time and the final set of outcomes. In addition, in applications to date, the development of the theory of change requires the input of various actors: program managers, sometimes the target clients or participants, collaborative agencies, and funders or investors. This process helps to align the expectations of the various actors and often uncovers conflicts among the various actors' theories of how the change would be generated and expected outcomes. In its fullest form, theory of change also calls for specifying benchmark measures for both intermediate stages and the final outcomes and a strategy for obtaining those measures.

The balanced score card approach is more a strategic planning, measurement, and feedback tool primarily for program managers. Like the theory of change requirement that multiple actors' perspectives be taken into account, the balanced score card calls for alternative perspectives (learning, business, customer, and financial) on the operations and outcomes of the activity and—even more than the theory of change approach—for separate measures (a separate score card), where necessary, for each of the perspectives. It appears that this approach calls more explicitly for dynamic feedback from the intermediate measures and reassessment and possible revision of the strategic plan.

Financial and Social Accounting Standards

One way to circumvent the counterfactual problem is to adapt investment standards to a social context. In a financial context, of course, one compares investments by reducing each to a rate of return (ignoring for this purpose the other usual parameter, the variance). Our challenge is to develop measurements of the social rate of return and to blend them with the financial rate of return to arrive at an overall rate of return.[15]

1. Financial measures of impact. Standard accounting procedures are used to derive a measure of profitability of an enterprise or an activity (the bottom line), which is then related to the investment resources (the internal rate of return).

2. Social accounting measures of impact. When no market valuations of inputs or outputs are available, measures of outputs to inputs are expressed in social internal rates of return. From the 1960s onward, these procedures were increasingly widely applied to assessing public sector activities. The major challenge with such measures is to define the nonmarket outcomes and develop a way to quantify and put a value on them. Quantifying social outputs can often be done in terms of counts (for example, number of employees with given characteristics), but developing values is usually more difficult and more controversial (see Boardman et al. 2005).

An alternative to the benefit-cost framework is cost-effectiveness. In it, outputs are counted but not valued and alternative projects or programs are compared on the cost per unit of the quantity produced (for example, cost per employee trained in computer skills). This, though, does not permit reduction to a rate of return on investment that can be blended with financial rates of return.

Sometimes a mixed procedure is resorted to. In the mixed procedure outcomes that can be are valued (priced) and the non-valued outcomes quantified. Then a rate of return is calculated for the valued outcomes. Next, sensitivity analysis is performed by posing the question: "What value would you have to put on these non-valued outcomes for the resultant rate of return to reach (a specific threshold)?" However, this strategy is seldom satisfying to those looking for a solid evaluation of impact because the subjective element is too significant and thus likely to generate contention.

Industry Standards of Accounting

As mentioned earlier, several large-scale attempts have been made to develop common standards for reporting CDFI performance. These include the Community Development Investment Impact System (CIIS) of the CDFI Fund; CARS™, the CDFI Assessment and Rating System, by the Opportunity Finance Network (2006); and the Impact Measurement Toolkit by the Community Development Venture Capital Alliance (2006). These systems parallel the financial and social accounting standards just discussed. What is different about them is that they focus on financial and social impact measures across a large group of CDFIs. The hope is that common standards and measures will facilitate comparisons across different strategies and different locations. However, there really has not been enough accumulated experience to assess the likely long-term effects of these measures. Furthermore, what these systems call impact is not what I have defined here as impact. They make no attempt to define and measure a counterfactual of any sort except what might arise from comparisons across CDFIs. For many of the reasons I outlined earlier, these would not represent reliable counterfactuals. These systems seem more like the performance measurement and standards systems developed and used in recent years, particularly for various federal programs.

QUALITY EVALUATIONS

Several examples of quality attempts to estimate the impact of certain CDFI or CDVC activities may prove helpful in several respects.[16] Even though these were judged to be quality studies, their shortcomings illustrate the sorts of issues that arise even in well-designed studies.[17] Several more recent attempts, though less comprehensive, are still a step toward improved analysis.

Kentucky Highlands Investment Corporation

Founded in 1968, Kentucky Highland Investment Corporation (KHIC) was in its early years funded with grants from the federal government's Office of Economic Opportunity. Its mission is to promote the economic development of ten largely rural counties in the Appalachian region of central Kentucky. Its focus is on promoting the growth of businesses to foster local employment opportunities.

Thomas Miller, a former KHIC president, conducted the assessment of KHIC's social impact shortly after he left the organization in 1993. His analysis covered KHIC's operations in the nearly twenty-five years between its founding and 1993. During this period, the company made 169 investments totaling $33.2 million in eighty enterprises and earned $9.1 million from net capital gains, interest on development loans, management fees, and rental income. It also earned $6 million from its earnings on idle cash balances. Its staff and operating costs over this period totaled about $13 million.

In his monograph, Miller explained that KHIC focused almost exclusively on business development. It did not try to influence the wages or benefits offered by its clients nor did it ask the firms to pursue other social goals. In one exception to this policy, it did require clients to contact local government employment agencies when seeking to fill open positions. KHIC included this requirement in its investment agreements.

For the most part, KHIC pursued what today would be called a community development venture capital strategy. A large part of this effort was devoted to getting existing firms to relocate to a rural target area. KHIC would start with a mix of debt and equity but jump in to take a controlling interest when the firms ran into trouble and could not meet their required financial commitments. Between 1968 and 1993, KHIC invested about $13 million in twenty such venture capital deals.

KHIC would also start its own businesses. In total, between 1968 and 1993, it launched ten concerns in which it invested $11.6 million. It would also provide debt financing to smaller firms in the region that had modest growth potential, investing $883,000 in twenty-two such deals in the same period.

To assess social impact, Miller relies solely on measures of changes in the employment levels at the firms assisted by KHIC and provides arguments for doing so rather than attempting something more ambitious. He does not report the details behind his measures of annual employment levels at the firms assisted by KHIC. He does not indicate, for example, how firms provided him with the data or how he treated part-time or seasonal employees. In the case of firms already operating in the region that secured KHIC financing, Miller appears to have only counted increases in their employment levels, but his report is not clear on this point. In addition, he does not attribute all of the increase in the firms' employment levels to KHIC. Unfortunately, the report does not provide raw employment levels, only those Miller attributes to KHIC. Nevertheless, one can use the information in the report to estimate the approximate raw numbers (see table 9.1).

Miller recognizes that some of the jobs might have been added even without the assistance of KHIC. The problem is to identify those that would not have

Table 9.1   Number of Additional Employees

1970	0
1975	364
1980	542
1985	876
1990	2,002
1993	3,130

Source: Caskey and Hollister (1999).

been added. Miller's solution is to use information from KHIC staff and the managers of some of KHIC's clients to develop an estimate for each firm in KHIC's portfolio of the share of new jobs that should be attributed to KHIC. These estimates range from 0 to 100 percent. In addition, Miller attributed to KHIC 25 percent of the employment increase in firms that received significant technical assistance but no financing. He arrived at this number based on KHIC staff descriptions of the role KHIC played in establishing and expanding these firms. These attribution weights combined to an overall rate of 84 percent.

Miller argues that the jobs that KHIC helped create benefited primarily lower-income, unemployed residents of the region. He bases this claim not on survey data, but on an analysis of the conditions of labor markets in the region and the type of jobs created by KHIC's clients. He acknowledges that new employment opportunities were unlikely to benefit the very poorest residents of the region. He also notes that there might be an employment multiplier for the jobs that KHIC helps to create, but that he has no idea what its magnitude might be and therefore decides to err on the side of conservatism by ignoring it altogether. He also points out that there could be other indirect benefits from KHIC's development activities, but that because he cannot quantify them, he leaves them out of the formal analysis. He does, however, list the indirect benefits that might occur.

Miller presents three different attempts at cost-benefit analysis, including one that uses the taxpayers' return on their investment. This is worth reviewing because such a perspective has been used elsewhere by others in somewhat misleading ways. Miller estimates the investment as the sum of grants plus administrative costs of the government in grant-making, plus the implicit interest costs taxpayers bear whenever their costs exceed the benefits received. He also estimates the benefits received as the sum of measures: savings from reduced unemployment insurance payments and reduced income support transfers as a result of the increased family incomes attributable to KHIC; increased tax revenue from the sales taxes, payroll taxes, and income taxes paid by the individuals employed in the KHIC-backed firms; and increased tax revenue from the corporate and property taxes paid by KHIC-backed firms. Miller must, of course, estimate each of these benefits and in his report he clearly presents all of the key assumptions behind his estimates. After filling in all the necessary measures, Miller concludes that, by 1993, gross returns to taxpayers were 224 percent of their cost of supporting KHIC.

There are many problems with these measures, but I note just a few. First is that the relevant measures of benefits would be derived from impact measures rather than outcome measures. This is particularly problematic here for two reasons: one, there are no direct estimates of what earnings would have been had there not been the KHIC activity and, two, many of the tax revenues key off the earnings estimates. To determine the correct net reduction in unemployment insurance benefits, one has to take into account the degree to which the job attributed to KHIC is truly a net new job. Otherwise, this employment may simply be displacing the employment that would have occurred in the absence of the KHIC activity. To the degree that there is displacement, the individual who would have gotten a job but did not may well claim unemployment insurance payments, income support transfers, and so on. Likewise, the tax revenues from corporate and property taxes will only be net increases to the degree that there is no displacement.

Finally, though it is always attractive to business and others to talk about saving taxes, it can be argued that the government does not invest in a CDFI to maximize subsequent taxes and savings on transfer payments. If this were the government's goal, it might find that investing in a golf course in a large urban area offers far better returns. The government invests in a CDFI such as KHIC because it believes that KHIC can be an effective tool for creating new employment opportunities in a low-income region, and that the new jobs will benefit low- and moderate-income households in the area. The relevant benefit to measure is the dollar benefit to lower-income households in the region as a result of KHIC's intervention. In spite of some of these shortcomings, Miller's is a good and thoughtful analysis that, for the most part, recognizes where it must make questionable assumptions.

Coastal Enterprises Incorporated

The second major early study of social impact of a CDFI concerned Coastal Enterprises Incorporated (CEI). CEI is located in Wiscasset, Maine, and provides financing and other assistance to firms located in or near the southeastern part of the state. Founded in 1977, CEI is thus, along with KHIC, one of the oldest CDFIs.

The author of the study, Josephine LaPlante (1996), examines the impact of CEI's operations between 1983 and 1995. As she recounts, over this period CEI had a number of economic development goals. It sought to increase the number of employment opportunities in the region that offer what it considered minimally adequate wages and benefits. That is, it wanted to help firms create "good" jobs. CEI also sought to increase self-employment opportunities for women, low-income individuals, refugees, and dislocated workers. It worked to help develop community facilities, environmentally beneficial industries, and low-income housing.

LaPlante's impact study examined only the job-creation and self-employment strategies of CEI. LaPlante bases her impact assessment on information gathered from the firms that CEI helped finance. She obtained this information by mailing a questionnaire to 114 businesses that CEI had financed from 1983 through 1995. Fifty-eight completed the survey and fifty-six of the responses were usable in her analysis. This low response rate plagued a number of the early evaluation studies.

The fifty-six firms reported that they employed about 575 full-time-equivalent (FTE) workers at the time of their initial loan closings with CEI. At the end of 1995, the combined employment level came to about 1,508 FTE workers, an increase of 933 FTE jobs. LaPlante does not provide information on whether reported job growth varied based on the number of years that had elapsed since a firm first received assistance from CEI. She also does not attempt to count the number of jobs maintained at the firms after they received CEI financing. CEI's goal is not simply to help create jobs but to help create jobs with minimally adequate wages and benefits. LaPlante argues that her survey data indicate CEI success in this regard. The survey did not ask about the characteristics of the jobs that firms added subsequent to CEI's financing, but did ask about the characteristics of jobs generally at these firms. As of 1995, CEI's clients paid an average hourly wage of $9.30. They reported that 68 percent of their employees are in skilled-labor or managerial positions. Eighty percent reported that they offer health insurance for full-time employees and 26 percent reported a pension plan for full-time employees. LaPlante's survey did not ask for any details on the characteristics of the health insurance or pension plans.

LaPlante tried to develop some sort of attribution of effects to CEI by asking a series of questions in her survey. These are presented in tables 9.2 and 9.3.

On the bases of these responses, LaPlante concludes that CEI's financing generally did not displace financing from other sources; that CEI deserves substantial credit for the improvements in business conditions cited by the majority of CEI clients; and that a significant share of the jobs added by CEI's clients are probably due to the financial and other assistance provided by CEI. In her cost-benefit analysis, LaPlante states that CEI probably deserves credit for at least 50 percent of the new jobs in the surveyed firms, but she also considers a more conservative estimate of 33 percent. LaPlante uses responses to questions about whether the firm would have gotten financing in the absence of CEI's to justify some of these claims. Many analysts are extremely skeptical about the value of responses to questions such as these and would be surprised if the consumers of CDFI evaluation studies would put much weight on them in their overall assessment.

Table 9.2   Survey: Financing and Contribution

Question	Firms' Responses
If CEI had turned you down for financing, do you believe that you could have obtained a loan from another source?	25 percent yes 42 percent no 33 percent do not know
Please estimate CEI's overall contribution to where your business is today by estimating the percentage of your company's economic value that you believe is attributable to CEI's financial and technical assistance.	Median. 30 percent Mean. 35 percent

Source: LaPlante (1996).

If 50 percent of the jobs added in the fifty-six firms that responded to the survey would not have existed were it not for CEI's assistance, then CEI deserves credit for 467 FTE jobs in these firms over twelve years. As LaPlante notes, extending this analysis to the fifty-eight firms that did not respond, assuming that they were similar to those that responded, implies that CEI deserves credit for an additional 516 FTE jobs over the period.

LaPlante provides suggestive data to support her conclusion that lower-income households were frequent beneficiaries of the new employment opportunities. In her survey, she asked whether they had increased the number of employees from lower-income households since the time of their loan from CEI. Sixty-four percent indicated that they had and that CEI was either important or very important for this development.

In addition to the survey of firms, LaPlante surveyed 155 employees across seventeen of the firms receiving loans from CEI. The survey asked what they had done before beginning work at the firm where they were currently employed. Fifty-five percent reported working full-time at another employer, 9 percent working part-time, 27 percent being mostly unemployed, and

Table 9.3   Survey: Progress

Indicator	Firms Citing CEI as "Important" or "Very Important" for Progress
Enhanced competitiveness	71 percent
Improved management practices	50 percent
Increased profitability	78 percent
New jobs created	78 percent

Source: LaPlante (1996).

8 percent having no steady job. In response to questions about their previous sources of income, 21 percent reported that they had received unemployment compensation, 13 percent food stamps, and 8 percent AFDC payments.

LaPlante notes that the jobs that CEI helped to create might lead to the creation of additional jobs in the region through employment multiplier effects. After a brief discussion of the ways that such multipliers might be estimated, she speculates that the multiplier might be in the range of 1.5 to 2.25. Most CDFI evaluations try to apply this sort of employment multiplier. A careful examination of the literature from which such multiplier estimates are drawn leaves me quite skeptical about their value. The fact of a possible multiplier effect can be mentioned but any precise magnitude should be given little weight.

In the final section of her study of the impact of CEI, LaPlante attempted a cost-benefit analysis. As a first step, she estimated CEI's operating costs from 1983 to 1994. She provides few details behind her estimates, other than to note that she tried to include only the costs related to CEI's development finance activities and did include the write-offs of bad loans but not the reserves set aside for future loan losses. In addition, LaPlante did not adjust the costs for changes in the price levels. Her explanation is that she did not count any benefits CEI produced before 1994, and did not want to make an offsetting adjustment to understate the costs. She did count a number of possible benefits from CEI's activities: benefits to the government from increased business taxes, taxes on wage income, state sales taxes, and saved transfer payments; benefits to individuals from increased incomes from new jobs; and benefits to the region from the financing leveraged by CEI. She estimates the value of these and other benefits for 1994. She then assumes that they will last for five years (the conservative assumptions) or twenty years (the optimistic assumption). She determines the present value of the benefits using two discount rates, 5 percent and 9 percent. Using her most conservative assumptions (five-year benefit duration, 9 percent discount rate, CEI responsible for 33 percent of employment gains at client firms, and an employment multiplier of 1.5), she then concludes that for each dollar of CEI operating costs, CEI created $14 of benefits. Using her most optimistic assumptions, she finds $159 of benefits for each $1 spent by CEI.

These results are powerful—in fact too powerful to be credible. They arise from errors in analysis. For one, LaPlante assumes that a person who takes a job paying $9.30 an hour receives a $9.30 an hour benefit. This in turn assumes that the opportunity cost of the individual's time is zero, an unreasonable assumption. She also counts as a benefit the money that other financial institutions provide in jointly financed CEI deals, which makes three mistakes. First, it assumes that this leveraged money would not have come into the economy through some other investment. Second, to the extent that this is a benefit, it is so because of the jobs and tax revenues generated by the funds, not because of the funds themselves. To count the jobs and tax revenues as a benefit, as well as the funds is to double count. Third, most of the funds leveraged are market-rate loans that need to be repaid. A $100,000 loan to a firm does not bring the same benefit as a $100,000 grant. Finally, for the reasons discussed when analyzing Thomas Miller's assessment of the costs and benefits of government support for Kentucky Highlands, I do not believe that increased tax revenues should count as benefits because they are not a goal of the initiative. To the extent that they do occur, they could count as an offset to government costs. Recognize, however, that these taxes come from workers' wages and employers' incomes, so the benefits to workers and employers must be reduced correspondingly.

LaPlante made an honest effort at a cost-benefit assessment. Though the results are flawed, the example illustrates how hard it is to generate sound cost-benefit estimates for CDFI activities.

Enterprise Corporation of the Delta

The third study of the social impact of a community development financial institution was conducted by John Caskey and Robinson Hollister (1999). It examined the operations and impact of the Enterprise Corporation of the Delta (ECD), a CDFI founded in 1994 that operates in numerous counties of Arkansas, Louisiana, and Mississippi that are located near the Mississippi River. When ECD booked its first development loan, it had about $2 million in assets. By the end of 1998, the end period for the study, it had almost $25 million.

ECD's area of operation is one of the poorest in the United States. At the time of this evaluation, ECD sought to promote the development of the region in several ways. Most important, it hoped to help firms in the region grow and expand employment. It also sought to help struggling firms stabilize to retain existing jobs. Last, it tried to facilitate the development of business ownership among minorities and women and to increase the wealth of the nonagricultural business community in the Delta.

In their assessment of the social impact of ECD, Caskey and Hollister focused only on ECD's job creation and retention goals. In promoting these, ECD provided debt (and occasionally equity) financing to small and medium-sized firms in the Delta. In selecting its clients, it originally gave priority to assisting businesses and industries whose major competitors were located outside the targeted region or that provided inputs to such "exporting" firms. The rationale was that the expansion of such businesses is unlikely to cause the contraction of other businesses in the region. In some cases, however, ECD helped small service sector firms selling primarily to local residents, because this would promote one of ECD's other goals of increasing ownership by minorities and women.

ECD's loan fees and interest rates were higher than commercial bank loans. It offered several justifications. Most important, the higher rates enabled ECD to cover part of the costs associated with providing basic management assistance to clients and with patching together funds from a variety of sources to meet a client's needs. They also helped ECD target its assistance, because bankable firms were less likely to seek higher priced financing. Additionally, ECD provided its clients with basic management assistance as well as financing. When clients required more assistance than ECD was willing or able to provide, it would refer them to third-party providers. In some cases, it offered the clients recoverable grants to pay for the assistance. Similar to Kentucky Highlands, ECD did not interfere in its clients' employment policies. It focused on strengthening firms and helping them grow. It did not tell the firms whom they should hire or try directly to influence the pay and benefits they provided.

Caskey and Hollister's basic strategy for monitoring changes in employment at ECD's clients was simple. In a series of surveys, they asked the owners and managers of the firms about their employment levels at the time of the first ECD loan closings and at later intervals. Then, based on that information, they made judgmental adjustments of the original responses to obtain steady-state FTE employment levels.[18]

Caskey and Hollister restricted their analysis to firms that ECD financed between late 1994 and July 1997. They did so because they were conducting their analysis in January 1999 and, at that point, the firms that ECD had financed for the first time after June 1997 did not have a long enough post-finance period to warrant preliminary judgments about employment effects. In total, ECD financed thirty-six firms between late 1994 and July 1997, but Caskey and Hollister restricted their analysis to the thirty-three firms for which they could obtain meaningful data. Among those, twelve had steady-state FTE employment levels that exceeded their employment levels at the time of their first loan closings. Twelve had ceased or never begun operations by January 1999 and did not employ anyone as of that time. In the remaining nine firms, employment levels either declined or stayed constant between the time of the first loan closing and the beginning of 1999.

The thirty-three firms in the data set employed a combined total of 483 FTE workers at the time of their initial ECD loan closings. By January 1999, the combined employment level at these firms was down to 397. Caskey and Hollister argued that this number is misleading. It includes, for example, one firm that employed sixty-eight workers at the time it borrowed money from ECD. A few months later, the firm decided to shut down production in the Delta because a new product was not developing as quickly as initially expected. The owners repaid the ECD loan and laid off all of the workers. This likely would have happened even if ECD had never become involved. Because of such cases, Caskey and Hollister argued that it is more instructive to estimate jobs created and jobs retained as separate categories. Twelve of the thirty-three firms in the data set increased employment levels over the relevant periods. The largest increase in a single firm was thirty FTE workers. The combined total increase across the twelve firms was 116 FTE employees.

Caskey and Hollister used this as an upper-bound estimate, stating that in its first two and a half years of operation, ECD could claim that it had created at most 116 FTE jobs directly through its loan activities.

In reporting this estimate, Caskey and Hollister noted two important qualifications. First, some firms may have added a few workers after the time of the first ECD loan closing but eliminated them by January 1999. If so, Caskey and Hollister's methodology does not credit ECD for creating short-term new jobs. Second, it is likely that some of the firms that ECD financed between 1995 and July 1997 will continue to grow even without additional assistance from ECD.

In a second step, Caskey and Hollister obtained an upper-bound estimate for the number of jobs retained. For simplicity, they start with the very strong assumption that all employment at all of the firms ECD assisted would have disappeared without ECD's intervention. Under this assumption, they concluded that, as of 1999, ECD's loan activities in its first two and a half years of operation directly retained 281 jobs. Some examples illustrate how they arrived at this estimate. If a firm employed eight people at the time of the closing of its first ECD loan and employed eight in January 1999, Caskey and Hollister assumed that the loan retained eight jobs. If a firm employed eight at the loan closing and four in January 1999, they assumed that it retained four. If the firm employed eight at the closing and twelve in January 1999, they assumed eight jobs retained and, as discussed previously, as many as four jobs created.

Paralleling the jobs-created discussion, Caskey and Hollister noted several qualifications. First, a firm might, from the time of the loan closing until late 1998, retain jobs that would otherwise have been lost, but be forced to lay off these workers just before the January 1999 employment survey. In this case, the methodology would not credit ECD for retaining some jobs for a short period. Second, one could imagine a firm that employs eight at the time of the loan closing and would have gone out of business without ECD's assistance. By January 1999, it employs four. However, by January 2000, it might again employ eight. If so, Caskey and Hollister's method of counting jobs retained will change over time, though it can never go higher than 483, the combined number of people employed at the thirty-three firms at the time of the initial loan closings.

Table 9.4 summarizes these estimates. As shown in the first row of the table, Caskey and Hollister's upper-bound estimate of the jobs that ECD directly created or retained to date as a result of its first two and a half years of operation is 397, the January 1999 employment level at the thirty-three firms in the sample. The second row of the table provide a more conservative estimate of 199. This simply credits ECD with half of the new jobs added and retained.

To provide a rationale for the more conservative estimate Caskey and Hollister recognize that ECD is unlikely to have a played a critical role in helping firms add or retain jobs in all of these cases. Some firms might have

Table 9.4   Direct Job-Impact Estimates for ECD Loans Closed 1995 to July 1997

	Jobs Created	Jobs Retained	Total
Upper bound	116	281	397
Conservative	58	141	199

Source: Author's compilation.
Note: Jobs created and retained as of January 1999.

gotten financing without ECD, some might have grown even without any financing, and some might have survived even without any outside financing. The authors do note that ECD's interest rate policy probably reduced the risk that many firms seeking financing could have obtained it from banks. They also interviewed a number of firm owners and reported the common response that ECD was a lender of last resort. Some firm owners explicitly attributed their firm's survival or growth to ECD, but this was not universal.

Caskey and Hollister do not take a stand on the share of job creation and retention that should be attributed to ECD. Rather, for illustrative purposes, they simply assume, for the conservative estimate, that ECD should be credited with half of the jobs created and retained.

Caskey and Hollister emphasized that one should not assume that unemployed or lower-income Delta residents necessarily benefited from the jobs that ECD helped firms create and retain. As they pointed out, there are frequently multiple barriers that keep these individuals unemployed or in the lowest-paying segments of the labor market. They did not propose a method to identify the extent to which lower-income households benefited. They did argue, however, that there should be a strong presumption that lower-income households shared in the benefits. This is because their interviews with the business owners revealed that many of the firms assisted by ECD employed moderate- and low-skilled workers. In addition, there is little in-migration from other regions to fill such jobs in the Delta.

Caskey and Hollister noted that there can be a multiplier effect from the jobs that ECD helped to retain or create. They did not argue in favor of any particular multiplier; for illustrative purposes they simply used a multiplier of two.

Caskey and Hollister also did not provide a cost-benefit analysis for ECD. Instead, they provided some estimates of the cost per job that ECD may have helped create or retain (essentially a cost-effectiveness type estimate). In doing so, they aggregated ECD's operating costs for 1994 through 1996. They excluded costs for the first half of 1997 on the theory that those expenditures were mainly for future growth. In aggregating the operating costs, they included the implicit costs of the in-kind donations that ECD received (mainly legal services and free office rent) and the provisions that it made for loan losses. Cumulative loan loss provisions totaled $750,000. These calculations implied that ECD's cumulative 1994 through 1996 operating cost was $3.6 million. Outstanding development loans averaged about $2 million, having begun at zero and risen to about $5.5 million as of July 1997. Caskey and Hollister assumed a 6 percent opportunity cost for these funds, implying a cumulative opportunity cost of about $300,000. Finally, ECD earned about $550,000 in interest and fees from its development loans between 1995 and July 1997. Based on these very rough numbers, they calculate the net cost of ECD's job creation efforts during its first two and a half years to be $3.35 million ($3.6 million + $300,000 − $550,000).

Using their upper-bound estimate of the number of jobs created or retained by ECD directly and indirectly, using an employment multiplier of two, Caskey and Hollister calculated that ECD's cost per job could have been as low as $4,220. Using the more conservative estimate of the number of jobs created or retained along with the employment multiplier of two, the cost per job was $8,440.

"We do not take these estimates very seriously," Caskey and Hollister said in reporting these estimates. "When one divides a number (the cost of creating or retaining jobs) about which there is a great deal of uncertainty by another number (jobs created or retained) with substantial uncertainty, the uncertainty associated with the result is magnified. Nevertheless, the exercise emphasizes that the cost per job created or retained by ECD might be low by the standards of most economic development initiatives." (Caskey and Hollister 1999 Appendix 1, 19)

MORE RECENT DEVELOPMENTS

Several recent efforts at impact-related analysis go beyond the three studies reviewed. A few comments on them are in order. These projects represent higher levels of effort than earlier studies, in terms of both data collection and trying to pin down issues of methods. The challenges, however, are much the same.

Further Efforts by CEI

CEI has followed up the initial study by LaPlante with several attempts at internal impact studies. Data gathering from their portfolio firms in 1998, 2000, and 2002 was designed to monitor net job creation and job quality in particular, distinguishing between microenterprises and small to medium-size enterprises. The efforts were plagued by a low response rate from the firms—around 50 percent for 1998 and 2000 but lower for 2002. They have had particular difficulty getting good, consistent financial data.

CEI undertook a major new effort, financed by the Ford Foundation and the Community Development Financial Institution Fund, to conduct a low-income longitudinal study of its employment training agreements (ETAG) program. CEI had pioneered combining financing agreements with efforts to shift financed firms' hiring patterns toward low-income persons through ETAGs. If the firm is approved for financing, under the ETAG it agrees to make CEI a first source of job candidates, usually with the goal that 50 percent to 75 percent of the new hires will be people with low incomes. To facilitate this process, CEI works as an intermediary between the financed firm and a network of workforce development organizations providing employment and training assistance to people with low incomes.

A major impetus for the study was to try to get some evidence on what differences ETAGs might have made. While doing so, however, the study took a broader perspective. Simply put, the goal was to monitor the economic and employment status of people hired by CEI-financed firms (referred to subsequently as participants) for three years. Eight questions were posed:

- How does the CEI job compare to other jobs in terms of quality (in terms of wages, benefits, and some nonmonetary benefits)?

- How long do people stay in the CEI job?

- Do they move on to a better job?

- How does the CEI job affect income?

- Do participants become self-sufficient?

- How does the CEI job affect asset accumulation?

- Is the job-brokering work associated with the ETAG effective in terms of placing low-income people in jobs?

- How do participants in CEI's workforce demonstration projects fare compared to those placed in jobs through ETAGs?

The study was made up of two types of data sources: first, telephone and in-person surveys of a sample of participants and, second, state unemployment insurance (UI) records for a larger sample of participants. The surveys began with a sample of contact information for 1,979 individuals hired into CEI-financed firms from 1995 through 1999 for whom CEI had social security numbers. In the first wave of interviews, which began in July 1999 and ended in May 2000, the survey group CEI contracted with to carry out the surveys was able to contact and interview only 24 percent of the people in the contact sample. The second wave of interviews took place between May 2001 and January 2002. In the second wave, they were able to contact and interview 381 of the wave 1 group, achieving an interview retention rate of 81 percent of the first wave completers. The low response rate was a major disappointment, but the questionnaires contained a rich set of measures, so even with the low response rate important insights were obtained.

The unemployment insurance records were sought initially to obtain earnings records data that would allow CEI to follow workers' experience with respect to earnings and employment beyond the period of the second (eighteen-month) interview. CEI asked the Maine Department of Labor (MDOL) for access to the UI earnings records data—to be used in a strictly confidential form in which no individual would be identified. The MDOL generously granted CEI access to quarterly individual-level wage records on all participants from 1996 (when MDOL began using their current database) through the summer of 2001.

The sample of people with UI records (1,800) was much larger than the completed survey sample (381). The UI results therefore gave CEI a far more complete picture of the wage history and progression of participants than the survey wage data. The records data provided little beyond employment and earnings, of course, whereas the survey data covered a rich array of topics. UI records enabled CEI to generalize some results beyond the smaller survey sample.

The study provided CEI with a good number of insights about the change in economic status over time of persons hired by the firms CEI financed. To give just one example, it was possible to compare their experience in the CEI job with the experience they had in jobs held before the CEI job and the jobs held after leaving CEI. In general, the CEI jobs provided were better than the ones held before CEI—a higher wage, faster wage growth, more hours. A higher percentage of the CEI jobs provided health insurance compared to both the pre- and post-CEI jobs.

The one finding that was disturbing and puzzling for the CEI staff arose from the comparison of the CEI job with the single job subsequent to the CEI job. The data showed that, for those respondents who had left the CEI job, more than one-third (37 percent) left for a job that had a lower starting wage than their ending wage at the CEI job. CEI staff probed the data more thoroughly to see if they could better understand why this happened. This analysis led them to reconsider the link between job quality and retention. Many factors outside the scope of the job and the workplace influence the length of stay at a job and people's decisions about where and whether to work. As a result, they developed new initiatives to address some of the post-employment support issues, particularly with regard to child care and through Managed Work Services, a Maine-based program that provides intense job coaching from an almost case management-type approach.

The UI data turned out to be useful beyond the originally conceived purpose of affording longer follow-up. From a comparison of the employment and earnings results from the larger UI sample it was found that the more limited survey sample had in general better earnings and employment experience both before, during, and after the CEI job than did those who were not interviewed through the survey but showed up in the UI records. However, the generalizations about the relatively better employment and earnings experience in the CEI job compared to the before and after jobs held up—though at lower-level earnings—as did the puzzling finding of taking post-CEI jobs with lower starting earnings.

Further ECD Efforts

The ECD has continued to strengthen and extend its self-evaluation capabilities. Building on the Caskey and Hollister procedures, it has completed annual surveys of its portfolio firms and has made a concerted effort to get responses from the firms, most recently reaching an 80 percent response rate.

For several years, ECD has issued an annual report that summarizes what it has found from the surveys. In early 2003, ECD issued its most recent report, *Program Monitoring Report—Commercial Lending 2002*. Among the findings highlighted in that report were:

- Twenty-three new businesses entered ECD's portfolio in 2002.

- Seventy-three percent of these had been in operation for less than two years.

- Fifty-nine percent of the new entrants to ECD's portfolio were businesses owned by minorities or women.

- Eighty-seven percent of all first-time borrowers that sought financing prior to working with ECD were denied financing by traditional lenders.

- ECD had sixty-one firms in its portfolio as of year-end 2002.

- Fifty-one returned the annual employment surveys. These firms had 818 FTEs as of year-end 2002.

- Thirteen of the firms that were in ECD's portfolio as of year-end 2001 left the portfolio in 2002 due to bankruptcy, foreclosure, or refinancings with other lenders.

- The surveyed firms in ECD's portfolio paid an average wage of $10.05.

- Sixty-seven percent of the firms with twenty-five to ninety-nine workers offered health benefits to their employees.

- Fewer than 10 percent of the smaller firms did so.

- ECD financed two child-care centers and one adult day care center.

- ECD made two equity investments in a broadband wireless telecommunications company to help it bring additional coverage to the Delta.

In addition, ECD has developed a much more extensive self-evaluation system, much of it related to new activities it has undertaken in recent years.

Roberts Enterprise Development Fund

The Roberts Enterprise Development Fund (REDF) has put a considerable effort into developing a methodology for attempting to estimate the social return on investment (SROI) for firms in its portfolio and has produced analyses applying the methods to specific firms.[19] REDF made a considerable effort at original data gathering over several years, carrying out extensive surveys of employees as well as firms. In their analysis, they attempt to estimate enterprise value, and separately social purpose value, and then blended value, which seeks to combine the two. They highlight some interesting questions and issues that they still face, which echo much of what has been said in this chapter (REDF 2006):

- How can we minimize the disadvantages of using public sector savings as a measure of success?

- How can we better address the attribution and causality challenges that are prevalent in SROI analysis?

- How can we capture the costs and benefits that are not reflected in our analysis?

- How can we improve the ways we offset our lack of industry comparables?

- How can the complexity and cost of SROI analysis be further reduced?

- How is REDF's SROI approach applicable to other fields of practice?

The reports of the SROI analysis for the individual firms are well worth looking at.

The Double Bottom Line Project

The Rockefeller Foundation's ProVenEx committee initiated the Double Bottom Line Project in 2002. A team made up of two business school professors and two independent economic consultants has been working on methods of assessing the social impact in Double Bottom Line Ventures.[20] The team has assembled a toolkit of methods for social impact assessment and examples of utilization of those tools, an overall framework for social impact assessment, and made some initial attempts to apply the framework to several of the investments in the ProVenEx portfolio.

The team has been careful to delineate different potential customers for a social impact assessment (such as managers of the venture and investors), and to suggest which tools are likely to best fit the needs and perspective of each type of customer. For example, and as noted earlier, they identified the balanced score card as an assessment tool most relevant for enterprise managers. They have also sought to make clear the distinction, stressed earlier in this chapter, between outcomes and impacts. They currently are at the stage of generating a final report on the project.

Pacific Community Ventures

Pacific Community Ventures (PCV) is an example of a ProVenEx investment project study that has done a good job providing some performance measures of possible social dimensions of the outcomes generated by their double bottom line enterprises (2004). A community development venture capital fund, it has developed an annual social assessment using employee surveys and financial and other characteristics data from the firms in its portfolio. It reports, for example, on the number of designated employees (individuals hired as hourly employees at wages of less than $20 an hour, who reside in low- to moderate-income zip code areas), average wages, percentage of businesses offering various benefit packages, extent of skill training, and rates of retention and advancement.

Monitoring Versus Impact

None of the examples cited as quality evaluative efforts would meet the highest standards of causal proof of impact of a CDFI activity.[21] Most were essentially before-and-after study designs. They should be characterized as monitoring performance rather than evaluating impact. Although they are not able to measure the impact of CDFI activities accurately, such studies—and their related information systems—do make very useful contributions to our assessments of the social as well as financial outcomes associated with CDFI activities.

CHALLENGES IN ADVANCING QUALITY OF EVALUATION OF CDFI OUTCOMES

As CDFI activities evolve, evaluators face a number of problems in trying to assess how to attribute outcomes to a given CDFI, particularly those that might be considered social rather than financial. These difficulties include the challenge of evaluating the effect of technical assistance, joint production problems, investments with special attributes, and the nonfinancial intermediary roles of CDFIs.

The Effect of Technical Assistance Efforts

CDFIs provide technical assistance to entities (businesses and community institutions) in a variety of ways. Loan officers in the due diligence phase, and often during the life of the loan, counsel businesses on many dimensions of their operations. Some CDFIs broker technical assistance for firms in their portfolio; that is, they match specialized technical assistance providers they have found to be high quality with the firm's specific need. Sometimes the CDFIs provide grants or loans to cover the cost of that technical assistance.

CDFIs that make equity investments generally provide their portfolio companies with various forms of technical assistance throughout the lives of such investments. Some CDFIs even provide technical assistance to firms with which they have no financial commitments. I know of no attempts to rigorously assess the effects of technical assistance efforts and have only limited ideas about how one might attempt to do so.

Joint Production Problems

CDFIs often invest jointly with other funders, such as commercial banks, state loan funds, or traditional venture funds. This may lead to double counting in trying to evaluate impact. It is also hard to know who mobilized whom; was the CDFI the key actor or did they pick up the riskier bits, thus reducing exposure for the other lenders (who might have funded the entire effort anyway)? It's hard to know how to deal with this attribution problem.

Recently CDFIs have sought to influence legislation at the state or local level or to try to change rules and regulations of the executive agencies at these levels. There are two challenges to assessing these types of activities: first, there are almost always other groups involved in the particular lobbying effort, so there is a joint product problem in attribution of any effects; second, it is usually quite difficult to quantify the benefits of the legislative or regulatory change.

Investments with Special Attributes

CDFIs often make investments with special characteristics that may add a "social dimension" to the supported activity. The problem is how to try to quantify what those dimensions might be.

Many CDFIs have made investments in charter schools, to take one example. Some people feel that there is a social benefit to such investments because charter schools provide alternatives to the often poor quality public schools that serve poor neighborhoods. A growing body of education economics literature attempts to assess whether charter schools enhance student academic or social performance (see, for example, Hanushek et al. 2005). Perhaps it will be possible to use some of this literature to construct some sort of a quantification of this special dimension.

CDFIs also make investments in and provide technical assistance to child-care providers, especially those serving low-income families. Is there a special dimension to the child-care sector that should be quantified?

Some CDFIs have facilitated major investments in community facilities, particularly in low-income neighborhoods. What might be a metric to quantify the "special dimension" that such investments provide?

CDFIs as Intermediaries

CDFIs are increasingly using their expertise to help bridge information gaps between business and government, business and community, and community and government. Some of this could fall under the topic of technical assistance, but again a few examples may help. Individuals working for businesses and non-profit organizations, who were interviewed by Caskey and Hollister as part of their studies of CDFIs, mentioned how the CDFI staff called their attention, and facilitated access to state or federal funds that could be obtained to subsidize worker training, provide wage subsidies, and offer technical assistance on production processes.

CDFI staff have provided assistance in tax filing to employees of companies in their portfolio and, sometimes, to a broader range of low-income people in their target communities. Particularly important has been their work informing people about their eligibility for the Earned Income Tax Credit (and providing them with an alternative to often expensive commercial tax preparers). In a few cases, CDFIs have provided general financial education to low- and moderate-income individuals.

Some CDFIs have been involved in developing major databases, along with geographic information system mapping capabilities, for use by non-profit community organizations, researchers, and state and local officials. In some cases, the CDFIs have gone in and reorganized basic records systems for agencies. They have sometimes used these systems to help city agencies better coordinate and geographically target their policies and operations.

Many CDFIs have become involved in identifying exploitive lending practices, particularly with respect to housing finance, within their target communities and, sometimes, citywide. It may be possible to quantify gains to particular community members as a result of these activities, but the author is not aware of any such quantifications.

REPRISE AND POINTS OF EMPHASIS

It is important to try to educate investors and managers so that they develop realistic expectations about what sorts and magnitudes of social impacts CDFIs might be able to generate, and to help them understand what an evaluation product assessing those impacts can reliably provide, and at what level of standard of proof. When the funder or manager starts with unrealistic expectations, pressure develops on the CDFI to resort to inflated evaluation claims they may know are questionable: "I know that measure isn't legitimate but it sells." One can hardly state strongly enough how important it is to try to get the customer (funder, manager) for the evaluation to have reasonable expectations about what outcomes are likely to be feasible and what quality of evaluation can in fact be provided. I was discouraged recently when discussing one CDFI project with a foundation officer. "We just want to be sure that this project will create 2000 jobs," she said. When I tried arguing that she couldn't reliably determine this, she waved the objections off and insisted again that this was the standard she would hold the project to.

Important elements in education about impact evaluation are the distinctions between outcomes and impacts and the central place of the concept of a counterfactual in establishing a causal link between a CDFI activity and a measured impact. It would be preferable if the term impact was used only in those rare cases in which the causal link could be reliably established, and otherwise to refer to the measured social dimensions as social outcomes.

It would also be a good idea to eliminate the term *social rate of return on investment*. This leads to an expectation that the evaluator can generate estimates reasonably comparable to those used to calculate a financial rate of return on investment. I argued earlier that such estimates are unlikely to be generated without a host of questionable assumptions. The rhetoric of a *blended rate return*, where the *financial rate of return* and the *social rate of return* are somehow intertwined, should certainly be abandoned.

There is a role, however limited, for random assignment experiments to determine, at the highest level of proof, the impact of certain components of CDFI activities. When situations arise that permit such experimental assessments of impacts, strenuous efforts should be made to ensure that such opportunities will be grasped.

More "sensitivity analysis" could be incorporated into evaluations. Sensitivity analysis is carried out by taking a basic calculation of a benefit or cost and seeing how the estimate changes when a slightly different assumption is used in some step of the estimation. The examples discussed—such as estimates of upper and lower bounds on jobs created or retained—show some of this.

Greater efforts should be made to marshal records data for use in evaluations. Original data collection for the purpose of evaluation can be expensive. Sometimes records data can be used instead. Data such as those from HMDA

(Housing Mortgage Disclosure Act public use files) and unemployment insurance records have been used in some CDFI evaluations. Although some are easily accessed public use files, others require special effort to meet concerns about data confidentiality.

In the spirit of "don't let the perfect be the enemy of the good," modest evaluations of performance on social dimensions can be useful in helping keep program managers focused on social as well as financial dimensions of their operations and to keep investors informed about both dimensions. I have argued that monitoring activities can fill this sort of role and have tried to point out what I consider some good examples of this type of evaluation.

APPENDIX: PROPENSITY SCORE MATCHING

A propensity score is estimated as a function of all the measured variables that are available for both "treatment group members" and members of the pool from which a comparison group is to be drawn. This is done as a logit equation where the dependent variable equals 1 if a treatment group member and 0 if a member of the comparison pool. The propensity score equation coefficients are used to generate a predicted probability of being in the treatment group for each member of both the treatment group and of the pool of possible comparisons by multiplying the coefficients times the value of the variables for that individual. A series of specification tests are done to assure that the distribution of predicted propensity scores across the comparison group is well balanced with the distribution of predicted propensity scores for the treatment group. If the results fail any of the specification tests, adjustments are made in the content of the logit equation and a new round of estimates of propensity scores and specification tests is carried out. Once all the tests have been passed, for each member of the treatment group a selection is made from the pool of potential comparison group members that has a predicted propensity score nearest to the predicted propensity score of that treatment group member. The resultant selected comparison sample is then used with the treatment sample to get a quasi-experimental estimate of impact by subtracting mean of the outcome variable for the selected comparison sample from the mean of the outcome variable for the treatment group. Propensity score matching is a truly complex procedure and I have not even attempted here to fill in all the necessary details.

NOTES

1. This chapter is based on my experience with CDFI evaluation, which has focused on business investments and employment outcomes. I have not studied dimensions of outcome measurement for housing or the environment and there may be measurements that can be made in

those dimensions that are less subject to the problems I outline. The chapter draws very heavily on a study John Caskey and I undertook at the request of and with funding from the Ford Foundation (Caskey and Hollister 2001).

2. A small community bank generally has about $100 million or less in assets. There are 3,617 such banks in the United States, or about half of all commercial banks. *Providing Capital, Building Communities, Creating Impact* reports that in its FY2003 sample of 316 CDFIs, average assets were $27 million. Note that this covers four types of CDFIs and the distribution of asset values is highly skewed, with bank CDFIs having much larger assets. Median asset size for all types of CDFIs in the sample was $4 million, whereas that for bank CDFIs was $116 million.

3. Some of this section was stimulated by a conversation with Kerwin Tesdale.

4. As quantitative evaluations began to emerge, they were challenged on one side by those who favored the program being evaluated on the grounds that the study "underestimated the real positive effects of this program" and on the other, by those opposing the program who challenged the study by claiming that the estimates grossly exaggerated the program's effects. Both groups enlisted technicians—mostly academic— who would attack weaknesses in the methodology employed. A classic case of this occurred when congressional opponents of the Job Corps challenged positive estimates of the program's impacts. The then named Bureau of the Budget (now OMB) appointed an expert panel to review and assess the evaluation study. They gave it a stamp of approval and the Job Corps survived for another period of time.

5. The Panel Survey of Income Dynamics and the two-part National Longitudinal Survey: National Longitudinal Surveys of Young Men and Older, National Longitudinal Surveys of Young Women and Mature Women.

6. Many have noted that rigorous evaluation standards seemed to be demanded and applied almost exclusively to projects and programs that targeted on low-income persons or communities.

7. In their recently established Community Investment Impact System, the CDFI Fund asks for information on, for example, proportions of financial activity by the individual fund involving faith-based organizations, geographic areas, hot spot zones, minority-owned, women-owned, specific racial groups, and the like. It explains that the system will help determine community impacts (see http://www.cdfifund.gov/what_we_do/ciis.asp).

8. Many of the aspects of this discussion are developed in more detail in Hollister and Hill (1995).

9. This is often referred to in econometric literature as a difference in difference estimator, that is to say, we have a measure of change for the communities where the intervention occurred and a measure of the change in the comparison communities (these are the second difference) and then by subtracting one from the other we have the difference in the change between to two types of communities (the first difference).

10. This is because the balance of characteristics between the two groups who have been randomly assigned increases as the size of the groups increases. Think of the case of randomly assigning just two individuals, one to treatment and one to control, the probability that they will have the same characteristics, for example, age, income, family background, is virtually zero. As the size of the two groups randomly assigned increases, however, the probability of balance of characteristics increases.

11. In a useful review of methods of estimating the impact of local economic development policies, Timothy Bartik (2002) suggests an experimental design to assess the impact of local economic development services. The design he proposes is really an "encouragement design" sometimes used in marketing analysis (Bradlow 1998) and Biostatistics (Hirano et al. 2000). I doubt the feasibility of implementation of this design and the estimation of the impact of the treatment (CDFI services in this case) as opposed to the impact of the encouragement per se is complicated (Hirano et al. 2000)

12. One example of a set experimental studies that come close to this type of design are random assignment experiments testing the impact of entrepreneurship training offered to Unemployment Insurance recipients in two demonstration programs, one in the State of Washington and the other one in Massachusetts (reported in Benus, Wood, and Grover 1994)

13. Examples of these types of problems arising in attempts to estimate the impacts of micro-finance lending in developing countries are provided in a very sophisticated review by Jonathan Morduch (1999).

14. Although it is not exactly analogous to the methods discussed in this section, Timothy Bartik (1991) provides a rich discussion of econometric studies of the effects of state and local economic development policies. He outlines difficulties with the methods used to obtain the estimates.

15.   I am familiar with two examples of attempts to carry out "blended" financial and social rates of return, both of which are discussed in this chapter: the work over several years of REDF (Roberts Enterprise Development Fund 2006) on developing a social rate of return methodology and Catherine Clark and William Rosenzweig, with David Long and Sara Olsen (forthcoming).

16.   Three of the studies covered in this section are reviewed and critiqued in more detail in Caskey and Hollister 2000.

17.   The studies reviewed should not be taken to represent estimates of the current status of the particular CDFI mentioned; in most cases the size and operations of the CDFI have changed substantially.

18.   As Caskey and Hollister (2001) noted, this approach means that their estimates of a firm's employment levels are subject to a margin of error: "Candidly, a firm might increase its steady-state FTE employment level from 5 to 7 over two years and we might mistakenly conclude that employment levels had not changed. We are confident, however, that we are picking up cases where firms increase employment levels from 5 to 12 or from 30 to 45" (Appendix 1, 15n4).

19.   The document "A Report from the Good Ship SROI" by Cynthia Gair provides a nice summary of their methods and applications (for descriptions of the methods and for specific firm analyses, see http://www.redf.org).

20.   The team is Catherine Clark of Columbia Business School, William Rosenzweig of Hass School of Business at UC Berkeley, David Long of Abt Associates, and Sara Olsen of SVT Consulting.

21.   One of the activity/investments cited by the Double Bottom Line Project as an example for use of some of the evaluative methods is Teach for America. Teach for America has in fact been assessed by a random assignment experimental study (see Decker, Mayer, and Glazerman 2004).

REFERENCES

Agodini, Roberto, & Dynarksi, Mark. 2004. "Are Experiments the Only Option? A Look at Dropout Prevention Programs." *Review of Economics and Statistics* 86(1): 180–94

Arveson, Paul. 1998. "What is the Balanced Scorecard?" The Balanced Scorecard Institute. Accessed at http://www.balancedscorecard.org/basics/bsc1.html.

Aspen Institute. 2006. "Theory of Change." Accessed at http://www.theory ofchange.org/html/basics.html.

Bartik, Timothy J. 1991. *Who Benefits from State and Local Economic Development Policies?* Kalamazoo, Mich.: W. E. Upjohn Institute for Employment Research.

————. 2002. "Evaluating the Impacts of Local Economic Development Policies on Local Economic Outcomes: What Has Been Done and What is Doable?" Upjohn Institute Staff Working Paper No. 03-89. Kalamazoo, Mich.: W. E. Upjohn Institute for Employment Research. Accessed at http://www.upjohninstitute.org/publications/wp/03-89.pdf.

Benus, Jacob M., Michelle Wood, and Neelima Grover. 1994. *A Comparative Analysis of the Washington and Massachusetts UI Self-Employment Demonstrations.* Unpublished report prepared for the U.S. Department of Labor, Employment and Training Administration.

Boardman, Anthony, David Greenberg, Aidan Vining, and David Weimer. 2005. *Cost-Benefit Analysis: Concepts and Practice,* 3rd edition. Toronto, Ontario: Prentice Hall.

Bradlow, Eric T. 1998. "Encouragement Designs: An Approach to Self-Selected Samples in an Experimental Design." *Marketing Letters* 98(4): 383–91.

Caskey, John P., and Robinson Hollister. 1999. "Final Report on the Job Impact of the Enterprise Corporation of the Delta." Unpublished report to the Pew and Walton Foundations.

————. 2000. "The Impact of Community Development Business Financial Institutions: A Review of Three Studies." Unpublished paper, Swarthmore College, May 2000.

————. 2001. "Evaluating the Social Impact of Business Development Financial Institutions and Community Development Credit Unions." Unpublished report to the Ford Foundation.

Clark, Catherine, and William Rosenzweig, with David Long and Sara Olsen. Forthcoming. *Double Bottom Line Project: Assessing Social Impact in Double Bottom Line Ventures.* A Project for the ProVenEx Committee of the Rockefeller Foundation.

Community Development Financial Institutions Fund. 2006. Accessed at http://www.cdfifund.gov.

Community Development Venture Capital Alliance. 2006. "CDVCA Measuring Impacts Toolkit." Accessed at http://www.cdvca.org/media/research/mit.php.

Connell, James, and Karen A. Kubisch. 1998. "Applying a Theory of Change Approach to the Evaluation of Comprehensive Community Initiatives: Progress, Prospects, and Problems." In *New Approaches to Evaluating Community Initiatives: Theory, Measurement, and Analysis,* Volume 2, edited by Karen Fulbright-Anderson, Anne C. Kubisch and James P. Connell. Washington: The Aspen Institute.

Coulton, Claudia, and Robinson Hollister. 1998. "Measuring Comprehensive Community Initiatives: Outcomes Using Data Available for Small Areas." In *New Approaches to Evaluating Community Initiatives: Theory, Measurement, and Analysis,* Volume 2, edited by Karen Fulbright-Anderson, Anne C. Kubisch, and James P. Connell. Washington: The Aspen Institute.

Decker, Paul T., Daniel P. Mayer, and Steven Glazerman. 2004. *The Effects of Teach for America on Students: Findings from a National Evaluation.* Princeton, N.J.: Mathematica Policy Research. Accessed at http://www.mathematica-mpr.com/publications/pdfs/teach.pdf.

Dehejia, Rajeev H., and Sadek Wahba. 1999. "Causal Effects in Non-Experimental Studies: Reevaluating the Evaluation of Training Programs." *Journal of the American Statistical Association* 94(448): 1053–62.

The Foundation Center. 2005. "What Is a Program-Related Investment?" Accessed at http://foundationcenter.org/getstarted/faqs/html/pri.html.

Friedlander, Daniel, and Philip K. Robins. 1995. "Evaluating Program Evaluations: New Evidence on Commonly Used Non-Experimental Methods." *American Economic Review* 85(4): 923–37.

Garasky, Steven, and Barnow, Burt S. 1992. "Demonstration Evaluations and Cost Neutrality: Using Caseload Models to Determine the Federal Cost Neutrality of New Jersey's REACH Demonstration." *Journal of Policy Analysis and Management* 11(1992): 624–36

Hanushek, Eric A., John F. Kain, Steven G. Rivkin, and Gregory F. Branch. 2005. *Charter School Quality and Parental Decision Making with School Choice.* NBER Working Paper 11252. Cambridge, Mass.: National Bureau of Economic Research. Accessed at http://www.nber.org/papers/w11252.

Hirano, Keisuke, Guido W. Imbens, Donald B. Rubin, and Xiao-Hua Zhou. 2000. "Assessing the Effect of an Influenza Vaccine in an Encouragement Design." *Biostatistics* 1 (1): 68–88

Hollister, Robinson, and Jennifer Hill. 1995. "Problems in the Evaluation of Community Wide Initiatives." In *New Approaches to Evaluating Community Initiatives: Concepts, Methods, and Contexts,* Volume 1, edited by James A. Connell, Anne C. Kubisch, Lisbeth B. Schorr, and Carol H. Weiss. Washington: The Aspen Institute.

LaPlante, Josephine. 1996. *Evaluating Social and Economic Effects of Small Business Development Assistance.* Portland, Me.: Edmund Muskie Institute of Public Affairs, University of Southern Maine.

McNess, Stephen. 1995. "An Assessment of the 'Official' Economic Forecasts." *New England Economic Review* 7/8(July/August): 13–23.

Michalopoulos, Charles, Bloom, Howard, & Hill, Carolyn J. (2004). "Can Propensity Score Methods Match the Findings from a Random Assignment

Evaluation of Mandatory Welfare-to-work Programs?" *Review of Economics and Statistics* 86(1): 156–79

Miller, Thomas. 1993. *Of These Hills: A Review of Kentucky Highlands Investment Corporation.* Unpublished manuscript.

Morduch, Jonathan. 1999. "The Microfinance Promise." *Journal of Economic Literature* 37(4): 1569–614.

Opportunity Finance Network. 2006. "Cars, the CDFI Assessment and Rating System." Accessed at http://www.opportunityfinance.net/financing/finance_sub4.aspx?id=56.

Pacific Community Ventures. 2004. "Investing for Change." BTW Consultants—Informing Change, April 2004. Accessed at http://www.pacificcommunityventures.org/newsroom/2003-PCV-Executive Summary.pdf.

Roberts Enterprise Development Fund. 2006. "Measuring Results." Accessed at http://www.redf.org/about-results.htm.

W. K. Kellogg Foundation. 2004. *Logic Model Development Guide.* Battle Creek, Mich.: W. K. Kellogg Foundation. Accessed at http://www.wkkf.org/Pubs/Tools/Evaluation/Pub3669.pdf.

Weiss, Carol. 1995. "Nothing as Practical as Good Theory: Exploring Theory-Based Evaluation for Comprehensive Community Initiatives for Children and Families." In *New Approaches To Evaluating Community Initiatives: Concepts, Methods, and Contexts,* edited by James A. Connell, Anne C. Kubisch, Lisbeth B. Schorr and Carol H. Weiss. Washington: The Aspen Institute.

Wilde, Elizabeth Ty, and Robinson Hollister. 2007. "How Close Is Close Enough? Evaluating Propensity Score Matching Using Data from a Class Size Reduction Experiment." *Journal of Public Policy Analysis and Management.* 26(4): 455–80

INDEX

ments, 130; legal structure, 129; Pacific Community Ventures, 300; pension fund investments, 142–3; political environment, 131–2; providers, 128; research overview, 6; role of, 128; securitization, 147; social outcomes, 152n11; strategic planning, 148; sustainability, 140; vs. traditional venture capitalists, 128–9; types of, 130

community economic development (CED) loans, 146, 147

Community Express, 111

Community Investment Program (CIP), 191

Community Organized Investment Network (COIN), 140–1

Community Reinvestment Act (CRA) (1977): bank requirements, 3, 39, 129, 132–4, 136, 137, 192, 193; CDFI advocacy, 127; and community development banks, 161; criticisms of, 199; enforcement of, 3, 132, 232, 241–2; predatory lending detection, 241–2; purpose of, 3, 132

Community Reinvestment Fund (CRF), 146

Community Renewal Tax Relief Act (2000), 4, 134, 139

Congressional Budget Office, 186

Connecticut, anti-predatory lending laws in, 247

conservatives, 199–200, 214n14

consumer debt. See debt, consumer

Consumer Federation of America, 73, 85

Consumer Literacy Consortium, 73

consumer loan data, 167–8

consumer protection laws, 244

consumption, 29–30

contract law, 244

Cooperative Extension System, 73, 79

Corporation for Enterprise Development (CFED), 45

cost-effectiveness, 283–4

counseling, financial. See financial education and counseling

counterfactuals, 267–8, 271–8, 283

Count Me In, 105

CRA (Community Reinvestment Act). See Community Reinvestment Act (CRA) (1977)

creative finance, 187–8

credit card debt, 19, 29–30, 80

credit scoring, 38–39, 104

credit unions: business loans, 165, 166; community development credit union designation, 160, 172–7; customer income analysis, 165–6; definition of, 160; deposit insurance, 160–1; financial education programs, 85–86; governance, 165; growth of, 164; guiding principle of, 165; low-income credit union designation, 160, 170–2; low-income customers, 39, 165–70; mandate under Federal Credit Union Act, 39; market share, 164; median income of members, 39; membership in, 160, 170; nonprofit status, 168; number of in U.S., 49; origins of, 164; partnerships with check cashers, 176; products and services, 169–70; types of, 160

CRF (Community Reinvestment Fund), 146

criminal prosecution, of predatory lenders, 242–3

cross-national comparison, of saving rates, 22–23

CTC (Child Tax Credit), 46

Cummings, J., 193

Curley, J., 45, **82**

Current Population Survey, 268

Danes, S., **81, 83**

databases, 302

data collection and sources: CDFIs, 100–101, 303–4; consumer loan data, 167–68; cross-national savings data, 22; microenterprise development organizations, 100–101, 106

debt, consumer: charge-off rates, 80; components of, 19; credit cards, 19, 29–30, 80; and financial education, 74; median value of, 19; percentage of households with, 19

deceptive practices, in lending, 230

Defense Department, 85